Cambridge Studies in Histor

THE ICONOGRAPHY
OF LANDSCAPE

Cambridge Studies in Historical Geography

Series editors:

ALAN R. H. BAKER   J. B. HARLEY   DAVID WARD

Cambridge Studies in Historical Geography encourages exploration of the philosophies, methodologies and techniques of historical geography and publishes the results of new research within all branches of the subject. It endeavours to secure the marriage of traditional scholarship with innovative approaches to problems and to sources, aiming in this way to provide a focus for the discipline and to contribute towards its development. The series is an international forum for publication in historical geography which also promotes contact with workers in cognate disciplines.

* *Also available in paperback*

THE ICONOGRAPHY OF LANDSCAPE

Essays on the symbolic representation, design and use of past environments

Edited by

DENIS COSGROVE

Senior Lecturer in Geography, Loughborough University

and

STEPHEN DANIELS

Lecturer in Geography, University of Nottingham

CAMBRIDGE
UNIVERSITY PRESS

Published by the Press Syndicate of the University of Cambridge
The Pitt Building, Trumpington Street, Cambridge CB2 1RP
40 West 20th Street, New York, NY 10011–4211, USA
10 Stamford Road, Oakleigh, Victoria 3166, Australia

First published 1988
Reprinted 1989, 1992

Printed in Great Britain at the University Press, Cambridge

British Library cataloguing in publication data

The iconography of landscape: essays on
the symbolic representation, design and
use of past environments. – (Cambridge
studies in historical geography; 9).
1. Landscape – Social aspects
I. Cosgrove, Denis   II. Daniels, Stephen
719'.09182'1   GF50

Library of Congress cataloguing in publication data

The iconography of landscape: essays on the symbolic representation,
design and use of past environments/edited by Denis Cosgrove and
Stephen Daniels.
      p.   cm. – (Cambridge studies in historical geography: 9)
Includes index.
ISBN 0 521 32437 8
1. Landscape in art. 2. Nature (Aesthetics) 3. Arts, Modern –
Themes, motives. 4. Arts and society. I. Cosgrove, Denis.
II. Daniels, Stephen.   III. Series.
NX650.L34I26 1988   87-17205   CIP
700—dc19

ISBN 0 521 32437 8 hardback
ISBN 0 521 38915 1 paperback

BS

Contents

Contributors

DENIS COSGROVE is Senior Lecturer in Geography at Loughborough University.

STEPHEN DANIELS is Lecturer in Geography at the University of Nottingham.

DOUGLAS DAVIES is Lecturer in Theology at the University of Nottingham.

DAVID FRASER is Assistant Curator at the Museum and Art Gallery, Derby.

PETER FULLER is an author and critic.

ERIC GRANT is a Principal Lecturer in Geography at Middlesex Polytechnic.

J. B. HARLEY is Professor of Geography at the University of Wisconsin-Milwaukee.

MARK HARRISON, formerly a research fellow in history at King's College, Cambridge, works for the BBC in Bristol.

G. MALCOLM LEWIS is Senior Lecturer in Geography at the University of Sheffield.

JOHN LUCAS is Professor of English and Drama at Loughborough University.

BRIAN S. OSBORNE is Professor of Geography at Queen's University, Kingston, Ontario.

HUGH PRINCE is Reader in Geography at University College London.

TREVOR R. PRINGLE, formerly of the Department of Geography at Loughborough University, now works in education for Bedfordshire County Council.

PENELOPE WOOLF, formerly of the Department of Geography at University College London, is a researcher for the Royal Society of Arts.

Preface

Except for those by Harley and Woolf, the following essays were originally presented as papers to a conference, Iconography in Historical Geography, convened by the volume editors for the Historical Geography Research Group, at the University of Nottingham in July 1984. Thanks are due to the HGRG for financial assistance with some of the illustrations in this volume.

Introduction: iconography and landscape

STEPHEN DANIELS AND
DENIS COSGROVE

A landscape is a cultural image, a pictorial way of representing, structuring or symbolising surroundings. This is not to say that landscapes are immaterial. They may be represented in a variety of materials and on many surfaces – in paint on canvas, in writing on paper, in earth, stone, water and vegetation on the ground. A landscape park is more palpable but no more real, nor less imaginary, than a landscape painting or poem. Indeed the meanings of verbal, visual and built landscapes have a complex interwoven history. To understand a built landscape, say an eighteenth-century English park, it is usually necessary to understand written and verbal representations of it, not as 'illustrations', images standing outside it, but as constituent images of its meaning or meanings. And of course, every study of a landscape further transforms its meaning, depositing yet another layer of cultural representation. In human geography the interpretation of landscape and culture has a tendency to reify landscape as an object of empiricist investigation,[1] but often its practitioners do gesture towards landscape as a cultural symbol or image, notably when likening landscape to a text and its interpretation to 'reading'.[2] This essay, and the collection which it introduces, explicate more fully the status of landscape as image and symbol and in doing so establish common ground between practitioners from a variety of different disciplines concerned with landscape and culture: geography, fine art, literature, social history and anthropology.[3] The discussion here is structured around the fertile concept of iconography: the theoretical and historical study of symbolic imagery.

Iconographies

The interpretation of symbolic imagery reaches back to Cesare Ripa's *Iconologia*, the first of many Renaissance handbooks acting as guides to an art which made systematic use of symbols, allegories and images from the Classical repertoire.[4] The terms iconography and iconology were revived this century, initially again in the interpretation of Renaissance imagery, by the school of art history associated with Aby Warburg. In opposition to the purely formalistic tradition of art interpretation associated with Heinrich Wölfflin (which analysed pictures purely in terms of the surface patterns of colour, chiaroscuro, line and volume, relating them principally to other works of art), iconographic study sought to probe meaning in a work of art by setting it in its historical context and, in particular, to analyse the ideas implicated in its imagery. While, by definition, all art history translates the visual into the verbal, the iconographic approach consciously sought to conceptualise pictures as encoded texts to be deciphered by those cognisant of the culture as a whole in which they were produced. The approach was systematically formulated by Warburg's pupil, Erwin Panofsky.

Panofsky distinguished between iconography 'in the narrower sense of the word' and iconography 'in a deeper sense'. Initially he labelled these two approaches 'iconographical analysis' and 'iconographical interpretation [or] synthesis' but eventually revived the term 'iconology' to describe 'iconography turned interpretative'.[5] Iconography 'in the narrower' sense was the identification of conventional, consciously inscribed symbols, say a lamb signifying Christ, or the winged lion of St Mark signifying in Venetian art the Republic and its power. Iconology probed a deeper stratum of meaning.[6] It excavated what Panofsky called the 'intrinsic meaning' of a work of art 'by ascertaining those underlying principles which reveal the basic attitude of a nation, a period, a class, a religious or philosophical persuasion – unconsciously qualified by one personality and condensed into one work'. There were no established conventions or specific methods that would ascertain these principles; they were to be reconstructed by a kind of detective synthesis, searching out analogies between overtly disparate forms like poetry, philosophy, social institutions and political life: 'To grasp these principles', wrote Panofsky, 'we need a mental faculty comparable to that of a diagnostician.' It was here in the interpretative search for such principles that 'the various humanistic disciplines meet on a common plane instead of serving as handmaidens to each other'.[7]

In a reference to the philosophy of Ernst Cassirer, Panofsky's colleague at the Warburg Library and author of *The philosophy of symbolic forms* (1923–9), Panofsky contended that iconology involved the identification of symbols, not in 'the ordinary sense e.g. the Cross, or the Tower of Chastity' but in the 'Cassirerian' sense; it involved the search for 'what Ernst Cassirer has called "symbolical" values'.[8] For Cassirer symbols were not

mere figures which refer to some given reality by means of suggestion or allegorical renderings, but in the sense of forces, each of which produces and posits a world of its own. The question as to what reality is apart from these forms, and what are its independent attributes, becomes irrelevant here. For the mind, only that can be visible which has some definite form; but every form of existence has its source in some peculiar way of seeing, some intellectual formulation and intuition of meaning.[9]

In the same year, 1925, as Cassirer made this case in the *Studien der Biblio-tek Warburg*, Panofsky deployed the concept of symbolic form in his own essay: 'Die Perspektive als "symbolische Form" ', a study of changing modes of perceiving and representing space, not as mere 'conventions' (to be taken up or not at will) or as true or false beliefs, but, much as Cassirer held language or mathematics to be, as 'symbolic forms' which structured the world according to specific cultural demands.[10] As an example of the interpretation of perspective as symbolic form Panofsky compared two pictures in which the subjects 'seem to hang loose in space in violation of the laws of gravity': *The Three Magi*, painted in the fifteenth century by Roger van der Weyden, in which the infant Jesus hovers in mid-air, and an Ottonian miniature of around 1000 AD in which 'a whole city is represented in the middle of an empty space while the figures taking part in the action stand on solid ground'. An inexperienced observer might assume that

the town is meant to be suspended in mid-air by some sort of magic. Yet in this case the lack of support does not imply a miraculous invalidation of the laws of nature ... In a miniature of around 1000 'empty space' does not count as a real, three-dimensional medium, as it does in a more realistic period, but serves as an abstract, unreal background ... Thus while the figure in the van der Weyden counts as an apparition, the floating city in the Ottonian miniature has no such miraculous connotation.

As experienced observers we may grasp this 'in a fraction of a second' but this still involves 'reading "what we see" according to the manner in which objects and events are expressed by forms under varying historical conditions'.[11]

Panofsky applied this approach of 'reading what we see' to built as well as to painted forms. He argued that designers of gothic cathedrals 'began to conceive of the forms they shaped, not so much in terms of isolated solids as in terms of a comprehensive "picture space" ', just as contemporary Church Fathers were conceiving of their textual apologetics as tightly articu-lated *summae* wherein the whole structure of the argument could be read off from the table of its contents and textual subdivisions. Thus, Panofsky pointed out, the entire constructional order of ribs and vaults may be read off from the cross-section of a single nave shaft. While acknowledging its status as building he found it fertile to regard gothic architecture as text, not just 'a way of seeing – or rather designing', but as a 'mode of literary representation', a treatise in stone, an architectural scholasticism.

Caen and Durham were to be read as cultural symbols of a whole age by being set in the full context of their spatial and intellectual articulation.[12]

If the medieval 'Age of Faith' wove the meaning of its world out of images and signs it was not in this respect fundamentally different from any culture. Thus when Panofsky likened iconography to ethnography[13] he pointed to a broad truth for all cultural study, one stressed in modern anthropology. Clifford Geertz's conceptualisation of culture as a 'text' and his dual method of 'thick description' ('setting down the meaning particular social actions have for the actors whose actions they are') and 'diagnosis' ('stating as explicitly as we can manage, what the knowledge thus attained demonstrates about the society in which it is found and about social life as such') have much in common with Panofsky's notions of iconography and iconology.[14] It was perhaps inevitable that Geertz was eventually to uphold iconographic art history (in the writings of Michael Baxandall) as a model for ethnography.[15] Since the 1970s ethnography, often of an explicitly Geertzian kind, has greatly influenced social history. In his essay 'A bourgeois puts his world in order: the city as a text', Geertz's colleague, Robert Darnton, analyses the representations of Montpellier in an account of the city written in 1768 by 'an anonymous but solidly middle-class citizen'. The first half of the account translated into writing the idiom of the urban procession. Such a procession 'expressed the corporate order of urban society . . . it was a statement unfurled in the streets through which the city represented itself to itself – and sometimes to God, for it also took place when Montpellier was threatened by drought or famine'. By 1768, however, 'the language of processions was archaic. It could not convey the shifting alignments within the social order that resulted from the economic expansion of the mid-century years.' In the second part of his account the author 'began to grope for an adequate terminology . . . the city no longer appeared as a parade of *dignités*. It became a three-tiered structure of "estates" (états).' And finally, and culturally more congenial for the author, the city became 'the scene of a style of living' made up of musical, masonic and educational institutions.[16] By his 'thick' description of this account, through a dialogue of 'text' and 'context', Darnton captures the shifting iconography of a modernising urban landscape.[17]

The iconography of landscape

A scholar of Renaissance art, Panofsky never addressed the European tradition of self-consciously landscape art and painting that became firmly established in the seventeenth century. The first great art critic and historian to devote his attention primarily to that tradition was the Victorian, John Ruskin. Over the past decade there has been a marked revival of interest in Ruskin's writings not only because they place landscape so squarely at the centre of social, political and environmental morality, but because his way of seeing and conceptualising has certain similarities to sensibilities today. Indeed, Peter Fuller has proclaimed Ruskin as 'the true prophet of the "post-modern" and "post-industrial" era'.[18] In the most recent major biography of John Ruskin, John Dixon Hunt has pointed out how his great eclectic collections or 'cabinets' of materials – mineral, floral and artifactual specimens, so typical of the Victorian intellectual sensibility – faithfully mirror Ruskin's mind in which 'everything was more or less reflected in everything else'.[19] We are reminded of Fredric Jameson's characterisation of late twentieth-century post-modern art as 'no longer unified or organic, but now [a] virtual grab-bag or lumber room of disjointed sub-systems and random raw materials and impulses of all kinds'.[20] In landscape Ruskin sought a stable ground in which a consistent order of divine design could be recognised in underlying form. Landscape he treated as a text, taking his method from biblical exegesis, seeking the reassurance of order in the face of the apparent chaos of industrialising Britain.[21] Thus the central purpose of his first great text, *Modern painters* (1843), was to locate landscape in a broader context than the study of form and the history of style. The 'higher landscape' depended upon a humble submission of men to the great laws of nature, a close observation of the natural world and the application of the greatest skill and imagination in its representation. In the hands of a master like Turner, landscape became in Ruskin's eyes a suitable subject for examining the deepest moral and artistic truths, rather as history painting had been viewed within the academic tradition.

In some respects Ruskin's was a conservative attempt to wrest order from that quintessentially modern anarchic interplay of images and feelings which his own prose so often betrays, and which every sensitive Victorian faced as the onrush of modernisation and the faith-shattering impact of Darwin made 'all that is solid melt into air'.[22] But while Ruskin proclaimed himself, like his father, a Tory 'of the old school', he also, and without apparent contradiction, styled himself a communist, 'reddest also of the red'. He was indeed one of the fiercest critics of the demoralisation and alienation of industrialism. In *The stones of Venice* (1851–3) he claimed to find in late medieval Venice a perfect society, one that followed the hierarchical order of nature. A voluntary submission to the laws which run through all creation had produced a community where a wise and just patriciate governed a state in which other orders of men and women found the spiritual freedom to express their truest being, a state therefore which became a collective work of art and the beauty of whose architecture and landscape still express the disciplined human liberation which comes only through faith.[23] Perhaps it is not surprising that it should be at the very juncture of the medieval world with its vision of nature as an illuminated text replete with the signatures of divinity, glossed at the margins by the insights of faith, and the Renaissance world of deeply engraved symbolism that Ruskin's vision should find its most comfortable resting point. Perhaps, too, it is appropriate that Ruskin should be rediscovered in today's world, so saturated in reproduced images

> that nature itself threatens to become what it was for the Middle Ages: an encyclopaedic, illuminated book overlaid with ornamentation and marginal glosses, every object converted into an image with its proper label or signature ... The quintessential modern experience of this new 'book of nature' is the stroll through the scenic wonders of a national park with a plastic earphone that responds to electronic triggers embedded at strategic locations along the path.[24]

Ruskin's modern appeal lies as much in this radical representation of nature as a complex interplay of images as in his appeal to a 'green' ideology of social harmony with a nature whose laws are incommensurable, irreducible to the analytic rules of positivist science and the profit-seeking logic of technology.[25]

The landscape tradition in painting which Ruskin did so much to promote and which peaked in England during his lifetime has been the subject of an increasing corpus of iconographical study that reaches beyond the disciplinary boundaries of art history. In his pioneering *Landscape into art* (1949), Kenneth Clark, himself a great admirer of Ruskin, attempted to place different styles of Western landscape painting – emblematic, empiricist, naturalistic, fantastic – in their philosophical and, occasionally, their sociological contexts. Seventeenth-century Dutch art, 'the landscape of fact', was, with its emphasis on '*recognisable* experiences', Clark asserted, 'a bourgeois form of art' for it represented the experiential world of the rising middle-class merchant patrons of Amsterdam and Haarlem.[26] Taking his title, *Ways of seeing*, from one of Panofsky's key phrases, but drawing too upon the marxist aesthetics of Walter Benjamin, John Berger took issue with Clark's interpretative emphasis on the philosophical as opposed to the social and economic in works of art and also in the idea that the history of high art was an expression of a unitary history of 'civilisation'.[27] Clark had described Gainsborough's *Mr and Mrs Andrews* as an 'enchanting work', a 'naturalistic' landscape painting expressing the artist's 'Rousseauism'; 'They are not a couple in nature as Rousseau imagined nature', countered Berger, 'they are landowners and their proprietory attitude towards what surrounds them is visible in their stance and their expressions ... the pleasure of seeing themselves depicted as landowners ... was enhanced by the ability of oil paint to render their land in all its substantiality.' A way of seeing the world which 'was ultimately determined by new attitudes to property and exchange, found its visual expression in the oil painting: ... not so much a framed window onto the world as a safe let into the wall, a safe in which the visible has been deposited'.[28]

Berger thus reformulated Panofsky's layers of meaning in terms of a marxist stratigraphy of economic base and cultural superstructure, the ideology of representation in English eighteenth-century landscape art serving to naturalise, and hence to mystify, basic property relations.

Around the same time as Berger, Raymond Williams conducted a similar polemical critique of landscape in English literature and by implication in polite English culture as a whole:

a working country is hardly ever a landscape. The very idea of landscape implies separation and observation. It is possible and useful to trace the internal histories of landscape painting, and landscape writing, landscape gardening and landscape architecture, but in any final analysis we must relate these histories to the common history of a land and its society.[29]

Berger and Williams inaugurated and often directly influenced a series of studies in many disciplines on the social implications of landscape imagery. Not all of them have been so confident as Berger and Williams in opposing a 'real' history of 'land' to an 'ideological' history of 'landscape', nor have they all been willing to reduce landscape aesthetics entirely to ideology.[30] But all have been intent to decipher the social power of landscape imagery, to identify, in the title of James Turner's study of seventeenth-century prospect poetry, the 'politics of landscape'.[31] Turner shows that many topographical and prospect poems went beyond the single vantage point of a spectator, perhaps by deploying conventions of mapping or inventory to 'work up an idea of human geography, a view of country life and regional character'.[32] While landscape for these poets connoted an attractive, elevated, comprehensive, disengaged and orderly view of the world – and hence a reliably objective one – so it was also distrusted (sometimes by the same poets) as a pernicious delusion, a dazzling trick designed to distort the world and its workings.

This sense of the duplicity of landscape imagery is characteristically 'postmodern', and it is no accident that Turner's study took shape under the influence of a critic best known for his decoding of modern advertising as well as painting and literature, Roland Barthes.[33] Commenting on such criticism W. J. T. Mitchell states that

language and images have become enigmas, problems to be explained, prison houses which lock understanding away from the world. The commonplace of modern studies of images, in fact, is that they must be understood as a kind of language; instead of providing a transparent window on the world, images are now regarded as the sort of sign that presents a deceptive appearance of naturalness and transparence concealing an opaque, distorting, arbitrary mechanism of representation, a process of ideological mystification.[34]

The post-modern apprehension of the world emphasises the inherent instability of meaning, our ability to invert signs and symbols, to recycle them in a different context and thus transform their reference. Earlier and less commercial cultures may sustain more stable symbolic codes[35] but every culture weaves its world out of image and symbol. For this reason the iconographic method remains central to cultural enquiry. But the liberation of meaning in modern society, the freedom of intertextuality which Ruskin's writings implicitly acknowledge, emphasises surface rather than depth. The conservative picture of a 'deep' England with its stable layers of historical accretion, so profoundly threatened by modernisation, that W. G. Hoskins framed from his window in North Oxfordshire in the closing pages of *The making of the English landscape*,[36] and the more radical and demotic, but no less composed, England sketched by Raymond Williams looking out from the window in Cambridgeshire where he wrote *The country and the city*[37] represent alternative attempts to achieve that stability of meaning in landscape which Ruskin sought and which has become a characteristic and honourable response to the perceived chaos of the modern world. At the same time we recognise these Englands for what they are: images, further glosses upon an already deeply layered text. These images might also be seen as additional reflections to a more dazzling and more superficial pattern. From such a post-modern perspective landscape seems less like a palimpsest whose 'real' or 'authentic' meanings can somehow be recovered with the correct techniques, theories or ideologies, than a flickering text displayed on the word-processor screen whose meaning can be created, extended, altered, elaborated and finally obliterated by the merest touch of a button.[38]

NOTES

1   D. E. Cosgrove, *Social formation and symbolic landscape* (London, 1984), pp. 13–38.
2   D. W. Meinig, 'Reading the landscape: an appreciation of W. G. Hoskins and J. B. Jackson', in D. W. Meinig (ed.), *The interpretation of ordinary landscapes* (Oxford, 1979), pp. 195–244; Pierce F. Lewis, 'Axioms for reading the landscape', in *ibid.*, pp. 11–32; James S. Duncan, 'Individual action and political power: a structuration perspective', in R. J. Johnston, *The future of geography* (London, 1985), pp. 174–89.
3   Similar common ground between those from different disciplines interested in landscape was sought in the symposium organised by the Landscape Research Group in Exeter, 1983, whose proceedings are published in *Landscape Research* 9, 3 (1984).
4   W. J. T. Mitchell, *Iconology: image, text, ideology* (Chicago, 1986), p. 2.
5   Erwin Panofsky, *Studies in iconology: humanistic themes in the art of the Renaissance* (Oxford, 1939), p. 14; 'Iconography and iconology: an introduction to

the study of Renaissance art', in Erwin Panofsky, *Meaning in the visual arts* (Harmondsworth, 1970), pp. 51–81, quotations on pp. 57–8.

6 Panofsky's stratigraphic metaphor for iconology forced him to suggest that the meaning of a work of art was somehow secreted below its surface configuration. For a criticism of this approach see Svetlana Alpers, *The art of describing: Dutch art in the seventeenth century* (Chicago, 1983), pp. xxiii–xxiv.

7 Panofsky, 'Iconography and iconology', pp. 55, 64, 65.

8 *Studies in iconology*, p. 6 fn. 1; 'Iconography and iconology', p. 56.

9 Ernst Cassirer, *Language and myth* (New York, 1946), p. 8; originally published as *Sprache und Mythos*, No. 6 in *Studien der Bibliothek Warburg*, quoted in Samuel Y. Edgerton Jr, *The Renaissance rediscovery of linear perspective* (New York, 1975), p. 156. We owe the recognition of the importance of Cassirer to Panofsky to pp. 153–65 of Edgerton's book.

10 Erwin Panofsky, 'Die Perspektive als "symbolische Form"', *Vorträge der Bibliothek Warburg: 1924–5* (Leipzig, 1927), pp. 258–331.

11 Panofsky, 'Iconography and iconology', pp. 59–61.

12 Erwin Panofsky, *Gothic architecture and scholasticism* (New York, 1957), pp. 17, 58.

13 Panofsky, 'Iconography and iconology', pp. 51–2.

14 Clifford Geertz, 'Thick description: toward an interpretative theory of culture' in *The interpretation of cultures: selected essays* (New York, 1973), pp. 3–30, quotations on p. 27.

15 Clifford Geertz, 'Art as a cultural system', in *Local knowledge: further essays in interpretative anthropology* (New York, 1983), pp. 94–120, esp. 102–9.

16 Robert Darnton, 'A bourgeois puts his world in order: the city as a text', in *The great cat massacre and other episodes in French cultural history* (London, 1984), pp. 107–43, quotations on pp. 120, 124, 140.

17 For similar analyses of the ritual meaning of urban landscapes see Edwin Muir, *Civic ritual in Renaissance Venice* (Princeton, 1981); and David Cannadine, 'The context, performance and meaning of ritual: the British monarchy and the "invention of tradition", c. 1820–1977', in Eric Hobsbawm and Terence Ranger (eds.), *The invention of tradition* (Cambridge, 1983), pp. 101–64.

18 Peter Fuller, 'John Ruskin: a radical conservative', in Peter Fuller, *Images of God: the consolation of lost illusions* (London, 1985), pp. 277–83, quotation on p. 283.

19 John Dixon Hunt, *The wider sea: a life of John Ruskin* (London, 1982). The quotation is from Kenneth Clark, *Ruskin today* (Harmondsworth, 1967), p. xiii.

20 Fredric Jameson, 'Postmodernism, or the cultural logic of late capitalism', *New Left Review*, 146 (1984), pp. 53–92.

21 D. E. Cosgrove, 'John Ruskin and the geographical imagination', *Geographical Review* 69 (1979), pp. 43–62.

22 This is the title of Marshall Berman's essay on modernism: *All that is solid melts into air* (London, 1981). The quotation is originally from Karl Marx discussing 'the bourgeois epoch' in *The communist manifesto*.

10   Stephen Daniels and Denis Cosgrove

23 Denis Cosgrove, 'The myth and the stones of Venice: the historical geography of a symbolic landscape', *Journal of Historical Geography* 8 (1982), pp. 145–69.
24 W. J. T. Mitchell, 'Editor's note: the language of images', *Critical Inquiry*, 6 (1980), p. 359.
25 Fuller argues that his holistic, ecological approach is the main reason for Ruskin's contemporary appeal: 'Mother nature', in *Images of God*, pp. 77–82.
26 Kenneth Clark, *Landscape into art* (Harmondsworth, 1956), p. 43.
27 John Berger, *Ways of seeing* (London, 1972).
28 *Ibid.*, pp. 106–9.
29 Raymond Williams, *The country and the city* (London, 1973), p. 120.
30 See respectively John Barrell, *The idea of landscape and the sense of place 1730–1840: an approach to the poetry of John Clare* (Cambridge, 1972), and Peter Fuller, *Seeing Berger: a re-evaluation* (London, 1980).
31 James Turner, *The politics of landscape: rural scenery and society in English poetry 1630–1660* (Oxford, 1979).
32 *Ibid.*, p. 24.
33 *Ibid.*, pp. 188–9. John Berger and Raymond Williams have also addressed advertising; see Berger, *Ways of seeing*, pp. 28–43, and Williams, 'Advertizing: the magic system' in *Problems in materialism and culture* (London, 1980), pp. 170–95.
34 Mitchell, *Iconology*, p. 2.
35 Marshall Sahlins, *Culture and practical reason* (Chicago, 1976).
36 W. G. Hoskins, *The making of the English landscape* (Harmondsworth, 1970), pp. 298–303.
37 Williams, *The country and the city*, p. 3.
38 We are grateful to Mike Heffernan for his comments on earlier drafts of this essay.

1

The geography of Mother Nature

PETER FULLER

Recently, I told a fellow art critic that a group of geographers had expressed an interest in some of the ideas which I had been putting forward: I could see from his expression that he was perplexed. I might just as well have told him that a gaggle of arms dealers, or pet food manufacturers, had responded to my aesthetic ideas. He could clearly discern no connection between the study and pursuit of art and those disciplines which are concerned with our knowledge of the natural world.

I do not think that my colleague was in any way exceptional; 'perplexity' is symptomatic of that chaos and confusion which prevails within today's art world. No one is certain any more about where aesthetic values come from; and it is the exception, rather than the rule, to think that they bear any relationship to our responses to nature.

Things were not always so: the early aesthetic philosophers – Alexander Baumgarten, Immanuel Kant, and Edmund Burke among them – recognised that the aesthetic response was evinced by natural forms and phenomena as much as by the objects created by artists. Similarly, there was a time when no one would have thought it odd for an artist to take a professional interest in, say, anatomy, zoology, botany, or meteorology. Indeed, it was generally assumed that such disciplines were keys to the successful creation of aesthetic effects in the visual arts. But that phenomenon which art historians refer to as 'Modernism' drove a wedge between the pursuit of art and the study of nature – a wedge which sadly seems to have remained firmly in place in the era of 'Post-Modernism' which, we are told, we have recently entered.

The modernist flight from the world of nature took a variety of forms. Some looked to the paradigms of mechanical, as opposed to natural, production. Others urged a form of 'art for art's sake' which insisted there was no correspondence between the 'Significant Forms' (of art) which give rise to aesthetic experience and *natural* forms. After the second world war, this severance became chronic. Studies related to the natural sciences and observation of the natural environment disappeared from our art schools. They were replaced – where they were replaced by anything which might be legitimately described as 'study' at all – by 'Basic Design', media studies, sociology, and so forth.

But this perplexity about the point of contact between art criticism and those disciplines concerned with the study of the natural world is as 'symptomatic' of the latter as of the former. For example, there was a time when geographers would have regarded aesthetic considerations as integral to their professional practice. I am, of course, referring to something more fundamental than, say, the aesthetic component in cartography, although it may be significant that this was once regarded as a central geographic preoccupation, one which has recently become, at best, peripheral.

As long ago as 1920, Sir Francis Younghusband, in his Presidential Address to the Royal Geographical Society, felt it necessary to advocate the systematic study of the beauties of scenery which, he said, constituted the neglected aesthetic dimension of geography. His call did not go entirely unheeded: for example, Vaughan Cornish produced a stream of books on this subject – all of them now neglected by aestheticians and geographers alike. 'Mainstream' academic geography was to develop in a very different sort of way. As I understand what happened – and I must beg forbearance because I have no specialist knowledge whatever concerning the geographer's discipline – geography became stripped in the post-second-world-war years of its aesthetic and ethical dimensions. In the 1950s and throughout the 1960s, a positivistic 'scientism' began to fall, if not like a cloud, then at least like an exhalation of academic exhaust fumes across the discipline.

Of course, it was not just geography that was so affected; we have all heard about that 'dissociation of sensibility' whose origins T. S. Eliot located in the Renaissance, and about the 'Two Cultures' which, according to C. P. Snow, were its extreme, contemporary expression. But I am trying to suggest something which runs even deeper than that. Back in the 1940s, Kenneth Clark, the art critic and historian, wrote vividly about the loss of that sense of 'intimacy and love' with which it had been possible 'to contemplate the old anthropocentric nature'. He commented on a spreading lack of faith in any idea of a 'natural order'.[1] More recently, that versatile anthropologist, Gregory Bateson, has described the acceleration of this loss. 'Most of us', Bateson writes, 'have lost that sense of unity of biosphere and humanity which would bind and reassure us all with an affirmation of beauty.'[2] Both Clark and Bateson imply there is a vicious circle connecting our changed response to the natural world and the impoverishment of our aesthetic lives. Aesthetic sensibility becomes a tepid and stunted – some might say decadent – faculty when it is severed from our evaluative responses to nature as a whole. Conversely, our response to nature is depleted and distorted when it is detached from aesthetic considerations. For Clark and Bateson, as for me, these were far from matters of merely specialist concern. The implications of this parting of the ways stretch far beyond the future of geography, or, come to that, the future of art. They touch upon the destiny of our culture as a whole, and perhaps even our survival upon this planet.

But not even Bateson took an entirely negative view. He was prepared to hint at the possibility of the emergence of a new sort of aesthetic response to nature. He argued that there were signs that men and women were 'beginning to play with ideas of ecology'. Although he believed we tend to trivialise such ideas into commerce or politics, he nonetheless felt able to detect 'an impulse still in the human breast to unify and thereby sanctify the total natural world, of which we are'.[3]

Many will not need reminding of the scattered signs of this impulse which, today, are sprouting up even at the oddest and most unexpected points on the shifting political spectrum. For example, I would cite the waning of belief in ever-increasing production as the means for the implementation of utopia. On both the left and the right, we see the re-emergence of debate about qualitative, rather than quantitative, aspects of both work and the environment. More generally, there are many signs of a widespread concern with, as it were, the ecology of our individual bodies, as organisms dependent upon a natural world which nurtures and supports them. All this seems to connect with the more public preoccupations of the conservationist and peace movements. As Raymond Williams has so vividly put it, there is now at least a possibility of replacing the idea of production by that of livelihood.[4]

Indeed, Williams's words seem to echo those of an even greater thinker: 'THERE IS NO WEALTH BUT LIFE' must be one of the most quoted of all John Ruskin's sentences – perhaps not surprisingly as he himself wrote it in capitals. There are many of us today who from different positions and disciplines find ourselves thinking about an idea of livelihood which regards man in unity with nature, rather than an idea of production which sets him against it. Inevitably, we have been drawn back to Ruskin. I know from the fascinating papers I have read by Denis Cosgrove and others that this is certainly happening to at least some geographers.[5] It has also happened to more than one art critic, myself included.

When I was a student in the mid-1960s, Ruskin seemed to be virtually unread. There was an extensive pseudo scholarship into such matters as the precise events of his wedding night. (The most recent research suggests it was menstrual blood, and not pubic hair, which precipitated his chronic aversion to the female genitals, and the sexual act.) But, to the literary establishment, Ruskin was just another forgotten Victorian, an eccentric embedded within the amber of Victorian celibacy, whose worthwhile reforms had all been incorporated into the modern welfare state, or at least into the reformist goals of the labour movement. Despite his concern with art and society, and his opposition to capitalism, Ruskin was deemed far too moralistic and reactionary to be taken up by the cultural radicals of the 1960s. Indeed, I well remember how when I gave Ruskin a very half-hearted sort of endorsement in an undergraduate essay, a fellow student took this as a betrayal, not just of the modernist movement in art but also of the revolutionary politics to which so many of us in those days felt committed without reservation. But, in the 1970s, like so many others, I slowly began to re-read Ruskin, and I no longer saw him as I had done in 1968, nor yet as some kind of tame and tepid prophet of the modern welfare state.

To set out to read Ruskin's work today is to start to climb an unknown mountain, a flawed and contradictory mountain, yes, and one on which it is easy to lose one's way among all those granite stubbornnesses, dangerous crevices, valleys clogged with the silt of dead ideas, and confusion of the strata of categories. It is a mountain upon which one constantly encounters strange fossils of thoughts, glacial drifts of verbiage, springs of brilliant insight, and the frequent glints of an almost unnaturally acute perception. Despite the arduous rocky passages where the going just gets so tough that one wants to give up, it is also an infinitely varied mountain, fascinating for its dappled surface, rich in filigreed rocks and luminous hoar-frost, and for the spectacular changes of view and mazes of argument which it offers at every turn. And, above all, it is a majestic mountain, with its foothills and lower slopes rooted firmly in the common-or-garden facts of nature and physical being, but soaring up towards those giddy and sublime heights, swathed in clouds of rapture, where an atheist like myself must leave Ruskin to tramp on by himself to meet with his maker.

But Ruskin is not, as some of his anthologists would have us believe, a kind of quarry of paradoxes and purple passages. For what he is saying, and, come to that, the way in which he says it, is all of a unity – that kind of unity in profusion and contradiction which one gets in those Gothic cathedrals whose beauties he did so much to popularise. This unity, however, was at odds not just with the *laissez-faire* capitalism of mid-nineteenth-century Britain; it springs out of the 39 volumes of the Library Edition of Ruskin's work as an even more formidable indictment of twentieth-century monopoly capitalism and its sad, technist apology for a human culture.

I believe that Ruskin is far more radical than many of his commentators give him credit for; but his radicalism is of an intensely unfashionable and, in many respects, a deeply conservative kind. Ruskin was only a founding father of British socialism in the sense that like the early socialists, he was an opponent of competitive, industrial capitalism. In the 1870s, Ruskin began to issue his eccentric monthly letters for working men, *Fors Clavigera*, in the seventh number of which he announced: 'Indeed I am myself a Communist of the old school, reddest also of the red.' But just three issues later, he is saying: 'I will tell you plainly. I am, and my father was before me, a violent Tory of the old school.' Now this contradiction is much less risible than it might appear if one remembers that Ruskin believed that a significant potentiality of human life, which had been realised in the past, was being suppressed in the present – even though it might be brought to life again in a changed future.

What then was that potentiality, or rather cluster of related potentialities? It was everything Ruskin came to express through his notion of 'The Gothic', which, in as far as it was for him not a purely historical category, might be described as those conditions under which the 'aesthetic dimension' in human culture can flourish. This aesthetic potentiality was denied and thwarted by nineteenth-century capitalism; but, until very recently, it has also been ignored by many of those who oppose themselves to it. And herein lies the importance of Ruskin's views about nature, and about work alike. It is the former which I am concerned with here, although the latter are also rewarding, and, I believe, relevant in our 'post-modern', 'post-industrial' age.[6]

We have to be careful about attributing an interest in the 'aesthetic dimension' to John Ruskin, if only because he himself distinguished between what he called *aesthesis*, or the response to merely sensuous pleasure (about which he was rather dismissive), and *theoria*, or the response to beauty of one's whole moral being. When I used the term 'aesthetic dimension' as a synonym for Ruskin's concept of Gothic, I was clearly referring to something closer to the latter, to *theoria*, than to the former, *aesthesis* – the simply sensuous response. Because Ruskin made this distinction, he has been much berated in the twentieth century for his allegedly 'moralistic' approach to art; but we should remember that he meant something much richer by his appeal to morality than narrowly ethical considerations. For Ruskin, 'morals' encompassed everything we would identify under such categories as human affections and emotions, structures of feeling, indeed the whole rich terrain of imaginative and symbolic thought. Ruskin was critical of 'the general tendency of modern art under the guidance of Paris', because he thought it was in pursuit of mere *aesthesis* in isolation from *theoria*. This was the true secret of his notorious quarrel with Whistler, which ended up in the law courts. As Ruskin put it, 'I take no notice of the feelings of the beautiful we share with spiders and flies.'

Ruskin had Impressionism in mind when he made these criticisms; but had he seen, say, the 'post-painterly' products of the School of New York, in the 1960s, he would certainly have felt that his fears about the 'general tendency of modern art' had been fully realised. And unless one believes that our response to, say, a beautiful red scarf is in every significant respect equatable with, say, our response to the ceiling of the Sistine Chapel, it seems to me not only must one admit that Ruskin had a point, but also that it was a very powerful one indeed.

A problem arises, however, because Ruskin's discussion of this 'response to beauty of one's whole moral being' is inevitably enmeshed with his ideas about nature and about God, and these are likely to seem nigh on impenetrable to anyone living in the latter part of the twentieth century who is fortunate enough to have escaped a theologically-infected childhood. Nonetheless, it is important to emphasise that even Ruskin's most 'eccentric' and 'idiosyncratic' aesthetic ideas turn out, on closer inspection, to have been broadly consonant with informed Protestant opinion in the early nineteenth century. One can get some idea of Ruskin's way of seeing things by thinking about St Hilary's question: 'Who can look on nature and not see God?' The immanence of God within his creation was a traditional element of Christian teaching; thus even Gregory the Great had regarded 'the wonders of visible creation' as 'the foot-prints of our creator'. But ideas of this kind were to acquire an unprecedented importance in early nineteenth-century Protestant thought – as ideas tend to do when the suspicion begins to arise in certain minds that they might not be true. The majority of nineteenth-century scientists and divines believed that nature revealed God's handiwork. This was true of the catastrophists, like William Buckland, who thought he knew the exact date of the creation of the world, and had an immediate, personal influence over Ruskin during the latter's time at Oxford. (Ruskin used to draw the diagrams and illustrations for his lectures.) But it was also true of more subtle thinkers, like Adam Sedgwick, of Cambridge, a pioneer geologist and churchman responsible for the exemplary museum of fossils and minerals which is still extant.

In 1833, Sedgwick argued that the 'beautiful and harmonious movements in the vast mechanism of nature' proved the existence of God; and that every portion of the visible world bore the impress of his wisdom and power. Sedgwick assumed that 'the adaptation of our senses to the constitution of the material world' led immediately to the discovery of theological truths. His museum would not only instruct the young men of Cambridge; it would also confirm their faith. But Sedgwick also readily acknowledged that nature spoke equally to what he called 'our imaginative and poetic feelings'. He wrote: 'It is certain that the glories of the external world are so fitted to our imaginative powers as to give them a perception of the Godhead and a glimpse of his attributes.' He quotes enthusiastically from the psalmist: 'The heavens declare the glory of God, and the firmament sheweth his handy work.'[7]

Ten years after Sedgwick had written these words, the young John Ruskin began what he intended to be a brochure in reply to scoffing press criticisms of Turner's painting: in fact, this work swelled into the five long volumes of *Modern painters* in which Ruskin changed his views about art and much else besides. But when he set out, he wanted to show that Turner had paid greater attention to nature, and depicted it more truthfully, than any of the old masters, or, indeed, any of his contemporaries. But, for Ruskin, this did not mean that Turner simply reproduced appearances more effectively than other artists. Like Sedgwick, and most other men who had thought seriously about such matters in the early 1840s, Ruskin – at least, the Ruskin of the first volume of *Modern painters* – believed 'Nature' was little more than a synonym for the handiwork of God. Like Sedgwick, too, Ruskin argued that it was possible to be 'tone deaf', as it were, to these evidences of the divine within nature. Nonetheless, Ruskin maintained that if a man developed his responses, he learned to *see* a leaf not just as vegetable tissue, but rather as the embodiment of religious and moral truth. Under these circumstances, he argued, 'the simplest forms of nature are strangely animated by the sense of Divine presence, the trees and flowers seem all, in a sort, children of God'. Turner was more of a realist than other painters because he had this kind of divinely attuned perception to an exceptional degree. Thus, as Ruskin put it, 'each exertion of [Turner's] mighty mind' might be 'both hymn and prophecy; adoration to the Deity, revelation to mankind'.[8]

These ideas are the key to Ruskin's early aesthetic theories. As George Landow has shown us, just as the evangelical preachers Ruskin had heard in his youth sermonised from the 'Types' they perceived in the natural world, so Ruskin saw 'Typical Beauty' in organic forms, which he believed to be God's handiwork.[9] Long before Ruskin, Schlegel had said: 'as God is to his creation, so is the artist to his own'. But in the early Ruskin at least, the natural world is seen, quite literally, as an expressive work of art produced through the supreme imaginative and creative capacities of the divine creator, God. And this is why – indeed it is the only reason why – for Ruskin, nature was the model of artistic creativity. Because God, as it were, seemed to Ruskin to have gone for diversity in unity, Ruskin looked for such things in the art and architecture of men and women. Ruskin attends to nature with such obsessive detail in those extraordinary passages on mountains and clouds in part, at least, because he wants to know quite literally how God went about making things. Thus in one famous passage in *Modern painters*, he imagines the Alps as a 'great plain, with its infinite treasures of natural beauty, and happy human life, gathered up in God's hands from one edge of the horizon to the other, like a woven garment, and shaken in deep folds, as the robes droop from a king's shoulders'.[10] And as late as 1870, Ruskin could compare the splendours of Chartres Cathedral's vault unfavourably with nature, i.e. with 'the work of His fingers', and 'the stars of the strange vault which He has ordained'.[11]

All this undoubtedly sounds rather quaint to us; but most of Ruskin's readers would not have found it so. Natural theology, or at least a theological naturalism, was something of a mania among the British middle-classes in the early nineteenth century. Many women spent much of their spare time gathering wild flowers, which they later painted or pressed. Many men collected minerals which, like Ruskin, they arranged in rows in cabinets. Both sexes, alike, compulsively combed beaches and probed rock-pools in search of sea creatures.[12]

A vast literature, at every level of sophistication, met these enthusiasts' needs. Little of this writing had much to do with natural *history*: rather its purpose was often simply to reiterate the theme that nature, rightly seen, revealed moral and religious truths. As Mrs Meredith put it in her soppy, but successful, *The romance of nature*: 'I love flowers as forming one of the sweetest lines in the GOD-WRITTEN Poetry of Nature.' In his great classic of the genre, *Glaucus or the wonders of the shore*, published in 1855, Charles Kingsley professed to be able to trace the reflection of God in the crabs and sea-anemones he saw in a rock-pool on the beach; 'the naturalist', he explained, 'acknowledges the finger-mark of God, and wonders, and worships'.

When Ruskin stepped forward – albeit with a certain nervousness concerning their possible Puseyism, or worse – to defend the Pre-Raphaelites, he picked out Charles Collins's *Convent Thoughts* (Fig. 1) for special discussion in his letter to *The Times*.[13] This painting is redolent with natural symbolism. Collins shows a nun standing in front of a pool of goldfish in an *hortus conclusus*, or enclosed garden. She stares at a passion flower, so-called because its stamens form a cross symbolising the crucifixion of Christ.[14] Ruskin's defence of Pre-Raphaelitism followed exactly the same lines as his defence of Turner. (In fact, the pamphlet he subsequently wrote about Pre-Raphaelitism was largely about Turner.) Insofar as he admired them, the Pre-Raphaelites were true to nature: through their heightened perception of it they revealed God. Perfect naturalism and revelation of divine, or spiritual, truth were thus one and the same thing. All Ruskin needed to do to defend the Pre-Raphaelites to a public well-versed in the arguments of natural theology was to stress the accuracy of their work. And so, he wrote of the water-lily growing in the pond in Collins's painting, 'I happen to have a special acquaintance with the water plant *Alisma Plantago*. And I never saw it so thoroughly or so well drawn.' To have drawn the leaf so well was not just to have revealed its associations with purity, maidenhood, and divinity, but, as Ruskin argued elsewhere, to show how

Fig. 1 Charles Collins, *Convent Thoughts*, 1850. Oil on canvas. Ashmolean Museum, Oxford.

it conformed to one of the great formal 'types' through which God struc- tured his world.[15]

Such a reading of the details in this painting sounds distinctly odd today:

it is therefore perhaps worth pointing out that at just the moment when Collins was painting his nun in an enclosed garden studying a passion flower with a pool of goldfish at her feet, the Victorian craze for Wardian cases, or exotic fern gardens enclosed in glass cabinets, was reaching its peak. The aquarium vogue was just about to take off. In 1850, Robert Warington set up the first twelve-gallon container of fishes, snails, and plants, which he saw as a sort of microcosm of nature itself. (He believed that it would be indefinitely self-sustaining – a matter on which any subsequent aquarist could quickly have put him right.) Within a couple of years, no self-respecting middle-class household was without one.[16]

Again, this interest in Wardian cases and aquaria was moral and religious. Charles Kingsley argued that the cases were much better for young ladies than 'fancy work' or 'dreamy idleness'. But more specific instruction could be derived from these glazed boxes than that. In 1853 Philip Gosse set up the Aquarium at the London Zoo, and, the following year, published *The aquarium*, a handbook which told everyone how to do it at home. This was tremendously successful.

Gosse saw every organism as revelatory of some small part of God's 'mighty plan', and described it accordingly. For example, a rare bladder sea-weed, which he knew as *Cystoseira ericoides*, showed none of its virtues when taken out of the water, but, Gosse wrote, 'the moment the plant is submerged all its glory returns: the pale olive branches become invested with a most brilliant flush or iridescent light blue, not changeable in tint, though varying in intensity according to the play of light that falls upon it'. Thus, Gosse continued, 'it may be compared to some Christians, who are dull and profitless in prosperity, but whose graces shine out gloriously when they are plunged into the deep floods of affliction'.[17] And so it was that mid-nineteenth-century Victorians assumed that artists and naturalists alike could draw close to the deepest spiritual truths through a relentless, empirical naturalism.

This inter-dependence of natural science, theology, and art was also reflected in architecture. One of the few contemporary buildings Ruskin actually praised was William Butterfield's All Saints Church in Margaret Street, London, begun in 1849 as an exemplary building for the High Church Cambridge Camden Society.[18] This place of worship celebrates Butterfield's belief in 'constructional polychromy'; inside, a profusion of beautiful minerals have been gathered together, cut, and polished into a complex ornamental system which was intended to reveal how the very stones were animated with the glory of their creator.

Butterfield interpreted the idea of a Ruskinian church as being a sacred museum; conversely, a Ruskinian museum turned out to be a secular cathedral. We have already seen how Adam Sedgwick hoped his mineral collection would provide the students of Cambridge with a theological as well as a geological lesson. Ruskin, too, was a compulsive collector of stones and mineral specimens from which he did not hesitate to draw ethical and aesthetic truths. One of the greatest buildings inspired by his influence was the Oxford Museum. He was closely involved with its construction until, characteristically, he went sour on the scheme and withdrew in a huff.[19] The marvellous colonnades there consist of pillars, each of which has been made out of a different stone, to illustrate geological strata. Many of the capitals are vigorously carved. The ceiling, though of iron and glass, is vaulted, and, in the original conception, the specimens were presented as a complete vision of nature comparable to that celebrated in a Gothic cathedral. Alfred Waterhouse, too, was influenced by Ruskin when he designed the Natural History Museum at South Kensington. He adapted the design, and the ornamental system, from cathedral architecture.[20] As long as nature could be seen as God's handiwork there was no paradox in this. The museums were built in the same spirit as the cathedrals, that is as man's expression of his knowledge of, and delight in, God's work, i.e. nature.

But what if there was no God? Unlike St Hilary, or Gregory the Great, Ruskin could never be sure. Indeed, the year *before* he had compared Chartres Cathedral unfavourably with 'the work of *His* fingers', Ruskin had concluded that there was 'no Eternal Father ... man has no helper but himself', and admitted this conclusion brought with it 'great unhappiness'. More generally, we can say that by the middle of the nineteenth century, the very urgency with which it was asserted that every organism in nature revealed God could be correlated with the dawning of the realisation that it did not. There was fear about what might happen if the system of natural theology broke down altogether. Perhaps the significance of nature would turn out to be sexual rather than spiritual. Ruskin was not alone in begging the 'gentle and happy scholar of flowers' to have nothing to do with the 'obscene processes and prurient apparitions' of the secular biologists with all their talk of sexual activity, even among the plants.[21]

But there was a more frightening prospect even than this. Perhaps nature would turn out to be actually *meaningless*, simply mindless matter, shaped not by God, but by the blind vicissitudes of chance. This fear, I think, was at the root of Ruskin's revulsion against Poussin's great, grey painting of *Winter*, or *The Deluge*. Ruskin believed not only that Poussin's atheism had rendered him unable to paint wetness, but also that it had led him into a 'sense of spiritual destitution' which had fastened on his mind 'together with the hopeless perception of ruin and decay in the existing world', ending up in a monochromatic vision of the extinction of all life. Ruskin knew that it was just such a vision that he himself had to struggle to avoid; but even by 1851, it was pursuing him. In his essay on Pre-Raphaelitism, he wrote: 'The man who has gone, hammer in hand, over the surface of a romantic country, feels no longer, in the mountain ranges he has so laboriously explored, the sublimity or mystery with which they were veiled when he first beheld them.' Of course, Ruskin adds quickly, even detailed knowledge of the strata leads back 'to the unity of purpose and everlastingly consistent providence of the Maker of all things'. But elsewhere he admitted to hearing the clink of the geologists' hammers at the end of every biblical sentence.[22]

If a stone is a stone is a stone, or a passion flower is a passion flower is a passion flower, then, of course, there can be no Pre-Raphaelite aesthetic, and no Turner. Nor was this just some sort of private, psychological dilemma for John Ruskin. For example, just compare Holman Hunt's celebratory, paradisial landscapes of the early 1850s with those he produced a few years later: in the middle of this decisive decade, Hunt determined to reverse the process of God's disappearance from nature by setting off on an ill-considered journey to the Holy Land itself; but not even there could he detect the divine presence in the landscape. Instead of his Redeemer, he found only a mangy goat which dropped dead on him beside the Dead Sea. 'It is black,' he wrote of the landscape there, 'full of asphalte scum – and in the hand slimy, and smarting as a sting – No one can stand and say it is not accursed of God.'[23] He came back not with a celebration of the incarnation, but with a terrible image of *The Scapegoat* (Fig. 2), of the world as a god-forsaken wasteland, a heap of broken images where the sun beats.

Meanwhile, back home, the natural theologians were becoming ever more ingenious at accommodating the facts of nature to a threatened natural theology. In 1857, Philip Gosse argued desperately that just as there was no evidence that God had created Adam without a navel, so there was no reason to assume he had not invested the rocks themselves with their own history.[24] God had created the strata and fossils too. And he had done so precisely in order to test man's faith. But who else could possibly believe that the contemplation of a fossil led 'naturally' to Philip Gosse's theory?

The following year William Dyce began one of the last of the 'classical' Pre-Raphaelite landscapes, *Pegwell Bay* (Fig. 3). Dyce, incidentally, was a friend of Ruskin, and the first to insist to him that he should attend to what the Pre-Raphaelites were doing. He was also responsible for the mosaics in All Saints, William Butterfield's great mineral church. How far *Pegwell Bay* takes us from the stained-glass, noon-day brilliance of Collins's *Convent Thoughts* or Hunt's *The Hireling Shepherd*, of the early years of the decade. Dyce was a keen and knowledgeable amateur geologist; he was naturally drawn to the coast-line at Pegwell Bay, with its exposed chalk cliffs and abundance of fossils. He shows us a group of women and

Fig. 2   William Holman Hunt, *The Scapegoat*, 1854. Oil on canvas. The Lady Lever Art Gallery, Port Sunlight.

Fig. 3   William Dyce, *Pegwell Bay, Kent – A Recollection of October 5th 1858*, 1859–60. Oil on canvas. The Tate Gallery, London.

children engaged in the familiar pursuit of looking for specimens on the sea-shore. But they are not finding 'types' of the glory of God! The whole painting is filled with menace and foreboding. Overhead a comet, a symbol of impending doom and calamity, passes by unnoticed. Before Dyce had finished this painting, Darwin published *On the origin of species*. The old natural theology had been dealt what would turn out to be its most devastating blow; the great debate between Wilberforce and Huxley took place in the museum Ruskin had helped to design. Predictably, Ruskin himself took up an entrenched anti-Darwinian position. The moment of the Pre-Raphaelite landscape aesthetic had definitively passed. Those who followed could no longer pretend to hope that by staring at the stamen of a passion flower one could see God, or that he would reveal himself among the dry stones.

And so in later life, despite attempts – with varying degrees of success – to retrieve the consolations of religious belief, Ruskin was dogged by a sense of the *failure of nature*, by, as it were, the feeling that nature had been reduced to the grey lifeless monotone that had so repelled him as a young man in that late painting by Poussin. Indeed, soon after he admitted that there was no God, Ruskin began to detect what he was to describe as 'The Storm Cloud of the 19th Century', and its accompanying 'Plague Wind', which led him finally to his bleak vision that this 'failure of nature' (which he felt had somehow been brought about by the blasphemous actions of men) was leading to ultimate annihilation, to, as he put it, 'blanched Sun, – blighted grass, blinded man'.[25] At such times, of course, even his beloved Turners lost all meaning for him and he would order his considerable retinue of servants to take them out of the house.

Now it is often said that all this is a matter of Ruskin's delusion, of, in effect, his madness. And he did, of course, go quite mad. Nonetheless, I believe that some of Ruskin's most significant insights are to be found precisely here. It isn't just that, after the mid-nineteenth century, a 'Higher Landscape' painting became increasingly impossible: I think that we live in a world where both nature and art are widely seen as having lost their meaning in just the sort of way that Ruskin described. We live in an anti-aesthetic, or anaesthetic, environment whose paradigm is, in a sense, the grey monochrome. Indeed, as I have argued elsewhere, Ruskin's perception that the actions of men might be leading to a *real* failure in nature, and to a potential annihilation of human life, may turn out to be his most prophetic insights in this era of acid rain, ecological devastation, and potential nuclear winter.[26]

Gregory Bateson was no more of a believer than I am. But he once pointed out how the erosion of the concept of divine immanence was leading men and women to see the world around them as mindless, and hence as not worthy of ethical or aesthetic consideration. This led them to see themselves as set apart from nature. When this loss of a sense of organic unity was combined with an advanced technology, Bateson argued, 'your likelihood of survival will be that of a snowball in hell'. Once the illusion that the world was the handiwork of God had been jettisoned, then the whole base of aesthetics needed to be re-examined. All that, you could say, is pure Ruskin. Bateson went on to argue that, if we wanted to survive, we needed 'an ecology of mind', or a recognition of the fact that if nature is not itself the product of mind, then 'mind is immanent in the total evolutionary structure', and indeed is objectively discernible outside of ourselves.[27] I think that Ruskin, who did not have the advantage of twentieth-century biological and psychological knowledge, expressed very similar sorts of insights through concepts of divine immanence and 'the failure of nature'.

And this, in a sense, takes us right back to where we set out. For there are signs that a new aesthetic – which will be of importance not just for geographers, and artists, but for mankind as a whole – is beginning to be explored.[28] But how can this aesthetic win our hearts and minds if the illusion that the world is the purposeful and harmonious creation of a loving God has been destroyed for ever, and the naked shingles have been exposed for all to see? We need, I would suggest, secular equivalents of the religious illusion.

Bateson's suggestion that if nature is not the product of mind, then mind is the product of nature, provides us with one possible line of inquiry, one possible explanation of how we can recognise ourselves in the forms and patterns of nature, and feel at one with them, even if we do not believe in God. But there is another quite different route into this issue.

Some readers may know of the importance I have placed on the writings of the British psychoanalyst, D. W. Winnicott. Winnicott argues that, in the beginning, each of us entertains the illusion that we created the mother (and, by extension, the world) who nurtures and supports us. But as the child develops, it gradually intuits the separateness of the world, and accepts the disillusioning idea that it did not create that world.[29]

At this time, Winnicott argued, the infant establishes a 'potential space' in which through play, toys, and so on, the fantasised and the real are mingled imaginatively in consoling and creative ways. In aesthetically and spiritually healthy societies, there is a continuity between such infantile activities and culture itself, as realised in creative work, religious and artistic pursuits. But with the decline of belief, and the industrialisation of labour, 'the potential space' was squeezed out of ordinary life.

It came to reside in those imaginary worlds which painters created behind the picture plane; I am not, of course, suggesting that this was a matter of regressing to the lost paradise of early infancy. Rather, the painter sought to create an *adult* equivalent which drew upon developed sentiments, acquired skills, and mature perceptions of the external world. The pictures the painter offered comprised 'other realities within the existing one'. Those who enjoyed them did not 'read' them as reflections of the world they already knew. Rather these pictures bore witness to a vision of a world transformed, which was both memory and promise, personal, and potentially historic.

But we have seen how as the nineteenth century progressed, it became harder and harder for landscape painters to offer such reconciling illusions. The outside world seemed to develop a resilience to imaginative transformation! It was easy enough for landscape painters to avert their eyes from the impinging apparatus of modern industry, and most, of course, did. But it proved much harder to evade the changes in the structure of feeling which the continued retraction of religious belief, rise of uncreative factory work, and estrangement from nature brought about.

Recently, sociologically inclined art historians have insistently argued that the omission of, say, rural poverty, and the signs of industrialisation from much nineteenth-century landscape painting, was somehow morally, or imaginatively, reprehensible – 'escapist', rather than desirably 'realist'.

But I believe this argument needs to be stood on its head: for the Higher Landscape was wrecked not so much by a flight from reality, as through its progressive intrusion and impingement in a way which threatened the 'potential space'. As Ian Jeffrey has written, 'Prosaic matter crops up again and again in paintings by Ford Madox Brown, William Holman Hunt and John Everett Millais, in views and close-ups seemingly cut at random from Nature.'[30]

The question arises, Jeffrey continues, 'Why this rather than some other more or less insignificant sample of earth?' These were the first intimations of the landscape painter's historic crisis: the growing inability to transfigure the world convincingly even in imaginative illusion. And this, of course, was not 'merely' an aesthetic problem. In the later nineteenth century, Ruskin was not alone in fearing a 'failure of nature'. Indeed, the image of nature as a harmonious garden, an *hortus conclusus*, in which the Madonna played with her child, disappears altogether; or rather it survives only as a sentimental residue which fails to command the finest imaginative minds. For a brief moment, a negative version of the sublime 'Higher Landscape' dominated painting. I have in mind Millais's *Chill October* (1870), a compelling but bleak expression of nature as a 'darkling plane'. In Europe, too, there was a short phase of 'Higher Landscape' based on European perception of the North African desert.[31] But then the use of landscape as symbol disappears altogether, or, to be more exact, it collapses

Fig. 4   Arthur Boyd, *Bathers with Skates and Halley's Comet*, 1985. Oil on canvas.
Photograph courtesy Fischer Fine Art.

into topography, on the one hand, and abstraction on the other. The min-
gling of subjective and objective seems no longer possible, even in imaginative illusion.

Indeed, we have to wait almost a hundred years for a new 'Higher Landscape' painting: ironically, this first came into being through war artists
– Paul Nash, Graham Sutherland, and John Piper. But it found its fullest
expression not here in Britain, but in Australia, through the great explosion
of desert painting in the 1940s. One of the finest of the painters of the
desert was Sidney Nolan, who has sometimes been criticised for the way
in which he tried to depict the alienness of the desert void. Kenneth Clark
always admired Nolan, and perceived that his work was about the affirmation of values as much as the depiction of appearances; but many modernist
art historians have accused him of parasitising this landscape, and of project-
ing into it his own anxiety in a negative form of the pathetic fallacy –
in short, of simply refusing to accept its intractable, unsignifying otherness.
As one artist has complained, in Nolan's painting, 'The void of the land
is forced to signify, ignoring the suture that it offers.'[32]

But I have been studying this Australian landscape recently.[33] And it
is not, as is sometimes said, that Nolan, Arthur Boyd (Fig. 4), or Fred
Williams – who painted the desert in a different, but also compelling, way
(Fig. 5) – borrowed conventions from Europe that are inappropriate to

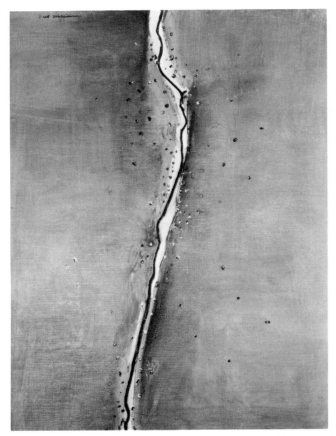

Fig. 5   Fred Williams, *Riverbed (A)*, 1978. Oil on canvas. Photograph courtesy Fischer Fine Art.

the depiction of the Antipodes. Rather, I think that the Australian desert landscape provides a better metaphor for all of us today than does the idyll of an English country garden. We have left the garden of Eden; or rather it is over-run with the metallic snakes of Cruise. We live, all of us, and not just the Australians among us, on the periphery of a potential desert. Even the Nature Conservancy Council is warning about the return of Constable's Suffolk to the condition of a prairie. We have become peculiarly ill at ease in the nature that nurtures us, constantly worried that through our own actions we will cause it to fail, certain that no God resides within the rocks and trees to save and console, sure that not much is for the best in this, our only possible world. (Even in biology, the panglossian fallacy of the traditional adaptationists is passing out of fashion.) The stubborn refusal of a Sidney Nolan, or a Fred Williams, to accept the intractability of the Australian landscape, their insistence upon realising an aesthetic response to it, was not only something new and admirable in art: it also bore witness to that irrepressible 'impulse in the human breast' to affirm beauty in, and unity with, the natural world, *regardless*.

NOTES

1 Kenneth Clark, *Landscape into art* (London, 1949), p. 141.
2 Gregory Bateson, *Mind and Nature* (London, 1980), p. 27.
3 *Ibid.*
4 *The Guardian*, June 1984.
5 Denis Cosgrove, 'John Ruskin and the geographical imagination', *Geographical Review*, 69 (1979), pp. 43–62; Denis Cosgrove and John Thornes, 'The truth of clouds: John Ruskin and the moral order in landscape', in D. C. D. Pocock (ed.), *Humanistic geography* (London, 1982), pp. 20–46.
6 The best and most original of recent accounts of Ruskin's theory of labour is by P. D. Anthony (*John Ruskin's labour* (London, 1983)).
7 *A discourse on the studies of the university* (London, 1833; republished Leicester, 1969), p. 18. See also Colin Speakman, *Adam Sedgwick: geologist and dalesman* (London, 1982).
8 *The works of John Ruskin*, Library Edition, ed. E. T. Cook and Alexander Wedderburn, 39 vols. (London, 1903–12), Vol. 3, pp. 630–1.
9 George Landow, *The aesthetic and critical theories of John Ruskin* (Princeton, 1971).
10 Ruskin, *Works*, Vol. 6, p. 119.
11 *Ibid.*, Vol. 20, p. 70.
12 See David Elliston Allen, *The naturalist in Britain* (London, 1976), and Lynn Barber, *The heyday of natural history* (London, 1980).
13 Ruskin, *Works*, Vol. 12, pp. 319ff.
14 For a detailed discussion of the symbolism in this painting, see the Tate Gallery catalogue, *The Pre-Raphaelites* (London, 1984), pp. 87–8.
15 For a detailed discussion of Ruskin's analysis of the leaf forms of *Alisma Plantago*, and the way in which he sought to relate them to other 'typical' forms, and for a more detailed discussion of many of the other issues raised in this text, see my own *Theoria*, forthcoming from Chatto and Windus.
16 Robert Warington, 'Notice of observations on the adjustment of the relations between the animal and vegetable kingdoms, by which the vital functions of both are permanently maintained', *Quarterly Journal of the Chemical Society of London* (1850), pp. 52–4. For origins of the Wardian cases craze see, Nathaniel Bagshaw Ward, *On the growth of plants in closely glazed cases* (London, 1842).
17 Philip Gosse, *The Aquarium* (London, 1854), p. 100. For further information on the aquarium craze, see also *The Aquarium* (2nd edn, London, 1856), which

contains additional material on the spread of this fashion; and *A handbook to the marine aquarium* (London, 1856). Apart from Gosse's writings, see Shirley Hibberd's many and various books including *Book of the water cabinet* (London, 1856), *The book of the fresh-water aquarium* (London, 1856), *The book of the marine aquarium* (London, 1856), *Rustic adornments for homes of taste, and recreation for town folk in the study and imitation of nature* (London, 1856), *The book of the aquarium* (London, 1860); and Francis S. Merton, *Handbook to the aquarium* (London, 1856). See also the writings of George Sowerby, including *Popular history of the aquarium of marine and freshwater animals and plants* (London, 1857); and *Companion to Mr. Kingsley's Glaucus* (London, 1858).

18 See Paul Thompson, *William Butterfield* (London, 1971).

19 For an informed discussion of Ruskin's involvement in the Oxford Museum see Eve Blau, *Ruskinian Gothic* (London, 1982) – also for its excellent analysis and history of the building itself.

20 See Mark Girouard, *Alfred Waterhouse and the Natural History Museum* (London, 1981).

21 Interestingly, Stanley Spencer was to elaborate just the sort of pan-sexual vision Ruskin feared, embracing even vegetable life, when his own religious faith dimmed: his 'prurient apparitions' were displayed in canvases like *Sunflower and Dog Worship* of 1937.

22 Ruskin, *Works*, Vol. 12, pp. 391–2; Vol. 26, p. 115.

23 See Judith Bronkhurst, ' "An interesting series of adventures to look back upon": William Holman Hunt's visit to the Dead Sea in November 1854', in Leslie Parris (ed.), *Pre-Raphaelite papers* (London, 1984), pp. 111–25.

24 Philip Henry Gosse, *Creation (Omphalos): an attempt to untie the geological knot* (London, 1857).

25 Ruskin, *Works*, Vol. 34, p. 40.

26 See, for example, 'Aesthetics and nuclear anaesthesia', in Peter Fuller, *The naked artist* (London, 1983), pp. 35–45.

27 See Gregory Bateson, *Steps to an ecology of mind* (London, 1973).

28 An example is the formation of groups like Common Ground, whose function is specifically to explore and support those involved in the aesthetic aspects of conservation and response to the natural world.

29 For my views on Winnicott see *The naked artist*, pp. 233–40. This and the following paragraphs have been adapted from my essay, 'Mother Nature', in *Images of God: the consolations of lost illusions* (London, 1985), pp. 77–82.

30 Ian Jeffrey, 'Public problems and private experience in British art and literature', in the Arts Council catalogue, *Landscape in Britain, 1850–1950* (London, 1983), pp. 22–33.

31 The best account of the European fascination with the African desert is to be found in the catalogue of a Royal Academy exhibition, *The Orientalists: Delacroix to Matisse, European painters in North Africa and the Near East* (London, 1984).

32 Joan Davila, 'Landscape art in western Australia', *Praxism*, No. 2 (July 1983).

33 For a detailed discussion of the significance of Australian landscape, and of many of the other themes of this essay, see Peter Fuller, *The Australian scapegoat: towards an Antipodean aesthetic* (Perth, 1986). In this book, I attempt to explore the symbolic geography of the Antipodes, and its relationship to European culture.

2

The evocative symbolism of trees

DOUGLAS DAVIES

And God held in His hand
A small globe. Look He said
The Son looked. Far off,
As through water, he saw . . .

On a bare
Hill a bare tree saddened
The sky. Many people
Held out their thin arms
To it as though waiting
For a vanished April

To return to its crossed boughs.
The Son watched them. Let me go there he said.

R. S. Thomas, *The Coming*

In an astute essay on 'theoretical landscapes' Anne Salmond has recently shown how widely metaphors of territory and journey have been used in the West to frame our talk about knowledge itself.[1] Like her, though with a shift of metaphor in a more arboreal direction, we also wish to see how natural phenomena assist thought. In scaling the tree of knowledge without getting too far out on any limb, in exploring the many branches of thought, and in attempting to get at the root of the matter, we pursue a branching task. For not only do we show how certain trees have served as symbols, but we also reflect on some of the complex aspects of symbolic thought itself.

In the history of Western thought the active and passive voices have been particularly dominant. 'I see the tree' and 'The tree is struck by lightning' exemplify a mode of thought implying a notion of causality which is far too simplistic for interpreting theories of symbolism. Standing over and against each other as they do such unidirectional notions of cause and effect result in contrary theories of knowledge which can best be typified as projectionist and revelationist. The former regards human thought as generating ideas which are subsequently projected onto the external world. Myths and other imaginative constructs appear to possess a reality of their own but none such objectively exists. This view was classically expressed in philosophy by Feuerbach, in psychology by Freud, and in sociology by Durkheim. Social scientists often view religious systems of thought in this way, while theologians for their part have traditionally espoused the opposite view and spoken of direct revelation from God to humanity. Mankind passively receives the divine input. This kind of revelationist stance will always be found to contradict the projectionist view in a conflict which cannot be creative. For our purposes it is certainly true that neither the stark projectionist nor the crude revelationist approach is at all helpful. Hence the adoption of what we call the evocationist or evocative theory of symbolic thought.

To speak of symbolism as an evocative mode of thought is to presume that both perceiver and perceived are set within a mutual system of information yielding a higher order knowledge than exists at the outset. The integrity of subject and object is maintained as the active and passive modes are reduced as antitheses, and in fact become more equal factors in the total process of symbolization. So the symbolic arena embraces the thinker, the object of thought – a tree for example – and the medium of historical and cultural imagination which integrates them in the act of symbolic reflection. I do not simply see the tree but am attracted to it by some inhering attribute whilst also conceiving it through cultural and historical precedent. Within my own autobiography it assumes a higher order significance than hitherto. To revert to our earlier analogy, the tree is not simply struck by lightning since it plays a part in attracting the devastating power.

Thus symbols are not arbitrary. They possess a peculiar appropriateness arising from their historical significance and their physical features. Very often symbols are what might be called a physical manifestation of ideas. They aid the process of gaining access to and of manipulating otherwise abstract concepts like those of kinship, manhood, womanhood, self-sacrifice, and so on. Symbols demand attention, they stimulate thought to produce new levels of association, they also afford a publicly accessible means of sharing concepts which are otherwise abstract or idiosyncratic.

We are now in a position to say that the attractiveness of trees lies both in their physical nature and in the creative metaphorical capacity of the human mind. As cultural and historical animals human beings are inevitably subject to existing symbolic expressions, not least those provided by trees and their associated environments. The attraction of trees thus unites their immediate botanical attributes and their established conventional attributes. Having once served as a focus of attention they are readily available to serve new, though perhaps derived, symbolic purposes as circumstance and imagination change. So the symbolic language of trees is likely to include some ideas of longstanding significance while also bearing the capacity for new expressions to flourish. At the glibbest level we could say that it is just because certain trees came to bear a meaning as parkland features that they have subsequently borne significance in suburbs. In what follows we first examine some physical features of trees which have fitted them for cultural service, and then we explore at greater length how certain of these cultural ideas have developed.

Practical symbolism

The tree presents itself as a medium of thought in a direct and obvious way through its possession of trunk, roots, and branches. Other factors such as type of bark, flower, fruit, and colour all add subsidiary themes, as does the fact that the tree is a habitat for many other creatures. It also stands, both literally and metaphorically, as a living entity spanning many human generations. As such it avails itself as a historical marker and social focus of events. As links with the past, be it actual or mythical, particular trees make ideas more realistic and dynamic in the present. So we have the Bo tree under which the Buddha attained his enlightenment, the Glastonbury Thorn with its supposed link with St Joseph, while several trees at Amritsar's Golden Temple serve the memory of some former Sikh Gurus. To borrow a well-worn anthropological dictum normally used of totemism we can say that trees are not simply good to climb, they are good to think. Much of their wood is fuel for metaphorical fires.

Victor Turner was perhaps the one recent anthropologist who did most in tracing through extensive detail the meaning of interlinked symbols within one tribal people, the Ndembu of North-west Zambia. Not a few Ndembu rituals utilize trees, and it is no accident that one of his fullest works is entitled (after a phrase of Baudelaire) *The forest of symbols*.[2] We can but hint at the richness of the Ndembu symbolic universe and of Turner's ethnography as we furnish a few examples associated with the *Isoma* ritual. This rite was intended to ensure the fertility of women, their matrilineage, and good conjugal relations with their husbands, all at a time when there is some misfortune caused by ancestral shades. Central to the ritual is the use of medical substances collected beforehand from specific trees. In front of a *kapwipu* tree, *Swartzia madagascariensis*, the ritual leader lays a model of the woman who is to be treated. Her former pregnancy and its failure are rehearsed and the tree asked to make her strong to bear future children. The hardness of the tree's wood is seen as a source of strength for the woman herself. Wood chips from sixteen other trees are also employed and many layers of meaning surround the reasons given for their use. Some are exceptionally prolific in fruit production, a fruition which is begged for the woman. All chips represent trees from which bark-string cannot be made which, in Ndembu theories of causation, means that her fertility will not be tied up and stopped. The *chikoli* tree, *Strychnos spinosa*, also has some of its leaves taken, for it is renowned for its toughness and according to local etymology it is a tree which the elephant cannot push over. This inhering power will assist women in childbirth just as it influences circumcised boys in its ability to confer exceptional virility. The *mulendi* tree, *Sterculia quinqueloba*, whose slippery bark can easily make climbers fall, is associated with the slipping of the foetus from the womb before its appointed delivery time. Yet another tree produces numerous small fruit used as bait in trapping small animals; just as this fruit of the *musoli*, *Vangueriopsis lanciflora*, makes small animals appear so it is also thought to be effective in making little babies appear. All these examples demonstrate what we have already said about evocative symbols, a point very neatly summarized by Turner elsewhere when he argued that there is in the semantics of such symbols a 'union of ecology and intellect that results in the materialization of an idea'.[3] For the Ndembu it is the association of ideas grounded in folk etymology which links arboreal characteristics and imaginative reflection and then implements the outcome in ritual. A final example from this culture shows something of the abstract sophistication inhering in the ritual; this time it involves not a particular species of tree but any type of tree whose roots are habitually exposed. Classified as *wuvumbu*, from a verb to unearth, the use of medicines from this category of plant is said to bring everything to the surface in the sense of helping to reveal the meaning and purpose of the rites.

For a somewhat different symbolic use of trees we move to Siberia and Central Asia, the traditional homeland of the shaman, that ritual figure whose trances are the focal point of community dramas intended to heal the sick and remedy discords within social life. In North and South America similar ritual experts are found who resemble the European shaman in taking journeys into supernatural realms while undergoing a trance. This technique of ecstasy, as it was called by Mircea Eliade the great scholar of shamanism,[4] is directly related to the notion of the cosmic or world tree which is believed to exist at the centre of the world, often at the apex of the world mountain. Its roots lie in the underworld, its branches touch heaven, while its trunk is the more accessible source of life and contact with these other dimensions and realms. In darkness and with dramatic behaviour the shaman sets out on his journey by mounting steps cut into a birch trunk set up for the purpose in the public gathering place. This particular birch represents the cosmic tree of legend and mythology. He or she (and the shaman is often a woman) then creates a kind of supernatural geography, a cosmic habitat in which dealings with the gods or other mythical figures occur. In yet other cultural contexts the tree is viewed as a ladder set up to heaven from earth and is widely known in Jewish, Christian, and Islamic traditions. In North America a pole stands for the cosmic tree and further similarities exist with the world tree of Mayan civilization under which the dead rest after the weariness of life.[5]

Certainly the Asian cosmic tree is depicted as a source of life, power, eternity, and strength, acting as a focal point for organizing thought about life's intrinsic mystery. On its branches perch the souls of the unborn waiting for an opportunity to gain an earthly abode, a desire the shaman may assist by his mystic journey. Aiding his own movement the shaman plays a drum reckoned to be made from the wood of the cosmic tree. Ritually speaking the cosmic journey is enhanced by the rhythmic music of the drum from the cosmic tree whose trunk is also the means of transport between the mundane realm and its transcendent complement. The three-fold symbolic segmentation of tree into root, trunk, and branch affords ease of reflection upon the infernal, earthly, and heavenly domains into which the shaman may venture on community errands.

Ideological symbols: pagan

While this kind of discussion stresses the immediate features of trees, and inevitably sets such attributes within local traditions, the fact that some cultures are non-literate and lack a written history and historiography means that the role of symbolism is not quite the same as it is in European thought. To exemplify this we move from practical and immediate uses of symbolic trees to what might be called ideological trees. What we have already said about shamans and cosmic trees has prepared the way for this shift of attention precisely because motifs involving cosmic trees have already become part of the literary heritage of Western thought. C. G. Jung, for example, used the picture of the world tree in discussing images desired by modern individuals who feel themselves disinherited in their own world.[6] Historians of religion have also traced similar uses of symbolic trees and show how they span many centuries of cultural reflection.

We begin with classical Greece and Homer's Odyssey as we follow the analysis so delightfully constructed by Hugo Rahner.[7] Odysseus is commanded to journey to Hades, to that dreadful realm of tall poplars and the fruit-destroying willows, a term whose meaning will soon become clear. Rahner traces it from Homer into early Christian theology and on into the medieval period; we simply sketch important episodes in that progression.[8]

Odysseus reaches the gates of Hades where he has been carried by mysterious winds and where unearthly light pervades that realm of darkness. He is overwhelmed by pangs of homesickness for Ithaca where, as in the

Greece of real life, willows were associated with water and life on the one hand, and with burial mounds and death on the other. On his return journey he has to be bound to the ship's mast lest he be fatally attracted by the devastating song of the Sirens, a song unheard by his crew whose ears have been carefully stopped against the alluring sound. Early Christian theology took these motifs of willow and mast and developed them in ways which show how mythological thought is as creative as it is elaborate. Their development shows, above all else, the longing to give vent to new ideas through older forms of reflection.

The Greeks had long observed that willows appeared to cast off their blossom before fruit had set. But more significant still the willow seemed to reproduce more by means of suckers from existing roots than by seed. Here, as Rahner pinpointed it, was a 'starting point for the dialectic of mythological growth, for this living tree is the murderer of its own fruit. Both life and death are at work in this tree that continually dies to itself and is at the same time its own procreator.'[9] Here in our terms is the basis for the attraction inherent in the willow which gives it great potential as a symbol, a potential not simply for one dichotomy, as in the case of life and death, but for virginity and fecundity and other ideals. This is a good example of what Victor Turner called the multivocal or polysemic nature of symbols, where one meaning is related to others in an increasingly deep pool of potential meanings available for exploitation by future interpreters.[10]

The Thesmophoria, an ancient Greek rite for women, affords an example. Treating the themes of fertile fields and fertile wombs in dramatic form it employed beds of willow wands on which the women slept. Two ideas were enshrined in this act, those of virgin and mother, and of sexual continence and maternal fertility, and both were capable of expression through the willows from which the wands were taken. Virginity and chastity were associated with the willow's dying blossom, while fecundity was grounded in its capacity to produce suckers from its own substance. The Greeks derived their word for the willow from the verb to go. The similarity between the Greeks and the Ndembu is of some passing interest since both employ etymology as the rationale for ritual. Similarly, the Romans said that the willow, *Salix* derived its name from the verb *salire*, to jump. The causal relations expressed in such etymologies allow us to relate the evocative theory of symbols to earlier anthropological ideas which seldom attract attention today. Sir James Frazer's discussion of sympathetic magic and homeopathic magic in *The Golden Bough* sought to depict ways in which primitive peoples reflected on the world.[11] Objects which looked, or which had once been, united could exert a subsequent influence upon each other. Causality and association of objects were thus related ideas; this was also argued by Lévy-Bruhl in his notion of participation.[12] Our discussion of the evocative nature of symbols also suggests that thinkers participate in certain ideas through associations afforded by symbolic phenomena. A final Greek example will support this point. It says in an old proverb that when the willow or chaste-tree blossoms the grape will soon be ripe. The folk-meaning is that the strength welling up in the production of flower is not utilized for fruit on the parent tree and thus becomes a kind of free energy available to benefit the ripening grapes. The dried flower of the willow was also believed to aid chastity by restraining sexual lust and by reducing the vitality of male seed.

Ideological symbols: Christian

For early Christians inhabiting the Greek-minded Mediterranean world these mythological motifs were not without some power. They were not abandoned as pagan and false, but were adopted as stories enshrining partial truths awaiting transformation into Christian crowning insight given the proper sort of interpretation. The fruit-destroying willow which had grown in Homer at the gates of Hades is now portrayed as standing at the gates of heaven and becomes a major symbol within the Christian dialectic on death and life. Some Old Testament passages were used to validate this willow symbolism. For example, the Jewish Feast of Tabernacles involved the ritual use of tents made from branches which recalled the temporary shelters of Jews escaping Egyptian captivity. The Greek translation of the Old Testament did something interesting when it came to Leviticus 23:40, a passage instructing Jews to use willow branches for the festival, for the Greek text comes to be embroidered with the addition of the poplar to the willow thus recalling Homer's picture of homesick Odysseus. Psalm 137, which tells of exiles mourning by the waters of Babylon also came into its own as the negative mood of willows in Hades is recalled and echoed through the willows on whose branches the languishing Jews hung up their muted harps as they longed for Zion. St Ambrose added the poplar to the willow and spoke of a Christian homesickness for heaven generated within this present life. Odysseus and the Christian both share a homesickness as they also anticipate a homecoming journey before them. Other strands of the tradition take up the dichotomy between virgin fruitlessness and dynamic fruitfulness. Jerome saw the newly baptized as a new sprouting willow, but one which does bear fruit. He uses the convention of fruitlessness as the basis for the Christian miracle of grace which makes even barren things to be productive. A slight variant on this regards willows as representing the virginity of the martyrs whose earthly life is fruitless but whose heavenly reward will make them fruitful indeed. These are they who have willow garlands as triumphal crowns.

The Shepherd of Hermas, a text from about 150 A.D. which was regarded as practically canonical by some early Christians, extends the tree motif in yet another direction beginning with some Old Testament ideas (Ezek. 47:12) of a tree of the Lord's planting which grows to cover the earth. The writer depicts a great willow which grows to be like a protective roof for hill and vale and into whose shadow come all those called in the Lord's name. A glorious angel gives each one a twig of willow which is immediately handed back for grafting onto the parent tree, but only after half the twig is withered through the wickedness of its handler. On reconnection with the tree the twigs flourish once more. By distinctive contrast martyrs hand back not only flourishing branches but ones possessing what appears to be fruit. Martyrdom thus makes men more than human, the fruit-destroying willow becomes productive for those possessing divine grace. So too the Book of Revelation, the Apocalypse concluding the New Testament, which portrays a tree of life near the heavenly river whose fruit was yielded each month and whose leaves were for the healing of the nations. The mythology linking the trees of Eden with the heavenly tree of redemption is no simple one. Indeed its central motif is still unexamined and it is to this we now turn in the symbolism of Christ's crucifixion.

The cross as tree of life

The New Testament contains several direct references to the cross as a tree on which Christ died. The First Letter of Peter (1:24) says that 'He himself bore our sins in his body on the tree', while the Acts of the Apostles (13:29) talks of those who 'took him down from the tree and laid him in a tomb'. The preaching of subsequent Christian generations extended these direct texts in increasingly figurative directions. So the poem of Pseudo-Cyprian from the third century tells of a place regarded by Christians as the centre of the world and called Golgotha by the Jews. There stands the tree of life embracing the world with the spring of baptism at its roots and affording everlasting life. The poem ends:

> Inde iter ad caelum per ramos arboris altae
> Hoc lignum vitae cunctis credentibus.
>
> (Thence we go to heaven by way of the branches of the high tree
> This is the wood of life to all that believe.)

Traditions then flourished as interpretations grew on how Eden and Golgotha were related. One told how Seth was sent to Paradise to fetch fruit from the tree of life to succour his father Adam who lay dying. The guardian angels gave him only three kernels which grew into the cedar, cypress, and pine. The last ultimately sprang from the dead man's mouth and ultimately yielded the wood from which the cross of Christ was fashioned. This itself was the source of eternal life and afforded access to that tree in heaven whose leaves are for the healing of the nations. The third century Hippolytus of Rome summarized this symbolism perfectly.

This tree, wide as the heavens itself, has grown up into heaven from the earth. It is an immortal growth, it is the fulcrum of all things, it is the foundation of the round world, the centre of the cosmos. In it all the diversities in our human nature are formed into a unity. It is held together by invisible nails of the Spirit so that it may not break loose from the divine. It touches the highest summit of heaven and makes the earth firm beneath its foot, and it grasps the middle regions between them with immeasurable arms. O crucified one, thou leader of the mystical dances. O joy of the universe by which dark death is destroyed and life returns to all and the gates of heaven are opened.

Another arboreal metaphor within the early Christian period is worth noting for it facilitated yet more creative thought within theology. It is that of the plantation. This too has an Old Testament source for Isaiah (5:1–7) described the people of Israel as Yahweh's vineyard: 'Let me sing for my beloved a love song concerning his vineyard. My beloved had a vineyard on a very fertile hill. He digged it, cleared it, and planted it . . . and he looked to it to yield grapes, but it yielded wild grapes.' The same image of the vine recurs in several forms in the New Testament and is quite complex. St Paul (Romans 11:17–24) speaks of the relation of Jewish and Gentile Christians through a metaphor of vine pruning, while St John (15:1–6) takes the vine to represent the relation between Jesus and his disciples.

The plantation motif extends beyond vines. The Jewish community of Qumran, for example, saw itself as the eternal plantation watered by the rivers of Eden, and some Christian traditions identified the gospels with those four rivers and saw the church as the ground they sustained. New converts were, of course, called neophytes, the newly planted ones, than which no metaphor could be more direct. Ignatius of Antioch (35–107 A.D.) talked of believers as branches of the cross, while Asterius, a fourth-century Sophist, refers directly to Christ as the tree of life and the devil as the tree of death. On the tree of life the apostles are branches, while it has words for leaves and baptism for its root. Iconographic representation often sets the tree of the cross with its root in a baptismal font.[13]

A large number of hymns from the Reformation to the present have used the tree cross motif as central themes of devotion. Others have been translated from much earlier hymns but these too attest to the popularity and to the continuing attractiveness of the image. Charles Wesley could sing in *O Love Divine* of the co-eternal Son, who 'bore all my sins upon the tree', and John Ellerton echoed him in *Throned upon the aweful Tree*.

It would be possible to extend this discussion of tree symbolism to embrace further cultures, but enough has been said to show how attractive a symbol is the tree as it confronts human imagination. A final reference will suffice to encompass the themes of cosmic tree and of creative suffering which have implicitly entwined themselves throughout the preceding descriptions. In Norse mythology the gigantic ash Yggdrasil stands as the universal tree with its roots in the nether world and the mythical spring about its base. Its evergreen leaves afford pasture to the stag whose dripping horns watered the earth. Eagles in the highest branches scan the earth, while the tale-bearing squirrel Ratatosk gossips between the higher and lower denizens of the heavenly and earthly realms. Odin, the god of wisdom, who knows that wisdom is gained only by sacrifice, hung for nine days and nights on that tree, looking all the while into the depths of the land of mists. 'And to Odin offered Myself to Myself, on that tree of which no one knows from what root it spring.'[14]

Sir James Frazer, whose *Golden Bough* is itself the single most celebrated mythology of a tree, thought it quite intelligible that the Aryan race in Europe had used tree symbolism so much since forests had been the dominant habitat from time immemorial.[15] While we cannot doubt that familiarity is one factor in the elective affinity between trees and human thought, we have been more anxious to stress the intrinsic suggestivity and the inherent attractiveness of trees as the basis of and for evocative symbolic responses. After all is said it remains true that grass, the most universal and successful of plants, has seldom fed the flames of creative thought to any marked extent. Trees have done so because they possess not only a variety of parts but because they stand over and against human generations in a way which demands acknowledgment.

NOTES

1   A. Salmond, 'Theoretical landscapes', in D. Parkin (ed.), *Semantic anthropology* (London, 1982), pp. 65–88.
2   V. Turner, *The forest of symbols* (Cornell, 1967).
3   V. Turner, *The ritual process* (London, 1969), p. 26.
4   M. Eliade, *Shamanism* (Princeton, 1964).
5   A. Hultkranz, *The religions of the American Indians* (Berkeley, 1979), pp. 23–5.
6   C. G. Jung, *Four archetypes* (London, 1972), pp. 126ff.
7   H. Rahner, *Greek myths and Christian mystery* (New York, 1971).
8   M. I. Finley, *Aspects of antiquity* (Harmondsworth, 1977).
9   Rahner, *Greek myths*, pp. 1ff.
10   Turner, *The forest of symbols*, p. 27.
11   J. G. Frazer, *The Golden Bough*, abridged edn (London, 1963), pp. 1ff.
12   R. Needham, *Belief, language and experience* (Oxford, 1972), pp. 160ff.

13 Rahner, *Greek myths*, p. 79. See for example Sir Edwin Landseer's *The Baptismal Font*.

14 H. A. Guerber, *Myths of the Norsemen* (New York, 1919), pp. 234ff.

15 Frazer, *The Golden Bough*, pp. 144ff.

3

The political iconography of woodland in later Georgian England

STEPHEN DANIELS

Hail, old *Patrician* Trees, so great and good!
Hail, ye *Plebeian* underwood!

Abraham Cowley, Of Solitude (1668)

In its way a nation is like a forest and the aim of war planning is to secure the survival of the great trees ... If all the great trees and much of the brushwood are felled a forest may not regenerate for centuries. If a sufficient number of great trees is left ... if felling is to some extent selective and controlled, recovery is swift.

North East Thames contingency plans for a nuclear war, quoted
in The Guardian, 14 May 1983

Trees and woodland have proved as rich a symbolic resource as a material one, frequently being exploited to represent ideas of social order. In his survey of English attitudes to the natural world between 1500 and 1800 Keith Thomas notes that trees 'provided a visible symbol of human society', and a stabilizing one in a period of accelerating social change.[1] In this essay I will show how in later Georgian England woodland imagery was deployed to symbolize, and so 'naturalize', varying and conflicting views of what social order was or ought to have been. There was, in short, a political iconography of woodland.[2] This was articulated in the selection, siting and arrangement of trees in written, pictorial and parkland images. Here I will survey major issues in the political iconography of woodland for the period 1770–1830, before focussing on writings by three leading theorists of the picturesque to examine, in a local context for the period of the Napoleonic Wars, the role of trees in the political iconography of landscape improvement.

Planting and power

By 1800 England was one of the least wooded of all north European nations.[3] Despite this, or probably because of it, English enthusiasm for trees and woodland seems never to have been higher. If the number and variety of publications on the subject is a reliable guide, enthusiasm escalated from the second half of the eighteenth century.[4] The interests of planters, land agents, landowners, landscape gardeners, painters, poets and political theorists overlapped in a large and often contentious literature.[5] The depletion of what little forest was left sharpened the taste for its scenery. But mindful of the continuing association of forests with lawlessness, connoisseurs of woodland were usually careful to distinguish areas which were effectively appropriated and managed from those which were not.[6] William Gilpin's taste for the scenery of the New Forest was spoiled by his feelings about the foresters, 'an indolent race', living by 'forest pilfer ... deer stealing, poaching or purloining timber'.[7] Impatient to improve the scenic or commercial value of forests, polite observers barely perceived their complex network of customary uses and meanings. Areas resistant to the improving imagination were, in the words of a reporter on the New Forest to the Board of Agriculture, a 'nest and conservatory of sloth, idleness and misery'.[8] The most agreeable woodland was that tidily planted or securely partitioned on landed estates. Here trees confirmed the power of property.

The association of planting with property was enshrined in law. Conditions of strict settlement often protected trees like land as part of the capital of an estate. Tenants for life could be prevented from felling timber trees (usually oak, ash and elm beyond a specified age and size, and in places beech and birch) and constrained also from felling trees planted for shelter or amenity.[9] The eighteenth century witnessed a progressive protection of private woodland in criminal law. The 'Black Act' (9 Geo. I c.22) of 1722 made it a capital offence to 'cut down or otherwise destroy any trees planted in any avenue, or growing in any garden, orchard or plantation, for ornament, shelter or profit'. An act of 1766 (6 Geo. III c.48) firmly established the criminality of wood gathering from plantations, copses and hedges. 'Where records survive, it would seem that wood theft was the most common form of crime in the countryside', concludes Robert Bushaway, 'possibly the most common way in which the laws and rights of landed property were infringed.'[10] As the value of timber as a commodity appreciated during the Napoleonic Wars, so the law was used more frequently to seal off private woodland from common use. In *The Parish*, John Clare complained:

> A shadow reigns, yclept a woodland king,
> Enthroned mid thorns and briers, a clownish wight,
> My Lord's chief woodman in his title's height.
> The bugbear devil of the boys is he,
> Who once for swine picked acorns 'neath the tree,
> Who gleaned their scraps of fuel from the wood; . . .

But Turks imperial of the woodland bough
Forbid their trespass in such trifles now.[11]

In the shadow of the law, forest communities, notably in Hampshire, Wilt-shire and Berkshire, continued to affirm their customary rights, gleaning faggots and offal wood, cutting young trees for maypoles and green oak-boughs for Maytime processions and, on occasion, mutilating or destroying trees in plantations to signify their disaffection with the encroaching gentry.[12]

Planting accentuated the impression of power in the land. Avenues, rid-ings, belts, clumps and screens were arranged to emphasize the apparent as well as the actual extent and unity of an estate. Formal styles of parkland planting, with long vistas radiating from the country house, expressed a military sense of command. Informal styles were more artful but no less domineering. The site, size and tonality of Capability Brown's clumps enhanced the size of a park and the pleasure of running ones eyes posses-sively over its contours. In his influential *Observations on modern gardening* (1770) Thomas Whately, an advocate for Brown, recommended ridings around a park '*to extend the idea of a seat* and appropriate a whole country to a mansion'. Such ridings were to be 'distinguished' from 'common roads' by their '*design*', such as 'plantations of firs, whether placed in the sides of the way, or in clumps or woods in the view'.[13] More picturesque land-scaping distinguished the park less explicitly from the country beyond, a quality its advocates found less oppressive. In *The English Garden*, William Mason advised landscapers to reject exotic species of conifer for native hardwoods, to take account of features of the working countryside and to incorporate in the 'sylvan scene' signs of rustic happiness – 'the scattered village', 'holy spire' and 'azure curl of smoke' from a cottage 'beneath the sheltering coppice'.[14] Picturesque landscaping was discreet, sometimes merely a matter of planting a few trees in a distant hedgerow or lopping some branches of a parkland tree to disclose a view. This both softened the impression of property and, by composing the countryside as a whole as a picture, strengthened it. Humphry Repton's alterations to estates were more modest and superficial than those by Capability Brown but their basis was still 'appropriation ... that charm which only belongs to owner-ship, the *exclusive right* of enjoyment, with the power of refusing that others should share our pleasure'.[15]

Conservative political theorists elaborated the analogy of the State with a landed estate and that of statecraft with estate improvement. Many novels, poems, essays and tracts did likewise.[16] While naturalizing the connection of landed property with political power, they were sufficiently flexible to allow moral criticism of landed opinions and tastes, usually by contrasting plain and careful gentry who managed their estates conservatively with speculative and extravagant gentry who did not. The importance of trees

and woodland to the appearance and economy of landed estates made
their mismanagement, especially their bulk felling to pay gambling debts
or realize quick profits, a recurring reason for censure. The condition of
the nation might be measured by the way landowners treated their trees,
as in William Cowper's *The Task* (1785):

> Were England now
> What England was, plain, hospitable, kind,
> And undebauched. But we have bid farewell
> To all the virtues of those better days,
> And all their honest pleasures. Mansions once
> Knew their own masters, and laborious hinds,
> That had survived the father served the son.
> Now the legitimate and rightful lord
> Is but a transient guest, newly arrived
> And soon to be supplanted. He that saw
> His patrimonial timber cast its leaf,
> Sells the last scantling, and transfers the price
> To some shrewd sharper, ere it buds again.[17]

Edmund Burke constructed a politics of landscape which counterposed
the chiaroscuro of maturely wooded English parkland to the clarity and
brilliance of 'experimental' landscapes like the 'geometrical constitution'
of revolutionary France. In nature, Burke observed, light was refracted
to create a unifying atmosphere.

But now all is to be changed. All the pleasing illusions which made power gentle,
and obedience liberal, which harmonized the different shades of life, and which,
by a bland assimilation, incorporated into politics the sentiments which beautify
and soften private society, are to be dissolved by this new conquering empire of
light and reason.[18]

Burke warned the Duke of Bedford, renowned for his 'experimental philosophy' in both politics and estate improvement, that the 'geometricians'
of revolutionary France 'want new lands for new trials' and while they
'have an eye on his Grace's lands', their fellow 'chemists are not less taken
with his buildings'.[19]

Economic and social threats to the conservative image of the landed
estate only served to cement it more firmly, if only nostalgically, as a picture
of England. From outside the property and the patronage of the gentry
this picture dissolved. In the face of financial speculation William Cobbett
offered himself as a populist spokesman for Old England, even if his views
of the old country were decisively influenced by his experience of American
agriculture and agrarianism. Cobbett's advice on tree planting and management, like his advice on cabbages and maize, was part of a politics of
smallholding and consciously opposed to that of estate ownership: 'it is

not the extent of a plantation: it is the height and bulk of trees; it is the quantity of timber, and not the breadth of land, that a man ought to look at'.[20] In his twopenny *Political Register* Cobbett's populism had a more radical edge. In an address to the 'People of the United States of America' on the famine and incendiarism in the southern counties in May 1816, Cobbett recalled

a book that we used to look at a great deal entitled '*A Picture of England*'. It contained views of *Country Seats* and of fine hills and valleys ... Alas! This was no picture of *England*, if by England we mean anything more than a certain portion of Houses, Trees and Herbage. If, by England, we mean the English *nation*; and if, by the nation we mean the *great body of the people*.[21]

Planting and patriotism

The development of Georgian Britain as a mercantile nation, dependent upon shipbuilding for expanding and defending its economic and political interests, cemented the patriotic associations of planting. The elision of woodland and maritime strength was a commonplace. The phrase 'wooden walls' became a cliché in exhortations to plant to defend the national interest.[22] Writing in the wake of the Battle of Trafalgar, the planter William Pontey announced:

The splendid Victory lately achieved, has proved our Wooden Walls to be an essential part of the Title, by which not only *Estates*, but every species of property, is held. Let, then, all who are anxious to preserve their property, remember the last order of that Patriot and Hero, the immortal NELSON ... let it be *especially* and *perpetually* sounded in the ears of British Timber owners.[23]

New plantations were named after Nelson and other victorious British admirals; some in Sherwood Forest had triumphal columns erected among the trees.[24] Writers on planting voiced their alarm at the depletion of timber near the coasts, accessible to shipyards. William Marshall calculated the impressive amount of timber, 2,000 well grown oaks, needed to build a 'third rate' 74 gun warship. Believing 'our existence as a nation depends upon the oak', he demanded a <u>census of the species</u>, every parish listing the location of oaks suitable for shipbuilding and their distance from water-carriage.[25] In the introduction to his updated editions of Evelyn's *Sylva* (still the seminal text on woodland management), Alexander Hunter quoted William Mason's exhortation to nourish 'Those sapling oaks, which at Britannia's call,/ May heave their trunks into the main,/ And float the bulwarks of her liberty.'[26] There was nothing new about complaints or forebodings of timber shortage for the navy but by the late eighteenth century the growth of intercontinental trade and the acceleration of the naval arms race made shipbuilding a major consumer of timber.[27] During the Napoleonic Wars there was a real shortage of oak, although devotion to the supposedly superior qualities of English oak trees delayed importing it from abroad.[28] The more picturesque the oak, the more valuable it often was. Single oaks growing unrestricted in parks or hedges developed open crowns of curved and bent branches, the compass timber that was in short supply for shipbuilding.[29] While oak and other hardwoods like elm and beech were important for building hulls, pine and spruce were essential for masts and spars but the pictorial and patriotic qualities of such conifers were less widely appreciated.[30]

The patriotism of planting was pronounced despite, or perhaps because of, the pressure from other uses of land. Wheat contended with oaks for the best soils in England. During the inflationary years between 1790 and 1812 increases in wheat prices ran ahead of those for oaks and plantations were grubbed up for arable fields. 'Even if the ultimate profit from raising oaks would be as great – and that was often doubtful – the immediate returns from a grain crop were more appealing to the landowner than the remote prospect of a timber felling by one of his descendants a century later.'[31] Furthermore, the growing of corn had an established political iconography which was forcibly reaffirmed in writing, painting and landscaping during the Napoleonic Wars.[32] A field of wheat proved as patriotic a spectacle as a grove of oaks and for some writers eclipsed the virtues of woodland. Protesting in 1791 against the holding of oak groves in 'maritime mortmain' while the country was forced to import wheat, Dr Thomas Preston of Suffolk told a Commons committee 'The Scarcity of Timber ought never to be regretted, for it is certain proof of National Improvement; and for Royal Navies, Countries yet barbarous are the right and only proper nurseries.'[33]

Deciduous and coniferous symbolism

The oldest, richest and most complex associations adhered to the oak. Like the ideal landed family, oaks were claimed to be venerable, patriarchal, stately, guardian and quintessentially English. The analogy of great trees to great families was firmly established before Burke described the English aristocracy as 'the great oaks which shade a country'.[34] As parkland styles became more informal and (as a consequence) country houses were made less obtrusive, so oaks seem to have become imbued with even more of the patrician qualities associated with country houses. Old oaks not planted by landed families were readily appropriated by them, framed in parkland views or used in portraits to amplify their pedigree.[35] In Zoffany's portrait of the Drummond family (Fig. 1), the banker Andrew Drummond is (posthumously) aligned to the trunk of an oak situated on a rise in his park at Stanmore improved by one of his most substantial clients, Capability

Fig. 1 Johann Joseph Zoffany, *The Drummond Family*, c.1769. Oil on canvas. Paul Mellon Collection, Yale Center for British Art, New Haven, Conn.

Brown; successive generations on the male line are positioned respectively beneath its branches and leaves.[36]

Other hardwoods acquired patrician associations as parkland trees. 'In stateliness and grandeur of outline, the Beech vies with the oak', observed William Marshall.[37] The role of the beech as an amenity tree, the subtle lighting effects of its foliage and the suitability of its wood for fine furniture and joinery, made it a favourite among connoisseurs.[38] The coolness of its shade gave the beech a reputation as a hospitable tree, in Evelyn's quotation of Virgil, 'sweet, and of all the rest, most refreshing to the weary shepherd'.[39]

Elms were planted as parkland trees and celebrated as such in verse[40] but their cultural associations were most closely tied to the working countryside in which they featured so prominently. They were used to signify farming interests. A poet of prudent husbandry, John Scott, beheld 'Stansted's farms inclos'd / With aged elms in rows dispos'd'.[41] In *The Reapers* George Stubbs deployed a lofty elm to frame a rich harvest and amplify the figure of a farmer supervising his labourers.[42] Elms feature as repoussoirs in many of Constable's celebrations of flourishing farming and in *Boatbuilding* (1814) as timber in every stage of a narrative of the building and floating of the barges which both imported the night soil to fertilize the fields of the Stour valley and exported their rich harvest of grain.[43] In contrast to these managerial images of the elm John Clare in 'To a Fallen Elm' used the tree to recall a homely pre-enclosure countryside the farming interest had erased.[44] The viticultural technique of 'marrying' vines to elms is a key image in the opening lines of Virgil's *Georgics* and English poets exploited its sexual as well as agrarian potential. 'What makes the Vine about the Elme to dance / With turnings, windings and embracements round' demanded Sir John Davies.[45] Wordsworth grafted this classical literary symbol to the native folk symbol of the maypole in his image of the 'The JOYFUL ELM / Around whose trunk the maidens dance in May'.[46]

The very antiquity of hardwoods, and the antiquity of their associations as places of communal assembly and ritual, made them available as symbols for popular, even anti-landed interests. In *The Deserted Village* (1770) Oliver Goldsmith opposed the 'spreading tree' on a village green to the plantations of a landscaped park. The poem emphasizes the belligerent power of parkland ('its vistas strike, its palaces surprize') by evoking the genial egalitarian scenes an emparking landlord had erased

> And all the village train, from labour free,
> Led up their sports beneath the spreading tree:
> While many a pastime circled in the shade,
> The young contending as the old survey'd;[47]

The felling of old familiar trees – oaks and hawthorns as well as elms

– are episodes in the poems John Clare wrote against Parliamentary enclosure: 'Thou art the cause that levels every tree / And woods bow down to clear a way for thee'.[48] In 1816 Robert Southey extended the virtues of oaks to small farmers evicted or dispossessed in the interests of improved agriculture: 'the yeoman had his roots in this soil: this was the right English tree in which our heart of oak was nurtured . . . But old tenants have been cut down with as little remorse and as little discrimination as old timber.'[49] Patrician spokesmen were anxious to arrogate the popular conservatism symbolized especially by oaks to a reassuring consensus. The illustrations of stately trees in Jacob George Strutt's *Sylva Britannica* (1822), a lavish volume subscribed to by gentry and aristocracy, show labourers maintaining the trees as they are sheltered by them; and the text emphasizes that the sight of a favourite and long remembered tree is cherished equally by rich and poor,

by the nobleman, who may be reminded, as its branches wave over his head, whilst wandering in his hereditary domains, of the illustrious ancestors by whom it may have been planted; and by the peasant who, passing it in his way to his daily labours, recalls, as he looks at it, the sports of his infancy round its venerable trunk, and regards it at once as his chronicler and land-mark.[50]

Fast growing and tolerant of thin soils, conifers were always acceptable to most landowners and their planting increased appreciably in late Georgian years on the heaths and commons then being rapidly enclosed. Larches and pines were welcomed by improving owners of great estates with extensive areas of poor soils and moorland. On the sandy soils of Welbeck the Duke of Portland nurtured them 'with as much pride as [his] oaks'; Thomas Coke was nicknamed 'King Pine' for the thousands of conifers he planted at Holkham.[51] Not surprisingly, the amount of writing on conifers increased appreciably in these years. Professional planters championed them vigorously, often against the ingrained opinions of those devoted to old English hardwoods. William Pontey declared firs to be 'unjustly degraded' and (perhaps because of his work for the progressive Duke of Bedford) was denounced by the *Anti-Jacobin Review*: 'His theoretical speculations are not only superficial', it charged, 'but highly dangerous.'[52] Pontey emphasized the political prudence of his ideas. As well as providing timber for ships to fight 'tyranny and injustice', the fir and the larch would increase the value and fertility of moorland and turn 'the once cheerless and solitary wilds into the social haunts of men'.[53] It was, in every way, good management to admit the poor into plantations, 'against the custom in many places', to gather rotten boughs.[54] The Lincolnshire landowner Sir Cecil Wray found his plantations of Scots fir a prudent, indeed a benevolent, scene of estate management. The green boughs were grazed by deer and sheep, the timber was good for farmhouses and fencing and 'the poor people supply themselves with very good fuel by gathering the fir apples and rotten wood;

you will sometimes see twenty children in my plantations *appleing* as they call it'.[55]

For some writers coniferous and deciduous trees made an agreeable mixture, for reasons of both beauty and profit. In his essays on 'Picturesque farming', Thomas Ruggles (a planter of 4,000 pines and firs on his own Suffolk estate) described how the 'lovely green of the larch' tinted deciduous plantations in summer and declared that the colour of conifers in winter 'is superior to any of the other species'. The 'prophetic eye of taste' could look forward to the time 'when the firs have amply repaid the planter's expense [and] see the deciduous trees lofty towering in the air, and gratifying our descendants with their beauty and magnificence'. On barren heaths the Scots pine 'will become a noble tree; but it is not ungrateful for a better and quite a different soil'.[56]

The precocity of conifers alarmed many conservative observers, especially when they displaced traditional hardwoods. In his *Guide to the Lakes*, written in 1810, Wordsworth contrasted the depletion of 'venerable woods' of oak with the recent encroachment of conifers.

Larch and fir plantations have been spread, not merely with a view to profit, but in many instances for the sake of ornament. To those who plant for profit, and are thrusting every other tree out of the way to make way for the favourite, The Larch, I would utterly regret that they have selected these lovely vales for their vegetable manufactory.

Such trees disrupted 'that fine connexion of parts, that sympathy and organization, if I may so express myself, which pervades the whole of the natural wood'.[57] Conifers in traditionally deciduous landscapes were, like garish modern villas, signs of the disruptive influence of the new, often industrially, rich who were then moving into the Lake District, and symptoms of an industrial order that Wordsworth accused of disrupting the community of dalesmen. In his *Two addresses to the freeholders of Westmorland* (1818), written to support the local Tory interest, Wordsworth complained that the 'rapacious speculation' and 'spread of manufactories' during the Napoleonic Wars had broken the bonds of affection between rich and poor. And he appealed to the oaken politics of Burke, 'the most sagacious politician of his age'. The 'stock of ancient virtue' needed careful manuring and pruning not the 'corrosive compounds' spread on its roots by 'Malignants' who, 'pretending to invigorate the tree', destroyed it.[58]

Trees in the radical imagination

Conservative spokesmen did not monopolize the symbolism of trees.[59] As a riposte to Burke's conservative use of the oak, Tom Paine protested about the 'deeply rooted' governments of the Old World and, adapting a phrase from St Matthew's gospel, called on the people to 'Lay the axe to the root and teach Governments humanity'. Since republican depredations on royalist woodlands in the seventeenth century, the felling of old trees had in England been associated with levelling politics; Paine did not abandon trees as radical symbols, rather he repossessed them by concentrating on their budding branches, emblems of energy and progress. At the end of *The rights of man* he wrote:

It is now towards the end of February. Were I to take a turn into the country the trees would present a leafless wintry appearance. As people are apt to pluck twigs as they walk along, I perhaps might do the same, and by chance might observe that a *single bud* on that branch had begun to swell. I should reason very unnaturally, or rather not reason at all, to suppose *this* was the *only* bud in England which had this appearance. Instead of deciding thus, I should instantly conclude that the same appearance was beginning or about to begin, everywhere; and though the vegetable sleep will continue longer on some trees and plants than on others, and though some of them may not *blossom* for two or three years, all will be in leaf in the summer, except those which are *rotten*. What pace the political summer will keep with the natural, no human foresight can determine. It is, however, not difficult to perceive that the spring is begun.[60]

The revolutionary imagery of renovating heat and light was graphically portrayed by a friend and supporter of Paine, William Blake. In Blake's works of the 1780s, particularly the *Songs of Innocence*, oaks are still symbols of strength and security, spreading trees on the village green, in images of communal content (Fig. 2).[61] In the prophetic books of the 1790s, inspired by the French Revolution, oaks stand for political repression. The 'Preludium' of *America* (1793) (Fig. 3) opens with the figure of Orc, the embodiment of revolutionary energy, chained to the base of a massive oaklike tree rooted in a repressive underworld. Orc is both Christlike, drawn in an attitude of crucifixion, and, in his sexual power, Satanic, 'wreath'd round the accursed tree' like the serpent coiled around the Tree of Knowledge. Rending his chains, Orc uncoils, rising through the earth to redeem it (Fig. 4): 'free are the wrists of fire / Round the terrific loins he seiz'd the panting struggling womb: / It joy'd'. In a flaming sunrise the deadening oak is replaced by a symbol of fertility, a lithe vine whose tendrils curl into the calligraphy of the text.[62]

I know thee, I have found thee & will not let thee go;
Thou art the image of God who dwells in darkness of Africa
And thou art fall'n to give me life in regions of dark death
On my American plains I feel the struggling afflictions
Endur'd by roots that writhe their arms, into the nether deep; . . .
O what limb rending pains I feel thy fire and my frost.

In the 'Prophecy' of *America* the newborn man is depicted lying in a luxuriant crop of corn.

Fig. 2   William Blake, 'The Ecchoing Green', from *Songs of Innocence and Experience* (1789), fol. 6. Relief etching, finished in pen and watercolour, on paper. Fitzwilliam Museum, Cambridge.

> They cannot smite the wheat, nor quench the fatness of the earth . . .
> They cannot bring the stubbed oak to overgrow the hills.
> For terrible men stand on the shores, & in their robes I see
> Children take shelter from the lightnings, there stands Washington
> And Paine and Warren with their foreheads reared towards the east.

Even the oak was reclaimed as revolutionary symbol. In *Common sense* Tom Paine likened the growth of America's 'continental union' to the growth of an oak tree.[63] American revolutionaries used young oaks as Liberty Trees. They were not strictly particular about species – the original

Fig. 3   William Blake, *America, A Prophecy* (1793), fol. 3. Relief etching, finished in pen and watercolour, on paper. Fitzwilliam Museum, Cambridge.

Fig. 4   William Blake, *America, A Prophecy* (1793), fol. 4. Relief etching, finished in pen and watercolour, on paper. Fitzwilliam Museum, Cambridge.

Liberty Tree in Boston was an elm – only that the chosen trees should cast no tyrannical shade; daylight emphasized the natural equality of those who encircled them. The Liberty Tree politicized the fertility symbolism of the maypole; in the 1790s Joel Barlow claimed to trace its genealogy further to the phallic cults of ancient Egypt.[64] The centrality of the Liberty Tree to the rituals and rhetoric of revolutionary France made it feature prominently in anti-republican imagery in Britain, usually counterposed to the conservatism of the native oak. In James Gillray's etching of 1798 (Fig. 5) the Tree of Liberty is depicted as a political Tree of Knowledge; a doltish John Bull, having picked the virtuous fruits of the British Royal Oak, is unsuccessfully tempted with the apple of Reform by a serpentine Charles James Fox.[65]

Trees and the politics of the picturesque, 1794–1816

The issues I have so far surveyed are implicated in arguments on picturesque improvements to landscape during the Napoleonic Wars. This was, and was felt to be at the time, a period of turbulence in almost every sphere of British life. The wars aggravated economic fluctuations, food shortages, financial speculation, social disaffection and fears about them. Reports of a small French force landing on the Pembrokeshire coast in 1797 to rally the Welsh spread alarm throughout the country and created an enduring fear of invasion and insurrection. With their reputation for vandalizing the countryside, poaching and cutting down wood for fires, the English militia scarcely calmed the interests of property. The most critical periods were probably the famine years of 1795 and 1812, the latter inflamed by Luddism in the textile districts.[66] Taste in landscape became no less contentious an issue than famine, financial speculation or invasion if only because it became implicated with these issues. Connoisseurs of the picturesque found it increasingly difficult to abstract the formal qualities of landscape features from their social associations.[67] Always difficult to objectify, trees and woodland became still more sensitive as signifiers of social order or disorder. I will now examine in detail the role of trees and woodland in the politics of picturesque improvement during the war years, focussing on the views of three leading theorists: Uvedale Price, Richard Payne Knight and Humphry Repton.

Uvedale Price

'It is in the arrangement and management of trees, that the great art of improvement consists', declared Uvedale Price in his *Essay on the picturesque*, 'they alone form a canopy over us, and a varied frame to all other objects which they admit, exclude, and group with, almost at the will of

Fig. 5   James Gillray, *The Tree of LIBERTY – with the Devil tempting John Bull* (23 May 1798), etching, from *The works of James Gillray* (1842), University of Nottingham Library.

the improver . . . their beauty is compleat and perfect in itself, while that of every other object absolutely requires their assistance'.[68] Price's own estate at Foxley in Herefordshire was well wooded with mature trees, notably with beech, his favourite tree. Gainsborough, a family friend, had portrayed beech trees at Foxley (Fig. 6) and Price took care to show beech trees to advantage on the ground.[69] Visitors sought out Foxley for the fine picture collection (especially of seventeenth-century Dutch Masters) in the house and for the pictorial character of the grounds, 'fine trees forming a kind of woody ampitheatre around the mansion . . . the distance being formed by various hills retiring in perspective . . . and the foreground by rich masses of wood'.[70]

Price's ideas of picturesque improvement are informed by a sense of social management which owes much to his role as a watchful squire.[71] In the *Annals of Agriculture* for 1786 he had called for stricter laws to make 'careless' landowners prevent 'rapacious' tenants and 'wanton' labourers stripping elms and cropping oaks for hedgewood and fuel, a practice which lessened both the pictorial attractions and the economic value of landed property as well as depleting the timber reserves of the nation.[72] Price revealed a more benevolent, but no less authoritarian, idea of improvement in *Thoughts on the defence of property* (1797). This was addressed to landowners in Herefordshire in response to news that the French had landed in Wales. Price warned that the local poor, maddened by hunger, might take advantage of an invasion to redress their grievances. Not trusting the militia, Price advised some armed training for property owners, but maintained that kindliness would be a more effective strategy: 'he who can scarcely buy bread, will hardly buy arms unless driven to despair by long ill treatment'. Those who paraded their power in vast parks, in splendid isolation, would be dangerously 'exposed to the outrage of a savage rabble'.[73] Such was the effect of Brown-style landscaping, which made no less military an impression on Price than formal styles, the clumps of trees 'drilled for parade . . . like compact bodies of soldiers'.[74] At a time of tension and disaffection in the country it was dangerously despotic. Clearing such signs of community as cottages, roads and churches from a gentleman's purview created a moral vacuum, 'the vacancy of solitary grandeur and power'. The 'ambitious views' of such landowners destroyed the 'local attachments' on which social order rested.[75]

Price argued that a more painterly style of landscaping, especially one modelled on Dutch or Flemish painting, implied a more humane one, for 'the lover of painting considers the dwellings, the inhabitants, and the marks of their intercourse, as ornaments to the landscape'. The moral landscape was an intimate one. For Price 'persons not conversant in pictures and drawings' were 'much more attentive to distant objects than to near ones'.[76] This echoes Burke who emphasized the moral indifference of 'geometri-

Fig. 6   Thomas Gainsborough, *Study of Beech Trees at Foxley*, 1760. Brown chalk, watercolour and bodycolour over pencil. Whitworth Art Gallery, University of Manchester.

cians' in politics whose 'long views' were drawn towards the vanishing point of linear perspective: 'their humanity is at their horizon – and like the horizon it always flies before them'.[77] Deciduous trees in the Dutch pictorial style Price favoured function not so much as frames for long views but as occlusive features. They hold a spectator's attention to the foreground by the gravity of their trunks and branches, the texture of their bark and foliage and the emphasis on their rooting. They effectively ground the gaze. Gainsborough depicted many woodland scenes in such a style. As Ronald Paulson points out they draw the spectator down into 'a green shade' through a series of descending curves in earth banks, tree trunks, branches and foliage.[78] Gainsborough's drawing of a beech wood at Foxley (Fig. 6) has these qualities. While one magnificent tree is the compositional centre of the picture it also draws the spectator down its embankment into a shady dell to the left. A narrow vista does open between the embowering branches only to be closed by a focus of local community, the parish church.

Price claimed his own family had shown 'attentive kindness' in their improvements, allowing villagers to walk through their park and improving the village itself which bore 'strong marks' of their benevolence; they were repaid by 'affectionate regard and reverence'. If practised more widely in the country, such a style of landownership 'would do much more towards guarding us against democratical opinions than twenty thousand soldiers arm'd in proof'.[79] For Price prudent landscape improvement involved blurring social boundaries to compose a picture of community in the countryside: 'although the separation of the different ranks and their gradations, like those of visible objects, is known and ascertained,' he acknowledged, 'yet from the beneficial mixture, and frequent intercommunication of high and low, that separation is happily disguised and does not sensibly operate on the general mind'.[80]

For Price the axiom of improvement was 'connection', the harmonizing of differing features of the natural and social world to create a painterly landscape. Deciduous trees of varying shapes and sizes were integral to a well-connected landscape. 'Connection' was a principle flagrantly violated by Capability Brown and his followers: 'One of their first operations is to clear away the humbler trees, those bonds of connection which the painter admires, and which the judicious improver always touches with a cautious hand.' Price complained about the fashion for conifers. When there was a space between two woods it was usual 'to fill it up with firs, larches &c; if this be done with the idea of *connecting* these woods, (and that *should* be the object), nothing can be more opposite than the effect'. The quickness of their growth, their shape and colour made them disagreeably conspicuous: 'it is a melancholy thing to compare the slow progress of beauty, with the upstart growth of deformity'. Felling humble trees and planting conifers were equally examples of 'levelling': 'To level, in the very usual sense of the word, means to take away all distinctions; a principle that, when made general, and brought into action by any determined improver either of grounds or governments, occasions such mischiefs, as time slowly, if ever, repairs.'[81]

Valuing a landscape with distinctions but not divisions, Price was particularly sensitive to routeways and borders. Embowered 'hollow lanes and bye roads' provided a paradigm for the improver because they were not designed but the product of piecemeal indiscriminate changes, some human, some natural. Here were 'no cut edges, no distinct lines of separation; all is mixed and blended together'. This effect might be destroyed by grubbing up the trees, by planting conifers or by the 'military style . . . smoothing and levelling' which he observed in two country lanes bordering pleasure grounds 'within thirty miles of London and in a district full of expensive embellishments', the territory of the newly rich. The social and aesthetic texture of each lane had been destroyed. The first had been dominated by a single spreading beech on a high bank on the sides of which sheep had made their tracks between the roots; the new owner had filled in the bank, smoothing the surface, emphasizing the disjunction of routeway and property. On the other lane the banks had been higher and trees loftier, their branches stretching from side to side, 'high-over arch'd imbower'. The new owner put a row of white pales at the foot of each bank and on that next to his pleasure ground a 'peat wall as upright as it could stand' planted with a row of laurels 'cut quite flat at the top'.[82] For Price an avenue of oaks was sacrosanct, the 'image of a grand gothic aisle with its natural aisle and vaulted roof'. He knew of one in Cheshire: 'Mr. Brown absolutely condemned it; but now it stands, a noble monument to the triumph of the natural feelings of the owner'.[83]

Embedded in Price's distinction between nature and artifice is not just a social distinction between benevolence and brutality but also one between sophistication and vulgarity. Underscoring many of Price's complaints about landscape improvement is the contempt of the connoisseur for the professional. Price made much of his role as a gentleman amateur, personally thinning and pruning to compose or, as he saw it, release the 'pictures in every tangled wood and thicket'.[84] While he accused professional improvement of disrupting the subtleties of organic woodland development, fundamentally at issue is the challenge of professional control of the landscape to Price's own. Commenting in 1811 on Price's improvements at Foxley, Wordsworth noted that 'a man little by little becomes so delicate and fastidious with respect to forms in scenery, where he has a power to exercise a controul over them, that if they do not exactly please him in all moods, and every point of view, his power becomes his law'; Foxley lacked the 'relish of humanity'.[85]

Arranging the finer points of his immediate surroundings was a way Price managed the tensions and divisions beyond. Writing 'in the present crisis' of 1795 he encouraged picturesque improvement, 'Till Albion smile / One ample theatre of sylvan grace', a quotation from William Mason and a description that fitted the arrangement of woodland around Price's own house.[86] And after confessing his anxiety in 1803 about hostilities between Britain and France, Price declared: 'The only tactics I know, or even wish to know, is that of arranging and disposing trees.'[87]

Richard Payne Knight

Richard Payne Knight's views on landscape improvement are conventionally paired with those of Price and undoubtedly some are similar. Knight's Downton estate was just 20 miles from Price's Foxley. The two men met frequently to exchange ideas and probably also techniques – Knight was as enthusiastic a lopper of branches as Price. Knight's long poem *The Landscape*, first published in 1794, the main vehicle for his views on improvement, is addressed to Price. He invited Price to publish his *Essay on the picturesque* together with the poem; Price did not do so but he did allude to and quote from it.[88]

Price and Knight were Foxite Whigs but Knight proclaimed a more radical politics of picturesque improvement. They both emphasized liberty in landscape and politics but whereas for Price freedom was a 'steady influence, like that of a fine evening, [which] gives at once a glowing warmth, and a union to all within its sphere', for Knight freedom was more volatile, 'the rays of genius that inflame / The free-born soul'.[89] Price emphasized order in nature and society, Knight energy. This difference in emphasis in their writings reflects their respective circumstances. Dominated by woodland, Foxley was an agrarian estate, and one Price sometimes found difficult to afford.[90] Downton was more an industrial estate and a more lucrative one. A family of ironmasters, the Knights had purchased it earlier in the century, as part of a group of properties, for its industrial potential. As much as local limestone and coal, the wood and water at Downton were seen as industrial resources. Richard Payne Knight was not as actively involved in iron manufacture as other members of the family, but he did own a number of forges and furnaces. While manufacturing *per se* never features explicitly in his taste for landscape he did admire powerful scenes of industrial potential, especially waterfalls, and at Downton created walks through the woods to display the dramatic character of the Teme gorge.[91] Knight's taste for a less settled landscape than that admired by Price was, of course, no less sophisticated, but it was less respectable. There is nothing of the piety of Price's picturesque in Knight's writing. Altogether, Knight cut a much less respectable figure. While Price was pleased to enjoy with his family 'the beauty, comfort and connection of my place' (and indeed was reluctant to leave it),[92] Knight, a bachelor with at least one mistress, spent much more time in London cultivating a raffish reputation as a free thinker and dilettante. By 1787 he had already outraged respectable opinion with a treatise on ancient phallic cults, in which he suggested that the cross was originally a phallic symbol 'serv[ing] as an emblem of creation and generation before the Church adopted it as a sign of salvation'.[93]

In a parody of Humphry Repton's technique of contrasting improved and unimproved landscapes, Knight illustrated *The Landscape* with a pair of views by Thomas Hearne (Fig. 7) showing a scene 'dressed in the modern style' to which he was opposed and the same scene 'undressed'. The dressed scene shows a typical Capability Brown landscape, a Palladian mansion surrounded by shaven lawns, clumps of trees and the still water of a serpentine river or lake. The undressed scene shows a more elaborate landscape, an ornate Elizabethan-style mansion and small garden surrounded by the shaggy trees, rampant undergrowth, exposed rocks and an agitated stream, the edge of what is described in the poem as an 'ancient forest'. (That

Fig. 7   Benjamin Pouncey after Thomas Hearne, contrasting plates from Richard Payne Knight, *The Landscape: A Didactic Poem* (1794).

this scene is reminiscent of Knight's estate is perhaps not surprising, still less so given that Hearne had already made a series of views of Downton.) In the Brownian landscape the power of property is directly apparent, the spectator's eye conducted to the brightly lit mansion along the serpentine water and path. For Knight the mansion is remote, standing 'unconnected' in 'solitary pride'. In the undressed scene the mansion is still a focal point 'rising to the view' but, 'mix'd and blended' with the abundant foreground detail, brought into short focus, 'a mere component part of what you see'. Like Price, Knight emphasizes the power of an enriched foreground to arrest the attention ('as the field of vision is confined, / Shews all its parts collected to the mind'), using as his model Dutch art and also the drawings of Claude Lorrain of which he was an avid collector.[94]

The politics of Knight's picturesque has both a conservative and a radical strain. He reads a strict social hierarchy into the 'ancient forest':

> Some [trees], towering upwards, spread their arms in state;
> And others, bending low, appear'd to wait:
> While scatter'd thorns, brows'd by the goat and deer,
> Rose all around, and let no lines appear.
> Such groups did Claude's light pencil often trace,
> The foreground of some classic scene to grace;[95]

Planting broad leaved trees like oak, elm and beech maintained this harmonious arrangement but planting conifers subverted it: 'Banish the formal fir's unsocial shade', Knight demanded, 'And crop the aspiring larch's saucy head'.[96] Knight considered picturesque landscape 'naturalized by use', that is naturalized by tradition; but a more radical notion of nature is discernible in Knight's description of the forest rising collectively in 'savage pride', 'Where every shaggy shrub and spreading tree / Proclaimed the seat of native liberty'.[97] If the conservative harmony of the forest implied its permeation by the social order of the Elizabethan mansion, Knight here implies the subordination of the mansion to the more ancient social order of the forest, one whose antiquity is emphasized, not qualified, by his description of the forest as a rival 'seat' of power. Read at a time when landed authority was in question this had seditious implications. When Knight recommends vandalizing Brownian parks to allow forest to regenerate his point is as much to revolutionize landscape as to restore it. Releasing the primordial power of wild nature would, Knight argues, make nature progressively more productive. While Knight refers only to productive farmland, his is as much an industrial as an agrarian point of view. Towards the end of *The Landscape*, at the climax of the poem, Knight expresses an unambiguously radical politics of natural rights as he likens the 'undressing' of a Brown-style lake to revolutionary liberation.

> As the dull, stagnant pool, that's mantled o'er
> With the green weeds of its own muddy shore,

No bright reflections on its surface shows,
Nor murmuring surge, nor foaming ripple knows;
But ever peaceful, motionless and dead,
In one smooth sheet its torpid waters spread:
So by oppression's iron hand confined,
In calm and peaceful torpor sleeps mankind;
Unfelt the rays of genius, that inflame
The free-born soul, and bid it pant for fame.
But break the mound, and let the waters flow;
Headlong and fierce their turbid currents go;
Sweep down the fences, and tear up the soil;
And roar along, 'midst havock, waste and spoil;
Till spent their fury: – then their moisture feeds
The deepening verdure of the fertile meads;
Bids vernal flowr's fragrant turf adorn,
And rising juices swell the wavy corn:
So when rebellion breaks the despot's chain,
First wasteful ruin marks the rabble's reign;
Till tir'd their fury, and their vengeance spent,
One common int'rest bids their hearts relent;
Then temp'rate order from confusion springs,
And, fann'd by freedom, genius spreads its wings.[98]

Knight closed the poem with a five page footnote on the French Revolution, lamenting the direction it had taken during the Terror but not disassociating himself from its impulse.

Reactionary readers were outraged. 'Knight's system appears to me the jacobinism of taste', wrote Anna Seward to Dr Johnson, '[he] would have nature as well as man indulged in that uncurbed and wild luxuriance, which must soon render our landscape-island rank, weedy, damp and unwholesome as the incultivate savannas of America'.[99] Seward's friend Humphry Repton found Knight's deduction of picturesque principles from wild scenery an experiment of 'untried theoretical improvement', inimical to the spirit of both English gardening and the English constitution.[100] Horace Walpole complained to William Mason about 'this pretended and ill-warranted dictator to all taste, who Jacobinically would level the purity of gardens, who would as malignantly as Tom Paine or Priestley guillotine Mr. Brown'.[101] And William Marshall saw the spectre of the guillotine in Knight's call to 'crop the aspiring larch's saucy head'; as a useful species for shipbuilding, the larch was for Marshall a symbol of national security but 'the adventurous Poet on behalf of that harmony which the larch may hereafter secure to this island calls down vengeance on its head'.[102] In a long postscript to the second edition of *The Landscape*, published in 1795 at a time of pronounced social alarm, Knight tried to undo the connection he had made between picturesque landscape and radical politics. His critics had taken him too literally, he protested: 'All that I entreat is, that they will not at this time, when men's minds are so full of plots and conspiracies, endeavour to find analogies between picturesque composition and political confusion; or suppose that the preservation of trees and terraces has any connection with the destruction of states and kingdoms.'[103]

Knight reaffirmed a correspondence between aesthetics and politics in his second didactic poem, *The Progress of Civil Society* (1796). This opens with a sceptical view of the origins of the cosmos, closes with an apologia for the French Revolution and includes an attack on the indissolubility of marriage. As in *The Landscape*, Knight's radicalism is driven by a sense of subversive energy and its repression. His protest at how sexual feeling 'stagnates' in marriage, 'fix'd by laws and limited by rules', parallels his protest in *The Landscape* at the repression of nature in a Brownian park, damned in a 'dull stagnant pool'.[104] Knight's description of sexual feeling as 'the fires of love' is one of a series of explicitly inflammatory metaphors in *The Progress of Civil Society*, some describing technological progress.[105] It is little wonder that in its parody of the poem the *Anti-Jacobin* referred its readers to Tom Paine and also to Joseph Priestley, distrusted by reactionaries as much for his experiments with light and oxygen as for his views on the rights of men.[106] William Mason's pious views were even more offended by Knight's second poem than his first. He found it sufficiently seditious to suggest to Horace Walpole that Knight's 'principles ought to be exposed before the next election, that such honest freeholders, who detest the French Jacobins, may be led to make it a point of conscience not to vote for him'.[107]

Humphry Repton

Price and Knight first published their writings on picturesque improvement in 1794, just in advance of, and perhaps to forestall, a book by Humphry Repton, *Sketches and hints on landscape gardening*. In five years Repton had established himself as the leading landscaper in the country and his book consisted largely of extracts from the manuscript Red Books of his commissions. Repton had met with Price and Knight on their estates and discussed his ideas with them, apparently amicably. But when Repton read their books he discovered they had attacked him arrogantly and often unfairly. They singled him out as the exemplar of professionalism in landscaping, adjudging his designs insufficiently pictorial. Knight accused Repton of mapping the possessiveness of his clients, relying on 'charts, pedometers and rules' rather than the pencil and palette.[108]

In reply Repton drew a distinction between landscape gardening and landscape painting, maintaining that he designed landscapes to be lived in not merely to be looked at.[109] But while Repton frequently emphasized 'utility' in landscaping his style was nevertheless always pictorial and based less on surveying (which he learned from canal engineers) than on his talent as a watercolourist.[110] Maps, the vehicle of Capability Brown's designs, were only incidental to Repton's and often not geometrically surveyed. Repton's Red Books were made up of watercolour sketches explained by a discursive text sometimes in verse. The misrepresentation of Repton by Price and Knight, especially their likening of his style to that of Brown, obscured the degree to which their views and their approach to landscaping agreed with his. Indeed Repton implied that Price and Knight had stolen his ideas.[111] By the turn of the century the dispute had blown over. And it was precisely at this time, when he was becoming increasingly sensitive to social issues, that Repton began to incorporate the views of his former adversaries in an explicit politics of landscape improvement.

Repton always shared the conservatism of the Portland Whigs who helped launch his career. During the first and most successful decade of Repton's career in the 1790s conservatism only tints his ideas on landscape improvement; after 1800 it saturates them. He became increasingly alarmed by such wartime conditions as the threat of invasion, the pressure of war taxes on the established gentry, the ascendancy of financial speculators and the disaffection of the poor: 'everyone trembled for the safety of old England' he recalled.[112] He was all the more mindful of these conditions because they threatened his own career. Demand for his talents decreased; those who did commission him tended to be parvenus with neither pedigree nor taste; and even aristocratic clients seemed to be infected by finance, sacrificing beauty for money in estate improvements.[113] In 1816 he recalled a time when his art 'seemed likely to extend its influence till all England would become one landscape garden'; but 'the eager pursuit of gain has, of late, extended from the new proprietor, whose habits have been connected with trade, to the ancient hereditary gentleman'.[114] Provoking this familiar conservative complaint were a number of related developments. These included 'the prevailing rage for agriculture', brought on by the escalating prices of the war years, which involved an unambiguously calculating attitude to estate management. Also the large and unregulated increase in the issue of banknotes troubled Repton. He saw this as destabilizing both the economy and society of the country by providing what seemed (in contrast to land) a baseless source of wealth and political power.[115] Like Burke he feared 'a paper circulation and a stock-jobbing constitution'.[116]

Repton's early views on planting tended to be formalistic. In *Sketches and hints* (1794) he recommended conifers as complements to classical architecture for the same qualities of shape, size and lighting that he recommended deciduous trees as complements to gothic architecture.[117] After the turn of the century, as his style became more emblematic, Repton distinguished softwoods and hardwoods more by their social associations. In *Observations on the theory and practice of landscape gardening* (1803) he was confident the 'man of taste' would not destroy an avenue of oaks 'for his hand is not guided by the levelling principles or sudden innovation of modern fashion'; he would protect each oak sapling 'which promises with improving beauty to spread a grateful shade for future "tenants of the soil"'.[118] Repton became increasingly intolerant of conifers and of those who planted them. In 1803, while travelling on the road between Ludlow and Worcester, returning from a commission near Knight's Downton, Repton realized the reason for Knight's 'enthusiastic abhorrence' for modern improvement: here, in the orbit of Birmingham, were the glaring red houses of the newly rich with 'plantations of firs and larches and Lombardy poplars'.[119] In his 1812 commission at Hewell, even closer to the city, he was alarmed to discover such plantations on an aristocratic estate and quoted Knight's lines about the 'unsocial fir' and 'aspiring larch' to sanction his contempt for 'that generation of Firs, Larches and Lombardy poplars which presently disgrace the character of Hewell'.[120] The following year at Beaudesert in Staffordshire he was relieved to discover that Lord Uxbridge was planning to restore the house and park to a style 'worthy of the rank and antiquity of its ancestors'. The place should be sharply distinguished from 'the spruce modern seat of modern affluence' and Repton implored him to grub up belts of 'spiral spruce firs and larches'; 'if the improvement of places such as Beaudesert is to be computed by the rule of pounds, shillings and pence, it would certainly be better to cut down all the trees, kill the deer and plough up the park'.[121] The more Repton was forced to take on parvenus as clients, the more he identified them with conifers. Of one he complained:

how could I hope to suggest an idea to this man who shewed me what he called 'the LARGEST ACORN he had ever seen!' at the same time producing the CONE of a STONE PINE that grew near an oak and had fallen among the acorns! (fit emblem of him I thought who had fallen among Gentlemen but could NOT be mistaken for one).[122]

Only at Sheringham in Norfolk in 1812 did Repton find a client who fully shared his ideas. On a coast exposed to the threat of French invasion Repton thought it 'an apt lesson to the Planter as well as the Moralist' that oaks should be grouped:

While Ocean's breath may blast a Single tree
England's combined Oaks resist the Sea
Emblem of Strength, increas'd by Unity

The unity of England at this time was precisely in question. To Repton the combined pressure of repression and disaffection had destabilized the country. 'Rebellious principles' were rife in the manufacturing districts, farmers were driving hungry labourers harder to reap high wheat prices and landlords were using the game laws to turn the poor into 'idle thieves and poachers'. To promote the impression of class unity at Sheringham he recommended a regime of estate management flavoured by custom; allowing villagers into the woods, perhaps once a month 'under the eye of a keeper to pick up dead sticks for firing' (for in places where this was done 'no wood is stolen, no trees are lop'd or disfigured') and creating a village green with 'a *May pole*; that almost forgotten Emblem of rural happiness and festivity'.[123]

Repton devoted a chapter in his last published work *Fragments on the theory and practice of landscape gardening* (1816) to the moral delinquency of modern improvement.[124] In a parody of his own technique (Fig. 8) he contrasted a recent 'improved' view of an estate 'in a distant county' with an unimproved view made from the same spot when he was passing ten years earlier. During this time the estate had been sold by an aristocratic 'ancient proprietor' to a 'very rich man' (by implication a newly rich one) who had transformed its organization and appearance. For Repton the changes symbolized the cultural decline of the country as a whole.[125] While Repton claims to have witnessed the two scenes and cites 'an old labourer' as his source on how the changes came about, his account is actually a pastiche of his own observations and other polemics on landscape improvement, notably by Uvedale Price and Richard Payne Knight.

The view during the benevolent regime of the 'ancient proprietor' is dominated by deciduous trees. To the left in the park, intermixed with hawthorns, are 'venerable ... large spreading trees', prominently an 'aged beech' in the left foreground. This extends its shade over the road, its branches pointing to a family resting on a thoughtfully placed bench. Its trunk marks the spot where a stile gives public access to the park. To the right is a wooded common, edged with what seem to be hawthorns in the middle distance and prominently in the right foreground an elm or perhaps a birch.[126] The foreground trees frame the scene, and with the hawthorns in the park and common, embower it. In the style of Price's and Knight's picturesque ideal, the foreground dominates the view, filling the picture space with finely deciduous texture. The impression of stability is further emphasized by the gesture of the aged beech to the resting couple. Indeed the middle distance can be seen as a vague echo of the foreground, the bough of the beech tree there pointing towards two hazy figures on the path. Divisions between the park, the road and the common are not clearly marked and the effect of the trees is to soften them further. It is a quintessential landscape of 'connection'. The effect for the spectator is to be taken into, not past, the estate, into an arena of landed benevolence.

Fig. 8   Humphry Repton, 'Improvements', from *Fragments on the theory and practice of landscape gardening* (1816).

The changes made by the new owner, for whom 'money supersedes every other consideration' destroy this landscape.

By cutting down the timber and getting an act to enclose the common, he had doubled all the rents. The old mossy and ivy-covered pale was replaced by a new and lofty close paling; not to confine the deer, but to exclude mankind, and to protect a miserable narrow belt of firs and Lombardy poplars: the bench was gone, the ladder-stile was changed to a caution about man-traps and spring-guns, and a notice that the footpath was stopped by order of the commissioners. As I read the board, the old man said 'It is very true, and I am forced to walk a mile further round every night after a hard day's work'.

Repton's letters of this period reveal that he often projected the personal hardships of his old age, in particular his failing career and health, into the decline in English society he narrated in published writings.[127] The figure with a stick in the middle distance may then represent Repton himself. It would be understandable for Repton to identify with a day labourer, when, as he complained, so many of his calculating new clients were treating him as just that. Once he had enjoyed the hospitality of the aristocracy, now the newly rich merely employed him for a few hours to fix a spot for their villas and 'one day is much like another'.[128]

The new regime of the estate is as uninviting for Repton as it is for the labourer. Money has dissolved the bonds of connection on which Repton's idea of landscape is based. No longer is the spectator's gaze drawn gently into the landscape but is driven rapidly through it. In the former view the eye winds along a downward spiral defined by the lower branches and trunk of the foreground beech, the fence and path, the outline of the hawthorn in the middle distance and finally the lower bough and trunk of the further beech, to disperse into the dappled shade of the park. In the improved view the straightened road, the new palings, the line of conifers and the ploughed field form a pyramid of linear perspective.[129] A streamlined vista conducts the eye abruptly to the horizon where, with little loss of clarity, we see a figure (the new owner?) pointing to (directing?) a ploughman, the conventional figure of rural toil. The landscape is, in every way, so severe as to be for Repton, or for any other lover of the picturesque, scarcely a landscape at all.

Picturesque practitioners did not abandon linear for aerial perspective – the framework of Repton's improved view is discernible in the unimproved one, if only to make his comparison between them possible. But they did seek to soften linear perspective with chiaroscuro and a more curvilinear geometry, building on a tradition of benevolent landscape that had since the seventeenth century consciously obscured the clarity of long views with enveloping shade. The hard-hearted owner in Repton's homily has an ancestry that reaches back through the oppressors in Price and Burke at least to the 'tyrant' of Thomas Wincoll's *Plantagent's Tragicall Story* (1649) who 'seems to cut down ev'ry Tree / That clouds th'ambitious prospect of his eye'.[130]

Picturesque England

Price, Knight and Repton exploited the rich reserves of English woodland symbolism to construct a political iconography articulated as much in the form of landscape as in its subject matter. Within their work two sensibilities combine, sometimes uneasily: on one hand a critical sensibility which actively engages social and economic issues, indeed articulates them comprehensively in landscape terms; and, on the other hand, a complacent sensibility which regards landscape as something separate from and opposed to human society and deploys its imagery to obscure social and economic issues. Repton's eventual despair at the possibility of 'improvement' and his creation of an introspective and consoling imagery of nostalgia and sentiment are symptoms of this sensibility which is more characteristic of Victorian than Georgian England (indeed Victorians tended to represent Repton's work as a whole in these terms).[131]

As social and economic concern shifted to the burgeoning industrial towns so the political power of the picturesque faded.[132] But it remained in reserve for the long period of the nation's industrial decline. Throughout the present century the picturesque has been mobilized to articulate English society and often again with a sense of its duplicity as both the 'true' England and a world of make believe.[133] In a recent example *Greening the Tories* (1985), Andrew Sullivan reminds his readers that picturesque England is one of those 'illusions important to the political life of nations'. Integral to this England are old English trees: 'they are not simply large outcrops of vegetation'. Sullivan maintains 'they are part of our social and political history . . . they represent moreover a sense of continuity and cultural unity that conservatives might do well not to ignore.'[134]

NOTES

1 Keith Thomas, *Man and the natural world: changing attitudes in England 1500–1800* (London, 1983), p. 219.
2 Elaborating Marx's discussion of the cherry tree in *The German ideology*, Roland Barthes suggests that the ideological power of trees as symbols resides in their particular compound of the 'natural' and the 'political'. Their 'political quality' (the social facts of their cultivation and management) 'fades', 'purified' by the discourse of the 'natural'. But the political power of trees can be discursively reconstituted as readily as it is dissolved, 'decorated, adapted to a certain type of consumption, laden with literary self-indulgence, revolt, images, in short with a type of social *usage*'. Trees and woodland can be used at once to politicize social relations and to naturalize them. Roland Barthes, 'Myth today', in *Mythologies* (St Albans, 1972), pp. 109–58, quotations on pp. 144, 109.

3 H. C. Prince, 'England *circa* 1800', in H. C. Darby (ed.), *A new historical geography of England after 1600* (Cambridge, 1976), pp. 89–164, see esp. p. 164.

4 N. D. G. James, *A history of English forestry* (Oxford, 1981), pp. 167–77, 317–19; Thomas, *Man and the natural world*, p. 213.

5 These various interests were compiled in single publications, notably Alexander Hunter's revised editions of John Evelyn's *Sylva*, published in four editions: 1777, 1786, 1801, 1812.

6 Thomas, *Man and the natural world*, p. 195.

7 William Gilpin, *Remarks on forest scenery* (London, 1791), Vol. 1, pp. 40–1.

8 Charles Vancouver, *General view of the agriculture of Hampshire* (London, 1813), p. 496.

9 Roger Miles, *Forestry in the English landscape* (London, 1967), p. 46.

10 R. W. Bushaway, 'Grovely, grovely, grovely and all grovely: custom, crime and conflict in English woodland', *History Today*, 31 (1981), pp. 37–43, quotation on p. 38; R. W. Bushaway, 'From custom to crime: wood gathering in eighteenth and early nineteenth century England, a focus for conflict in Hampshire, Wiltshire and the South', in John Rule (ed.), *Outside the law: studies in crime and order, 1650–1850* (Exeter, 1982), pp. 65–101, quotation on p. 66.

11 Quoted in Bushaway, 'From custom to crime', p. 99.

12 Bushaway, 'Grovely, grovely', and 'From custom to crime', *passim*. E. P. Thompson, *Whigs and hunters: the origin of the Black Act* (London, 1975), pp. 144–5, 229–30, 246, 255.

13 Thomas Whately, *Observations on modern gardening* (London, 1770), p. 227. It was an outlook that fitted with Whately's explicitly political polemics. As Secretary for the Treasury, in *Remarks on the budget* (1765), he declared that when 'power is supported by property, the subjects have the only security the nature of government will admit of'. I owe this reference to Nigel Everett, 'Country justice: the literature of landscape improvement and English conservatism, with particular reference to the 1790s' (unpublished PhD thesis, University of Cambridge, 1977), p. 27n.

14 William Mason, *The English Garden*, Book II, lines 225–31, 261, 351, 357–67, 398–9, 403–5, in *The works of William Mason*, Vol. 1 (London, 1811), pp. 265, 37, 250–1.

15 Humphry Repton, *Fragments on the theory and practice of landscape gardening* (London, 1816), p. 233.

16 Everett, 'Country justice', *passim*. Alisdair M. Duckworth, *The improvement of the estate: a study of Jane Austen's novels* (Baltimore, 1971), pp. 35–80; Alisdair M. Duckworth, 'Fiction and the uses of the country house setting from Richardson to Scott', in David C. Streatfield and Alisdair M. Duckworth (eds.), *Landscape in the gardens and literature of eighteenth century England* (Los Angeles, 1981), pp. 91–128. Raymond Williams, *The country and the city* (London, 1973), pp. 60–7, 108–26.

17 William Cowper, *The Task* (1785), Book III, lines 746–55, in William Cowper, *The task and selections from the minor poems*, ed. Henry Thomas Griffiths (London, 1926), p. 68.

18 Edmund Burke, *Reflections on the revolution in France* (1790; Harmondsworth, 1979), p. 171.

19 Edmund Burke, *Letter to a noble lord* (1796; London, 1831), p. 49.

20 William Cobbett, *The woodlands* (London, 1825), n.p., section 82. See also Cobbett's defence of forested commons, section 64. For a discussion of the politics of Cobbett's rural views see Raymond Williams, *Cobbett* (Oxford, 1973).

21 *Cobbett's Weekly Political Register*, 30, No. 20 (18 May 1816).

22 The earliest use of the phrase I know is in Lord Coventry's 1635 speech to the judges of England, quoted in James, *English forestry*, p. 139. Hunter uses it on the first page of his introduction to his editions of Evelyn's *Sylva*.

23 William Pontey, *The forest pruner* (Huddersfield, 1805), p. 27.

24 Hunter's annotation to pp. 299–300 of his 1812 edition of John Evelyn's *Sylva*.

25 William Marshall, *Planting and ornamental gardening* (London, 1785), pp. 485, 314, 315.

26 Hunter, 1812 edition of Evelyn's *Sylva*, p. 1n.

27 Oliver Rackham, *The history of the countryside* (London, 1986), pp. 91–2.

28 Thomas, *Man and the natural world*, p. 220.

29 Gilpin, *Forest scenery*, p. 25; James, *English forestry*, p. 151.

30 James Thomson did appreciate conifers in his vignette of the port of London in *The Seasons*, like 'a long wintry forest, groves of masts / shot up like spies'. James Thomson, 'Autumn', lines 124–5, from *The Seasons* (1746 edn), in James Thomson, *The Seasons and the castle of indolence*, ed. James Sambrook (Oxford, 1972), p. 92.

31 Robert Greenbaugh Albion, *Forests and sea power* (Cambridge, Mass., 1926), p. 118.

32 Michael Rosenthal, *British landscape painting* (Oxford, 1982), pp. 92–118; Michael Rosenthal, *Constable, the painter and his landscape* (New Haven and London, 1983), pp. 74–89. Stephen Daniels, 'Humphry Repton and the morality of landscape', in John R. Gold and Jacquelin Burgess (eds.), *Valued environments* (London, 1982), pp. 115–44, see esp. pp. 134–6.

33 Quoted in Albion, *Forests and sea power*, p. 119.

34 Thomas, *Man and the natural world*, p. 218.

35 For examples of framing ancient oaks see Humphry Repton, *Plans, hints and views for the improvement of Welbeck in Nottinghamshire* (1790), n.p., private collection; Ronald Paulson, *Emblem and expression: meaning in English art of the eighteenth century* (London, 1975), p. 115.

36 Hector Bolitho and Derek Peel, *The Drummonds of Charing Cross* (London, 1967); Peter Willis, 'Capability Brown's account with Drummond's Bank, 1753–83', *Architectural History*, 27 (1984), pp. 382–91. For a fuller analysis of the painting in terms of 'the iconography of possessions' see Palson, *Emblem and expression*, p. 155.

37 Marshall, *Planting and ornamental gardening*, p. 166.

38 Marcia Allentuck, 'Sir Uvedale Price and the picturesque garden: the evidence of the Coleorton papers', in Niklaus Pevsner (ed.), *The picturesque garden and its influence outside the British Isles* (Washington DC, 1974), pp. 59–76, see esp. p. 76. Richard Payne Knight, *The Landscape* (London, 2nd edn, 1795), Book III, lines 81–90, p. 73.

39 Hunter, 1812 edition of Evelyn's *Sylva*, p. 135.

40 The most notable elm planting was probably the great avenue at Wimpole, Cambridgeshire, planted c.1718. The elms in front of the house were relics of the lost village of Wimpole. See Rackham, *The history of the countryside*, p. 238. A notable celebration in verse occurs in *The Seasons* where Thomson describes 'the rural seat / whose lofty elms and reverable oaks / Invite the rook': 'Spring', lines 76–8 in Thomson, *The Seasons*, p. 24.

41 John Scott, 'Ode I, To Leisure', in *The poetical works of John Scott* (London, 1782), p. 167.

42 The 1783 version is in the National Trust Bearsted Collection, Upton House, and is reproduced in Constance-Anne Parker, *Mr. Stubbs the horse painter* (London, 1971), p. 126. Cf. Stubbs's use of an oak in *The Grosvenor Hunt* (1762, collection of His Grace the Duke of Westminster) to concentrate attention on Lord Grosvenor viewing a stag at bay on his Eaton Hall estate. This painting is reproduced on p. 66 of the 1984 Tate Gallery catalogue, *George Stubbs 1724–1806*. I owe the references to the Scott poem and the Stubbs painting (but not my interpretation) to R. H. Richens, *Elm* (Cambridge, 1983), pp. 143 and 168.

43 Rosenthal, *Constable*, pp. 87–9.

44 Gerald Wilkinson, *Epitaph for the elm* (London, 1978), p. 27. See also John Lucas's discussion of Clare's use of the elm in 'Places and dwellings', ch. 4 in this book.

45 Quoted in Richens, *Elm*, pp. 156–8.

46 William Wordsworth, *The Excursion* (1814 edn), Book VII, lines 621–2, in William Wordsworth, *Poetical works*, ed. Ernest de Selincourt (Oxford, 1969), p. 675.

47 Oliver Goldsmith, *The Deserted Village*, lines 16–20. John Barrell points out that while the 'agrarian egalitarianism' of *The Deserted Village* might have been found disturbing to its first readers in 1770, in the mid-1790s it would have seemed dangerously radical. See John Barrell, *The dark side of the landscape: the rural poor in English painting 1730–1840* (Cambridge, 1980), pp. 81–2.

48 John Clare, 'Helpston', lines 133–4, in Eric Robinson and David Powell (eds.), *John Clare* (Oxford, 1984), p. 4.

49 Robert Southey, 'On the state of the poor' (1816), in *Essays, moral and political*, 2 vols. (London, 1832), Vol. 1, pp. 159–247, quotation on p. 180.

50 Jacob George Strutt, *Silva Britannica* (London, 1822), n.p.

51 Prince, 'England *circa* 1800', pp. 126–7. Tom Williamson and Liz Bellamy, *Property and landscape: a social history of land ownership and the English countryside* (London, 1987), p. 193.

52 Pontey, *The forest pruner*, p. 4. The attack on Pontey by the *Anti-Jacobin Review* is reprinted in Pontey's riposte to it, *The rotten reviewers* (n.p., n.d.), p. 6.

53 William Pontey, *The profitable planter* (Huddersfield, 1800), p. 94.

54 Pontey, *The forest pruner*, p. 140n.

55 William Marshall's 1811 *Review of the Reports to the Board of Agriculture from the Eastern Department of England*, quoted in James, *English forestry*, p. 123.

56 *Annals of Agriculture*, 5 (1786), pp. 180, 185; 8 (1787), pp. 90–1.

57 William Wordsworth, *Guide to the Lakes* (5th edn, London, 1835), pp. 57–92, quotations on pp. 82 and 86. William Mason accepted conifers as nurses for oaks till their charges 'possesst / Of native strength, they learn alike to scorn / The blast *and their protectors*' (my emphasis): lines 244–57 of Book I of *The English Garden*, in Mason, *Works*, Vol. 1, p. 220.

58 William Wordsworth, *Two addresses to the freeholders of Westmorland* (Kendal, 1818), pp. 70, 11, 70.

59 I owe much of the argument of this section and many of the references to Ronald Paulson, *Representations of revolution (1789–1820)* (New Haven and London, 1983).

60 Thomas Paine, *The rights of man* (1791–2; London, 1969), pp. 151, 32.

61 David Bindman, *William Blake: his art and times* (London, 1982), pp. 24, 37, 99.

62 This interpretation is based on Paulson, *Representations of revolution*, p. 88, and Geoffrey Keynes's introduction to the facsimile edition of Blake's *America* (London, 1963).

63 Winthrop Jordan, 'Familial politics: Thomas Paine and the killing of the King', *Journal of American History*, 60 (1973–4), pp. 294–308, quotation on p. 305.

64 Arthur M. Schlesinger, 'Liberty Tree: a genealogy', *New England Quarterly*, 25 (1952), pp. 435–58. James H. Billington, *Fire in the minds of men: origins of the revolutionary faith* (London, 1980), pp. 46–53.

65 On Gillray's politics see Paulson, *Representations of revolution*, p. 190; and Draper Hill, *Mr. Gillray, the caricaturist* (London, 1965), pp. 46–7. After 1793 Gillray endorsed the Tory attitude towards Fox but this cartoon suggests his anti-monarchism had not been extinguished.

66 On the aggravating effects of the wars see Clive Emsley, *British society and the French wars 1793–1815* (London, 1979).

67 Even William Gilpin, who popularized a formalistic picturesque, found it difficult. See especially his *Moral contrasts* (Lymington, 1798), which contrasts the conduct of the reckless Sir James Leigh, who is forced to fell all his timber to pay his debts, with that of the prudent Mr Willoughby: 'what timber he cut down, was only such as called for the axe; and in its room he planted thousands of trees all over his domain'. Willoughby's careful regime of estate management is rewarded by the gratitude of his tenants and labourers. The 'associationist' aesthetics of Archibald Alison, expressed in his *Essays on the nature and principles of taste* (Edinburgh, 1790), became extremely influential on landscape theorists, painters and designers. See Rosenthal, *Constable*,

pp. 74–5; Andrew Hemingway, 'Meaning in Cotman's Norfolk subjects', *Art History*, 7 (1984), pp. 57–77.

68 Uvedale Price, *An essay on the picturesque* (London, 1794), pp. 206–9. Price expanded his essay in two-volume editions in 1796–8 and 1810.

69 Many of the trees at Foxley were planted by Price's father, Robert. On Robert Price's improvements and benevolence to the poor in times of hardship see 'Character of Robert Price Esq.' in W. Coxe (ed.), *The literary life and select works of Benjamin Stillingfleet*, 2 vols. (London, 1811), Vol. 1, pp. 169–82. A collector of landscape art, especially seventeenth-century Dutch paintings and drawings, Robert Price was himself a keen sketcher and painter of landscape. Gainsborough sketched with him at Foxley and wandered over the grounds with the young Uvedale. On Gainsborough at Foxley see Jack Lindsay, *Thomas Gainsborough: his life and work* (St Albans, 1981), pp. 55, 65.

70 *The beauties of England and Wales*, Vol. 6 (1806), quoted in Allentuck, 'Uvedale Price', p. 74.

71 Price's sense of social and economic balance in landscape probably reflects the reputation of Herefordshire generally as a county with a preponderance of minor gentry and owner occupiers (and an absence of aristocratic grandees) and also a healthy mixture of flourishing farms and small industry. See Barrell, *Dark side*, pp. 173–4.

72 Uvedale Price, 'On the bad effects of stripping and cropping trees', *Annals of Agriculture*, 5 (1786), pp. 241–50.

73 Uvedale Price, *Thoughts on the defence of property* (Hereford, 1797), pp. 10–11, 20.

74 Price, *Essay* (1810 edn), Vol. 1, pp. 246, 246n.

75 Price, *Defence of property*, p. 19.

76 Price, *Essay* (1796 edn), Vol. 1, p. 103. John Murdoch points out that Price struggled 'with the fact that landscape painting, to which he looked for ultimate authority, did not much deal with subjects in vivid close-up' and was 'compelled to make some special pleading in favour of the enriched foreground'. See 'Foregrounds and focus: changes in the perception of landscape c.1800', in *The Lake District: a sort of national property* (London, 1986), pp. 43–59, quotation on p. 55. This essay, which came too late to my attention to address in the text, has many points of connection with my subsequent arguments on the morality of short focus picturesque landscape.

77 Burke, *Letter to a noble lord*, p. 49. Thanking Price for sending him a copy of his *Essay*, Burke expressed his 'happiness to agree with you in almost everything you have to say about Brownism'; Price's 'pleasing, ingenious and instructive Book' gave Burke 'a few hours very reasonable relief from Books of a very different kind, which teach but too clearly the art, not of improving, but of laying waste a Country': Burke to Uvedale Price, 1 June 1794, in *The correspondence of Edmund Burke*, Vol. 7 (Cambridge, 1968), pp. 547–8.

78 Paulson, *Emblem and expression*, pp. 218–21.

79 Price, *Essay* (1794 edn), pp. 278–80.

80 Uvedale Price, *A letter to H. Repton Esq.* (London, 1795), p. 160.

81 Price, *Essay* (1794 edn), pp. 213, 216n, 218, 28n; (1796 edn), pp. 261–2. On 'connection' see also Price's *Letter to Repton*, p. 95, and *Defence of property*, pp. 14, 28. In condemning Brown, Price broke the correspondence between the reform in English politics and in gardening, between English constitutional liberty and informal Brownian landscaping. Whereas the Glorious Revolution was, Price maintained, 'the steady, considerate and connected arrangement of enlightened minds', the revolution in taste was carried out by 'the lower and less enlightened part of mankind': *Essay* (1798 edn), Vol. 2, pp. 175–6.

82 Price, *Essay* (1794 edn), pp. 21, 27–33. Cf. William Mason's complaints about the weekend retreats of city gentlemen with their 'trim domain', their 'milk-white palisades' a blemish on 'the sylvan scene' in *The English Garden*, Book II, lines 355–61 in *Works*, Vol. 1, p. 359.

83 Price, *Essay* (1794 edn), p. 196n. On the late eighteenth-century view of woods as ecclesiastical landscapes see Thomas, *Man and the natural world*, p. 216.

84 Uvedale Price to Lady Beaumont, 5 December 1817, quoted in Allentuck, 'Uvedale Price', p. 75. See also Price's letter to Sir George Beaumont, 12 September 1824, quoted in *ibid.*, p. 73.

85 William Wordsworth to Sir George Beaumont, 28 August 1811, in Ernest de Selincourt (ed.), *The letters of William and Dorothy Wordworth: the middle years* (Oxford, 1937), p. 467. Both Wordsworth and Price advised the Beaumonts on improvements to their grounds at Coleorton, Leicestershire.

86 Price, *Letter to Repton*, p. 161.

87 Uvedale Price to Lady Beaumont, August 1803, quoted in Allentuck, 'Uvedale Price', p. 75.

88 For example the phrase 'high-over arch'd imbower' quoted above is from *The Landscape*, Book II, line 137, p. 37.

89 Price, *Letter to Repton*, pp. 159–160. Knight, *The Landscape*, Book II, line 400, p. 92.

90 In March 1798 Price considered selling Foxley, 'this beautiful but expensive place'. Uvedale Price to Sir George Beaumont, 18 March 1798, Coleorton Papers MA 1581 (Price), 16.

91 Nicolas Penny, 'Richard Payne Knight: a brief life', 'Architecture and landscape at Downton', in Michael Clarke and Nicolas Penny (eds.), *The arrogant connoisseur: Richard Payne Knight 1751–1824* (Manchester, 1982), pp. 1–18, 32–49, esp. 1, 47–8 and 111 n. 113.

92 Uvedale Price to Sir George Beaumont, 24 July 1812, quoted in Allentuck, 'Uvedale Price', p. 71. Price's reluctance to leave Foxley is a recurring theme in his letters to the Beaumonts.

93 Richard Payne Knight, *The worship of priapus*, quoted in Peter Funnell, 'The symbolical language of antiquity', in Clarke and Penny (eds.), *The arrogant connoisseur*, pp. 56–64, quoted on p. 62. On the relationship between tree symbolism and that of the Cross, see Douglas Davies's essay 'The evocative symbolism of trees', ch. 2 in this book.

94 Knight, *The Landscape*, Book I, lines 185, 221, 255–6, 218–20, pp. 13, 16, 17, 16. On Knight's picture collection see Michael Clarke, 'Collecting paintings and drawings', in Clarke and Penny (eds.), *The arrogant connoisseur*,

pp. 93–109. On Thomas Hearne's views of Downton see 'Catalogue' to *ibid.*, pp. 156–8.

95 Knight, *The Landscape*, Book II, lines 45–8, p. 33.

96 *Ibid.*, Book III, lines 59–60, p. 72.

97 *Ibid.*, Book II, lines 31, 39–40, pp. 54, 32–3.

98 *Ibid.*, Book III, lines 377–400, pp. 91–2.

99 Quoted in Frank J. Messman, *Richard Payne Knight: the twilight of virtuosity* (The Hague, 1974), p. 83. Seward appears here to recall Shakespeare's lines condemning the state of England under the Yorkist Richard II in *Richard II*, Act III, Sc. 4. For other examples of Seward's conservatism in landscape taste see her poems 'The Lake' and 'On the Pleasures of Rural Life', in Anna Seward, *Poetical works*, 3 vols. (Edinburgh, 1810), Vol. 3, pp. 35–8, 291–301.

100 Humphry Repton, *Sketches and hints on landscape gardening* (1794), in J. C. Loudon (ed.), *The landscape gardening and landscape architecture of the late Humphry Repton Esq.* (London, 1840), p. 106n.

101 Quoted in Messman, *Knight*, p. 83.

102 William Marshall, *A review of the landscape* (London, 1795), p. 25. For Marshall's views on the larch see his *Planting and ornamental gardening*, pp. 283–4.

103 Knight, *The Landscape*, p. 104.

104 Richard Payne Knight, *The Progress of Civil Society: A Didactic Poem* (London, 1796), Book III, lines 150–2, p. 55; *The Landscape*, Book III, line 377, p. 91. On the importance of sexual energy to Knight's aesthetics see Gordon McKenzie, *Critical responsiveness: a study of the psychological current in later eighteenth century criticism* (Berkeley, 1949), pp. 79, 169–71.

105 Knight, *Civil Society*, Book III, line 163, p. 55, lines 1–36, pp. 49–50.

106 Messman, *Knight*, p. 88.

107 Quoted *ibid.*, p. 94.

108 Quotation from Knight, *The Landscape*, Book I, line 276, p. 21. On the quarrel between Repton, Knight and Price see Patrick Goode, 'The picturesque controversy', in George Carter, Patrick Goode and Kedrun Laurie (eds.), *Humphry Repton, landscape gardener 1752–1818* (Norwich, 1982), pp. 34–41.

109 Humphry Repton, *A letter to Uvedale Price Esq.*, Appendix to *Sketches and hints* in Loudon (ed.), *Repton's landscape gardening*, pp. 104–9.

110 Kedrun Laurie, 'Humphry Repton' in Carter *et al.* (eds.), *Humphry Repton*, pp. 14–15.

111 Humphry Repton, *An inquiry into the changes of taste in landscape gardening* (1806), in Loudon (ed.), *Repton's landscape gardening*, p. 353.

112 On Repton's politics and their implication for his art see Stephen Daniels, 'The political landscape', in Carter *et al.* (eds.), *Humphry Repton*, pp. 110–21. Quotation from Repton's *Memoir* on p. 114, British Museum, Add. MSS 62112.

113 Daniels, 'The political landscape'.

114 Repton, *Fragments*, p. 110.

115 Stephen Daniels, 'Cankerous blossom. Troubles in the later career of Humphry Repton documented in the Repton correspondence in the Huntington Library', *Journal of Garden History*, 6 (1986), pp. 146–61, see esp. p. 149.

116 Burke, *Reflections*, p. 142.

117 Repton, *Sketches and hints*, in Loudon (ed.), *Repton's landscape gardening*, pp. 56–60.

118 Humphry Repton, *Observations on the theory and practice of landscape gardening* (1803), in Loudon (ed.), *Repton's landscape gardening*, p. 195.

119 Repton, *Fragments*, pp. 33–4.

120 Humphry Repton, *Plans for Hewell* (1812), n.p., private collection.

121 Repton, *Fragments*, pp. 48, 46.

122 Humphry Repton, *Memoir*, Part 2, draft, n.d., p. 170.

123 Humphry Repton with the assistance of John Adey Repton, *Plans for Sherringham in Norfolk* (1812), n.p., private collection, on loan to Drawings collection of Royal Institute of British Architects, London, and published as one of a boxed set of three Red Books in Edward Malins (ed.), *The Red Books of Humphry Repton* (London, 1976). For a detailed discussion of the Sheringham commission see Daniels, 'Humphry Repton and the morality of landscape', pp. 124–44.

124 Repton, *Fragments*, pp. 191–4.

125 The estate may be based in part on Thorngrove in Worcestershire. I am grateful to Miss M. Sanders of Worcester City Library for responding so fully to my enquiries on a likely location for the estate.

126 This wooded common recalls the practice of Robert Marsham, Repton's mentor on planting. On his estate at Stratton Strawless in Norfolk he refused to deprive local commoners of their rights by enclosing the common but planted trees along the road to improve its appearance. See Nigel Harvey, 'Marsham the tree planter', *Journal of the Land Agents Society*, 58 (1954), pp. 78–9. Repton extols Marsham's methods of planting commons in *Observations* in Loudon (ed.), *Repton's landscape gardening*, pp. 73–4. On Repton and Marsham and the roots of Repton's conservatism in his years before his career as a landscape gardener, living in a Norfolk village, see Stephen Daniels, 'Humphry Repton at Sustead', *Garden History*, 11 (1983), pp. 57–64.

127 Daniels, 'Cankerous blossom', *passim.*

128 Daniels, 'The political landscape', p. 115.

129 For a discussion of the ideological implications of the spiral form as opposed to the pyramid form of visual perspective see W. J. T. Mitchell, 'Metamorphoses of the vortex: Hogarth, Turner and Blake', in Richard Wendorf (ed.), *Articulate images: the sister arts from Hogarth to Tennyson* (Minneapolis, 1983), pp. 125–68, esp. 130–3.

130 Quoted in James Turner, *The politics of landscape: rural scenery and society in English poetry 1630–1660* (Oxford, 1979), p. 45.

131 Daniels, 'The political landscape', p. 118; Daniels, 'Cankerous blossom', pp. 153–8.

132 Barrell, *Dark side*, pp. 32–3; Everett, 'Country justice', pp. 313–19: Rosenthal, *British landscape painting*, pp. 128–30; Daniels, 'The political landscape', p. 118.

133 Martin J. Wiener, *English culture and the decline of the industrial spirit 1850–1980* (Cambridge, 1981). Peter Fuller, '"Neo-Romanticism": a defence

of English pastoralism' in *Images of God: the consolation of lost illusions* (London, 1985), pp. 83–91.

134 Andrew Sullivan, *Greening the Tories: new policies on the environment* (London, 1985), pp. 9, 10.

I am grateful to Denis Cosgrove, Susanne Seymour and Charles Watkins for their helpful comments on earlier drafts of this essay.

4

Places and dwellings: Wordsworth, Clare and the anti-picturesque

JOHN LUCAS

We are unlikely nowadays to think of the picturesque as a purely aesthetic matter. For although its theorists and champions insisted on its 'dissociation of visual, pictorial, or generally aesthetic elements from other values in contemplating a scene', it is clear that this cannot be done.[1] I have elsewhere argued that 'the picturesque aims not at tragedy, but at pathos, and the pathetic is inseparable from a certain complacency precisely because it invites us to consider that nothing can be, other than what is'.[2] In other words, the picturesque frequently renders what it chooses to term 'the principle of change' as an immutable law.[3] In the present essay, I want to dicuss some poems by two great poets who, in their challenge to this complacency, this apparent immutability, offer something that approaches a tragic vision of the changes that occur within so-called 'picturesque' landscapes; and I shall suggest that they read the landscape through a very un-picturesque attention to apparently random details whose ultimate significance radically upsets the kinds of aesthetic categorisation which the theorists of the picturesque took for granted. Moreover, such concern with detail is itself something of a challenge to the picturesque concern with a distanced viewpoint and 'vague emotion, expressed in shadowy mass and luminous base'.[4]

Wordsworth

Although in Book XI of the 1805 *Prelude* Wordsworth denied that he had ever been much in the habit of giving way to what he calls the 'strong infection of the age', you have only to look at such early poems as 'An Evening Walk', 'The Vale of Esthwaite' and 'Descriptive Sketches' to see how in thrall to the picturesque he was as a young man. The very titles of these poems imply as much, and nothing in their contents challenges it.[5] On the other hand, by the time Wordsworth came to write the poems that were included in *Lyrical Ballads* he had undoubtedly freed himself from the infection. Among the poems that appeared in this revolutionary volume are some that are best thought of as decisive rebukes to the picturesque sensibility and others that go beyond this to an altogether more original concern with place.

As an example of Wordsworth's rebuke to the picturesque we might choose the poem whose full title is 'Old Man Travelling; Animal Tranquillity and Decay, a Sketch'. Such a title may well suggest that Wordsworth is still labouring under the infection of the age. Martin Price notes that the picturesque frequently turns to 'the sketch, which precedes formal perfection,' and that among its formal properties are 'aged men'.[6] Wordsworth's poem not only promises a sketch, its capitalising of the sub-title 'ANIMAL TRANQUILLITY AND DECAY' suggests an aesthetically pleasing absorption of his aged man into an overall mood of gentle pathos; this old man is as natural a 'ruin' as the mouldering castles, churches and cottages which are habitual to the picturesque landscape. The fact that the poem even opens with a half-line further indicates its sketch-like nature.

> The little hedgerow birds
> That peck along the road regard him not.

But in what follows we find ourselves taken well beyond anything the picturesque poem or painting would deem necessary or desirable. This is partly because the old man becomes one of those visionary figures you often find in Wordsworth's greatest work, a deep symbol of human perseverance, suffering, knowledge, of .... But any attentive reader of Wordsworth knows how nearly impossible it is to find a verbal equivalent for what the poet uniquely provides in such figures as the leech gatherer, the old soldier (of Book IV of the *Prelude*), Margaret (of the 'Ruined Cottage'), and many more. As St Augustine said when he was asked the meaning of time: 'I know if you don't ask me.'[7] What *is* true is that Wordsworth's brooding concern with the old man has nothing of the picturesque about it. On the contrary, its rapt gravity, its very intensity, denies the adequacy of that distanced view – 'observation' or 'marking' – which characterises the picturesque vantage point.

Nevertheless, the poet provides what may seem to be the authoritative vision/interpretation of the old man. Until, that is, the poem's closing lines. Then the old man speaks, and the awkward prosaicism of his words breaks open the framing element of the poem's contemplative stance, so that all sense of him as an object to be observed is insistently dispelled.

> I asked him whither he was bound, and what
> The object of his journey; he replied
> 'Sir! I am going many miles to take
> A last leave of my son, a mariner,

Who from a sea-fight has been brought to Falmouth,
And there is dying in an hospital.'[8]

The stubborn matter-of-factness of these words has seemed to many commentators ludicrous. Yet they are essential to Wordsworth's intention. For
in giving the old man his voice, and in having him say what he does, the
poet dislocates the poem's unified tone, its overall mood of what might
be characterised as reflective melancholy. The distance between observer
and observed is closed, and the man's speech provides among other things
an implied rebuke to the containing imagination: it brings him ungovernably
alive. Until he speaks he appears a type – 'one' – to be opposed to the
poet's highly specialised sensibility. But when he speaks it is the *poet* who
becomes a type – 'Sir!'; and the old man is individualised by his words
which after all may well be embarrassing to the kind of person who supported the war against Napoleon, as Wordsworth did, and as a result of
which other men (non-sirs, non-gentlemen) did most of the dying. The
old man's words thus importantly intrude on the poet's aesthetic containment, imply a social-political thrust which has hitherto been denied.

'Old Man Travelling' is a fine, original poem – at least, it is in the version
that was published in 1798. But by 1800 Wordsworth seems to have become
worried by his own originality, for in the second edition of the *Lyrical
Ballads* the old man's words are given as reported speech, a tactic which
greatly diminishes their force. Worse was to follow. In the two-volume
edition of his *Poems*, published in 1807, Wordsworth gets rid of the speech
altogether, so that the poem, now called 'Animal Tranquillity and Decay',
ends with precisely that image of 'framed' melancholy which can be
absorbed into the picturesque aesthetic.

> He is by nature led
> To peace so perfect, that the young behold
> With envy, what the old man hardly feels.

The absence of anything to qualify that distanced view of the old man
as 'one who' hardly feels – made possible by the cutting of his own words –
means that a poem which had in its first version been an important antidote to
the infection of the age now virtually succumbs to the infection. I think there
can be little doubt that the reason for this is Wordsworth's growing conservatism. But his great period is one where rejection of the picturesque is crucial
to much of his finest work, and pre-eminent among that work is 'Michael'.

'Michael' is one of the great poems of the language and there is no
point in trying to give a full account of it in the present context. I want
merely to touch on aspects that are relevant to the concern of the present
essay, and also to suggest that, great poem though it undoubtedly is, there
is perhaps something slightly evasive about it, especially when it is considered in the context of a letter which Wordsworth wrote to Charles James

Fox, in which he purports to discuss the poem's meaning. 'Michael' opens
with some lines that seem very close to the kind of *Guide to the Lakes*[9]
which any well-bred town traveller would have taken with him when, in
obedience to Gilpin and others, he went in search of the picturesque.

> If from the public way you turn your steps
> Up the tumultuous brook of Green-head Gill,
> You will suppose that with an upright path
> Your feet must struggle; in such bold ascent
> The pastoral Mountains front you, face to face.
> But, courage! for beside that boisterous brook
> The mountains have all open'd out themselves,
> And made a hidden valley of their own.
> No habitation there is seen; but such
> As journey thither find themselves alone
> With a few sheep, with rocks and stones, and kites
> That overhead are sailing in the sky.[10]

The tone is courteous to the gentle reader – 'you' – of the *Lyrical Ballads*.
'No habitation there is seen'. Good. For the traveller in search of the
picturesque might well be looking for the 'utter solitude' which Wordsworth
immediately goes on to tell 'you' will be found here. And yet: 'Beside
the brook / There is a straggling heap of unhewn stones!' As the admonitory
exclamation mark suggests, this matters in a way that takes us beyond
the picturesque, which would see nothing noteworthy in the detail; and
it points to the heart of a near-tragic experience in which the poem's story
is rooted.

   It is a story set in the past, and is about events from which 'you' are
made to feel ignorantly excluded. Yet such events, Wordsworth insists,
are of profound human importance.

> It was the first,
> The earliest of those tales that spake to me
> Of Shepherds, dwellers in the vallies, men
> Whom I already lov'd, not verily
> For their own sakes, but for the fields and hills
> Where was their occupation and abode.

It would be easy to misunderstand these lines and see in them a preference
for nature over men. But the truth is that Wordsworth is making his love
of the shepherds dependent, not on the aesthetic contemplation of fields
and hills, but on 'occupation and abode', on 'dwelling', in a word. The
story itself begins: 'Upon the Forestside in Grasmere Vale / There dwelt
a shepherd, Michael was his name'; and 'dwell' recurs in other poems
of the period, where Wordsworth is preoccupied with the deep interconnectedness of people and places, for example 'She Dwelt among Th'untrodden
Ways'; 'The Reverie of Poor Susan', 'Simon Lee', 'We Are Seven'.

Dwell: dwelling. The words are now archaic, virtually obsolete. But they had a vital currency for Wordsworth. In his great *Dictionary of the English Language*, Johnson defined dwell as 'to inhabit; to live in a place; to reside', and he defined occupation as 'the act of taking possession; employment, business'. The ambiguity of this word's meaning is of considerable importance. 'Occupation and abode' can be read as 'occupation of abode'. Living and working go together, and these interconnections, commitments and rooted concerns are an inseparable part of the meaning of 'dwell'. In 'Michael' Wordsworth writes about the destruction of a dwelling, with the loss of meaning for a society that this necessarily implies: the loss of a dwelling is the loss of a word and the loss of values embodied in that word. What makes the landscape where Michael dwells cherishable has nothing to do with its picturesque properties, as 'you' are brought to realise. Instead, it has to do with endeavour, work, and all that is contained in the key terms 'occupation', 'abode', 'dwelling'. It is because of these things that the fields and hills where Michael dwells

> . . . had laid
> Strong hold on his affections, were to him
> A pleasurable feeling of blind love,
> The pleasure which there is in life itself.

Such pleasure, such love, imply a passionate repudiation of the 'love' of landscape which is to be found in the cliché formulations of picturesque poetry: 'I love to mark', or 'I love to see' or 'note' or 'hear'.

Thomas Hardy famously remarked that a beautiful scene in nature is unimportant compared with the wear of a foot on a threshold, and for Michael the landscape is to be read – marked – in terms of work, love and aspiration, the three terms being indissolubly fused. In the letter to Charles James Fox which accompanied a copy of the *Lyrical Ballads*, Wordsworth drew the great Whig statesman's attention to 'Michael' in particular, and to the sources from which it came. He remarked of the shepherd 'class of men' from whom Michael was drawn, that

Their little tract of land serves as a kind of permanent rallying point for their domestic feelings, as a tablet upon which they are written which makes them objects of memory in a thousand instances when they would otherwise be forgotten. It is a fountain fitted to the nature of social man from which supplies of affection, as pure as his heart was intended for, are daily drawn.[11]

Both here and in the poem Wordsworth is touching on a matter which becomes almost an obsession with nineteenth-century writers, for whom time takes on a significance it scarcely had or could have had for previous generations of writers. It is not now 'the principle of change' that concerns them, but the agencies of destruction, of radical alteration; so that continuity is itself called into question and is, indeed, again and again denied.

In the letter Wordsworth identifies as one of the agents of this destruction the new manufacturing industries, which take men from the land and so obliterate all signs of 'occupation and abode'. 'Parents are separated from their children', he writes, 'and children from their parents; the wife no longer prepares with her own hands a meal for her husband, the produce of his labour; there is little doing in his house in which his affections can be interested, and but little left in it which he can love.'[12]

There is nothing odd about Wordsworth sending his poems to Fox. Even though he was no longer sure about the value of the French Revolution, Wordsworth was still radical enough to sympathise with Fox's stands against the jobbing Tories, against city money and corruption; and he would have approved of Fox's championing of 'the people'.[13] Yet it is perhaps odd that the tragedy which overtakes Michael is not caused by those agencies of change which Wordsworth identifies in his letter, still less by the practice of enclosure which was affecting thousands of small farmers throughout the country, and which it is natural to suppose will be the cause of Michael's own downfall. Instead, what destroys him is a freakish occurrence: he has allowed himself to be a bondsman for a nephew, and when the nephew suddenly finds himself heavily in debt, Michael is 'summon'd to discharge the forfeiture, / A grievous penalty, but little less / Than half his substance'. I do not pretend to know why in the letter Wordsworth should make a general case out of the exceptional circumstances of Michael's disaster (a disaster which no doubt was built on fact); but it is at least possible that he does not mention the fact of enclosure and *its* terrible consequences because he knew that Fox's money – much of which he gambled and drank away – came from the land. And it may be worth noting that not long after this Wordsworth himself received the gift of a freehold at Applethwaite from Sir George Beaumont: 'a few old houses with two fields attached to them', as he described the gift to his brother, Richard.[14]

To say this is in no way to detract from the greatness of Wordsworth's poem. It is however to suggest that he may not have felt himself in a position to identify – either there or in the letter to Fox – Michael's sufferings and the eventual loss of his estate as those forced upon the victims of enclosure, even though that is how the end of the poem seems to work. Or, to speak more accurately, the last lines tell of the loss of Michael's estate in a manner which makes clear that his identity is uprooted, that the rememberable has been obliterated:

> . . . the estate
> Was sold, and went into a stranger's hand.
> The Cottage which was nam'd The Evening Star
> Is gone, the ploughshare has been through the ground
> On which it stood; great changes have been wrought
> In all the neighbourhood . . .

Reading those lines out of context you could be forgiven for thinking that they must come from a poem dealing with the miseries of enclosure. That they don't may, perhaps, have to do with the fact that in the last analysis Wordsworth belonged to a class for which enclosure was more of a benefit than a curse. And this may then explain the passive verbs, which make what has happened seem as though it had inevitably to happen. This is perilously close to 'the principle of change'.

Clare

John Clare, by contrast, belonged to the class which was endlessly the victim of enclosure. 'Thou art the bar that keeps from being fed / And thine our loss of labour and of bread', he wrote in his poem 'Helpston'; and added, 'Thou art the cause that levels every tree / And woods bow down to clear a way for thee'. There is a sermon in that straggling heap of unhewn stones towards which Wordsworth directs our attention at the start of 'Michael'. Unremarkable as they may seem to the casual observer, they tell of broken hopes, of the destruction of continuity, of the obliteration of a family and even of community, for they had been gathered for a sheepfold which Michael had intended to build with and for the son, who was to have been the inheritor of his land. They are thus marked with a human significance which outweighs any value they may have as pictures-que objects. (And indeed as picturesque objects they have precious little value, so that the gentle reader is surprised by having his attention drawn to them in the first place.) For Clare, the landscape is similarly and inti-mately known through its human associations.

It is significant that when his publisher, John Taylor, paid a visit to Help-ston, he couldn't see why Clare was so deeply committed to writing about the place. To Taylor the landscape was boringly, ordinarily dull: there was nothing picturesque about it at all. But for Clare, Helpston and its neighbourhood were of the deepest human significance, and to change the look of the land was to wound the lives of those who lived on and through it. Clare has no doubts about what causes his and others' sufferings, and there is nothing freakish about it: enclosure denies him work, dwelling – occupation and abode – and its decisive altering of the physical landscape obliterates 'objects of memory'. It is not surprising, therefore, that Clare's patron, Lord Radstock, thought that the lines I have just quoted smacked of 'radical slang', and insisted that they be cut from the poem when it appeared in *Poems descriptive of rural life and scenery* in 1820.

The story of editorial interference with and mangling of Clare's poems is not one I can pursue here, even though it involved a denial of his identity almost as complete as the experience of enclosure. Instead, I wish to com-ment on two great poems of his, 'The Flitting' and 'To a Fallen Elm', both of which are about the interconnectedness of place and identity, and both of which testify to the tragic scale of the loss that results from the enforced separation of person from place. In neither poem does Clare gaze on or contemplate a landscape from a distance; he is not concerned with the picturesque vantage point.[15] On the contrary: he is within a highly particularised landscape, in which details are seen close to and are known, and named, with a loving familiarity which is utterly different from the generalised effects of the landscapes of picturesque poetry and painting. Moreover, the poems are very decidedly political in their way of talking about ownership, belonging, community, and it is probably this which has made Clare's commentators so uneasy with them. At all events, they are rarely mentioned in discussions of his work.

It is true that both Mark Storey, in his *The poetry of John Clare*, and Edward Storey, in his biography, *A right to song*, say something about 'The Flitting', but their accounts seem to me woefully inadequate. Both of them try to explain the poem in purely biographical terms. It was written shortly after Clare had moved from Helpston to Northborough, and according to Mark Storey

> The importance of home is crucial: at this stage (the poem's opening stanzas) the cottage at Northborough is not transformed into the house he had hoped for. Home is still Helpstone [sic] . . . Home, like poesy, had the power to transform the ordinary into the magical. He dislikes what is new and strange.

But then we are to understand that Clare manages to make a connection between 'the past, unseen things, what he has lost, and the power of poetry to live'. As a result, he rejects all pomp and splendour for the 'poetry of nature' and 'turns his attention to the preservation of all living objects'. Every weed now means something to him:

> the realisation of this encourages the stoicism of the last two stanzas: parting is inevitable, as is change, but nature can 'make amends', because of the power of memory, related to the eternity of nature. Grandeur is seen to fade, but grass springs eternally. Here lies what hope there is for Clare, as his personal sorrow gives way to a comprehensive philosophy of the value of the poetry of nature.[16]

This account is not merely typical of the two Storeys, it fits in uncomfortably well with a prevailing attitude to Clare. The poetry of nature soothes away the hurts of the world, and Clare can be pensioned off to a modest but useful life as conservationist of little things.

One thing is obvious, to me at least. If Storey's account of 'The Flitting' is in any way accurate then the poem doesn't deserve much attention. He makes it sound like a branch line of that tradition which runs through (say) Langhorne's 'Country Justice', with its recommendation of 'the fair Vale, where REST, conceal'd in Flowers, / Lies in Sweet Ambush for thy careless Hours', and comes to rest with the Georgians. Storey in fact turns the poem into a proto-Georgian piece of soft, sentimental, evasive mush. Yet, 'The Flitting' is a great poem, and although the move to Northborough may have triggered it off, it isn't about that at all. A moment's reflection is enough to prove this to be so. For you may know nothing about such a move and still find the poem completely intelligible.

'The Flitting' is about dispossession. It is a grieving, eloquent utterance of a sense of being denied ownership of, or relationship with, all that you feel most intensely to be yours, all that feels so intimately connected with you that it is integral to your sense of selfhood. Here is the first stanza.

> Ive left mine own old home of homes
> Green fields and every pleasant place
> The summer like a stranger comes
> I pause and hardly know her face
> I miss the hazels happy green
> The blue bells quiet hanging blooms
> Where envys sneer was never seen
> Where staring malice never comes[17]

The home isn't merely a house, it composes a neighbourhood. By contrast, the new place is one of strangeness and thus strangers. It is a denial of familiarity. As D. W. Harding points out in *Social psychology and individual values*, in homesickness 'it seems likely that although the conscious longing may be for familiar places and physical surroundings, the house, the village, the scenery and so on, these ultimately derive their value from associations with the people to whom we are attached; that very word 'familiar' underlines the fact'.[18] Whether Clare got on well or badly with particular Helpston neighbours is of no relevance whatsoever. For 'The Flitting' voices an experience that was and remains pervasive. It is not directly about the effects of enclosure, but it certainly registers the keen, wounding shock of being away from all that had been known and taken for granted. It could only have been written by someone who knew the dehumanising effects of the kinds of removals which enclosure helped to bring about, and/or who could imaginatively grasp what that meant for those who were their victims. 'Envys sneer' and 'staring malice' do not refer to local detractors but to that world which the poem comes to associate with the city, or with fashions that are inevitably hostile or indifferent to particular kinds of worth, and yet which, also inevitably, have power over other people's lives. In the last analysis this includes the power to enclose not only land, but also the language, and culture.

The former place is known intimately, is nameable: royce wood, Langley bush. It is where people 'dwell'. By contrast, in the new place 'The sun een seems to lose its way / Nor knows the quarter it is in'. You realise just how sharp Clare's sense of disorientation is as soon as you note that you would expect him to write 'know' rather than 'knows'. As it is, the two lines take for granted a kind of matter-of-fact common sense ('seems' is a key-word in the poem), while at the same time recording a dislocation that feels entire.

Clare also makes a crucial and precise link between his loss and the world of fashion. For in an important sense 'The Flitting' is about knowing yourself to be at the mercy of values you despise and yet which have ultimate power over you, because they are endorsed by and are an intimate expression of those whose authority is everywhere: in matters of art, politics, law. They are the owners. It is worth noting that Clare attacks this subject in two sonnets on Bloomfield, only one of which appeared in *The Rural Muse*. As we might expect, it is the more conventional of the two. 'Sweet unassuming minstrel not to thee / The dazzling fashions of the day belong' it begins; and it ends by claiming that Bloomfield's 'gentle muse' will linger on when the proud streams of the fashionable are 'summer burnt and dry'. The other sonnet is much better: a hard, angry, proud poem, which lashes those who sail in 'that gay ship popularity':

> Let not their fancys think tis muses fare
> While feeding on the publics gross supply
> Times wave rolls on – mortality must share
> A mortals fate and many a fame shall lie
> A dead wreck on the shore of dark posterity

Stanza 7 of 'The Flitting' begins, 'Alone and in a stranger scene / Far far from spots my heart esteems'; and two stanzas later Clare returns to that word 'esteems' in rejecting the comfort of books:

> For books they follow fashions new
> And throw all old esteems away
> In crowded streets flowers never grew
> But many there hath died away

There is no need to read biography into these lines, or to assume that in them Clare is sadly musing over his own lost fame in London. The four lines speak with an epigrammatic terseness of the eddies of taste which wash lightly over matters of worth, and which deny its value even in the act of praising it; and they inevitably link with the opening of stanza 7 because they express a disenchantment that belongs as much to the stranger scene as to books. Both have been arranged/ordered by others. This is the world of Vanity Fair – although to put it this way is to ignore the subtle tact by means of which Clare links power processes that are hatefully opposed to all that's implied by 'esteem'. (Johnson defined the word as 'reverential regard', and this is the sense in which Clare uses it.) Those who are ignorant of the feelings, values and relationships summed up in esteem compose a world of strangers: they are indifferent to the dear familiarity of a peopled place. 'Strange scenes mere shadows are to me / Vague

unpersonifying things', Clare writes in stanza 12, and then, in the following
stanzas:

> Here every tree is strange to me
> All foreign things where eer I go
> Theres none where boyhood made a swee [swing]
> Or clambered up to rob a crow
> No hollow tree or woodland bower
> Well known when joy was beating high
> Where beauty ran to shun a shower
> And love took pains to keep her dry
>
> And laid the shoaf upon the ground
> To keep her from the dripping grass
> And ran for stowks and set them round
> Till scarce a drop of rain could pass
> Through – where the maidens they reclined
> And sang sweet ballads now forgot
> Which brought sweet memorys to the mind
> But here a memory knows them not

What I find almost miraculously beautiful about those stanzas has something
to do with the way Clare takes over Augustan abstractions and rescues
them from the expected and the dull: 'Where beauty ran to shun a shower /
And love took pains to keep her dry'. The tender eroticism of those lines
is made firm by the carry-over into the next stanza, with its imaginative
exactness of recall, including the easy, unforced use of colloquial words
and ways of speaking. But then comes the bleak disenchantment of the
last line, the expulsion from a world of familiarity. In the following stanzas
the new, strange place contrasts with the old one, where 'Every weed and
blossom too / Was looking upward in my face / With friendships welcome
"how do ye do"'. Weeds, blossoms, grasses. The conventional language
of pastoral poetry. But in 'The Flitting' they carry a remarkable weight
of significance. First, and most obviously, they operate in contrast to the
trappings of the city:

> Give me no high flown fangled things
> No haughty pomp in marching chime
> Where muses play on golden strings
> And splendour passes for sublime
> Where citys stretch as far as fame
> And fancys straining eye can go

'Golden strings': as the context makes clear, Clare's sardonic use of the
cliché links poetry with money, power, class-bound assumptions of superiority. 'And splendour passes for sublime': this is art set upon a bough to
sing: tame, lacquered, contemptible. Art in a formal garden wants the
weeds away. Clare nurses 'A love for every simple weed'. He calls it 'an

ancient neighbour'. Johnson defined weed as a 'herb: noxious or useless', and thus makes clear the fact that the word has no botanical meaning. 'The Flitting' ends:

> Time looks on pomp with careless moods
> Or killing apathys disdain
> – So where old marble citys stood
> Poor persecuted weeds remain
> She feels a love for little things
> That very few can feel beside
> And still the grass eternal springs
> Where castles stood and grandeur died.

Where in these lines is the stoicism that Storey refers to? What first strikes me is the wit. Time will behave with exactly the same insolence towards Pomp as the pompous have done towards those over whom they lord matters, whose lives they have displaced, whose art they have derided. Moreover, by the end of the stanza the 'poor persecuted weeds' have become 'grass', and are clearly metaphoric of the people displaced by pomp. As Clare well knew, the well-tended fields of enclosure weeded out tenant-smallholders just as surely as they weeded out groundsel and shepherd's purse.

In *Man and the natural world*, Keith Thomas remarks that towards the end of the eighteenth century a botanical society in Lichfield produced a *System of Vegetables ... translated from ... the Systema Vegetabilium of the Late Professor Linneus*, in which the Vegetable Kingdom was divided into tribes and nations, 'the latter bearing titles which were more sociological than botanical: the grasses were "plebeians" – "the more they are taxed and trod upon the more they multiply"'.[19] *This* is the context in which to think of the last stanzas of Clare's great poem. I do not see how you can read them without recognising that they work towards a generous, even exuberant political affirmation, one which takes for granted and deliberately exploits the idea that to the owners of England its people are weeds or grass. Storey's obtuse and sentimental condescension to Clare – the recommendation of his 'stoicism' – misses the point about as completely as is possible. Clare's lines celebrate an act of reclamation that is radical. The grass *springs* where castles *stood* and grandeur *died*. This is an invading army, and the present tense of 'springs' shows that again and again rights will be asserted and won over those who denied them. In contrast the past tense of 'stood' shows grandeur dying in the act of defending those castles that the grass overwhelms. What we have here, then, reminds us that the poem was written at the time of Captain Swing and his activities, and of George Loveless and his companions. At the very least, the placing of the word 'springs', and the continuous affirmation of energy that it releases, ought to prevent us from reading the close of the poem as a

stoical exercise about coming to terms with the poetry of nature. For such
an exercise would, of course, return us precisely to that 'principle of change'
which is at the heart of the picturesque. 'The Flitting' denies such a principle,
just as it denies the propriety of melancholia or pathos as the emotionally
fitting response to the matters in which it deals.

   Much the same may be said of 'To a Fallen Elm'. It begins with the
affectionate familiarity of companiable talk:

> Old elm that murmured in our chimney top
> The sweetest anthem autumn ever made
> And into mellow whispering calms would drop
> When showers fell on thy many colored shade[20]

It is perhaps worth noting – at least in passing – that the elm becomes
at this time something of an unofficial symbol of England, a function which
it retains at least until the Great War; and although it perhaps has not
that status in Clare's poem it is obviously expressive of neighbourliness,
and can be linked to the language of community.[21] 'Murmured' has about
it the accent of unforced speech, of loving acquaintance. It is familiar,
intimate. And it is worth comparing Clare's use of the word with Hardy's,
as for example in 'Friends Beyond', where 'The Squire and Lady Susan
murmur mildly to me now'.

   In no sense is 'To a Fallen Elm' a melancholy meditation on the 'principle
of change'. Unlike Cowper's 'Yardley Oak' it has not fallen because of
old age, and Clare does not mourn for it in a manner that anticipates
Hopkins' grief over the thoughtless destruction of 'Binsey Poplars' and
the despoliation of a sweet, especial rural scene. This was intended. 'Self
interest saw thee stand in freedoms way / So thy old shadow must a tyrant
be'. This is not even enlightened self-interest; the destruction hasn't the
justification of being for the greater happiness of the majority. (Although
by the 1830s enlightened self-interest was becoming enshrined in Government law.) No, this is a 'freedom' which, in its ruthless selfishness, destroys
the freedom of others. The cutting down of the elm becomes the occasion
for Clare to voice a passionate, pointed anger, directed through the poem's
last 40 lines at those who claim ownership over the lives and circumstances
of others. It is impossible to quote from these lines without severing the
poem's driving pulse, its fierce, scornful anger. What can be said, however,
is that in them you hear very clearly the voice of English radicalism, the
voices of Byron, Cobbett, and others with whose work Clare was familiar.
And it identifies for its special contempt the abuse of the term 'freedom'.

> It grows the cant term of enslaving tools
> To wrong another by the name of right
> It grows a liscence with oer bearing fools
> To cheat plain honesty by force of might
> Thus came enclosure

A poem which starts from what might seem to be a pictorial image of the elm spreading above a cottage ends with the displacement of that image; and the tone of the opening lines, warm, tender, personal, ends in anger and public utterance. In other words, Clare rejects a picturesque treatment of his subject, although such a treatment would have been the orthodox one and would have supported a tone of gentle regret for the passage of time and how things must be. Clare knows that change occurs not through natural but through human agencies. There is thus a hard, bitter contempt in the poem which is very different from the principled sadness of some of Wordsworth's poems, including the two I have discussed in this essay; and the reason for the difference is that Clare is more ready to confront the cause of such sadness. This means that his placing of the picturesque – his understanding of the complacent amorality of its politics – is both more radical and more directly searching than even Wordsworth chooses to be. It is therefore not perhaps surprising that for so long his poems should have been marginalised or deliberately misunderstood.

NOTES

1   The quotation comes from Martin Price's essay, 'The picturesque moment', in F. W. Hilles and H. Bloom (eds.), *From sensibility to romanticism* (New York, 1965). While drawing on Christopher Hussey's classic study, *The picturesque* (London, 1927), Price also considers other secondary and primary material in order to produce the best single essay on the subject – considered especially from an aesthetic standpoint – that I know.

2   John Lucas, 'Wordsworth and the anti-picturesque', in John Lucas, *Romantic to modern literature: essays and ideas of culture, 1750–1900* (Brighton, 1982), pp. 50–67.

3   Price, 'The picturesque moment', p. 277.

4   See Christopher Salveson, *The landscape of memory: a study of Wordsworth's poetry* (London, 1965), p. 66.

5   For a fuller discussion of these poems, and especially 'An Evening Walk' see Lucas, 'Wordsworth and the anti-picturesque'.

6   Price, 'The picturesque moment', p. 285.

7   Wordsworth himself was not especially good at explaining such figures. In a letter to his future wife, Sarah Hutchinson, he rebuked her for not estimating the leech gatherer at his true value. 'It is of the utmost importance that you should have had pleasure from contemplating the fortitude, independence, persevering spirit, and the general moral dignity of this old man's character.' *Letters of William Wordsworth*, ed. P. Wayne (London, 1954), p. 51. I imagine that there are few readers for whom these are the most important, or arresting, characteristics of the old man.

8 *Wordsworth and Coleridge's Lyrical Ballads*, ed. R. L. Brett and A. R. Jones (London, 1963), p. 106.

9 The *Guide* was first written in 1812, although not published as a separate piece of work until 1822, after which it went into many editions during Wordsworth's own lifetime.

10 *Lyrical Ballads*, p. 220.

11 *Letters of William Wordsworth*, p. 40.

12 *Ibid.*, p. 39.

13 Although Fox was suspected by some radicals of being a mere 'rhetorician', far more held him in great respect, especially for his attitude to Warren Hastings, and because of his opposition to British anti-French hysteria.

14 For this see Mary Moorman, *Wordsworth: a biography: the early years 1770–1803* (Oxford, 1968), p. 588.

15 Of course, he knew about the picturesque, and on more than one occasion embarked on a poem that looks as though it belongs within the tradition. No doubt he was trawling for favour among his fashionable audience. Yet he seldom maintains the stance of picturesque observer for long. Sooner or later – and it is usually sooner – he breaks down the tactics and habits of 'survey' common to picturesque treatment, as John Barrell above all has shown in *The idea of landscape and the sense of place 1730–1840: an approach to the poetry of John Clare* (Cambridge, 1972).

16 Mark Storey, *The poetry of John Clare: a critical introduction* (London, 1974), pp. 142–5.

17 I use the text of The Oxford Authors *John Clare*, ed. E. Robinson and D. Powell (Oxford, 1984), p. 250, which improves on the version published in *The Midsummer Cushion*, ed. A. Tibble and R. K. R. Thornton (Manchester, 1978). They print from the version that originally appeared in *The rural muse* (1835).

18 D. W. Harding, *Social psychology and individual values* (London, 1953), p. 69.

19 Keith Thomas, *Man and the natural world: changing attitudes to England 1500–1800* (London, 1983), p. 66.

20 Text from *John Clare*, p. 96.

21 This is a complicated subject, and one I attempt to provide outlines for in my study of *Modern English poetry: Hardy to Hughes* (London, 1986). There is no doubt that the elm is seen as a kind of usable symbol of England (free from the taint of the oak and sycamore – from the Tolpuddle martyrs, Joseph Arch and royalty), and one that is drawn on by such very different figures as William Morris and E. M. Forster. For a survey of the political symbolism of trees in the late eighteenth and early nineteenth centuries see Stephen Daniels, 'The political iconography of woodland in later Georgian England', ch. 3 in this book.

5

Art and agrarian change, 1710–1815

HUGH PRINCE

A fruitless search for English eighteenth-century paintings that depict newly enclosed fields, newly built farmsteads, newly reclaimed heaths and newly introduced crops prompts the question why artists who were increasingly sensitive to landscape, and to that of the contemporary English countryside, seemed to ignore such graphic evidence of agrarian change.[1] Contemporary writers – poets and essayists as well as agricultural reporters – described agrarian changes to the land in great detail and pondered the social, economic and political implications of what they observed. John Barrell has drawn upon this literature to argue that landscape painters did in fact address agrarian change, less in empirical surveys of topographical features than in symbolic depictions of social relations and perceptions.[2] Barrell's approach has encouraged me to look for iconographic rather than empirical representations of the countryside, or rather to see empiricism in landscape painting as much an iconographic issue as its apparent absence.

From the point of view of a late twentieth-century historical geographer seeking records of agrarian change, eighteenth-century landscape paintings seem escapist fantasies.[3] Paintings in an Arcadian idiom evoke visions of classical antiquity. Picturesque views concentrate on crags, cliffs, waterfalls, woods, dead trees and crumbling ruins; romantic pictures seek to arouse powerful feelings of wonder and awe at the beauties and sublimities of cloud forms, geological structures and plant life. All these styles of painting seem to treat features of agricultural change as intrusions.

Not only did most eighteenth-century painters disregard agricultural innovations but landowners who purchased their work were at least as conformist – if not themselves leaders of taste – in preferring idealised views. One of the largest landowners, the Duke of Bedford, an early purchaser of New Leicester sheep, founder of the Woburn sheep shearings, experimenter with new ploughs and chaff cutting machines, promoter of irrigation schemes, builder of labourers' cottages and provider of cottage allotments, was also a leading patron of the arts. He commissioned

Lambert, Gainsborough and Stubbs to paint idyllic landscapes that are difficult to locate on a map and offer little or no indication of the new agricultural features pioneered on the duke's own estate.[4] Among private collections in country houses, especially those of prints, drawings and water-colours, are to be found some illustrations of agricultural activities. Many landowners commissioned paintings of their houses in parkland settings and ordered portraits of prize specimens of new breeds of livestock. For example George Stubbs portrayed a magnificent Lincolnshire ox with its owner, John Cribbens in a parkland setting at Long Sutton, and Lord Leicester, his shepherd and flock were portrayed against a background of Holkham Hall.[5] Newly planted hedges, banks and ditches appear as incidents in hunting scenes. Stubbs, Sawrey Gilpin, John Nost Sartorius and many other artists recorded prospects of hunting country in the mid-lands.[6] A few landscape paintings depicting newly enclosed districts were exhibited at the Royal Academy Summer Exhibitions but these amount to a very small proportion of the total number of views of named places listed in the annual catalogues.[7] For the most part the activities that trans-formed farming on light soils in eastern and southern England and improved the management of heavy soils in the midlands passed unrecorded by the leading painters of the period.

If painters and their patrons preferred to ignore agricultural scenes, ought not historical geographers to reconsider how much importance they should attach to literary evidence for agricultural change? Were the changes as momentous as historians and geographers have been led to think or have scholars propagated a myth of an 'agricultural revolution', as an analogue for an 'industrial revolution', based on the propagandist writings of Arthur Young, the Board of Agriculture reports and other essays by adherents to the farming interest? Does a study of paintings suggest that perceptions of change or stability remained more or less the same throughout England over the whole period from 1710 to 1815, or did artists' views differ from place to place and from time to time?

In order to focus upon these questions, I have chosen for study six oil paintings from public galleries that portray named places and identifiable landmarks. There can be no doubt that the artists and also their patrons regarded the topographical specificity of these pictures as critical for under-standing their contents. The first three pictures suggest a diminishing inter-est in details of farming practice. The first celebrates the task of haymaking in the Vale of Severn, the second commemorates the possession of produc-tive land on the Essex–Suffolk border, the third projects a vision of Arcadian tranquillity on the banks of the Thames. In the long interval between Wil-son's *The Thames at Twickenham* (1762) and Turner's *Ploughing up Turnips near Slough* (1809) I can find few pictures that represent farmland at named places. In the 1780s Stubbs painted haymaking and harvesting scenes but

Fig. 1   Artist unknown, *Dixton Manor, Haymaking*, c. 1710–20. Oil on canvas. Cheltenham Art Gallery and Museum.

the exact locations of these activities are not identified and none of Morland's vast output specifies a precise geographical locality. I have failed to find a picturesque view that depicts farming at a particular place, although picturesque mountains, rivers, forests and heaths are frequently named. The last three pictures I shall discuss were painted at the height of the Board of Agriculture's campaign to improve agriculture during the Napoleonic wars. In all three paintings agricultural activities occupy prominent positions in the foreground or middle distance: turnip lifting provides the subject for Turner's picture, ploughing in Constable's and wheat harvesting in Lewis's.

Haymaking

Dixton Manor, Haymaking (Fig. 1), by an unknown artist, takes in a wide prospect across the Vale of Severn towards the edge of the Cotswolds.[8] In the extent of ground delineated from an elevated viewpoint it resembles contemporary bird's-eye views of landed estates and their improvements

by such artists as Johannes Kip or Leonard Knyff. But in most of its features it is a highly unusual estate painting. Most bird's-eye views focus on the mansion as the centre of attention and while they sometimes include figures and activities signifying the economic and social well being of the estate these are usually strictly subordinate to an impression of property. A pendant to the harvesting scene looking west does show the manor house, a modest, vernacular building and pictorially unobtrusive. The artist does not depict the country house as the centre of its world, rather with his perspective fixed upon the city of Gloucester the artist makes it integral to a larger sense of a region.[9] The haymaking scene is unique in the genre of prospect painting in focusing on a working field.

From a height of several hundred feet and from a distance of several hundred yards, the artist surveys a large meadow where the villagers of Dixton are haymaking. From here we observe the movements and teamwork of the villagers but cannot make out their individual expressions and demeanour. A line of 23 mowers is cutting a last strip of grass in the middle of the field, about 50 other men and women are spreading and turning swathes, putting up haycocks and pitching cured hay into five wagons while the squire James Higford, accompanied by his wife and daughter, ride among the labourers. Large numbers were needed to gather the crop on the one or two fine days in the year when the grass was ready for cutting and could be dried. If the artist has accurately enumerated the scene, more than half the able-bodied people of the village are out in the field.[10] The picture demonstrates and commends a traditional method of organising haymaking. The sequence of mowing, tedding, cocking and carting is carried out by teams differently made up of men, women and children. Operational efficiency is achieved through the division of labour and the whole effort is co-ordinated under the eye of the squire. Beyond the meadow the landscape is neatly divided by timbered hedges into a chequerboard of largish fields, mostly under grass, well stocked with cattle and sheep, reaching to the summit of the hills.[11] It is a scene of good management. While the fields of Dixton were already enclosed in the sixteenth century, those of the parish of Alderton, with which Dixton was at this time combined, remained open until 1809,[12] and the painting, showing a vast meadow, is reminiscent of views of open field landscapes and the virtues that agriculturalists ascribed to them. William Marshall observed that 'at all times, the manager of the estate was better enabled to detect bad husbandry ... by having the whole spread under the eye, at once'.[13] John Barrell comments that an open field 'would thus present itself to the observer as a scene of continuous and simultaneous activity, carried on in all parts of the field yet visible "at a glance", and in which almost the entire village was engaged'.[14]

Dixton Manor, Haymaking is not just an efficient scene but a happy one too. The weather is fair, birds wheel in the sky, sheep graze on the hillsides, a line of Morris Men trip lightly from the meadow, the mowers swing their scythes in unison. The village is united in work and in diversions from work, a few villagers courting, others refreshing themselves with beer or cider. Indeed the painting has the ceremonial quality of seventeenth-century poems like Jonson's *To Penshurst* which celebrate the harmonious hierarchy of landed estates. The painting puts Michael Rosenthal in mind of more contemporary poems, of Thomson's opening line to a description of haymaking in *Summer*, first published in 1727, in which the poet rejoices that the village 'swarms ... o'er the jovial mead' and, in its political iconography, of Pope's celebration of the rural economy of Windsor Forest: 'Rich industry sits smiling upon the plains / And peace and plenty tell, a STUART reigns'.[15]

Landowning

No harvesters, nor even a solitary shepherd, intrude upon the peace and privacy of Robert Andrews, Esquire, and Frances, his new bride, portrayed in 1748 by Thomas Gainsborough (Fig. 2). While also depicting a well managed estate, this painting presents a very different view of agrarian life from *Dixton Manor, Haymaking*. Instead of celebrating the cultivation of the land and the mobilisation of communal labour under the personal supervision of the squire, the means of production are taken for granted: the crop of wheat, the venerable oak, fat sheep, wild partridges and everything else are appropriated by the landowner who stands complacently in front of these accumulated assets. The picture extols the present and prospective satisfactions of landownership and attendant possessions, offering a life of contented ease, a comely wife, fine clothes, broad acres, a bounteous harvest, an obedient hound at heel and the promise of good shooting ahead.[16] Mr and Mrs Andrews are too soft-skinned and unsuitably dressed to have toiled in the fields or even to have supervised others doing so and none of the people employed in producing their good fortune appears in the picture.

The estate belonging to the Andrews, the Auberies at Bulmer, occupies a plateau surface a hundred feet above the valley of the Stour. Had Gainsborough wished to place his sitters in the context of an agricultural region, he could have seated them at the top of Ballingdon Hill, opening an extensive vista over ploughland and meadows stretching across the valley towards Sudbury three miles away. But the domestic style of such a 'conversation piece', deployed on this occasion to celebrate a wedding, required a closed space. In choosing this spot on high grounds looking over a small declivity to a skyline bounded by mature woods Gainsborough has securely enclosed the private domain of the young couple. As an eyecatcher, glimpsed through a grove, the church tower of St Peter's Sudbury has been moved to a site apparently within the boundary of the Auberies estate. The artist and his patron have evidently preferred a parkland setting encompassed by belt plantations to a prospect over unadorned farmland. The farm pictured here is a ring fence holding, much larger than any in the Dixton painting.[17] Gainsborough has depicted a large, naturalistic Stour countryside *ferme ornée* of a kind described by Thomas Ruggles.[18]

The picture reveals that farming at the Auberies is conducted according to a new system employing up-to-date techniques. The wheat has been drilled, hawthorn hedges in the middle distance are neatly cut and laid, a new-style five-barred gate gives entry to the field where sheep are grazing and the sheep themselves are of the size and shape of breeds selected for feeding on turnips and artificial grasses. Robert Andrews was still active in promoting agricultural improvements 40 years after this picture was painted, in 1786 contributing a note on the smut in wheat to the *Annals of Agriculture*.[19]

Never again did Gainsborough portray such a confidently empirical and proprietorial view of the countryside, even in paintings of and for the gentry.

Fig. 2   Thomas Gainsborough, *Mr and Mrs Andrews*, 1748. Oil on canvas. The National Gallery, London.

He left his home town of Sudbury in 1752, returning at infrequent intervals to sketch woods and heaths that had yet to be touched by agricultural improvement. In the manner of Dutch painters – Rubens, Ruysdael, Cuyp – he depicted ancient elms, dead and dying oaks, bracken, gorse, banks of bare sand and pools of water. He peopled these rough retreats with poor people at ease: rustic lovers, romping children, a man fishing, a man resting beside a bundle of firewood, another riding a donkey, others accompanied by shaggy dogs. After 1760, as he perhaps became more pessimistic about the social condition of the countryside, the mood of Gainsborough's pastoral paintings darkens: they bear less and less resemblance to the domesticated scenes of his youth and shift towards wilder and more fantastic realms.[20] Shapes of trees are no longer recognisable as oaks or elms, tracks cease to lead to settlements, people on the light side of these landscapes are continually on the move in carts and wagons, the resident poor are thrown into shadow. In these unsettling scenes the appearance of cultivators and cultivation are presented as irredeemably distasteful.

Being in Arcadia

Richard Wilson's *The Thames at Twickenham* (1762) (Fig. 3) conveys a sense of unearthly stillness and timeless composure. The sailing barge on the water glides by without stirring a ripple. Its presence suggests the use of the waterway as a means of transport but it betrays none of the bustle of commercial activity. Two horses head along the towpath but because their legs are concealed by a bank, it is impossible to see whether they are walking or standing still. A bather and his companion are resting and every other object is motionless.

The structure of the picture carries sufficient reminders of a Claudean composition – contemplative figures in the foreground, the stream leading the eye sinuously towards a sylvan skyline, a villa half hidden by trees on the opposite bank of the river – but it does not transport the viewer to the Roman Campagna. The limpid atmosphere recalls the luminosity of a Claude but the light is the cool, soft light of an English summer morning not the burnished gold of an Italian autumn evening. The tree on the right-hand side does not, as in a painting by Claude, frame the view; it draws together rather than separates foreground and middle distance.[21] The manner is Italianate but the subject matter is essentially English.

The Thames near Twickenham is an elegant pastoral, exhibiting only the most noble features of nature: tall forest trees and a Thames fit to bathe in. It excludes vulgar, commonplace objects such as Mr and Mrs Andrews' wheat-sheaves and cut-and-laid hedges or such picturesque objects as donkeys and ragged rustics that Gainsborough introduced in his later landscapes. The pastoral distances itself from the workaday world,

Fig. 3   Richard Wilson, *The Thames at Twickenham*, 1762. Oil on canvas. Marble Hill House, Twickenham.

screening the village of Twickenham and shutting out any glimpse of the intensively cultivated farms and market gardens of south Middlesex.[22] It projects a vision of Arcadia where the landscape is enchantingly beautiful, everyone enjoys endless leisure, nothing changes, no one goes ragged and even the poor have youth and beauty.

The picture constructs a patrician image of social order and harmony very different from those formed in pictures of Dixton and the Auberies. The scene at Twickenham does not focus, as in the Gloucestershire hayfield, upon a traditional place of work where the squire, his neighbours and village swains come together and exert themselves for a common purpose. Nor does it exclude from view, as in the private domain of Mr and Mrs Andrews, all but the squire and his relations. The space in the foreground is open to the public and five or six figures can be seen there. They cannot be placed with certainty among the lower orders of eighteenth-century English society, rather they are generalised representatives of an ideal stable society. All except the bather and his companion are obscured in the shadow of the trees on the dark side of the landscape. The Thames interposes a barrier, but one that may be swum or sailed across, and on the opposite bank is a landscape garden inspired by Twickenham's poet, Alexander Pope. The Palladian villa, Marble Hill House, designed by Henry, Earl of Pembroke, for the Countess of Suffolk, looks over shaven lawns to the stretch of water that unites it visually to trees on the near side of the river.[23] The landscape garden connects three different parts of the picture: at its centre, a sunlit pediment; describing an arc around the stately home, a stretch of water, a channel for commerce; and on the periphery, the populace, contentedly reclining. Classical allusions endow this landscape with enduring values. At the sight of Marble Hill House, *cognoscenti* are reminded of Pope's verse, Palladio's architecture and Virgil's eclogues.

Turnip lifting

During the second half of the eighteenth century agricultural landscapes were being rapidly transformed by enclosure, reclamation, farm building and new systems of farming. But artists turned away from the evidence of innovation, indeed, from scenes of cultivation in general. A few painters followed Richard Wilson in pursuit of Arcadia but the interpretation of Arcadian imagery demanded the erudition of classically educated, hereditary landowners. Up and coming middle-class patrons preferred easily intelligible picturesque views in the manner of George Morland, depicting woods and wild scenery. By the end of the eighteenth century picturesque tourists were eulogising heaths and moors for their native roughness and playful disorder whilst agricultural writers complained loudly of the stubborn poverty of such villainous wastes. Conversely, to seekers after the picturesque cultivated land appeared disgusting or insipid, but to agriculturalists it seemed charming and luscious. During the first two decades of the nineteenth century some landscape painters did begin to express an agriculturalist view.

Turner's *Ploughing up Turnips near Slough* (1809) (Fig. 4) approaches a scene of work more closely and more particularly than any of the three pictures I have considered so far. We are sufficiently close to the turnip field to observe that the two nearest labourers are resting from their work, that three are inspecting a plough lying on its side and that two others are clutching armfuls of turnip tops. We cannot clearly read the expressions on their faces but their postures indicate that they are taking a break from tiring work. It is not a pastoral idyll of rustic ease nor a celebration of happy industriousness, but an encounter with the harsh routine of work on an early nineteenth-century farm. The scene is set in a muddy field on a cold grey day, the lifting of the roots follows no regular pattern, piles of leaves are scattered haphazardly here and there and lifters are seated in different positions, not all together, but in twos and threes.[24] We observe the weariness of individuals, not the united effort of a team.

The picture is constructed in a Claudean manner, so that the eye is drawn from turnips to labourers across a hazy middle distance to a silhouette of Windsor Castle on the horizon. Turner has drawn the castle somewhat larger than it actually appears at that distance from the higher river terrace

Fig. 4   J. M. W. Turner, *Ploughing up Turnips near Slough*, 1809. Oil on canvas. The Tate Gallery, London.

at Slough. Moreover, the height of the castle has been raised above the level of the uplands to the south so that the turreted skyline hides the plateau on which Sunninghill, Virginia Water, Ascot and Winkfield stand. The castle terminates the vista. The twilight atmosphere, that might equally well signify dusk or dawn, subdues tones, blurs details, renders distances indefinite. Fading light and mistiness dissolve the immediacy of this particular day's work, imparting an air of antiquity to the scene. A viewer's perception is distracted from the modernity of turnip growing and the employment of casual labour by attempts to decipher figures shrouded in mists of time and by intimations of Claude's golden age.

By placing this apparently immemorial scene against a background of Windsor Castle Turner induces powerful currents of association. Historically the castle is associated with crown forests and farmlands in the Honour of Windsor covering parts of south Buckinghamshire.[25] A strong patriotic current links turnip growing with the king, Farmer George, whose zeal for agricultural improvements is communicated in notes on sheep husbandry published in the *Annals of Agriculture* and in schemes designed to bring into cultivation light soils in and around Windsor. In Windsor Great Park two pioneer farms, Flemish Farm and Norfolk Farm, were carved out of sandy wastes and on the heath-covered gravels of south Buckinghamshire enclosures were promoted.[26] Land reclamation culminated in a ploughing-up campaign to increase food supplies during the Napoleonic wars. The cultivation of turnips near Slough reminds us of this patriotic duty.

Turner's picture is at once down to earth and allusive. It confronts the numbing drudgery of turnip lifting whilst implying that this unremitting age-old task served a higher purpose in wartime Britain as a loyal contribution to the defence of the realm. The picture lifts a workaday incident to the level of an epic; it raises landscape to the stature of a historical commemoration.

Ploughing

Like Turner, Constable drew inspiration for his *Landscape, Ploughing Scene in Suffolk* (Fig. 5) from an identifiable place less than a mile from his birthplace in East Bergholt, a locality where he lived and worked throughout his youth and early manhood, the shapes of whose fields and woods were as familiar to him as the back of his hand. Constable's attachment to his native place was stronger and more intense than that of any other English painter. In a letter to a friend, John Dunthorne, written in 1814 while he was working on this picture, he expressed the depth of his concern for the conservation of the scene he was painting: 'I dread these feilds falling into Coleman's hands as I think he will clear them a good deal and cut the trees – but we cannot help these things.'[27] Not only did he gain his deepest satisfaction from painting in Dedham Vale, he recorded its features with painstaking care and studied it with scientific curiosity. Although he could easily have worked from memory he constructed his pictures from detailed sketches made on the spot. Preliminary pencil notes of ploughmen, ploughs, trees and other features for the *Ploughing Scene* were sketched out of doors in June 1813 and the composition was put together on canvas in February 1814.[28]

The picture takes in a distant prospect but otherwise does not follow Claude's method of arrangement. The eye is not conducted along a winding path from foreground to horizon. The vista is not framed by trees, nor are distances demarcated by overlapping wings as in theatrical scenery. Unlike a Claudean foreground, Constable's is exposed and unshaded by trees. The middle distance is divided by a dark wedge of trees and another band of trees separates middle distance from background. Successive zones are presented as alternating layers of light and dark colours. A horizontal emphasis is absolutely dominant. The largest features are flattened as if a giant roller had passed over the surface. The entire prospect is wide

Fig. 5 John Constable, replica of *Landscape, Ploughing Scene in Suffolk*, 1824. Oil on canvas. Paul Mellon Collection, Yale Center for British Art, New Haven, Conn.

open. Nothing is hidden, everything is spacious, the panorama is immensely flat, calm, unexciting.

The sky is vast, the fields are large, woods are of indeterminate extent. The two ploughmen are reduced to the size of toys. The landscape is looked down upon from an elevated viewpoint: it is under control. The ploughmen recede into the distance; they are figures without faces, occupying subordinate positions within the natural environment. We do not meet them eye to eye; they do not disclose their individuality to us. We see them only in their relation to the landscape, following the plough, bound to the soil, performing their duties as labourers. Our eye commands the landscape and the landscape contains two faceless ploughmen.

The *Ploughing Scene* requires the presence of the lowly ploughmen as much as *Mr and Mrs Andrews* requires the presence of a landed estate, and it is instructive to compare these two different views of Stour landscapes painted by native artists over 60 years apart. Gainsborough's picture places landowners in the foreground, enjoying exclusive possession of harvest field and game coverts, their comfort and privacy undisturbed by any other people. Not even a roof of another person's house may be seen within the private domain. Constable's picture, by contrast, conceals all explicit signs of landownership, although the artist shared a family interest in some of the land and remarked upon the acquisitive designs of a neighbour.[29] In the scene before us no boundary of private property can be detected, no Palladian villa or royal castle emerges above the trees, no sign of a landlord's improvement is to be seen, no gentleman rides across his fields.

If a social structure is to be discerned in this flat landscape, it is an indistinct reflection of a divinely ordered ecosystem. Two churches stand on high ground, towering above and presiding over two red and white farmhouses which rise up from the ground cleaved by two ploughs. The ploughs are wheel ploughs with high carriages, proclaiming their East Anglian provenance as distinctively as the friable loam soils, timber-framed red-tiled houses and tall church towers.[30] Constable clearly intended the vernacular relationship between ploughmen and soil to provide a key to understanding the picture. In the Royal Academy catalogue he included a couplet from Robert Bloomfield's *Farmer's Boy*: 'But, unassisted through each toilsome day / With smiling brow the Plowman cleaves his way'.[31] Bloomfield was a native Suffolk poet, a ploughboy from near Bury St Edmunds. Central to the interpretation of the poem is the notion that the work of tilling the soil provides a connection between the individual and nature. The ploughman is a creature of his environment both in the sense that he creates and domesticates the landscape and also in the sense of being sustained by and wresting a living from the soil. Of others who depend upon this productive relationship Constable alludes in passing only to farmers' houses and the church. He ignores landowners, corn merchants, tax collectors and excludes all the vagrant, idle poor who staff picturesque scenes by Morland and later works by Gainsborough.

As John Barrell points out the phrase, 'smiling brow', taken literally, makes no sense unless it is read as 'a brow puckered as in a gesture of smiling'.[32] The mixed metaphor may express a tension between opposing sensations experienced by the ploughmen: on the one hand, feeling worn out by physical labour; on the other hand, feeling contented at accomplishing a necessary and useful job cultivating the soil. Constable's picture avoids this tension by showing the ploughmen bent over their ploughs in close harmony with the ploughed field and so far away that we cannot see whether they are weary, wretched or content. Constable made no attempt to contrive a false impression of contentment. He was acutely aware of and felt threatened by the distress and discontent that prevailed among the labouring poor in his home region.[33]

In order to account for the condition of the ploughmen Constable draws upon the imagery of environmentalism. He presses the figures down into the earth, diminishing their stature, whilst amplifying the vastness, the flatness, the crushing power of the environment.[34] They are small, distant creatures not permitted the 'glorious sight' afforded by Bloomfield:

> That glads the Plowman's Sunday-morning's round,
> When on some eminence he takes his stand,
> To judge the smiling produce of the land.[35]

The diminutive size and, by analogy, lowly status of Constable's ploughmen were imposed upon them by the bleak surroundings in which they lived. Again and again, Constable reminds us that he is simply recording the true condition of Suffolk and nothing but Suffolk. Down to the last detail of farm building, plough construction, breed of horse, even illustrative verse – everything owes its character to this particular place. Overworked, underpaid ploughmen require no special explanation.

Constable was at pains to show how little the landscape had been altered by modern innovations. A peculiarly archaic feature of the scene is ploughing during the summer while trees are still in full leaf – albeit on a blustery day. Only fallow land – summerland – was ploughed at this season. Throughout eastern England fallows had been greatly reduced following the introduction of artificial grasses and root crops and the adoption of perennial courses of cropping, such as the Norfolk four-course rotation. Constable implies that in this district an earlier system of husbandry survived.

Harvesting

No prospect could be more reassuringly old-fashioned than *Hereford from Haywood Lodge* (Fig. 6), painted around 1815 by George Robert Lewis. It presents a traditional view of rural landscape at harvest time on a sunny

Fig. 6   George Robert Lewis, *Hereford from Haywood Lodge*, 1815. Oil on canvas.
The Tate Gallery, London.

afternoon in late summer. It expresses a conservative view of rural
labourers, working collectively, bringing home the harvest, pausing awhile
to pass round refreshing flagons of cider. It commemorates an old-enclosed,
mixed farming country, scarcely touched by modern improvements, apart
from seven rectilinear intakes inscribed on the distant Malvern Hills on
the far right of the picture.

Lewis perceptively recognised that he had found nearly the right place
at almost the right time to mirror a comforting early eighteenth-century
ideal of a Georgical landscape, a landscape in which the fertility of the
soil and the efforts of the cultivator united to yield a good harvest and
a measure of satisfaction to the harvesters. The Wye valley between Hereford and Dinedor was almost the perfect place to realise the Georgical
ideal because it possessed a congenial climate, soils made productive under
traditional methods of farming and it underwent few changes during the
period of parliamentary enclosures. From the early eighteenth century,
several poets, including Alexander Pope, William Diaper and John Dyer,
regarded the district, in Barrell's phrase, as 'the home of English Georgic'.[36]
The author of the first Board of Agriculture report for Herefordshire, John
Clark, considered that the county's economy 'derives its whole vigour from
no other resources than the mere production of its own native soil. Health,

peace and plenty smile in the countenance of its very peasantry.'[37] Clark attributed the prosperity of agriculture to the production of fine wool. John Duncumb, author of the second report in 1804, attached greater importance to wheat growing on heavy soils and thought the diversity of farming enterprises a source of strength and stability. He also noted with mild approval the conservative attitude prevailing in the district:

> The old-fashioned farmer of Herefordshire receives any new experiment in agriculture with great hesitation, if not reluctance. When its utility is confirmed by repeated trials, he slowly and gradually falls into the practice; but he wisely leaves the experiment and the risque to those who recommend or suggest it; and happily the county at this moment is well provided with agriculturists who possess the means and the spirit to undertake the patriotic task.[38]

Here, then, was a place where people made a virtue of preserving old ways and were rewarded with good crops. The wheat depicted by Lewis is heavy in the ear, long in straw and abundant in the sheaf.

1815 was exactly the right year for the Georgical ideal to be revived. Prices of wheat and other farm produce rose high enough to keep farmers satisfied, ensuring that rents were paid and enabling adequate wages to be found for labourers. Everyone in and out of agriculture could feel proud that those who worked the land were serving the country and helping to defeat Napoleon. Lewis's harvesters are seasoned workers not fresh-faced youths and blushing maidens; nor are they servile and deferential hinds. In the absence of a farmer or bailiff, they carry themselves with a manly, assured self-respect. Those taking a break have enough stamina to remain on their feet. None lies exhausted as those illustrated by Rowlandson or Linnell.[39] They face each other unsmiling but do not appear dejected. They are clean and neatly dressed, their white shirts and coloured waistcoats adding a touch of individuality to their appearance. None of them would aspire to the dandy elegance of Stubbs's haymakers and reapers.[40] In almost any other part of England at this or any other time in the period from 1710 to 1815 Lewis's representation of the Georgical ideal would not ring true, but on this occasion it does and with a powerful resonance.

Changing and unchanging agrarian landscapes

These six paintings, chosen for their topographic accuracy, and, by implication, other landscape paintings, whose locations are less clearly identified, play down the impact of agrarian changes, dwell on aspects of continuity, emphasise ties with the past, highlight signs of ageing and allude to old traditions. None of the pictures I have seen provides any firm evidence that an agricultural revolution was taking place. I think this neglect may be attributed partly to artistic fashions, partly to patrons' preferences and partly to widespread feelings of nostalgia.

Eighteenth-century artistic fashions increasingly inhibited interest in modernity. The Georgical style ritualised time-honoured movements of haymaking at Dixton, extolling the virtues of ancient practices. The harvesting scene at Hereford, a century later, strenuously denied that change had occurred or was ever likely to occur. Both pictures assert an ideal of unchanging village communities united in the work of cultivation and harvest. An Arcadian vision portrayed the earth as a bountiful provider of the fruits of nature either for the benefit of its present owners, as in the picture of Mr and Mrs Andrews, or for all *cognoscenti*, rightful heirs and successors of classical bards and philosophers, who figure in the picture of the Thames at Twickenham. At the Auberies, agricultural activities are made to look like acts of providence; at Twickenham, all vestiges of farming are pushed out of sight. In both pictures everyone enjoys unlimited leisure, eternal youth and unfading beauty.

During the second half of the eighteenth century, in the most active period of agrarian change, painters turned to hills, wild heaths and deserted shores for inspiration. Farmed landscapes were spurned except by engravers of topographical and sporting prints. Artists remained indifferent to the spectacle of technical progress, environmental renewal and social unrest. One appeal of picturesque art was precisely its escape from the stresses and disturbances caused by agrarian changes. Turner and Constable transcended present discontents to discover new truths in the forms of clouds, in structures of mountains and the intricacies of plant life. In their pictures of farmland both Turner and Constable attempted to romanticise farmwork, not by denying its essential drudgery but by investing it with a divine and patriotic purpose. In lifting turnips near Slough, Turner's labourers are performing a noble duty for their country; in ploughing the summer field at East Bergholt, Constable's ploughmen retrace the furrows cut by generations of East Anglians – all are creatures of their environment.

Artistic fashions were to some extent dictated by large landowners, the principal patrons of landscape painting. Landowners were proud of their achievements as breeders of livestock, especially racehorses and hounds. They took pleasure in exploits of the hunting field, in the extent of their parks, in the refinements of their country houses. Farming was less a subject for display in the hall than a matter to be transacted in the estate office. Landowners did not want pictures of new enclosures or new machines or new farmsteads and they certainly did not think of themselves as transforming the countryside. They were not in the business of revolutionising rural society. On the contrary, they saw their role as pillars of stable communities and their efforts were devoted to securing and perpetuating their position at the top of the social hierarchy. The notion of an agricultural revolution is not an eighteenth-century concept. Arguably, agrarian improvements were regarded at the time as restoring the order and composure attained in a classical golden age, dispelling the ignorance and superstition that had supervened during the gothic middle ages. Romantic artists, themselves not unsympathetic towards medieval ideas, proclaimed the truth of their feelings of harmony with nature to be universal and eternal. Agrarian change was subsumed within a time-scale so long that only the most enduring and unchanging elements were regarded as significant.[41]

NOTES

1 Most general histories of painting based on extensive studies of works exhibited in leading public and private collections treat agrarian change as a subject affording little interest even to artists specialising in landscape painting. See for example John Ruskin, 'On the novelty of landscape', *Modern painters*, 2nd edn (London, 1898), Vol. 3, pp. 153–60; E. H. Gombrich, *The story of art*, 11th edn (London, 1966), p. 369; Ellis Waterhouse, *Painting in Britain 1530 to 1790*, 4th edn (Harmondsworth, 1978), pp. 213–16. Michael Rosenthal, *British landscape painting* (Oxford, 1982), pp. 44–124, is an exception which discusses at length the question of representing agricultural activities in eighteenth- and early nineteenth-century paintings.

2 John Barrell, *The dark side of the landscape: the rural poor in English painting 1730–1840* (Cambridge, 1980).

3 Nicky Gregson, 'Conference report: iconography in historical geography', *Journal of Historical Geography*, 10 (1984), p. 409.

4 Barrell, *Dark side*, pp. 8, 22, 35, 42–6, 52; Hugh Prince, 'Landscape through painting', *Geography*, 69 (1984), pp. 11–12. Some notes on the Duke of Bedford's work as an agricultural improver in Bedfordshire appear in Thomas Batchelor, *General view of the agriculture of the county of Bedford* (London, 1808), pp. 27, 173, 484, 488, 537, 618.

5 Reproduced respectively in John Berger, *Ways of seeing* (London, 1972), p. 99, and R. A. C. Parker, *Coke of Norfolk* (Oxford, 1975), frontispiece.

6 Oliver Millar, *British sporting painting, 1650–1850* (London, 1974), pp. 48–57, 67–9; Anthony Vandervell and Charles Coles, *Game and the English landscape* (New York, 1980), pp. 47–116.

7 Peter Howard, 'Change in the landscape perceptions of artists', *Landscape Research*, 9 (1984), pp. 41–4; Peter Howard, 'Painters' preferred places', *Journal of Historical Geography*, 11 (1985), pp. 138–54.

8 John Harris, *The artist and the country house. A history of country house and garden view painting in Britain 1540–1870* (London, 1979), pp. 248–9, 270, offers the opinion that the picture might have been painted any time after 1725, but probably nearer to 1735. A date between 1710 and 1720 is ascribed to it by the Cheltenham Art Gallery and Museums.

9 The view of the manor house is reproduced in Harris, *The artist and the country house*, p. 270.

10 Robert Atkyns, *Ancient and present state of Gloucestershire* (London, 1712), p. 211, estimates the combined populations of Alderton and Dixton as 200; C. R. Elrington and Kathleen Morgan, 'Alderton with Dixton', *Victoria County History of Gloucestershire*, Vol. 6 (London, 1965), p. 190.

11 Dixton Tithe Award, 1839, records 430 acres in pasture, 70 acres in arable and 30 acres in wood. *V.C.H. Gloucestershire*, Vol. 6, p. 193.

12 *Ibid.*, p. 189.

13 Quoted in John Barrell, *The idea of landscape and the sense of place, 1730–1840: an approach to the poetry of John Clare* (Cambridge, 1972), p. 104.

14 *Ibid.*, p. 105.

15 Rosenthal, *British landscape painting*, p. 26.

16 Berger, *Ways of seeing*, pp. 107–9.

17 In the mid-nineteenth century the Auberies estate contained 1,524 acres whilst Dixton Manor Farm contained not more than 150 acres. Parliamentary Papers, *England and Wales: return of owners of land 1873*, c. 1097 (1875), 'Essex', Vol. 1, p. 7; *V.C.H. Gloucestershire*, Vol. 6, p. 194.

18 Thomas Ruggles, 'Picturesque farming', *Annals of Agriculture*, 6 (1786), pp. 175–84; *idem*, 7 (1787), pp. 20–8; *idem*, 8 (1787), pp. 89–97; *idem*, 9 (1788), pp. 1–15.

19 Robert Andrews, 'On the smut in wheat', *Annals of Agriculture*, 6 (1786), pp. 173–5.

20 Michael Rosenthal, 'Approaches to landscape painting', *Landscape Research*, 9 (1984), pp. 2–13, discusses the lack of empiricism in Gainsborough's later landscapes, pp. 7–11.

21 Wilson was steeped in classical learning, not only through studying art for seven years in Venice and Rome, where he received guidance from Zuccarelli and Vernet, but also by making himself an expert in Greek and Latin mythology. David H. Solkin, *Richard Wilson: the landscape of reaction* (London, 1982), pp. 37–55.

22 John Middleton, *View of the agriculture of Middlesex* (London, 1798), pp. 16–23, 254–72; G. B. G. Bull, 'Thomas Milne's land utilization map of the London area in 1800', *Geographical Journal*, 122 (1956), pp. 25–30.

23 James Lees-Milne, *Earls of creation* (London, 1962), pp. 79–92; J. T. Coppock and Hugh C. Prince (eds.), *Greater London* (London, 1964), p. 340.

24 Tate Gallery, *Turner 1775–1851* (London, 1974), p. 75. Note on exhibit 156.

25 J. C. Cox, 'Forestry', *V.C.H. Buckinghamshire*, Vol. 2 (London, Constable, 1908), p. 131; E. P. Thompson, *Whigs and hunters: the origin of the Black Act* (Harmondsworth, 1977), pp. 26–54, describes the geography of Windsor Forest in the eighteenth century.

26 The king wrote under a pseudonym as Ralph Robinson of Windsor. Ralph Robinson, 'On Mr Ducket's mode of cultivation', *Annals of Agriculture*, 7 (1787), pp. 65–71, and 'Further remarks on Mr Ducket's mode of cultivation', *Annals of Agriculture*, 7 (1787), pp. 332–6; H. B. Carter, *His Majesty's Spanish flock* (Sydney, 1964), pp. 115, 200; Hugh C. Prince, 'Georgian landscapes', in Alan R. H. Baker and J. B. Harley (eds.), *Man made the land* (Newton Abbot, 1973), p. 158. In 1799 and 1800 over 4,000 acres of open fields and

commons were enclosed in three neighbouring parishes of Horton, Wraysbury and Iver. Between 1808 and 1810 further acts were passed enclosing over 2,900 acres in Slough and adjoining parts of Upton cum Chalvey, Langley Marish, Datchet, Stoke Poges and Wexham. The process was rounded off by an enclosure act for Windsor Forest in 1813, covering parts of Bray. W. E. Tate edited by M. E. Turner, *A domesday of English enclosure acts and awards* (Reading, 1978), pp. 68–9.

27   R. B. Beckett (ed.), *John Constable's correspondence: the family at East Bergholt*, Vol. 1 (Ipswich, 1962), p. 101, cited in Michael Rosenthal, *Constable, the painter and his landscape* (New Haven and London, 1983), p. 69.

28   Leslie Parris, Ian Fleming-Williams and Conal Shields, *Constable: paintings, watercolours and drawings* (London, 1976), pp. 87–8, Tate Gallery catalogue description of exhibit 123.

29   Rosenthal, *Constable*, p. 70.

30   A measured drawing of a high carriage similar to that figured in Constable's painting is illustrated in Arthur Young, *General view of the agriculture of the county of Suffolk* (London, 1813), facing p. 35.

31   Robert Bloomfield, *The Farmer's Boy: Spring* (1800), lines 71–2, in William Wickert and Nicholas Duval, *The farmer's boy* (Lavenham, 1971), p. 72.

32   Barrell, *Dark side*, pp. 151–2; Rosenthal, *Constable*, pp. 71–8, especially discussion on p. 202.

33   Rosenthal, *Constable*, pp. 204–13.

34   A sense of a vast landscape reducing humans to the insignificance of flies crawling over a flat, featureless surface is evoked in Thomas Hardy, *Tess of the d'Urbervilles* (1891) (London, 1957), p. 322. The passage is examined in John Barrell, 'Geographies of Thomas Hardy's Wessex', *Journal of Historical Geography*, 8 (1982), p. 354.

35   Bloomfield, *Farmer's Boy: Summer*, lines 118–20.

36   Barrell, *Dark side*, pp. 114–17, 173, explained in n. 99.

37   John Clark, *A general view of the agriculture of the county of Hereford* (London, 1794), p. 32.

38   John Duncumb, *General view of the agriculture of the county of Hereford* (London, 1804), p. 35.

39   Thomas Rowlandson's *The Hedger and Ditcher* and *Labourers at Rest* (Mellon Collection) are discussed in Barrell, *Dark side*, pp. 29–30, 119–20. John Linnell's *Noonday Rest* (Tate Gallery) is mentioned in Rosenthal, *British landscape painting*, p. 128.

40   George Stubbs's *Haymakers* and *Reapers* (Tate Gallery) are discussed in Barrell, *Dark side*, pp. 25–31.

41   I am grateful to the University of Hull for inviting me to give the first Jay Appleton Lecture on this topic on 9 May 1985. I wish to thank David Lowenthal and Alison Martin of University College, London, for their valuable comments on an early draft and express my debt to Stephen Daniels for referring me to illuminating comparisons with other studies.

6

'Fields of radiance': the scientific and industrial scenes of Joseph Wright

DAVID FRASER

Historians of art, science and industry have long recognised the original subject-matter and unusually striking light-effects of Joseph Wright's paintings of scientific and industrial scenes; but much of the meaning these paintings had for their eighteenth-century audience is now obscure. This essay specifies the cultural, economic and locational context of Wright's scientific and industrial scenes in order to help clarify their meaning.[1]

Wright was born in Derby in 1734, the son of an attorney, and trained as a portrait-painter in the London studio of the fashionable Thomas Hudson during the years 1751–3 and 1756–7.[2] His father's business connections with local professional people and important local families must certainly have encouraged Joseph's earliest portrait commissions. Of solid middle-class stock, Wright remained throughout his career primarily a painter to the middle classes, working mostly in and around his native Derby, but with connections in mercantile centres like Liverpool and Manchester. His later patrons included innovating industrialists like Richard Arkwright, Jedediah Strutt, Samuel Oldknow and Josiah Wedgwood. Firmly established in Derby with a living from portraiture by the early 1760s, Wright began to produce non-commissioned subject-paintings which from 1765 he sent to the Society of Artists' annual exhibitions in London. In these paintings he departed from the narrow mainstream of eighteenth-century British portraiture to develop a style based on the work of seventeenth-century Dutch masters like Rembrandt, Honthorst and Terbrugghen. This style was characterised by striking contrasts of light and shadow, calculated to produce images of great visual intensity, as in his first contemporary scientific subject, *A Philosopher Lecturing on the Orrery* (Fig. 1), exhibited in 1766. Wright applied the same dramatic style to other modern subject-matter, such as scenes in drawing academies or iron forges.[3]

Science and the Sublime: *A Philosopher Lecturing on the Orrery*

As exceptional as Wright's pictorial mastery of light-effects, was his application of that mastery to modern and progressive subject-matter. His two

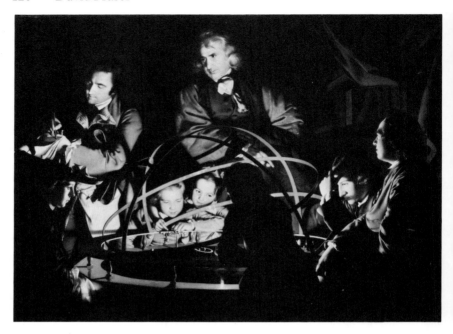

Fig. 1   Joseph Wright, *A Philosopher Lecturing on the Orrery*, 1766. Oil on canvas.
Derby Art Gallery.

contemporary scientific scenes, *A Philosopher Lecturing on the Orrery*
(1766) (Fig.1) and *Experiment on a Bird in the Air Pump* (1768), depict
subjects new to British painting. They express an informed interest in
science and technology that Wright undoubtedly owed to his personal
acquaintance with members of a provincial group that later came to be
known as the Lunar Society. Made up of prominent Midlands scientists,
industrialists and intellectuals, this group originated in the 1760s with the
friendship and mutal interest of three men: Matthew Boulton, Erasmus
Darwin and Derby clock-maker and geologist John Whitehurst.[4] Over ensu-
ing years it drew in James Watt, Joseph Priestley and Josiah Wedgwood
as well as various doctors, chemists and philosophers. Though no formal
record of their activities was kept, letters and other documentary evidence
indicate that members met in each others' homes to conduct experiments
and discuss current topics in such fields as medicine, chemistry, electricity,
botany, steam technology and civil engineering. The formulation of the
Lunar Society and like-minded groups in cther major provincial centres,
signified the spread of the Enlightenment in England far beyond London

circles, as also did the dissemination of scientific teaching by popular publications and journals aimed at the increasingly educated middle classes, by lectures and demonstrations given by touring lecturers in provincial towns, and by the teaching of experimental science in dissenting academies outside the metropolis.

Wright's association with the Lunar Society is most immediately apparent from his portraits of various of its members. He painted Erasmus Darwin c.1770, when the doctor was in Lichfield, and again in 1792–3, by which time Darwin had moved to Derby and founded a similar group, the Derby Philosophical Society, whose membership also included Wedgwood. About 1770, Wright painted the radical social philosopher, Thomas Day, who joined the Lunar Society c.1768, and around 1782–3 executed his portrait of founder-member John Whitehurst. A portrait of Wedgwood's three sons conducting an experiment to produce 'fixable air', projected c.1777, was never painted, though Wright did produce several works to Wedgwood's commission or which Wedgwood purchased during the 1780s.[5] Of all the Lunar Society members, Wright was undoubtedly closest to Darwin and Whitehurst.[6]

Between c.1765 and 1771, Wright painted two contemporary scenes of scientific demonstration and a historical one of scientific discovery. *A Philosopher Lecturing on the Orrery* (Fig. 1) and *An Experiment on a Bird in the Air Pump* were exhibited at the Society of Artists in London in 1766 and 1768 respectively; *The Alchemist Discovering Phosphorus*, was exhibited at the same venue in 1771. Wright's work was warmly commended by prominent artists such as Benjamin West, James Barry and James Northcote, who praised particularly his mastery of artificial light-effects.[7] The orrery and air pump subjects were engraved in mezzotint, along with other of Wright's exhibited paintings of the years 1765–72, a sign of his work's general popularity.

Wright's first scientific painting depicts a group of people in a darkened room, gathered round an orrery, a model of the solar system used to demonstrate the movement of the planets round the sun during the course of the year. The instrument was invented in the early 1700s to illustrate Newton's ideas and teachings on the order, regularity and harmony of the universe.[8] It was operated by turning a handle on the side, setting in motion, through a series of clockwork gearwheels, the planets on top around the sun. In Wright's painting, the scene is illuminated by a single light source, a lamp-wick burning in a glass of oil, almost hidden from our view by the elbow of the boy in the foreground. This is the lamp of the picture's full title, *A Philosopher Giving that Lecture on the Orrery, in which a Lamp is put in Place of the Sun.* Normally orreries had a brass ball on a supporting rod in the centre to represent the sun, but to demonstrate an eclipse (which is what Wright's philosopher seems to be pointing to) this ball was replaced with a lamp.[9]

Nicolson records several facts which bear on the genesis of this painting.[10] He discusses Wright's connection with Whitehurst who, as a clock-maker, would have understood all about orreries (though he is surely mistaken in accepting a contemporary identification of the lecturer in the painting as Whitehurst himself).[11] He also mentions the lectures given in Derby in 1762 by Whitehurst's correspondent, Scottish astronomer and lecturer James Ferguson.[12] These lectures, given four years before Wright exhibited his painting, possibly included a demonstration of the orrery, and if Wright was present, could have inspired the painting. Nicolson also refers to the shadowy connection between Wright, his friend Burdett (cartographer and artist, and identified as the note-taker in the painting) and Washington Shirley, 5th Earl Ferrers, of Staunton Harold, not far from Derby. This connection is significant because Earl Ferrers, an amateur astronomer, was elected to the Royal Society in 1761 after submitting a paper on the transit of Venus. It was Ferrers who purchased Wright's painting of the orrery scene.

What did the demonstration of the orrery mean to the audience in the painting? And, by extension, what did Wright's painting mean to its audience? Judging by their costume, as well as from documentary evidence on their identification, the spectators in the painting belong, like Wright, to the educated provincial middle class,[13] the group to whom a number of scientific treatises and lectures were then addressed to disseminate what Whitehurst called 'the sagacity of the immortal Newton'.[14] While the lecturer pauses to allow the note-taker time to write, the other figures gaze, deep in thought, at the spectacle before them.[15] All, except the children, seem serious and solitary. It is a scene of intense concentration. The overall impression is one of awestruck contemplation of the solar system, in whose vast expanses the spectators live their transient and infinitesimally small lives. The spectacle was, to use the contemporary term, 'Sublime'. Expressions of awestruck speculation about the universe can also be found in the work of eighteenth-century poets such as Thomson, Akenside, Blair and Young, and it is revealing to compare their writings with Wright's painting.[16]

Thomson was one of several poets who developed the 'excursion', a literary mode of describing voyages through space and round the earth, and pondering the origin and nature of what they would see there. Conscious of Newtonian concepts of the universe and of other scientific analyses of natural phenomena, these poets wrote verses that Wright, with his known interest in scientifically informed verse, could well have had in mind when painting *The Orrery*. In perhaps the most popular poem of the time, *The Seasons*, Thomson writes:

O Nature! all-sufficient! over all
Enrich me with the knowledge of thy works:
Snatch me to heaven; thy rolling wonders there
World beyond world, in infinite extent,
Profusely scattered o'er the blue universe,
Show me; their motions, periods and their laws
Give me to scan; through the disclosing deep
Light my blind way:

'Autumn' II: l.1352–9

Other poets influenced by Newtonian science, notably Mark Akenside in
The Pleasures of the Imagination (1744), Robert Blair in *The Grave* (1743)
and Edward Young in *Night Thoughts* (1742–5) also use similar imagery
of vast interplanetary space and moreover use light as a key element in
articulating that space by speculating on the time taken for light to travel
from distant stars. Akenside imagines

. . . fields of radiance, whose unfading light
Has travell'd the profound six thousand years
Nor yet arrives in sight of mortal things.

Six thousand years was then the estimated age of the universe and a sage
in Young's *Night Thoughts* also doubts if

beams, sent out at Nature's birth
Are yet arrived at this so foreign world
Though nothing half so rapid as their flight.

Blair's poem *The Grave* has a 'star-surveying sage' with his telescope who,
'travelling through the boundless length of space/Marks well the courses
of far-seen orbs'.

There are several parallels between the imagery of these poets and the
imagery in Wright's painting. In both cases, the central activity is contemplation of astronomical space. The expressions of Wright's spectators recall
Akenside's *Hymn to Science* (1744), where

The vast ambitious thoughts of man
Which range beyond control
Which seek eternity to trace,
Dive through the infinity of space,
And strain to grasp the whole.

In this poem Akenside specifically asks of his scientific muse: 'Let Number's,
Figure's, Motion's laws/Reveal'd before me stand' so that he can see
Nature's hand at work 'round the globe, and through the sky', just as
Thomson, in the passage quoted above, asked Nature to allow him to
scan the motions, periods and laws of the heavens. Both poets are referring
directly to the Newtonian view of the universe and the movement of the

planets, which the orrery was invented specifically to demonstrate. The most telling parallel concerns the use of light. In the *Hymn to Science*, Akenside describes science in terms of light illuminating the poet's mind:

> Science! thou fair effusive ray
> From the great source of mental day,
> Free, generous and refined!
> Descend with all thy treasures fraught
> Illumine each bewilder'd thought
> And bless my labouring mind.

The poet later hails science as the 'light of truth' and 'sun of his soul'. By analogy, in Wright's painting, the lamplight signifies far more than the sunlight, it signifies the knowledge and truth being imparted to the audience, illuminating and enlightening their minds. The light in Wright's painting brings their faces out of the surrounding darkness of the room and their minds out of ignorance.

Landscape and geology: Wright and Whitehurst

Scientific minds speculated on geological as well as astronomical conceptions of space and time; 'through the disclosing deep/Light my blind way: the mineral strata there', demanded James Thomson in *The Seasons*. Along with the works of Newton and their exegesis in popular writings, geological treatises helped shape eighteenth-century cosmology. Wright's friend John Whitehurst, besides making instruments such as clocks and barometers, wrote the seminal *Inquiry into the original state and formation of the earth*.[17] Whitehurst's geological interests and ideas, I will argue, can be discerned in Wright's art.

Whitehurst's *Inquiry* was first published in 1778 and earned him his Fellowship of the Royal Society the following year. However, it appears that the basic ideas were formulated much earlier; Benjamin Franklin told the author in a letter of 1763 that 'Your new Theory of the Earth is very sensible' and Wedgwood mentioned Whitehurst working on 'his world' in 1767.[18] Wright and Whitehurst would almost certainly have known each other by the early 1760s, since they were near neighbours and Whitehurst served as churchwarden at All Saints' Derby in 1761–2, whose organist, Mr Denby, held musical evenings in his house at which Wright played the flute. Denby is identified in an old print as the lecturer in *The Orrery*[19] and his name appears in the list of subscribers at the front of the first edition of Whitehurst's *Inquiry*. These associations suggest that Whitehurst's ideas, developed during the early 1760s, could at least have contributed to the sense of speculation with which Wright endowed his spectators in *The Orrery*, since the *Inquiry* deals not just with earth's geology and

Newton's observations on the planet but with the creation and origin of earth. In seeking 'to derive the nature of things from causes truly existent, and to inquire after those laws by which the Creator chose to form the world', Whitehurst strove to reconcile his deductions from 'FACTS and the LAWS of NATURE' with the Biblical account of creation and the Deluge.[20]

It is possible to identify specific iconographic parallels between Whitehurst's ideas and Wright's paintings. Whitehurst intended to establish a 'system of Subterraneous Geography', inquiring into the origins of earth's natural phenomena such as its 'craggy rocks and mountains, its steep, angular and impending shores, subterraneous caverns, etc.'. These 'romantic appearances', he deduced, resulted from tremendous convulsions which burst earth's strata and threw its fragments 'into all this confusion and disorder', principally when the waters of the Deluge met vast subterranean fires under the earth's surface. Whitehurst's dominant interest in 'Subterraneous Geography' and his ultimate conviction of 'the existence, force, and immensity of subterraneous fires' under the seas, mountains and continents,[21] evidenced particularly by volcanoes, extinct or active, explains a much-quoted comment of Wright. On 11th November 1774 he had just visited Naples and wrote to his brother from Rome:

Remember me with respect to all my friends; when you see Whitehurst, tell him I wished for his company when on Mount Vesuvius, his thoughts would have center'd in the bowels of the mountain, mine skimmed over the surface only; there was a very considerable eruption at the time, of which I am going to make a picture. 'Tis the most wonderful sight in nature.[22]

Wright made about thirty pictures of Vesuvius over the next twenty years, so much did the spectacle fascinate him. Most were painted in England, but a gouache study (Fig. 2) must have been made during an actual eruption judging from its sense of immediacy, its particularly vivid colour and light. An eruption would have appealed to Wright's sense of pictorial drama, and, despite his doubts about the penetration of his art, the gouache also suggests something of the vast, explosive fire in the earth's bowels identified by Whitehurst.

Other of Wright's landscapes depict the types of scenery and landscape features discussed by Whitehurst, and can be read in the light of Whitehurst's theory of 'Subterraneous Geography'. Amongst the artist's Italian scenes there are not just views of Vesuvius, but of other types of volcanic landscape, like the series of c.1790–2 depicting lakes Albano and Nemi situated in their extinct volcanic craters. In a view of Catania with Etna in the distance, Wright used heavy impasto and scumbles with touches of colourful hues in the foreground to suggest the particular surface texture of volcanic terrain. A series of cavern and grotto subjects, some executed

Fig. 2   Joseph Wright, *Vesuvius Erupting*, 1774. Gouache on paper. Derby Art Gallery.

in Italy in 1774 and others produced in England, are literally subterranean views, with light playing over the surface of the rock walls and ceilings. Wright's Derbyshire views regularly feature the distinctive limestone cliffs and crags discussed by Whitehurst. Wright probably felt the same standing on Matlock High Tor as he did on Vesuvius; whereas his thoughts were seized by appearances, Whitehurst's probed into the bowels of the earth. For Whitehurst, the bed of the River Derwent was 'a great *fissure* or *chasm*, filled up with the *fragments* of the *upper* and *adjacent strata*' which appeared to have been '*burst, dislocated* and *thrown* into *confusion*, by some violent convulsion of Nature', and he wondered 'that such immense masses of earth should have been thus totally absorbed into the bowels of the earth'.[23] To illustrate this structural analysis of the landscape in the *Inquiry* Whitehurst published a stratigraphic section of Matlock High Tor (Fig. 3), while Wright often used the raking light of an evening effect to articulate the surface of a limestone cliff, or scumbles and glazes to render the texture of stone.

   Wright celebrated Whitehurst's achievements as a geologist in a single portrait, painted c.1782–3 (Fig. 4). Its iconography is clear. Whitehurst is seated at his desk, drawing his pioneering *Section of the Strata at Matlock*

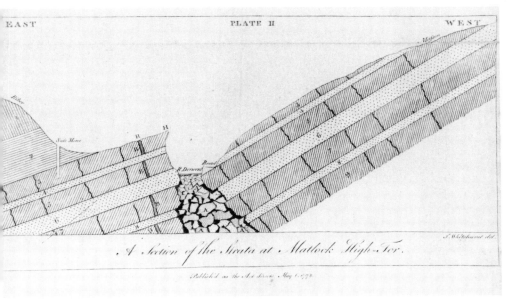

Fig. 3   Engraving after John Whitehurst, *A Section of the Strata at Matlock High Tor*, from John Whitehurst, *An inquiry into the original state and formation of the earth* (1778).

High Tor (Fig. 5) (which is shown in reverse in the engraving in the *Inquiry* (Fig. 3)). Through the window behind him we see a landscape with a volcano smoking on the horizon. The section shows the interleaving of toadstone with beds of limestone and the volcano refers to Whitehurst's discovery of the igneous origin of toadstone (which he deduced from comparing the texture and structure of Derbyshire toadstone with those of recent lava) as well as to his overall emphasis on vulcanicity as the primary geological force.

The link between science and industry was fundamental to Whitehurst, indeed the industrial exploitation of the Derbyshire landscape made his geological speculations possible. (His published section of Matlock Tor (Fig. 3) marks at 'R' one of the mine shafts which disclosed the strata.) In turn he hoped to benefit digging for copper, coal, lead, iron or water by encouraging reliable geological inferences from accurate sections.[24] It is then scarcely surprising that local industrialists subscribed to the *Inquiry*. As Wright portrayed Derbyshire industrialists with emblems of their enterprise – a sample of iron ore with Francis Hurt, a piece of muslin with

Fig. 4   Joseph Wright, *Portrait of John Whitehurst*, c.1782. Oil on canvas. Private collection.

Samuel Oldknow, a model spinning frame with Richard Arkwright (Fig. 6) – so he portrayed Whitehurst with the emblem of his contribution to local industry.[25]

Fig. 5   Detail from Wright, *Portrait of John Whitehurst*.

The morality of manufacture: Wright's smithies and forges

In the years 1771–3, Wright turned from painting scientific demonstrations to depicting manufacturing. He painted two similar versions of *The Blacksmith's Shop* (both dated 1771) (Fig. 7), *The Iron Forge* (1772) (Fig. 8) and *An Iron Forge Viewed from Without* (1773). A fifth scene, *A Farrier's Shop*, is lost and known only in Pether's engraving of 1771. Like Wright's scientific scenes they are all nocturnes showing figures in artificially illuminated interiors.

To his smithy and forge subjects Wright brought the same analytical approach that characterised his scientific scenes. He depicts precisely the process of making a horseshoe or forging iron, showing in detail what the various workers' tools and machines look like and what they do. Wright's knowledge was exact. Even the tumbledown blacksmith's shop

Fig. 6   Mezzotint, 1801, by J. R. Smith after Joseph Wright, *Portrait of Sir Richard Arkwright*, 1790. Derby Art Gallery (original oil painting in private collection).

Fig. 7   Joseph Wright, *The Blacksmith's Shop*, 1771. Oil on canvas. Derby Art Gallery.

with its thatched roof supported by rough wooden poles over the walls and arches of a ruined church, so reminiscent of Nativity scenes, may be explained not so much in terms of a deliberate religious symbolism (as

Fig. 8 Mezzotint, 1773, by Richard Earlom after Joseph Wright, *The Iron Forge*, 1772. Derby Art Gallery (original oil painting

Ronald Paulson suggests)[26] as by the contemporary practice of improvising workshops from disused buildings. Wright must have relished the overlap between the pictorial conventions of Biblical nocturnes (that would have been recognised by, and appealed to, those familiar with Old Masters) and the actuality of industrial practice.

There is a clear progression in the modernity of Wright's industrial subjects. The *Blacksmith's Shop* paintings show a blacksmith making a horseshoe for a traveller with a lame horse. Wright noted the original ideas for the subjects in his account book under the heading 'Subjects for Night Pieces', mentioning the traveller, the men hammering the white-hot metal (which acts as the primary light source), the poses of the workmen and the horseshoes on the wall.[27] The paintings adhere closely to the initial conception, except for variations in the workers' poses and the inclusion of a seated old man and some playful children. Like the *Farrier's Shop*, which also shows two smiths making a horseshoe, they depict a craft which could be found in villages, cities and on country estates throughout the country, and which had scarcely changed for centuries. The two *Iron Forge* scenes of 1772 (Fig. 8) and 1773 depict a more modern process using water-powered forges with tilt hammers, not exactly new, but certainly more sophisticated than blacksmithing in terms of both technology and organisation, and more representative of contemporary industrial changes.

The first *Iron Forge* (1772) (Fig. 8) was preceded by a study obviously made on the spot, recording the interior and machinery of the water-powered forge, but without figures. The finished painting retains the clear definition of the machinery, with the large drum visible which is turned by the waterwheel outside to lift the hammer beam. This type of machinery was installed by entrepreneurs and operated by ironmasters to perform a specialised function in a succession of manufacturing operations carried out in different hearths, if not in different locations. Eighteenth-century ironmasters would often lease buildings from local squires, again often converting old watermills or barns to forges, provided a river or stream was nearby to provide power. Different processes such as smelting, forging, rolling and slitting would be handled in different places at this time, and sometimes materials would travel some distance, perhaps by canal, between the locations where these operations were performed. Toward the end of the eighteenth century, as the factory system developed, the centralisation of operations in a complex on one site became a feature, whether in the iron, textile or other industries. It is not clear exactly which process Wright's ironworkers are performing as they hammer quite a large ingot; they could be preparing it for a rolling or slitting mill, like that erected on the Derwent in Derby in 1734.[28]

While the blacksmith and ironworker belonged to different systems of manufacture, Wright depicts both in the act of hammering metal. They

wear working clothes but nothing in their appearance, expressions or surroundings betokens poverty or hardship. Indeed they seem heroic. They
are masters of their craft, concentrating intelligently on their work, or
pausing to rest, the sturdy English artisans on whom, political economists
believed, the nation's wealth and well being was founded.[29] The presence
in Wright's smithies and forges of women and children amplifies this view
of working life, since it suggests the equation of honest labour with domestic
happiness.[30] The simultaneous representation of domestic contentment in
a scene of work is convincing in a picture of an industrial *interior* (moreover
a 'hearth') and in a picture with associations of the Nativity. The equation
is strongest in *The Iron Forge* (Fig. 8) where the workman behind the anvil
rests and gazes affectionately at the child in the arms of a woman who
is obviously his wife. Though not as overtly moralising and didactic as
Hogarth's *Industrious Prentice* engravings of 1747, Wright enshrines similar
values in this picture: the virtues of honest labour and application, which
bring to man dignity, social worth, satisfaction, domestic happiness, stability
in the home and in society. It is a bourgeois vision, natural enough for
Wright with his middle-class background and self-conscious professionalism, and in sympathy with the values of his industrial, mercantile and
landed patrons.[31] In particular, Wright's manufacturing scenes would surely
have appealed to those of his Derbyshire landowning patrons who had
industrial interests of their own, like Francis Hurt of Alderwasley, who
figured prominently in the development of Derbyshire's iron industry.
Wright's smithies and forges, sent to London for exhibition at the Society
of Artists, found buyers amongst the aristocracy and even royalty. The
first version of the *Blacksmith's Shop* was bought by Lord Melbourne;
Lord Palmerston bought the *Iron Forge* and the Empress of Russia the
Iron Forge Viewed from Without. It seems the interest in manufacturing
and its moral virtue was not peculiar to Wright's Lunar Society friends
and local industrialists, but rather was part of a broader consensus on the
virtues of 'improvement' in all spheres of economic life.

Industry and vulcanicity: *Arkwright's Mill by Moonlight*

As far as we know Wright painted no more experiments, smithies or forges
after 1773, in which year he went to Italy to study the antique. Returning
in 1775, his subject-matter diversified further to encompass a wider range
of landscape and literary subjects. However, Wright's scientific and industrial interests found another outlet during the 1780s and 1790s in his views
of Arkwright's cotton mill at Cromford, and in portraits of industrialists
posing with emblems of their industrial enterprise.

Richard Arkwright built his first mill at Cromford in 1771 to house and
operate the new water-powered cotton-spinning frame that he claimed to

Fig. 9   Joseph Wright, *Arkwright's Mill by Moonlight*, c.1782. Oil on canvas. Private collection.

have invented,[32] a model of which Wright included in his portrait of 1790 (Fig. 6). The water-frame probably constituted the most significant technical advance in the history of the cotton industry. In harness with managerial innovations that Arkwright also pioneered it helped to transform cotton manufacture into a fully fledged factory industry. Arkwright's mill was a symbol of that transformation. The mill complex at Cromford expanded in the 1770s and 80s, becoming a notable local landmark and something of a local pictorial motif, appearing in the work of visiting water-colourists like amateur artist and geologist William Day and also on Derby porcelain plates and dishes decorated c.1790 by Zachariah Boreman.[33] A cotton mill was however an unusual subject for an exhibition-size landscape in oils.[34]

A painting eccentric to the English landscape tradition, *Arkwright's Mill by Moonlight* (Fig. 9) is, I shall argue, a logical development of Wright's interests in industrial scenes and Derbyshire landscape. It is closest in conception to the 1773 *Iron Forge Viewed from Without*, though the forge is set in a more contrived landscape suggesting the Derwent valley rather than recording its topography in the more specific manner of the mill view. As a subject, *Arkwright's Mill* continues the progression in industrial technology and organisation recognisable in his smithy and forge paintings. Whereas Wright's earlier smithies and forges were dominated by individually characterised figures, *Arkwright's Mill* is devoid of characters; there is only a small and shadowy figure with a horse and cart in the foreground, eclipsed by the dazzling spectacle beyond. This corresponds to a change in industrial organisation, the loss of individual character and craftmanship in a mechanised factory operated by the semi- and unskilled labour of women and children. In Wright's smithies and forges, men are masters of technology; in *Arkwright's Mill*, technology itself seems the agent of production.

The mysterious rosy light illuminating the mill exterior may denote the particular 'candle-lighting at the cotton mills of Messrs. Arkwright & Co.' reported in the *Derby Mercury* in September 1776 and 1778 on the occasion of the millworkers' annual festive evening procession round the village. If so then the painting itself can be read as a celebration of the mill and its industry. The yellow-red light in the windows is the candlelight by which the night staff worked. It recalls the light of the sun in *The Orrery*, the glow of hot metal in smithy and forge, the volcanic eruptions of the Vesuvius pictures, and by implication Whitehurst's subterranean sea of fire.

A parallel can be drawn between the volcanic forces identified by Whitehurst in his *Inquiry* and the industrial forces represented by Wright in *Arkwright's Mill*. The valley sides enclose the glowing mill like a crater, suggesting the tension of a contained force in the landscape. More precisely, the view resembles Whitehurst's geological section in Wright's exactly contemporary portrait of Whitehurst (Fig. 5), drawn to demonstrate the igneous origin of the Derwent valley. The analogy of a mill to a volcano is persuasive and powerful. Just as the energy of an active volcano transforms the landscape, so does the energy of Arkwright's mill, not just the scenery, but the economic and social order too. The volatility of this new nocturnal landscape was recognised by others and viewed apprehensively by observers with landed opinions and tastes like Wordsworth [35] and John Byng; [36] both saw illuminated mills as 'unnatural'. Wright probably drew no tragic conclusions. To a disciple of Whitehurst, Arkwright's mill would have seemed as natural and creative a spectacle as the forces which shaped the Derwent valley itself, and indeed all post-diluvian landscapes. Much of the power of *Arkwright's Mill by Moonlight* can be seen to reside in the resonance of the primordial in the industrial.

Art and the industrial revolution

Wright's paintings of scientific experiments, so in tune with the spirit of contemporary scientific advance, stand apart from the rest of English eighteenth-century art. Of the paintings discussed in this essay, it is the industrial scenes which can be more easily linked to related subjects by contemporary and later artists like Paul Sandby, Ibbetson, de Loutherbourg, Constable and Turner.

As travelling artists like Sandby and Ibbetson toured and sketched the changing landscape of Britain so they recorded forges, factories, mines and quarries at sites of developing industrial importance. Some of their pictures recall Wright's of forges, but (almost by definition) they lack the local knowledge of Wright's paintings and also his symbolic depth.[37] A more comparable artist is Constable. Both Wright and Constable express a sensitive knowledge of the landscape of their native counties and a commitment to the technological and managerial innovations making these landscapes more productive. Michael Rosenthal shows that Constable's *Boat Building* (1814) represents the successive stages of constructing a barge,[38] clearly identifying the various tasks and recalling something of the analytical clarity with which Wright depicted the process of forging. Constable's fields and canals are worked as industriously as are Wright's forges. Flatford Mill is in Constable's paintings as much an emblem of productivity as Arkwright's mill in Wright's.

The two painters closest to Wright's sense of spectacle in industrial landscape are Philippe de Loutherbourg and J. M. W. Turner. De Loutherbourg exhibited and published views of Derbyshire, including pictures of the lead industry, and his stage scenery for the Drury Lane production *The Wonders of Derbyshire* (1779) included sets representing lead mines and ropemakers' cottages. Most dramatic, and most reminiscent of Wright, is de Loutherbourg's *Coalbrookdale by Night*, exhibited at the Royal Academy in 1801. Compositionally similar to *Arkwright's Mill by Moonlight*, it also presents a scene of concentrated energy, the pioneering site of the English iron industry appearing like a fiery crucible.[39] In his watercolours, Turner could explain the workings of industrial landscapes with great precision and also amplify their moral and social associations.[40] In his oils there is more impression of the fiery transmutation of matter and energy. Like Wright, Turner was fascinated by vulcanicity and the parallels between natural and industrial energy.[41] Towards the end of Turner's life the railway replaced the cotton mill as the key symbol of industrial power and transformation. As Wright developed a style of landscape painting to represent the harnessing of this power in *Arkwright's Mill by Moonlight*, so also did Turner in *Rain, Steam and Speed* (1844). They were the only English painters to do so.

NOTES

1 Any student of Wright is indebted to Benedict Nicolson, *Joseph Wright of Derby: painter of light*, 2 vols. (London, 1968), which first drew together much contextual and documentary material, providing a solid basis for further research.

2 Volume 1 of Nicolson provides full biographical details on Wright, and Volume 2 illustrations of paintings by Wright referred to but not reproduced in this essay.

3 Interestingly, both Wright's patrons, and the patrons of the Dutch artists who influenced Wright, were frequently merchants and businessmen. By painting in a recognisably continental manner, Wright probably increased the saleability of his work to those British collectors who, as Hogarth lamented earlier in the eighteenth century, preferred on the whole to buy continental paintings (even second-rate work) rather than the work of their own British contemporaries. Wright's continental style was surely more than a commercial ploy; in giving his work a recognised pedigree he was declaring his intention to establish himself in the historical mainstream of European art.

4 Robert E. Schofield, *The Lunar Society of Birmingham* (Oxford, 1963). The Lunar Society was so called because their meetings came to be held monthly on the Monday nearest the full moon, so they could ride home with the benefit of moonlight.

5 Nicolson, *Joseph Wright*, Vol. 1, pp. 143–9.

6 *Ibid.*

7 *Ibid.*, p. 4.

8 The fullest account of the development and use of orreries is Henry C. King and John R. Millburn, *Geared to the stars: the evolution of planetariums, orreries and astronomical clocks* (Toronto, 1978).

9 *Ibid.*, p. 156.

10 Nicolson, *Joseph Wright*, Vol. 1, pp. 111–22.

11 The features of the philosopher demonstrating the orrery simply are not those of Whitehurst as depicted in Wright's later single portrait of the latter (Fig. 4). The identification of the philosopher as Whitehurst is made in the memoirs of James Gandon, an architect and contemporary of Wright quoted by Nicolson (Vol. 1, p. 115) but in fact these memoirs were compiled and published in 1846, eighty years after Wright's painting was exhibited, ample time for Gandon's memory to develop inaccuracies.

12 See also King and Millburn, *Geared to the stars*, who devote a whole chapter (pp. 178–94) to Ferguson.

13 Documentary evidence confirms the audience is composed of individual portrait studies. Beside the memoir of James Gandon (fn. 11 above), there is also the memoir of Wright by his niece Hannah (1815), in Derby Public Library, which identifies the lecturer in *The Orrery* as an 'old John Wilton' or Wilson, of Derby Almshouses, of whom nothing more is known. Nicolson (p. 115) also cites an old print that names the lecturer as Mr Denby, organist at All Saints', Derby.

14 John Whitehurst, *An inquiry into the original state and formation of the earth*, 3rd edn (London, 1792), p. 3.

15 Ronald Paulson points out that Wright followed Hogarth's footsteps in 'trying to find ways to maintain the criterion of expression as he produced a history painting for his time', referring us back to the tradition whereby artists sought to depict a spectrum of responses to a focal centre of attention in a painting. See his *Emblem and expression: meaning in English art of the eighteenth century* (London, 1975), p. 193.

16 For an illuminating account of the impact of science on literature and poetry of eighteenth-century Britain, see Marjorie Hope Nicolson, *Newton demands the Muse* (Princeton, 1946), and *Mountain gloom and mountain glory: the development of the aesthetics of the infinite* (New York, 1959). I am much indebted to Kathleen Monaghan, formerly of Santa Barbara Museum of Art, for stimulating this line of inquiry. Some of the poetry quoted was popular for decades after it was written: Blair's *The Grave* was in its eighth edition by 1776 and Blake illustrated it in 1808, while Thomson's *Seasons* inspired paintings by Turner and Constable. Wright's own circle included poets William Hayley and Erasmus Darwin (who celebrated in verse science and industry amongst his other achievements). Wright himself illustrated literary subjects from Homer to Shakespeare, Sterne and Beattie, and had a library including contemporary poetry of industry and science. Though little is known of Wright's library now, ten books from his collection were with London booksellers Pickering and Chatto in 1984 (their catalogue No. 652, p. 124). These included a poem entitled *The Sciences* (Derby, 1783), and John Sargent's *The Mine: A Dramatic Poem* (London, 1785). A similar, although earlier, conjunction of interest in painting, literature and science is discussed by Denis Cosgrove, 'The geometry of landscape', ch. 13 in this book, although it is informed by the Copernican rather than the Newtonian system. The mystery of light was however a stimulus to both.

17 John Whitehurst, *An inquiry into the original state and formation of the earth* (1st edn, London, 1778); other editions following in 1786 and 1792, with a German edition in 1788.

18 Schofield, *Lunar Society*, p. 176.

19 See n. 13.

20 Whitehurst, *Inquiry* (1st edn), p. ii.

21 *Ibid.*, pp. ii, 49, 84.

22 Quoted in William Bemrose, *The life and works of Joseph Wright, A.R.A.* (London and Derby, 1885), pp. 34–5.

23 Whitehurst, *Inquiry* (1st edn), pp. 154–5.

24 *Ibid.*, pp. 144–5.

25 When we consider Wright's artistic preoccupation with light, his predilection for scientific matters and his relationship with Whitehurst, even his late, dramatic *Landscape with Rainbow* (1794–5), not an obviously scientific subject, can be seen to draw together the artist's dual interests in art and science. When rendering the rainbow, Wright may have had in mind Whitehurst's analysis of the rainbows in terms of refracted light, in Chapter XVI of the *Inquiry*. There also seems to be a connection between Whitehurst and another 'scientific' painter of the period, William Hodges (1744–97), a subscriber to Whitehurst's *Inquiry*

who painted volcanic craters and exotic mountains inspired by his trip to the south Pacific with Captain Cook in 1772–5. Brighton Art Gallery has a painting by Hodges of the interior of a crater in the Pacific. Nicolson suggests that Hodges knew Whitehurst personally, and possibly Wright too (see Nicolson, *Joseph Wright*, Vol. 1, p. 83 n. 3).

26 Paulson, *Emblem and expression*, pp. 190–2.

27 Quoted in Nicolson, *Joseph Wright*, Vol. 1, p. 51.

28 Stephen Glover, *History and gazetteer of the county of Derby* (Derby, 1829), Vol. 2, p. 424. There is no clue in the titles to the location of the forges, but the *Iron Forge Viewed from Without* has an almost identical setting to another painting of the same year, *The Earthstopper on the Banks of the Derwent* (1773). Presumably the similar limestone cliffs and river in both pictures are intended to suggest the Cromford–Matlock area, though it is not possible to pinpoint a particular forge from contemporary maps.

29 Maxine Berg, 'Political economy and the principles of manufacture 1700–1800', in Maxine Berg, Pat Hudson and Michael Sonenscher (eds.), *Manufacture in town and country before the factory* (Cambridge, 1983), pp. 33–58.

30 cf. John Barrell's analysis of some of Gainsborough's cottage scenes in his *The dark side of the landscape: the rural poor in English painting 1730–1840* (Cambridge, 1980), pp. 48–88.

31 In his second iron forge subject *An Iron Forge Viewed from Without*, Wright included amongst the figures an elegant, more fashionably dressed gentleman, who is most likely intended to be an ironmaster, or some type of proprietor or investor in the industry, presiding over his interests. Thus Wright has here expanded his representation of the different people, roles and social classes involved in the industry. The forge itself is set by a river in a landscape, so the source of water power is also visible, though the waterwheel itself is not.

32 Lunar Society members Boulton, Watt, Wedgwood and Darwin were all drawn into the highly contentious litigation surrounding the patent for Arkwright's water-powered spinning frame. See Schofield, *Lunar Society*, pp. 349–51. A celebration of Arkwright's mill by Erasmus Darwin appears in *The Botanic Garden* (1789). For a comprehensive account of Arkwright and his achievements see R. S. Fitton and A. P. Wadsworth, *The Strutts and the Arkwrights, 1758–1830* (Manchester, 1958).

33 Derby Art Gallery has eighteenth-century topographical views of Arkwright's mill by various artists, the most detailed being by William Day (1789). Examples of the mill depicted on porcelain are in the collection of Derby Museum.

34 In fact Wright did not exhibit the painting; it was purchased by Daniel Parker Coke, a barrister and M.P. for Derby (1775–80) and then Nottingham (1780–1812). As local industrial developments, including the cotton factories, would have figured prominently in his constituency affairs, Wright's painting must have embodied many of Coke's own interests. Coke appears in a group portrait by Wright of the same date as *Arkwright's Mill by Moonlight*, seated with his cousin Rev. D'Ewes Coke, and his cousin's wife. As a proprietor of local coal mines D'Ewes Coke had his own industrial interests.

35 William Wordsworth, *The Excursion* (London, 1814), Book VIII, lines 148–85.

36 John Byng, *The Torrington diaries*, Vol. 2 (London, 1935), pp. 194–6; Vol. 3 (London, 1936), pp. 81–2.

37 For a discussion of the industrial pictures of touring artists see Francis D. Klingender, *Art and the Industrial Revolution*, ed. and rev. by Arthur Elton (London, 1968), pp. 72–90.

38 Michael Rosenthal, *Constable, the painter and his landscape* (New Haven and London, 1983), p. 88.

39 See Leslie Parris's catalogue, to the Tate Gallery exhibition *Landscape in Britain c.1750–1850* (London, 1973), pp. 67–8. The de Loutherbourg entries and illustrations include a view of Dovedale, 1784 (cat. 131); a maquette for *The Wonders of Derbyshire*, 1779, depicting a cavern interior, possibly Peak Cavern at Castleton (cat. 130); and *Coalbrookdale by Night*, 1801 (cat. 133).

40 Stephen Daniels, 'The implications of industry: Turner and Leeds', *Turner Studies*, 6, no. 1 (1986), pp. 10–17.

41 Michel Serres, 'Turner translates Carnot', *Block*, 6 (1982), pp. 46–55.

7

The privation of history: Landseer, Victoria and the Highland myth[1]

TREVOR R. PRINGLE

The use of the Queen, in a dignified capacity, is incalculable. Without her in England, the present English Government would fail and pass away. Most people when they read that the Queen walked on the slopes at Windsor – that the Prince of Wales went to the Derby – have imagined too much thought and prominence were given to little things. But they have been in error; and it is nice to trace how the actions of a retired widow, and an unemployed youth become of such importance.

Walter Bagehot, 1867[2]

We used a great many words whose derivations we did not know – for instance the word myth – What does it come from – I was not given enough to reply beyond the common place facts about the word.

Frederick Keyl in conversation with Sir Edwin Landseer, 1867[3]

The reign of Queen Victoria saw the emergence of a new genre in painting, one which expressed a royal liking for the Highlands of Scotland. Through royal patronage painters such as Carl Haag and John Phillips rose to prominence in Britain. While many artists worked within this genre one name above all others came to be identified with the image of Queen Victoria and the royal family in the Highlands of Scotland, that of Edwin Landseer. Born in 1803, Landseer was a Regency dandy who rose to fame and fortune through his paintings of animal life and the Scottish Highlands. Further, he instructed both Queen Victoria and Prince Albert in the art of sketching and was in many ways the last of the court painters.[4]

Landseer's first painting of the royal family in the Highlands of Scotland was *Queen Victoria Sketching at Loch Laggan* (1847). In 1849 Queen Victoria purchased Landseer's *The Free Kirk*. Although not a royal commission, the Queen thought this work symbolised the peacefulness of the Highlands. Later that year she commissioned two Highland subjects from Landseer as Christmas presents for Prince Albert: *Highlander and Eagle* and *Highland Lassie Crossing a Stream*. In 1850 Landseer paid his first visit to Balmoral, leased by Victoria in 1848, and was a guest there the following autumn. It was on this first visit that the Queen discussed the details of the most important of Landseer's royal commissions, *Queen Victoria Meeting the Prince Consort on his Return from Deer Stalking in the Year 1850*. This work was exhibited at the Royal Academy in May 1854 in its unfinished form and received unfavourable reviews.[5] Landseer continued work on the painting until 1870 when it was exhibited for a second time at the Royal Academy. Critics tactfully passed it by.[6] The painting finally entered the royal collection around 1873 and was engraved by W. H. Simmons in 1874 under the title *Royal Sports on Hill and Loch*. It was destroyed by order of George V.[7]

From these paintings it is possible to discern the emergence of a Victorian Highland myth, a myth in which the contingent and historical are lost in an image of tranquil natural order. Further, I will argue that the loss of history inherent in the myth automatically entails the loss of geography, of the contingency of place. For the specifics of historical events to be veiled successfully by a constructed past which celebrates sectional interests, the specifics of location, place and environment wherein these events occurred must similarly be veiled by the construction of a mythical geography. Both history and geography are re-presented in the myth. The term 'myth' is of course problematic. In this discussion I refer to Roland Barthes' concept and analytic method which is briefly outlined here before being applied to the engraving of Landseer's *Royal Sports on Hill and Loch*.[8]

Barthes' semiology postulates a relation between two terms: a 'signifier' and a 'signified'. There is however a third term, the 'sign', which may be considered the associative total of the first two terms. In myth, the sequence of signifier, signified and sign again appears (Fig. 1). Myth is in essence what Barthes calls a second order semiological chain, one which is constructed from the chain which exists before it. That which is a sign in the first system becomes a mere signifier in the second. This second order signifier Barthes terms the 'form'. The signified in the second order semiological chain is the 'concept'. In the second order semiological chain the signification, or sign, is the myth itself. Barthes calls the sign of the first order semiological system the 'meaning'. In myth the mythical signifier, or form, is both full and empty. It is from the meaning that myth draws its nourishment. When the first order sign, or meaning, becomes the mythical signifier or form, its contingency is left behind. When this happens the mythical signifier or form leaves behind a whole system of values: a history, a geography, a morality. Barthes postulates a continuous alteration, a dialectic, between meaning and form. Meaning is a reservoir of history which the myth can call and dismiss at will. According to Barthes, it is this constant game of hide and seek between meaning and form which defines myth.

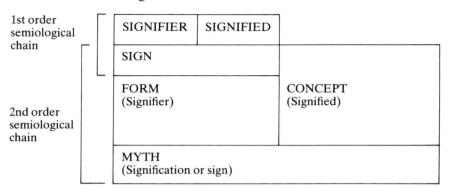

1st order semiological chain

2nd order semiological chain

SIGNIFIER	SIGNIFIED	
SIGN		
FORM (Signifier)		CONCEPT (Signified)
MYTH (Signification or sign)		

Fig. 1   The nature of myth. *Source:* R. Barthes, *Mythologies* (St Albans, 1972), p. 115.

Landseer, Victoria and the Highland myth

Royal Sports on Hill and Loch (Fig. 2) was the largest and most important of Landseer's royal commissions. According to Ormond, the picture was intended 'to identify the royal family with the spirit of the Highlands and the ennobling pursuit of hunting'.[9] Landseer's sketches for the work were undertaken at Balmoral in 1850 where Queen Victoria discussed the picture at length with him. Her Majesty was explicit in her wishes:

It is to be thus: I, stepping out of the boat at Loch Muich, Albert, in his Highland dress, assisting me out, & I am looking at a stag which he is supposed to have just killed. Bertie is on the deer pony with McDonald (whom Landseer much admires) standing behind, with rifles and plaids on his shoulder. In the water, holding the boat, are several of the men in their kilts, – salmon are also lying on the ground. The picture is intended to represent me meeting Albert, who has been stalking, whilst I have been fishing, & the whole is quite consonant with the truth. The solitude, the sport, the Highlanders in the water, &c will be, as Landseer says, a beautiful exemplification of peaceful times, & of the independent life we lead in the dear Highlands. It is quite a new conception, & I think the manner in which he has composed it, will be singularly dignified, poetical & totally novel, for no other Queen has ever enjoyed, what I am fortunate enough to enjoy in our peaceful happy life here. It will tell a great deal, & it is beautiful.[10]

As a commission from the reigning monarch, Landseer's *Royal Sports* does indeed tell a great deal about Queen Victoria's conception of, and identification with, the 'spirit of the Highlands'. Using Barthes' methodology, it is possible to identify the signifiers of a first order semiological

Fig. 2 W. H. Simmons, *Royal Sports on Hill and Loch*, 1874. Engraving after Sir Edwin Landseer, 1850. Copyright reserved. Reproduced by the gracious permission of Her Majesty The Queen.

chain. First, *Royal Sports on Hill and Loch* illustrates a British queen in the symbolic act of landing in Scotland.[11] Secondly, all eyes of the royal retainers are directed towards the Queen. All these are the first order signifiers. What do they signify? Apart from the symbolic connotation of the Queen landing and conquering Scotland, the signifiers proclaim that the Queen is great and that all her subjects serve her loyally regardless of nationality. There is no better retort to those contemporaries who would allege colonial imposition than the loyalty shown by the natives.[12] What is the sign? Quite simply, the sign is royalty in a loyal Highlands. At this level of understanding the meaning of the engraving would appear to be clear. However, if the engraving is examined carefully, what Barthes would call a second order semiological chain can be detected, one whose signifiers, or form, are already present in the sign of the first order system. It is this second order semiological chain which defines the myth.

The mythical signified or concept can have several signifiers. Further, as Barthes argues, it is the repetition of this concept through various signifiers that allows the observer to decipher the myth. Signifiers at this second level are present in the physical ascendency of Queen Victoria, the royal ensign and Prince Albert's adherence to the tartan and kilt, the invention of an English Quaker in 1727.[13] What do these signifiers signify? The concept signified here is royal imposition and appropriation of the Scottish landscape and Scottish history. Royal imposition and appropriation lie at the very heart of the myth. It is through the concept that a whole new history is implanted, for myth has one principle: it transforms history into nature. What then is the signification? It is the myth itself.[14] Myth is the process of de-politicisation of the image. Here what is lost from the image is not royal imposition and appropriation but the geographical and historical, the fabricated quality of this imposition and appropriation. The Victorian Highland myth (Fig. 3) is the naturalness of the image of Queen Victoria and the royal family in a tranquil loyal Highlands.[15]

The privation of history

'Myth deprives the object of which it speaks of all History'.[16] From the myth and its signification in Landseer's *Royal Sports* historical reality is transformed into an image of natural reality. The naturalness of the image in *Royal Sports* denies the struggles of the 1715 and 1745 Jacobite rebellions. Further, in *Royal Sports* and *Highlander and Eagle* the image of kilted and armed Highlanders seems to negate the tensions of the eighteenth century when such items of apparel were prohibited by Georgian statutes, statutes which had only been revoked in 1780.[17] The fact that George IV, the first reigning monarch to visit Scotland since Charles I, did so less than 30 years previously is easily forgotten. Myth has the task of giving

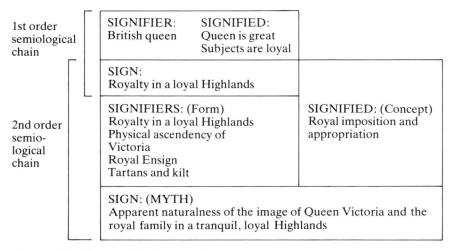

1st order semiological chain	SIGNIFIER: British queen	SIGNIFIED: Queen is great Subjects are loyal	
	SIGN: Royalty in a loyal Highlands		
2nd order semio- logical chain	SIGNIFIERS: (Form) Royalty in a loyal Highlands Physical ascendency of Victoria Royal Ensign Tartans and kilt	SIGNIFIED: (Concept) Royal imposition and appropriation	
	SIGN: (MYTH) Apparent naturalness of the image of Queen Victoria and the royal family in a tranquil, loyal Highlands		

Fig. 3   The Victorian Highland myth.

the historical, here Queen Victoria's presence in the Highlands, a natural justification. In doing so it makes contingency eternal: 'The world enters language [here the image] as a dialectical relation between activities, between human actions; it comes out of myth as a harmonious display of essences.'[18] These essences are those which saturate the 'spirit of the Highlands' and in this sense contribute not only to the privation of history but to the privation of geography.[19]

Myth and the privation of geography

The Highland myth contributes to the privation of both history and geography in its reduction of the landscape from a romantic construction to a bland container for what is ultimately a socially and historically determined myth.[20] The nature of this change in landscape representation under the agency of myth can be illustrated by comparative analysis of *Royal Sports on Hill and Loch* with other works of the Highland genre by Landseer. In *Queen Victoria Sketching at Loch Laggan* (Fig. 4), the first of Landseer's pictures of the royal family in the Scottish Highlands, the landscape component is strong. Here the setting, at the east end of Loch Laggan looking towards the East Binnein, is more than just a backdrop for the royal image; it forms an integral part of the meaning.[21] It is the landscape that Queen Victoria is in the act of sketching and as such it cannot be divorced from the meaning of the painting. Similarly, in the pastoral imagery of *Highland Lassie* (Fig. 5) the landscape component, although different in nature from that in the previous painting, remains strong. As with *Royal Sports on*

Fig. 4 Sir Edwin Landseer, *Queen Victoria Sketching at Loch Laggan*, 1847. Oil on panel. Copyright reserved. Reproduced by the gracious permission of Her Majesty The Queen.

Hill and Loch Queen Victoria was explicit in her wishes: *Highland Lassie* was to be all 'peace and sunshine'.[22] Examination of the painting shows that her wishes were respected. The wild animals no longer fear mankind, sheep graze peacefully in the background while, in the distance, smoke spirals upwards into a serene sky from the hearths of doubtlessly happy homes.

Highlander and Eagle (Fig. 6), the companion painting to *Highland Lassie*, appears radically different from the other royal commissions examined so far. Here the landscape component has been eradicated and the ruggedness of the Highlands personified in the highly romantic and powerful figure of the Queen's gillie, Peter Coutts. Further, the peaceful and tranquil imagery of the previous works has gone. This highly dramatic image is however the result of Landseer's disregard for the Queen's wishes. In a letter to Queen Victoria's dresser, Miss Skerrett, Landseer had asked whether the Queen would prefer the 'peaceful and sunny side' of the Highlander's character in preference to an 'action and bloodied' image.[23] In the reply that followed it was apparent that while Queen Victoria's equerry was eager for a stormy image the Queen herself was not.[24] Queen Victoria again expressed her wish for a pastoral image and thought that the Highlander should represent the 'natural spirit of the highlands'. The Queen in fact proposed a forester resting on his way home with the spoils of a day's sport silhouetted against a sunset over distant hills. Clearly Queen Victoria's wishes were ignored by Landseer in this instance in favour of a dramatic, powerful, highly romantic composition.

In his sketch for *Royal Sports* (Fig. 7) Landseer recovered the romantic image of landscape and nature. Here the actions of Queen Victoria and her retainers remain within the framework prescribed by nature, or at least the artist's conception of the natural world. Even the Queen in all her regality cannot rise above the peaks of the Highland landscape. In the completed version of *Royal Sports* (Fig. 2), however, the myth, in its privation of history, has brought about the privation of geography in at least three distinct ways. First, the landscape component of the painting has been subsumed if not eradicated by the myth of naturalness of royalty in a loyal Highlands. The landscape image undergoes change from the picturesque of *Queen Victoria Sketching at Loch Laggan* (Fig. 4) to the pastoral of *Highland Lassie* (Fig. 5), eventually to be subsumed in *Royal Sports* (Fig. 2) where Queen Victoria in all her regality is higher, and by implication greater, than all the surrounding natural world. Secondly, the animal kingdom has been completely subjugated by the royal presence. This is readily apparent on comparison of the artist's sketch with the final version. The number and species of dead game has increased while those animals which are not physically subjugated, such as the dogs at Queen Victoria's feet, pay homage like their human retainers to their royal master.

Fig. 5   Sir Edwin Landseer, *Highland Lassie Crossing a Stream*, 1850. Oil on canvas. Reproduced by the gracious permission of Her Majesty The Queen.

The third way in which the privation of geography occurs is related not to the specific content of the painting but the context in which the commission was undertaken. The transformation of social relations in Scottish

Fig. 6   Sir Edwin Landseer, *Highlander and Eagle*, 1850. Oil on canvas. Copyright reserved. Reproduced by the gracious permission of Her Majesty The Queen.

society and the resultant tensions that this transformation produced are implicitly denied. All the commissions discussed so far either illustrated or expressed the Queen's desire for a tranquil image of Highland life,

Fig. 7   Sir Edwin Landseer, artist's sketch for *Royal Sports on Hill and Loch*, 1850. Oil on canvas. Copyright reserved. Reproduced by the gracious permission of Her Majesty The Queen.

an image which ignores the transformation of Scottish social and economic
life which had been underway from the mid-eighteenth to the mid-nineteenth century: the history of Highland clearances, agrarian revolution,
political domination, colonisation, eviction and emigration.[25] Moreover,
Landseer's tranquil images mask fundamental changes in the structure of
social and economic life over the period 1820 to 1870.

By 1820 a significant proportion of the Scottish people had been transformed into a landless proletariat. A decade later the basis of industrial
capitalism had been laid: Scotland was on the brink of the transition to
a modern economy.[26] In 1841 despite the fact that only 32.7% of Scots
lived in towns of over 5,000 inhabitants over half the population lived
in parishes which were recognisably urban–industrial.[27] Between 1830 and
1870 industrialisation, centred on increasing factory production, finally
transformed the great majority of Scots into landless proletarians.[28] The
rise of Scotland's distinct form of client capitalism resulted in an irrevocable
break of the traditional ties between the Scottish people and the land.[29]
Rapid urbanisation resulted in poor sanitation, chronic overcrowding and
an inadequate supply of drinking water in many urban areas. In the cities
tuberculosis, typhus, measles, scarlet fever, dysentery and whooping cough
were all endemic until the second half of the century. Urban mortality
rates returned to seventeenth-century levels and on occasion were twice
as high as those of the countryside. In the early 1840s economic depression
was so acute that relief was given to the able-bodied unemployed and soup
kitchens established in almost all major Scottish towns.[30] For Scotland the
period 1832–55 was one of profound social and economic crisis. While the
vogue for tartan shawls following Victoria's initial visit to Scotland in 1842
may have temporarily eased Paisley's unemployment problem, the Highland myth veiled the harsh realities of Scottish urban existence and helped
propagate an increasingly false regional image of a tranquil rural Scotland.[31]

In masking the tensions inherent in Scottish society the Victorian Highland myth also masked tensions within Britain as a whole.[32] Landseer's
royal commissions and the emergence of the myth came at a time of great
administrative change and upheaval. To many contemporaries the climax
of the Chartist struggle in 1848, like the Jacobite risings of 1715 and 1745,
had seemed to threaten the very foundations of British society. In 1842
Queen Victoria on her first visit to Scotland had been forced by Peel to
undertake the journey by sea to avoid the chance of being caught up
in Chartist unrest in the north of England.[33] Indeed, in the months previous to this visit two direct attempts had been made on the Queen's
life.

In addition to Britain's internal problems, unrest throughout Europe
was widespread. The crowned heads of Europe communicated with each
other in despondent letters. On 26 February 1848 Queen Victoria's uncle

Leopold, King of the Belgians, wrote to his niece: 'I am unwell in consequence of the awful events at Paris . . . What will soon become of us God
alone knows; great efforts will be made to revolutionise this country; as
there are poor and wicked people in all countries it may succeed.'[34] Queen
Victoria in her reply could state:

Since 24th February I feel an uncertainty in everything existing, which . . . one
never felt before. When one thinks of one's children, their education, their future
– and prays for them – I always think and say to myself, 'Let them grow up fit
for whatever station they may be placed in – high or low'. This one never thought
of before, but I do always now. Altogether one's whole disposition is so changed
– bores and trifles . . . one looks upon as good things and quite a blessing – provided
one can keep one's position quiet![35]

It was no doubt these reasons amongst others that led to the Queen's
entourage of troops, present even during her 'peaceful happy highland
existence'. That this presence was noticeable in the Highlands there can
be no doubt. Landseer himself was to comment: 'The highlands – particularly the neighbourhood of Blair in Atholl present a new character – soldiers
and bustle. The Q and P.A. being the great attraction.'[36] Clearly the tensions present in Scottish and British society were apparent for all to see,
yet the Highland myth with its tranquil rural imagery denied them.

Propagating the myth

In Victorian Britain before the advent of photographic reproduction the
major medium for visual mass communication was the engraving. Following
the invention of the steel printing plate in 1840 and of stereotyping, the
duplicating of the printing plates themselves, the print business was revolu-
tionised. The very period in which Landseer painted royalty in the Scottish
Highlands saw a boom in the engraving trade.[37] In 1842 there were approximately 20 printsellers in London; by 1890, 126 printsellers had registered
with the Print Sellers Association, a body established to clamp down on
pirate engravings and prints.[38] Between 1847 and 1894 the number of plates
declared totalled 4,823. This figure excluded those printed privately.
Further, print piracy was rife. The fact that technical innovation, in particular stereotyping, enabled the plates to be duplicated, and that thousands
of engravings were taken from each plate ensured that the total number
of prints produced could be numbered in millions.

The cumulative effect of the production of multiple copies on a large
scale was to depress prices. However, substantial problems remained in
distribution of the end product. There was no national or international
network of retail outlets. One attempted solution was the foundation of
Art Unions, for example the Art Union of London which was established

Table 1. *Engraving record of Landseer's royal commissions*

Title	Engraver	Year of publication	Price
Queen Victoria	J. T. Willimore	1858	1 gn.
Sketching at Loch Laggan	W. Roffe	1881	—
*The Free Kirk**	T. L. Atkinson	1854	2 gns.
	R. Piercy	1885	1 gn.
Highland Lassie Crossing a Stream	J. Outrim	1864	2 gns.
Highlander and Eagle	J. Outrim	1856	1 gn.
	W. Roffe	1891	1 gn.
Royal Sports on Hill and Loch	W. H. Simmons	1874	3 gns.

* *The Free Kirk* has been included in the above table although not executed by royal commission.
Source: information derived from the catalogues of the Print Sellers Association (P.S.A.) and the Incorporated Print Sellers Association, London (Vol. 1, 1847–91).

in 1837.[39] Art Unions were really no more than glorified lotteries where members subscribed a guinea or more each year. Prize money was allocated by lottery and the winner could select a work of art currently on exhibition at the Royal Academy, the British Institute or the Society of Painters in Water Colours. The governing committees of the Art Unions annually commissioned an engraving after one of the winners' choices and prints were subsequently distributed to subscribers. Between 1838 and 1887 the Art Unions published 50 large plates, one of which was Landseer's *Highland Landscape* (1857). Despite the activities of the Art Unions, the annual subscription rates and the problems of distribution ensured that the engraving mass market was restricted largely to the Victorian middle classes. From a brief study of the engraving market it is possible to make some comment on the identity of those who purchased Landseer's works and thus became consumers of the myth.

All of Landseer's royal commissions and genre paintings discussed above were engraved. Table 1 shows that some were engraved more than once.[40] While it is impossible to provide any real estimate of the number of prints published, the prices charged for them are readily available and are given in Table 1. Such prices over the period 1854–91 were beyond the reach of the majority of the working classes. Clearly the mass market for the

Victorian Highland myth lay in the Victorian middle and upper classes, and perhaps in the aspiring labour aristocracy. Above all myth is a value, a bourgeois value.[41]

The myth in context

So far this discussion has examined the nature of the Highland myth and the medium through which it spread. However, in order to understand its meaning fully, it is necessary to relate it to the specific social, political, economic and cultural milieu within which it flourished.[42] Between 1820 and 1870 the British monarchy was at its most significant in terms of the real effective political power it wielded.[43] The monarchy was neither impartial nor above politics. As Cannadine has argued this continuing royal power made grand ceremonial unacceptable, while renewed royal unpopularity made it impossible.[44] Over the period 1820–70, due to various reasons such as Prince Albert's Germanic descent, the press as a whole remained hostile to the monarchy. The lack of pictures made even the greatest of royal ceremonies invisible to all but the most literate and wealthy. There was no cheap periodical press. The *Illustrated London News*, begun in 1842, sold at a shilling a copy and as a result had a very restricted readership,[45] as did the prints of Landseer's royal commissions. Both were restricted to the mass market of the Victorian middle classes.

It was a combination of these kind of factors that led Cannadine to conclude that royal ceremonies such as state visits to Scotland were not so much shared corporate events as remote inaccessible group rites, performed for the benefit of the few rather than the edification of the many.[46] It is within this historical context that the Highland genre and myth discussed above must be examined, for the Victorian Highland myth and the emergence of specific Scottish royal rituals are interconnected. Cannadine has argued that 'the nadir of Royal grandeur and ceremonial presence' occurred in the two decades following the Prince Consort's death in 1861.[47] However, in the Victorian Highland myth discussed above it is possible today to identify the emergence of a new royal ritual, a ritual which was intimately connected *not* with the invention, but with the creation and coming into being of a Scottish royal past.

Queen Victoria and the myth: a conscious creation?

Having identified and examined the nature of the Victorian Highland myth, it may be asked to what extent was the myth a conscious creation. Both Cannadine and Hobsbawm argue for the conscious creation or invention of tradition in the nineteenth century.[48] Given Queen Victoria's highly

personal reasons for her preference for the Highlands and her naive acceptance of Sir Walter Scott's romanticism such a stance here would be incorrect.[49] In *Mythologies* Barthes directs his attention to myths that are not
so much concocted as secreted and this is perhaps the best way to view
the Highland myth. To argue otherwise would be to practise a form of
reductionism akin to the 'Balmorality' of much late nineteenth- and early
twentieth-century Scottish nationalist thought.[50] It is not suggested that
Queen Victoria took the lease on Balmoral to appropriate Scotland physically and symbolically, nor is it suggested that Landseer's royal commissions
formed part of a conscious, ideological exercise to manufacture and appropriate a Highland tradition. To claim as much would be historically incorrect. There was no need for such measures, given the apparent naturalness
of the image of the Queen and the royal family in a tranquil, loyal Highlands.
Since the Victorian period the Highland myth has been appropriated, modified and propagated by the image makers of twentieth-century consumer
society. The Victorian Highland myth was no more a conscious creation,
and no less powerful, than the Royal Highland myth of today.[51]

NOTES

1   Thanks must be conveyed to Richard Ormond and Tony Dyson for their assist-
    ance in the preparation of this essay. All plates appear by the gracious per-
    mission of Her Majesty The Queen. The author wishes to acknowledge receipt
    of an E.S.R.C. studentship to fund the research upon which this essay is based
    and a grant from the Historical Geography Research Group towards the cost
    of illustrations.
2   W. Bagehot, *The English constitution*, 17th impression (originally published,
    1867, London, 1963), p. 82.
3   Keyl Papers, unpaginated MSS with the Surveyor of the Queen's Pictures,
    Lord Chamberlain's Office, St James's Palace, entry dated 1 March 1867. Keyl's
    personal record of dinner conversations with Landseer.
4   Little has been written on Landseer this century; for biographical details the
    following works are useful: F. G. Stephens, *Memoirs of Sir Edwin Landseer*
    (London, 1874); A. Graves, *Catalogue of the works of the late Sir Edwin Land-
    seer* (London, 1876); W. C. Monkhouse, *Sir Edwin Landseer's works with
    a history of his art life* (London, 1881); J. A. Manson, *Sir Edwin Landseer,
    R.A.* (London, 1902); C. Lennie, *Landseer: the Victorian paragon* (London,
    1976); R. Ormond, *Sir Edwin Landseer* (London, 1981).
5   'The connoisseur will not in the whole "land see a" better Landseer than
    the "Doctors visit to Poor Relations at the Zoological Gardens" (265) nor
    a worse, than the group of royal portraits to which Sir Edwin has not been
    ashamed to affix his name, but which it is charitable to hope he did not paint.'

From *Judy*, cited in C. S. Mann, *The works of Sir Edwin Landseer*, 4 vols. (1874–7) (National Art Library, MSS 86.BB.19–22), 1875, 86.BB.22, p. 173.

6 Ormond, *Landseer*, p. 163.

7 *Ibid.*

8 R. Barthes, *Mythologies* (1957; transl. by A. Lavers, St Albans, 1972). For critically informed discussions of Barthes' concept of myth, see P. Thody, *Roland Barthes: a conservative estimate* (London, 1977); A. Lavers, *Roland Barthes: structuralism and after* (London, 1982).

9 Ormond, *Landseer*, p. 160.

10 Extract from the Journal of Queen Victoria quoted in Ormond, *Landseer*, pp. 159–60. The Queen's account of her Highland existence has recently been called into question: 'Victoria's diary is a remarkable revelation of a monarch's ignorance about her kingdom, in spite of having travelled through it.' J. Brand, *The national movement in Scotland* (London, 1978), p. 93. While such accounts dispute the depth of the Queen's understanding they do not challenge the deep sincerity of her feelings for her Highland retreat.

11 The iconography of a monarch stepping onto land and symbolically 'capturing' it is not unique to Landseer; it has a long pedigree in the history of art.

12 However, at least one contemporary satirist thought otherwise: 'Yonder are "respectable" couples who have come specially to see Sir Edwin Landseer's portrayal of an interesting incident in the life of the Queen. They gaze on the picture with feelings of loyalty and flunkeyism intermingled: and among the people gathered around this work is sure to be a tall and solemn parson engaged probably in ponderous explanation of it. I profess of Sir Edwin's work the intelligent reader will derive much amusement from the faces of the gillies in the background who are gazing at the meeting of the Queen and her husband with looks of unmitigated disgust as if they would like to pitch the Prince Consort into the Loch.' Extract from *The Period*, cited in Mann, *The works of Landseer*, 1875, p. 173.

13 For an informative yet amusing account of the origin of the kilt see, H. Trevor-Roper, 'The invention of tradition: the highland tradition of Scotland', in E. Hobsbawm and T. Ranger (eds.), *The invention of tradition* (Cambridge, 1983), pp. 15–41.

14 Barthes, *Mythologies*, p. 121.

15 This naturalness is related to a broader issue noted by Bagehot: 'We have come to regard the Crown as the head of our morality. The virtues of Queen Victoria and the virtues of George III have sunk deep in the popular heart. We have come to believe that it is natural to have a virtuous sovereign, and that the domestic virtues are as likely to be found on thrones as they are eminent when there.' Bagehot was however to comment critically: 'But a little experience and less thought show that royalty cannot take credit for domestic excellence.' Bagehot, *English constitution*, p. 96.

16 Barthes, *Mythologies*, p. 151.

17 See 19 Geo.II c.39; 20 Geo.II c.51; 21 Geo. II c.34.

18 Barthes, *Mythologies*, p. 142. For Barthes' thoughts on painting as a language, see 'La peinture est-elle un langage?', *La Quinzaine Litteraire* (1 March 1969), p. 16.

19 That the privation of history necessarily also entails a privation of geography has hitherto been noted: 'The history-less robot society and the "brave new world" in which the deliberate falsification of history preserves the last shreds of the historical sense, is at the same time a geography-less society, for both time and space are reduced to mere dimensions.' Van Paassen quoted in J. A. May, *Kant's concept of geography and its relation to recent geographical thought* (University of Toronto Department of Geography Research Publications, No. 4, University of Toronto Press, 1970), p. 23.

20 The phrase 'socially and historically determined myth' should not be interpretated as implying a conscious creation of the Highland myth: 'Motivation is unavoidable. It is none the less very fragmentary. To start with, it is not "natural": it is history which supplies its analogies to the form.' Barthes, *Mythologies*, pp. 126–7.

21 Ormond, *Landseer*, p. 160.

22 Royal Archives, Add. C4/161 21/11/1849.

23 *Ibid.*, C4/160 20/11/1849.

24 *Ibid.*

25 For a critical reappraisal of this received history, see E. Richards, *A history of the highland clearances: agrarian transformation and the evictions 1746–1886* (London, 1982).

26 See B. Lenman, *An economic history of modern Scotland* (London, 1977), and *Integration, enlightenment and industrialisation in Scotland, 1745–1832* (London, 1981); I. Levitt and T. C. Smout, *The state of the Scottish working class in 1843: a statistical and spatial enquiry based on the data of the Poor Law Commission reports of 1844* (Edinburgh, 1979); A. Dickson (ed.), *Scottish capitalism: class, state and nation. From the union to the present* (London, 1980).

27 Levitt and Smout, *State of the Scottish working class in 1843*, p. 7.

28 K. Burgess, 'Workshop of the world: client capitalism at its zenith, 1830–1870', in Dickson (ed.), *Scottish capitalism*, pp. 181–243.

29 *Ibid.*

30 R. M. Mitchison, 'The making of the old Scottish poor law', *Past and Present*, 63 (1974), pp. 58–93; Levitt and Smout, *State of the Scottish working class in 1843*, pp. 160–1.

31 Levitt and Smout, *State of the Scottish working class in 1843*, p. 158.

32 This point is of course related to Bagehot's discussion of the role played by constitutional monarchy as 'a disguise' in times of transition: 'It enables our real leaders to change without heedless people knowing it. The masses of Englishmen are not fit for an elective government; if they knew how near they were to it, they would be surprised, and almost tremble.' Bagehot, *English constitution*, p. 97.

33 D. Duff (ed.), *Victoria in the Highlands: the personal journal of Her Majesty Queen Victoria* (London, 1968), p. 25.

34 A. C. Benson and Viscount Esher (eds.), *Letters of Queen Victoria: 1837–1861*, Vol. 2: *1844–1853* (London, 1908), p. 149.

160   Trevor R. Pringle

35 *Ibid.*, pp. 183–4.
36 Letter in the archive of the Royal Institution, London, dated 'Sunday 15th, 1844' (File No. 1, 70a).
37 For a recent discussion of Landseer and the engraving trade, see A. Dyson, 'Images interpretated: Landseer and the engraving trade', *Print Quarterly*, 1, 1 (March 1984), pp. 29–43.
38 H. Guise, *Great Victorian engravings* (London, 1981).
39 For a brief discussion of the rise of the Art Union of London, see E. Aslin, 'The rise and progress of the Art Union of London', *Apollo*, 85 (1967), pp. 12–16. For a full account of the Art Unions, see House of Commons, *Report and minutes of evidence; select committee on Art Unions* (1845).
40 For a brief discussion of the Print Sellers Association, see *A few words on art . . . containing a short history of the Association* (London, 1881).
41 Barthes, *Mythologies*, p. 123. Bagehot's comment on the Court Circular is perhaps pertinent here: 'We smile at the Court Circular; but remember how many people read the Court Circular! Its use is not in what it says, but in those to whom it speaks.' Bagehot, *English constitution*, p. 85.
42 Barthes made it clear that the structural study of myth could only yield half the truth. The other half must of necessity be obtained by empirical means of contextual study. Although Barthes made this point in his writings he never overstressed it for there was in contemporary Marxism a taboo on formalism. Semiology had to be affirmed in the teeth of the current Marxist orthodoxy, even if this meant a sacrificing or downgrading of empirical modes of analysis. Lavers, *Roland Barthes*, pp. 117, 125.
43 'If we look at history, we shall find that it is only during the period of the present reign that in England the duties of a constitutional sovereign have ever been well performed.' Bagehot, *English constitution*, p. 117.
44 D. Cannadine, 'The context, performance and meaning of ritual: the British monarchy and the "invention of tradition", c.1820–1977', in Hobsbawm and Ranger (eds.), *Invention of tradition*, pp. 101–64.
45 On the Victorian periodical press, see J. Shattock and M. Wolff (eds.), *The Victorian periodical press: samplings and soundings* (Leicester, 1982).
46 Cannadine, 'The context, performance and meaning of ritual', p. 111.
47 *Ibid.*, p. 118.
48 See Hobsbawm's introduction 'Inventing traditions', in Hobsbawm and Ranger, *Invention of tradition*, pp. 1–14.
49 Queen Victoria took the lease on Balmoral on the recommendation of her chief physician, Sir James Clark, who believed the climate would aid her rheumatism. In addition Prince Albert enjoyed both the solitude and the hunting while aspects of the Highland landscape reminded him of Saxe-Coburg.
50 On the development and nature of Scottish nationalism, see C. Harvie, *Scotland and nationalism, Scottish society and politics, 1770–1977* (London, 1977); Brand, *The national movement in Scotland*; R. Mitchison, 'Nineteenth century Scottish nationalism', in R. Mitchison (ed.), *The roots of nationalism: studies in northern Europe* (Edinburgh, 1980).

51 For examples of the Royal Highland myth of today see the various periodicals which proliferate such as *The Royal Magazine* or the frequent articles in the tabloid press. For example, 'Having a lovely time', Sunday Supplement, *News of the World*, 12 August 1984, pp. 16–18.

8

The iconography of nationhood in Canadian art

BRIAN S. OSBORNE

Every mature nation has its symbolic landscapes. They are part of the iconography of nationhood, part of the shared ideas and memories and feelings which bind a people together.

D. W. Meinig, 'Symbolic landscapes'[1]

Artists have been major contributors to the development of such national iconographies.[2] They have documented their periods and places; they have projected the perceptions and values of their sponsoring society; and some artists, mindful of the cultural and national implications of their work, have consciously expressed a corporate sense of cultural or national identity. Whatever their original purpose or meaning, some pictures of places, peoples, and events have become part of this corporate identity and some have become central to it.

For at least one commentator on Canadian cultural identity, the relationship between private and public visions of landscape is profound: 'Visual images form a continuum with our imaginative responses to our contemporary environment. They will if their currency can be increased help to prevent the destruction of many of the elements of our cultural values and respect for the varieties of cultural themes that constitute the cultural whole of Canada.'[3] In this essay, I will search for the development of distinctive Canadian iconography in artistic images of Canadian lands and peoples and in popular responses to these images. To this end I will place the styles and subject matter of several groups of Canadian artists in their geographical, social, intellectual, and political contexts without losing sight of the unique vision of individual artists.[4] Only then can the role of art in the development of a Canadian iconography be adequately understood.[5]

Domesticating a savage land

Northrop Frye, a scholar long concerned with the particulars of the Canadian identity, has concluded that 'Everywhere we turn in Canadian literature and painting, we are haunted by the natural world. Even the most sophisticated Canadian artist can hardly keep something very primitive and archaic out of our imagination.'[6] Nowhere is this more evident than in the art of Canada's indigenous peoples. 'Primitive' and 'archaic' though it may appear to some, it was none the less a sophisticated statement of an integral relationship with their spiritual and material worlds. Northern indigenous carvings on bone and stone, west coast wood carvings, the birch-bark scrolls and masks of the eastern woodlands, and pictography throughout several regions all demonstrate aesthetic as well as worldly and spiritual concerns. In the secular mode, images often represented messages, totemic identifications, simple maps, chronicles of experienced events, or even casual graffiti. Block images, forms, or line drawings could also constitute a pictography of sacred communications, spiritual identity, or chronicles of cosmological events. And often secular and spiritual meanings were not differentiated. Thus, the birch-bark scrolls of the Ojibwa Midewiwin shamans (Fig. 1) may be viewed as two dimensional plans of the ceremonial processional of the long-house as well as a four dimensional statement of arrangements in the spiritual world.[7] And as much as the subject matter, the very media of rock, wood, and bark underscore the primary concern with the natural world and man's place in it. These images reinforced the identity of indigenous peoples with an environment that was at once sacred and mundane.

This integrated view of a 'lived in world' stands in sharp contrast to the views introduced during the colonial period of settlement and development. European renderings of the 'natural world' of North America were more projections of European ideas, values, and tastes than reflections of American realities. Initially, there was an encyclopedic interest in the exotic flora, fauna, and aboriginals and the spirit of scientific empiricism ensured that these were recorded objectively and accurately. But by the mid-nineteenth century, North American landscapes were being moulded into categories advanced by Burke, Gilpin, and Ruskin and their representation was increasingly distorted by the artistic conventions developed in English landscape painting, notably by Constable and Turner. Denis Cosgrove's comment on the Canadian landscapist, George Heriot, is true of the works produced by the scores of other transient and resident artists of the period: 'as is so often the case, it was convention that framed his vision of the new environment he encountered rather than the environment which challenged that vision'.[8]

Thus, the native peoples came to be depicted in the patrician poses of Joseph Brant in William Berczy's portrait of the Mohawk leader, as mere staffage in Lieut. James Peachey's several views of the Loyalist settlements at Cataraqui on Lake Ontario, and as pastoral swain in Cornelius Krieghoff's Chippewa on Lake Superior.[9] But if the ethnographic accuracy of

164 Brian S. Osborne

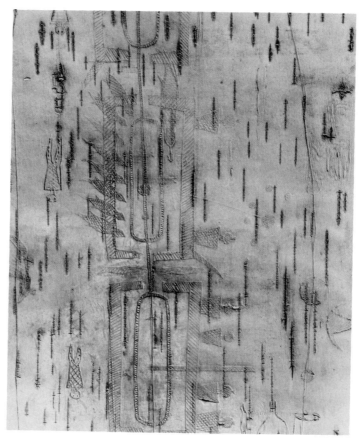

Fig. 1 Detail from an Ojibwa birch-bark scroll. Photograph from the Royal Ontario Museum, Toronto.

a George Catlin and Paul Kane was sacrificed to the Picturesque and Romantic depictions of the native population by others, so was topographical accuracy. The search for the Sublime was rewarded by the prospects of the Montmorency Falls, Niagara, and the Thousand Islands of the St Lawrence. And if the Picturesque was more elusive, William Bartlett or Cornelius Krieghoff could reproduce it in their images of new settlements, complete with a dash of bucolic comfort. Bartlett's forests are overbearing but his pioneers' homesteads look promising. If Krieghoff's winter scenes do not stint on snow they are Bruegelian in their jollity and contentment. For these and other European artists, a primitive and archaic Canada was appealingly picturesque.

For some Canadians, however, such imaginative renderings of their world

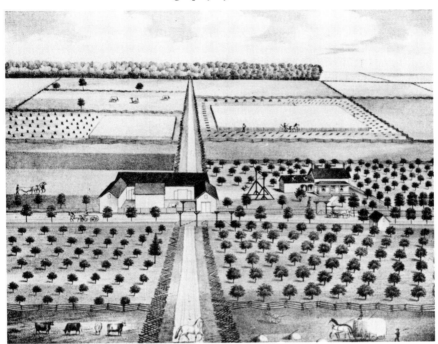

Fig. 2 'Residence of D. Y. Williams, J.P., Concession 5, Lot 69, Hiller Township, Ontario', from *The illustrated atlas of the counties of Hastings and Prince Edward, Ontario* (Toronto, 1878).

were an affront to hard won accomplishments and driving ambitions. The natural environment was being doggedly transformed into a cultural landscape and throughout much of Canada the first battle was with the forests. 'A Canadian settler hates a tree, regards it as his natural enemy, something to be destroyed, eradicated, annihilated by all and every means', noted one early nineteenth-century traveller through Ontario.[10] The disorderliness of the 'wilderness' was to be replaced by the cultivated and geometrical order of the domesticated world. Counties, townships, farmsteads, fields, and gardens, all were to be laid out, at least on paper, in patterns foreign to the natural world. Nowhere was this better achieved than in the genre of *Illustrated county atlases* which by the 1880s had become popular vehicles for recording the gentrification of much of rural Ontario and Quebec. The foregrounds of the plates (Fig. 2) are dominated by such symbols of domestic prosperity as the Georgian or Victorian Gothic house and its gardens and lawns; the middle ground is a landscape of productivity replete with crops, livestock, and progressive equipment. Only in the distant rear ground is the forest to be found, corseted into the productive woodlot of the 'back forty'.[11] Similar fabrications of accomplishment and progress are to be found in the work of rural primitives such as Joseph Swift, Ebenezer Birrell, and James Kenyon.[12] These itinerant artists obliged their rural patrons with images of farmland more improved by their brushes than by their patrons' labours, and stocked them with livestock that owe more to the stereotypical drawings in agricultural journals than to the actual results of the scientific breeding these journals advocated.

Even the winter had to go! The romanticization of such essential Canadian verities as snow, ice, and frontier life could not be allowed to obstruct the objectives of Canada's boosters. Accordingly, 'typical' Canadian scenes in the 1881 Christmas edition of the London *Graphic*, together with that season's Christmas greeting cards, provoked hostility because they contributed to 'our country's ill favoured reputation ... as a land of snow and ice, of Indians and half breeds, and of bears and fur overcoats'.[13] This editorial of 1881 in Kingston's *British Whig* was dramatically titled a 'Libel On Our Land'. It continued:

One might also doubt whether English artists ever get a glimpse of Canadian homes and public and private festivities, so prone are they to select scenes as foreign to the experience of the bulk of the people of the Dominion as they are curious to European eyes. A Xmas market in Kingston, for instance, would be a far worthier view than the 'Graphic' has yet produced in Canada's name.

The environment in its raw, alien, undisciplined state was an embarrassment, an unacceptable image in an improving world and running counter to the metropolitan aspirations and boosterism so typical of late nineteenth-century Canada. Artists were called upon to assist in the work of transformation.

Recording a nation's heritage

New images were needed for an increasingly self-confident young nation. The late nineteenth and early twentieth centuries were heady times for Canadian nationalism. Confederation had been only a constitutional start and Canadian national identity was much further advanced by the realization of the national dream of coast to coast rail communication, the completion of such major projects as the all-Canadian lock at Sault Ste Marie, and the participation of Canadians in World War I. By producing a national historiography, Canadian scholars such as H. A. Innis, D. Creighton, and A. R. M. Lower contributed much to this nascent national identity.[14] In the visual arts, picturesque and pioneering stereotypes gave way to attempts to represent the regionally distinctive cultural landscapes emerging throughout Canada. C. W. Jefferys, Daniel Fowler, and Homer Watson painted carefully the characteristic fences, lanes, and farmsteads of late nineteenth-century Ontario, bringing a regional landscape to national attention.[15] James Morrice and Maurice Cullen did the same for Quebec while with the help of the Canadian Pacific, Otto Jacobi, Lucius O'Brien, and John A. Fraser transferred their attention from eastern landscapes to popularize the grandeur of the Canadian west and so incorporated this region as a symbol of emerging national consciousness.[16]

Remarkably, a more didactic style of patriotic art did not develop. In late nineteenth-century Europe, realism in art and nationalist fervour found a mutual interest in the ordinary, the commonplace, the vernacular. America's 'West' was recorded and idealized – if not fictionalized – by Frederic Remington, Charles Russell, and others.[17] In Australia Tom Roberts, Arthur Streeton, and Charles Condor contributed substantially to an iconography of the 'outback'. Indeed, in 1890, Roberts asked: 'What Should Australian Artists Paint?', and himself answered: 'it should be the ambition of our artists to present on canvas the earnestness, vigour, pathos and heroism of the life around them'.[18] Roberts and his fellow artists did paint townscapes and portraits but it was their scenes of labour on sheep and cattle stations and mining claims, of the daily routine and unique events of life in the 'bush' that helped develop a special if stereotypical identity with the land and life of Australia. Canada lacked the 'hairy chested impressionism' so prominent in Australian and American art.[19] Its rural landscapes were being repatriated from European artistic conventions but the style of Jefferys, Fowler, and Cullen was bucolic rather than heroic, mundane not mythological.

Some Canadian artists were, however, attracted to chauvinistic themes. Despite her representations of scenes throughout rural Quebec, Frances Hopkins is best known for her sensitive depictions of canoe travel in all its forms (Fig. 3), including renderings of 'six fathom freight canoes', the 'canoe de maitre', 'three-and-a-half fathom express canoes', and their crews, cargoes, and passengers, gliding quietly through sylvan scenes, picking their way through mists on the Great Lakes, shooting through impressive rapids, or camped for the evening along the shore.[20] William Armstrong also recorded life on Canada's expanding western frontier. While he faithfully documented such technological wonders as Ontario's railroads and steamboats, as well as more prosaic emblems of progress such as Toronto's water-mains and rolling-mills, it was his images of the lands and peoples to the north and west of the Great Lakes which received public acclaim. Armstrong travelled west with the 1870 expedition sent to subdue the Riel Rebellion, an epic episode in nationalist history. His artistic record of the lands being traversed, and of the native population encountered, did much to incorporate this hitherto remote region in the national imagination at the same time as it was being incorporated politically on the ground.[21]

Fig. 3   Frances Hopkins, *Canoe Manned by Voyageurs*, 1869. Oil on canvas. Public Archives of Canada, Picture Division.

If chauvinism was rare in high art, it was certainly common and indeed powerful in such popular works of illustration as the Toronto Art Student's League calendars depicting scenes from Canadian life, in Henry Sandham's illustrations of the stories published by the Thomas Nelson company, in Adam Shirriff Scott's calendars commissioned to sell Molson's beer, and in Clarence Gagnon's illustrations of the life of 'les braves colons' for Louis Hemon's *Maria Chapdelaine*.[22] In Canada, as elsewhere, illustrators did much to further national identity through the wide circulation of their images.

C. W. Jefferys was both illustrator and fine-artist. He felt a responsibility to use his artistic talents to further a better appreciation of Canadian history and national identity and did so in over 2,000 illustrations. In an article in the *Canadian Historical Review* in 1936, Jefferys argued for the utility of 'imaginative reconstructions' in 'arousing popular interest in historical subjects'.[23] And in the preface to his three volume study, *The pictorial gallery of Canadian history*, Jefferys declared that

The history of a country is to be read not only in its written or printed records. These, while of the greatest value and importance, do not tell us all we desire to know. Old buildings, early architecture, tools, vehicles, weapons and clothing, contemporary pictures of people, places and events must be examined to fill out the story.[24]

It is thus not surprising that Jefferys moved on several fronts. He illustrated Canadian literary classics like Richardson's *Wacousta*, Kirby's *The golden dog*, Haliburton's *The clockmaker*, and several of Marjorie Pickthall's popular historical novels. Moreover, commissioned by the Ontario Department of Education to illustrate history texts, he created an idealized national history for future generations of Canadians with his Romantic representations of such events as Count Frontenac's landing at Cataraqui, the Battle of Lundy's Lane, and the 1837 rebels drilling in North York. Nor is it surprising that Jefferys also portrayed such mundane frontier scenes as the circuit rider, the village dance, grain threshing, preparing pearl ash, and clearing land. In pen and ink he recorded the paraphernalia of the everyday world – artillery and uniforms, carioles and sleighs, carpenters' tools and smithies – and interspersed them throughout his illustrations of Canada's past.[25] If Jefferys' settings are humble, his characters are often heroic, their proportions and poses reminiscent of European 'social realism' (Fig. 4). In the words of a modern admirer, Jefferys 'reserved his highest honours for men and women cast in heroic mould ... the pioneer homesteader, trapper, woodsman, and homemaker, those who stood at the frontier of many kinds, who stood face to face with life, and who begged no favours. He interpreted them with unfailing insight and compassion.'[26]

The search for a national symbol

While a national historical identity was well served by the efforts of Canada's historical illustrators, it was the work of Tom Thomson and the 'Group of Seven' which contributed most to the development of a national identification with a distinctive sense of place. Indeed, the Group's avowed mission was the enhancement of Canadian national identity. The catalogue to their 1920 exhibition trumpeted this patriotic purpose: 'The group of seven artists whose pictures are here exhibited have for several years held a like vision concerning Art in Canada. They are all imbued with the idea that an Art must grow and flower in the land before the country will be a real home for its people.'[27] This was an 'Art' that 'sincerely interprets the spirit of a nation's growth', one 'of real value to the country'.[28]

While individual members of the Group of Seven painted various subjects – portraits, still lifes, mining camps, townscapes and a range of regional landscapes – the Group collectively became known for their images of a primordial, unpeopled 'North' (Fig. 5). For Ronald Nasgaard the reason for this lies beyond the context of Canada alone; it must be sought in the broader setting of the Symbolist landscape movement in Finland, Norway, and Sweden, in which the 'North' was already a focus of nationalist feeling.[29] Nasgaard sees the first phase of this movement covering the period 1890 to 1910 and including the works of the Norwegians Edvard Munch and Harald Sohlberg, the Finn Akseli Gallen-Kallela, Ferdinand Hodler from Switzerland, Piet Mondrian from Holland, and Karl Nordstrom from Sweden. Tom Thomson and the core members of the Group of Seven became aware of these Scandinavian landscapists through an exhibition

Fig. 4   C. W. Jefferys, *Louis-Joseph Papineau Addressing an Election Crowd in the 1830s*, c.1921. Watercolour over pencil. Public Archives of Canada, Picture Division.

held in Buffalo in 1913. Indeed, Nasgaard argues that 'the Canadians, despite their originality within their own context, and their uncontestable vitality, invite classification as the final stage of nineteenth century northern Romantic landscape painting'.[30]

Also influential was the Theosophist view that a spiritual, cultural, and aesthetic renaissance would come from the 'North'. For one of the Group, Lawren Harris, a northern artistic focus would result in a 'clear native expression', a call 'from the clear, replenishing, Virgin north'. His 'Revelation of art in Canada' published in the *Canadian Theosophist* identifies several environmental determinants of Canadian greatness:

Fig. 5   Lawren Harris, *Icebergs, Davis Strait*, 1930. Oil on canvas. McMichael
Canadian Collection.

With us in Canada painting is the only art that has so far achieved a clear, native
expression and so the forming distinctive attitude, the creative direction of the
genius of our people, and their higher aspirations are to be detected in it. Indeed
a new vision is coming into art in Canada. It is a direct effect of the interplay
of capacity and environment and moves into manipulation straight through the
muddle of perishable imported notions.[31]

This interplay between 'capacity and environment' was much influenced
by very specific, and very 'Canadian', psycho-ecological forces which smack
of the racist and environmentalist credos of Canadian chauvinists a generation earlier. For one of these, George R. Parkin, Canada's national unity
was favoured by a 'northern climate' which excluded the 'negro', the 'Italian
organgrinder', and weaker races which would not fit in with 'Anglo-Saxon
institutions', a climate which furthered 'progress', 'democratic spirit', and
a 'high and powerful form of civilization'.[32] While not as inflammatory
as Parkin's, Harris' credo strikes the familiar environmentalist chords with
references to

the charged air, the clarity and spaciousness of our north country. For it has in it a call from the clear, replenishing, Virgin north that must resound in the greater, freer depths of the soul or there can be no response ... we are in the fringe of the great North and its living whiteness, its loneliness and replenishment, its resignations and release, its call and answer – its cleansing rhythms. It seems that the top of the continent is a source of spiritual flow that will ever shed clarity into the growing race of America, and we Canadians being closest to this source seem destined to produce an art somewhere different from our southern fellows – an art more spacious, of a greater living quiet, perhaps of a more certain conviction of eternal values. We were not placed between the Southern teeming of men and the ample replenishing North for nothing.[33]

The artist, 'because of his constant habit of awareness and his disciplined expression' is better equipped to 'interpret [the "North"] to others' and 'create living works' by using 'forms, colour, rhythms and moods, to make a harmonious home for the imaginative and spiritual meaning it has evoked in him'.[34] The 'North' was instilled into the artist's 'outlook' through 'the bodily effect of the very coolness and clarity of its air, the feel of soil and rocks, the rhythms of its hills and the roll of its valleys, from its clear skies, great waters, endless little lakes, streams and forests, from snows and horizons of swift silver'.[35] These were the defining themes of the Group of Seven: rock, rolling topography, expansive skies, water in all its forms, trees and forests, and the symbolic white snow and ice of the 'strong North'.

Whatever its lineage, the work of the Group of Seven came to dominate Canadians' self-images, or at least, the images of their country. An ideology of northern distinctiveness became central to the iconography of Canadian landscape.

Icons of nationhood

An artistic icon must be revered to be meaningful and by a significant proportion of the populace if it is to be an effective symbol of nationhood. Fine art, however appealing to the cognoscenti, has little opportunity to become part of the nationalist imagination if it is sequestered in the art galleries of metropolitan centres or the salons of high society. This is, of course, especially true if it is seen to exhibit foreign styles and subjects. And neither will 'primitive', 'folk', or 'popular' art become iconic. Illustrations in county atlases, paintings of rural homes by itinerants, and boosterish views of towns and cities may reveal the expectations and priorities of broader segments of society but they are too specific, in style and subject matter, to strike a responsive chord in the nation as a whole. But on occasion, a particular genre emerges which not only meets with the approval of the artistic community but becomes known by, and popular with, most citizens. This was the case with Canada's Group of Seven and, to some extent, with C. W. Jefferys and his fellow illustrators. Its success lay in the meeting of the artists' own sense of mission and a growing awareness of a discrete nationalism, propagated by various cultural and political agencies seeking to cultivate a distinctive Canadian, neither American nor British, sense of place.

But the consensus did not last. Tom Thomson and the Group of Seven's images of the Algonquin, the Shield 'north of Superior', and the symbolist polar landscapes of Harris' far north were inappropriate symbols for all of Canada. For some Canadians, they only represented a replacement of one set of foreign images by another equally removed, emanating from metropolitan Toronto, an 'Uppity Canada'. While the metaphor of the 'North' suited Harris' Theosophist formulations, it could not comprehend Canada's continental scope. The particulars of the Maritime east are better appreciated through the marine and littoral settings of Alex Colville, Tom Forrestall, Lawren Harris, Christopher Pratt, and Tom Zuick. The essence of rural Quebec can be approached through Andre Bieler's and Marc-Aurele Fortin's views of the Laurentians and Frances Hopkins' and A. Y. Jackson's renderings of the 'rangs'. And there was an Ontario to the south of Algonquin and Superior, a 'middle landscape' captured by Daniel Fowler and C. W. Jefferys. For the Prairies, William Kurelek and Robert Hurley looked along the lines of roads and fences and focussed on the intersections of horizontal skylines and vertical forms (Fig. 6). The Pacific coast had its own advocates: Edward Hughes, Donald Jarvis, Jack Shadbolt, F. H. Varley, and, most notably, Emily Carr developing images of the unique conjunction of Pacific shores and cordilleran forests.[36]

Even in art Canadian diversity is cultural as much as it is environmental. Carr's celebration of the Pacific coast peoples, Bieler's vignettes of community life in rural Quebec, and Kurelek's impressions of the vernacular world of the Prairies all serve to underscore the empty, natural worlds of the Canadian symbolic landscape tradition. Nowhere is the expression of cultural rather than environmental identity stronger than in the work of the so-called 'Indian Group of Seven' (Fig. 7). Founded in the early 1970s, and much influenced by the work of Norval Morrisseau, their work combines modern western art techniques with indigenous iconography. Indeed, it has been argued that this art constitutes 'a revival of traditional art forms as well as a redefinition of "Indianness" in the context of contemporary and multi-cultural Canadian society'.[37]

No one iconography can encompass Canada's diversity. As Northrop Frye maintains:

A culture which is the expression of a specific community is in contrast to a mass culture which tends towards uniformity rather than unity, and towards the obliterating of the specific and distinctive ... Every part of Canada is shut off by its geography. Everywhere ... we find solitudes touching solitudes: every part of Canada has strong separatist feelings, because every part of it is in fact a separation.[38]

Fig. 6   William Kurelek, *The Devil's Wedding*, 1967. Mixed media on masonite. Collection of James Richardson and Sons Ltd, Winnipeg, Manitoba.

Fig. 7   Roy Thomas, *Art of My People*, 1983. Acrylic on canvas. Collection of Lorraine Hullachen, Toronto.

But this is the case in nations other than Canada. Recent, cultural history suggests that the predictions by Marshall McLuhan of the erosion of cultural particularism in a 'global village' are premature, if not misplaced. 'Separatist feelings' are still vigorous and they derive their vigour from affirming their own iconographies against the forces which threaten them. To be sure, creating a cultural iconography may involve 'inventing' traditions as well as reviving them,[39] but this does not necessarily weaken it. Icons may continue to be effective, even if composed of base metal.

NOTES

1 D. W. Meinig, 'Symbolic landscapes: some idealizations of American communities', in D. W. Meinig (ed.), *The interpretation of ordinary landscapes* (Oxford, 1979), p. 164.
2 See also Brian S. Osborne, 'The artist as historical commentator: Thomas Burrowes and the Rideau Canal', *Archivaria*, 17 (1983–4), pp. 41–59; Brian S. Osborne, 'Art and the historical geography of nineteenth century Ontario: an humanistic approach', in F. Helleiner (ed.), *Cultural dimensions of Canada's geography: proceedings of the German-Canadian symposium, August 28–September 11, 1983* (Occasional Paper 10, Department of Geography, Trent University, Peterborough, 1984). Similar themes have also been developed in several excellent pieces by Ronald Rees: 'Images of the prairie: landscape painting and perception in Canadian art', *Canadian Geographer*, 20 (1976), pp. 259–78; 'Landscapes in art', in K. Butzer (ed.), *Dimensions of human geography* (Chicago, 1978); 'In a strange land . . . homesick pioneers on the Canadian prairie', *Landscape* (1982), pp. 1–9; *Land of earth and sky: landscape painting of western Canada* (Saskatoon, 1984). See also, Greg Spurgeon, 'Pictures and history: the art museum and visual arts archives', *Archivaria*, 17 (1983–4), pp. 60–74.
3 Michael Bell, 'Why look at this stuff?', *The roles of documentary art in understanding a cultural heritage* (Proceedings of a Conference held at the Art Gallery, Mount Saint Vincent University, Halifax, Nova Scotia, 31 October 1980), p. 40.
4 Michael Rosenthal argues that, like all historical documents, landscape paintings must be placed in the context of their times: 'The chief problem the art historian faces is the virtually insurmountable one of turning the visual into the verbal. If we are to consider a landscape painting in any way historically it is wilful to ignore any leads which might bear on the work. These may range from seeing to what extent, if any, the landscape painting may relate to some site . . . to comparing it with other pictures to see how typical or atypical it may be of its period. It may be useful to have biographical data for the artist. Or the historian might read through pages of nature poetry contemporary with the painting . . . All the time, though, it is accepted that any historical account of a picture must be approximate and, therefore, that anything which may tighten the focus must not be ignored.' Michael Rosenthal, 'Approaches to landscape painting', *Landscape Research*, 9 (1984), p. 2. Rosenthal is a leading practitioner

of a 'new' history of landscape art that emphasizes the social and ideological implications of painting. See also Michael Rosenthal, *Constable, the painter and his landscape* (New Haven and London, 1983); John Barrell, *The dark side of the landscape: the rural poor in English painting 1730–1840* (Cambridge, 1980); David Solkin, *Richard Wilson: the landscape of reaction* (London, 1982). More traditional art historians have their misgivings: 'The economic, social and ideological history affecting art is a subject art historians cannot afford to ignore ... But there are dangers which can attach to [this] approach: too hard a search for meaning in works of art, so that staffage, for example, may be invested with spurious symbolism, over-enthusiasm in the use of evidence in support of an hypothesis, an underlying rigidity in basic assumptions.' J. Hayes, 'The painture of prosperity', *The Times Literary Supplement*, 25 November 1983, pp. 1299–300.

5 For those not familiar with Canadian art, the following are excellent surveys: D. Reid, *A concise history of Canadian painting* (Toronto, 1973); J. R. Harper, *Painting in Canada: a history* (Toronto, 1974); M. Bell, *Painters in a new land* (Toronto, 1973); B. Lord, *The history of painting in Canada: toward a people's art* (Toronto, 1974). In this essay I will refer to some recent exhibitions which are suggesting alternative perspectives on Canadian art.

6 Northrop Frye, *Toronto Globe and Mail*, 18 October 1977; for a fuller development of this theme, see his *Bush garden: essays on the Canadian imagination* (Toronto, 1971).

7 Elizabeth McLuhan and Tom Hill, *Norval Morrisseau and the emergence of the image makers* (Toronto, 1984).

8 Denis Cosgrove, review of Gerald Finley, *George Heriot: Postmaster-Painter of the Canadas* (Toronto, 1983), in *American Review of Canadian Studies*, 14 (1984), pp. 234–7; see also, Hugh Honour, *The European vision of American* (Cleveland, 1975).

9 For more on this, see Osborne, 'The artist as historical commentator', and Honour, *European vision*.

10 Anna Jameson, *Winter studies and summer rambles in Canada* (Toronto, 1938; republished 1965).

11 B. May and F. McGuire, *County atlases of Canada: a descriptive catalogue* (Ottawa, 1970).

12 See also J. R. Harper, *A people's art: primitive, naive, and folk painting in Canada* (Toronto, 1974).

13 *Daily British Whig*, 6 December 1881.

14 C. Berger, *The writing of Canadian history* (Toronto, 1976).

15 F. K. Smith, *Daniel Fowler of Amherst Island, 1810–1894* (Kingston, 1979); R. Stacey, *Charles William Jefferys, 1869–1951* (Kingston, 1976).

16 D. Reid, *Our own country Canada: being an account of the principal landscape artists in Montreal and Toronto, 1860–1890* (Ottawa, 1975).

17 See Brian W. Dippie, *Remington and Russell* (Austin, 1982); also, John C. Ewers, 'Fact and fiction in the documentary art of the American west', in John F. McDermott (ed.), *The frontier re-examined* (Urbana, 1967).

18 Quoted in Virginia Spate, *Tom Roberts* (Melbourne, 1978), p. 86.

19 Michael McNay, 'A brush with the burning bush', *Manchester Guardian Weekly*, 27 May 1984, p. 21. McNay concludes: 'Painting is, after all, rooted in time and place and a cultural parochialism is the first essential of universality.' For Canada in the nineteenth century the work of William Cruikshank (1849–1922), Wyatt Eaton (1849–96), Robert Harris (1849–1919), Adolphe Vogt (1843–71), Homer Watson (1855–1936), and Inglis Sheldon-Williams (1870–1940) merit further attention as recorders of the vernacular and heroic.

20 M. Rand, 'Rediscovering voyageur artist Frances Hopkins', *Canadian Geographic Magazine*, 102 (1982), pp. 22–9.

21 Henry C. Campbell, *Early days on the Great Lakes: the art of William Armstrong* (Toronto, 1971).

22 Harper, *A People's art*; see also Fern Beyer, *The Ontario collection* (Toronto, 1984); Jim Burant, 'The visual world in the Victorian age', *Archivaria*, 19 (1984–5), pp. 110–21.

23 C. W. Jefferys, 'The visual reconstruction of history', *Canadian Historical Review*, 17 (1936), pp. 249–65.

24 Quoted in Robert Stacey, '"Salvage for us these fragments"': C. W. Jefferys and Ontario's historic architecture', *Ontario History*, 70 (1978), pp. 147–70.

25 For specific examples of Jefferys' illustrations of historical literature, see John Richardson, *Wacousta: a tale of the Pontiac conspiracy* (Chicago, 1906); William Kirby, *The golden dog: a romance of old Quebec* (Toronto, 1925); Marjorie L. C. Pickthall, *Dick's desertion: a boy's adventure in Canadian forests, a tale of the early settlement of Ontario* (London, 1906); Marjorie L. C. Pickthall, *The straight road: adventure in the backwoods of Canada* (Toronto, 1906); Marjorie L. C. Pickthall, *Billy's hero, or the valley of gold* (Toronto, 1908); C. W. Jefferys, *Sam Slick in pictures: the best of the humour of Thomas Chandler Haliburton* (Toronto, 1956). For more direct historical artistic commentary see his work in George Wrong, *The story of Canada* (Toronto, 1929); C. W. Jefferys, *Dramatic episodes in Canada's story* (Toronto, 1930); C. W. Jefferys, *The pictorial gallery of Canadian history*, 3 vols. (Toronto, 1942–50); Harry Symons, *Fences* (Toronto, 1958).

26 Lorne Pierce, Address at the unveiling of plaque commemorating C. W. Jefferys, York Mills, Ontario, 30 August 1960.

27 *Group of seven*, Catalogue to exhibition of paintings at Art Museum of Toronto, 7–27 May 1920 (Toronto, 1920) n.p.

28 *Ibid.*

29 Ronald Nasgaard, *The mystic north: symbolistic landscape painting in Northern Europe and North America, 1890–1940* (Toronto, 1984).

30 *Ibid.*, p. 8.

31 Lawren Harris, 'Revelation of art in Canada: a history', *The Canadian Theosophist* (1926), pp. 85–8.

32 George R. Parkin, *Imperial federalism: the problem of national unity* (London and New York, 1892). For more on this theme, see G. Rawlyk, 'Canadian-American relations: the view from the North' (Paper presented at the Meetings of Ontario Historical Geographers and Eastern Historical Geography Association, Kingston, 1984).

33 Harris, 'Revelation of art in Canada', pp. 85–6.

34 *Ibid.*, p. 86.
35 *Ibid.* An exhibition of Lawren Harris' work at the Art Gallery of Ontario in 1985 further explores the relationship between his art and Theosophy. See, *Atma Buddhi Manas: the later works of Lawren Harris* (Toronto, 1985).
36 P. White, review of 'Coasts, the sea and Canadian art' at The Gallery, Stratford, in *Toronto Globe and Mail*, 29 July 1978.
37 Ruth Phillips and Valda Blundell quoted in McLuhan and Hill, *Norval Morrisseau*, p. 26.
38 Frye, *Toronto Globe and Mail*, 18 October 1977.
39 See Eric Hobsbawm and Terence Ranger (eds.), *The invention of tradition* (Cambridge, 1983); Donald Horne, *The Great Museum: the re-presentation of history* (London, 1984). For a provocative discussion of emerging symbols of nation and region see Victoria Konrad, 'Symbolic landscapes of nationalism and regionalism' (Paper presented at the Conference of Australia and New Zealand Association of Canadian Studies, University of Canterbury, Christchurch, 1984).

9

Rhetoric of the western interior: modes of environmental description in American promotional literature of the nineteenth century

G. MALCOLM LEWIS

In the nineteenth century emigrant guides and the promotional publications of emigrant aid societies, territorial and state agencies and local interest groups were arguably the most effective disseminators of information about the western interior of the United States.[1] Now largely forgotten, somewhat difficult to retrieve and usually dismissed as vernacular, their content has not received as much retrospective attention as that of the region's literature of exploration and travel, official reports or accounts of scientific surveys. Yet, because they were written for outsiders – potential investors and intending transmigrants, settlers and tourists – they are invaluable sources of descriptions of what environments and landscapes were supposed to be, would be found to be or ought eventually to be like. Their importance as sources of this type of information is enhanced by the large number published between about 1820 and the end of the century and the variety of, as well as rate of change in, the natural environment and settlement conditions within the million square mile region which, in full or in part, they described and promoted.

This essay draws on 37 guides and 101 promotional publications. It focuses on purpose, meaning and the modes of environmental and landscape description they employed.

The literature

Emigrant guides were prominent in the period preceding the Civil War. Frequently substantial and sometimes impressive, they were produced for sale by publishing houses and printers in Europe as well as the United States. In most cases both the author and publisher seem to have hoped to profit solely from their sales and advertizing income. Promotional literature produced by land and cattle companies appeared from the 1820s onwards but as a genre it began to equal the emigrant guides in importance only with the emergence of railroad, territorial, state, county and local interests in the years immediately before the Civil War. Thereafter, it dominated and soon eclipsed the emigrant guides. It was almost all free, produced by the newest printing techniques and reflected fashionable concepts of style and design.

Both categories of literature were apparently authoritative, up to date and responsive to events within or impacting upon the interior. They were usually written specifically for potential investors, transmigrants, settlers and, last in time and of least importance, tourists. Content was often plagiarized, with or without acknowledgement of sources. After the Civil War, at least, they transmitted descriptions of environment and landscape over a wide geographical range with an efficacy not to be surpassed until the advent of popular cinema. The descriptions were intended to create images: images which, in turn, were calculated to influence decision making in favour of investment, migration, settlement and travel for pleasure.

Authorship, especially of promotional literature, was often unacknowledged but most authors are known to have had, or gave the impression of having, some experience of the area they described, gained in the course of work, trade or profession. Authors came from a wide spectrum of backgrounds, and included farmers, physicians, politicians, soldiers, lawyers, surveyors, government officials, newspaper editors, company directors, preachers, real estate dealers and sundry entrepreneurs.

Although illustrated by engravings, tables, maps and, towards the end of the century, photographs, most of the content consisted of text. Style of writing varied but tended to be popular and to become simpler with the ascendancy of promotional literature after mid-century and with the concern, after the Civil War, to attract less well-educated settlers from within and outside the United States.

By no means all the content was concerned with environment and landscape. Some was historical, some predictive and there was much practical advice concerning such issues as ways and means of getting to the interior, surviving the first few months, selecting and acquiring land, obtaining loans and deciding when to sow. Nevertheless, on average, descriptions of regions, environment, landscape and locale together occupied about 40 per cent of the text and vied for dominance with accounts of resources, livelihood, healthfulness, freedom, opportunity and predictions of ultimate prosperity.

Messages and modes

Guides and promotional literature were explicitly written to influence readers' decisions by attracting and facilitating selection. Guides stressed the principles of spatial selection in choosing between routes, places, areas and types of land. Promotional literature stressed the attractiveness of particular routes, places, areas and types of land. But the types of publication differed only in the balance of these purposes, and in practice they were often inextricably mixed. Influenced by a contemporary awareness of evolution, reflecting the widespread belief in social progress and the potential of science to solve problems, and fully aware of the major social and economic changes which were occurring or anticipated in the interior, both types of publication were strongly temporal. Focusing on the contemporary, they stressed the future and indicated the nature of changes by reference to past conditions which had already been modified or even disappeared. Since, almost without exception, the literature had utilitarian purposes, 'independent' description, presented for its own sake, was rare. 'Associative' and 'dissociative' descriptions were much commoner: the former to indicate or predict the association of desirable attributes with particular or generic types of landscape and environment, and the latter to indicate the absence of hazards and disadvantages known to exist in similar, adjacent or competing areas.

I shall examine these independent, dissociative and associative uses of environmental and landscape description and show how they deployed the techniques of classical rhetoric.

Independent description

Descriptions conveying images of landscape and environment but presented without an obvious utilitarian meaning were rare. Where they did occur their implicit intention was to attract by presenting a picturesque image, conveying a sense of variety or emphasizing the absence of landscapes which were either monotonous or austere. An emigrants' guide to Iowa Territory contained a long description of the 'Face of the Country' which ended with the summary statement that, unlike many prairie regions, the mixture of woodland with prairie was well suited 'to the wants and conveniences of the husbandman'. The earlier and longer part of the description had served to attract by conveying an impression of variety but without focusing on associated resources, potential or the absence of hazards and limitations:

The general aspect of the country is one of unrivalled beauty, ... it is what may be termed moderately undulating, no part of the territory being traversed by mountains, or even high hills, (if we except the northern or mineral region, where the hills and mounds are of considerable magnitude); on the margin of rivers, there are frequent ranges of 'bluffs', or calcareous strata of lime rock, intersected with ravines. The southern portion of the territory may be termed the most picturesque, abounding with grassy lawns and verdant vales, interspersed with groves and meandering rivulets. The northern parts would seem to partake more of the bold and striking. The traveller here beholds the hill-top covered with towering oaks to its lofty summit ... the river tumbling its crested form over precipitous ledges of cragged rocks ... the spiral cliffs and massy ledges grouped in fantastic forms amidst the cultivated valley ... The territory is remarkably well watered by beautiful rivers and creeks, the margins of which are skirted with woodlands and groves.[2]

This work was published in Britain where landscape studies were still dominated by the picturesque and where the fascination with geology was undimmed.

In promotional literature published within the United States such independent descriptions were rarer, shorter and less lyrical. They occurred occasionally, in literature promoting local areas. For example, according to a booklet promoting Fillmore County in southeastern Nebraska, 'No pen or pencil can give adequate portraiture to [its] ... topographical charms ..., which in common with the entire Blue river country, abounds in long reaches of graceful billowy prairie with intervening valleys coursed by clear, winding, forest-fringed streams and presents a pastoral landscape as fair and inviting as an oriental garden.'[3] The tourist literature published by the railroad companies towards the end of the century might have been expected to include more examples of such independent description, but it contains very little. Written to attract tourists to cross the interior, it extolled the scenic attractions of the Rocky Mountains and trans Rocky Mountain West ignoring the less spectacular scenery to be seen from the railcar window *en route*. The Santa Fe Route's lavish tour handbook, *To California and back*, was typical. The cis Rocky Mountain interior contained approximately 15 per cent of the route but received less than 1 per cent of the attention. On the outward journey the route beyond Hutchinson, Kansas, was merely described as following 'the windings of the Arkansas River, with only occasional digressions'.[4] On the return journey, at La Junta, Colorado, the 'marvels of the West' were said to have been 'left behind, and the tourist may be expected to be absorbed in pleasurable anticipation of his home-coming'.[5] Whenever the author assumed that the reader was neither faced with the prospect of settling, investing in or making his own way across the interior in the pre-railroad era, its landscapes and environments received very little attention.

Dissociative and associative descriptions

Dissociative and associative environmental descriptions served that part of rhetoric known as *style*. By the early nineteenth century the other four parts of rhetoric – invention, arrangement, memory and delivery – were in decline in the United States with the increasing concern to communicate with the common man in ways he could understand.[6] Style embraced the use of figures of words and figures of thought, devices or patterns of 'language in which meaning is changed or enhanced'.[7] Throughout the nineteenth century these continued to be used, particularly in popular expository prose, of which promotional literature was an important sub genre.

Dissociative descriptions

Dissociative descriptions were made in communicating the advantages of the area, place or route being promoted in relation to others which were better known, already settled or competing for attention. Each employed some form of *antithesis*. For example, in promoting Barnes County, North Dakota, the First National Bank of Valley City claimed that it was 'remarkably exempt from the casualties [droughts, floods and plagues of insects] which inflict the country south and west of it'.[8] Similarly, though at a vastly different scale, the Union Pacific Railway's Passenger Department claimed that Montana Territory did not have the equivalents of

the illimitable and monotonous level prairies which distinguish some Mississippi Valley States, the vast impenetrable forests which were encountered and struggled with for years away 'down East', and in which a settler could hardly carve a home in one life-time, or the marshy low lands of the [Great] Lake[s] region, whose enervating atmosphere needs no mention here.[9]

In promoting the idea of a transcontinental railroad Asa Whitney first suggested three possible routes across the interior: southern, central and northern. He was adopting a form of *division* (into kinds or classes). After describing each of these in general rather than engineering terms he then evaluated them, a form of *deliberato* (the evaluation of possible courses of action). Such evaluation was overwhelmingly in favour of the northern route because, among other things, he claimed it as the only one

which could furnish, on the commencement of its line, timber and materials for the work and for the settlement of the country for almost the entire line ... where the climate would permit us to take our vast products from the soil to the markets of all Asia [refrigeration had not then been developed so that food would deteriorate if transported by a more southerly route] ... where all the streams from ocean to ocean could be bridged ... [and] which could carry and sustain almost an entire line of settlement with it to the Pacific Ocean.[10]

Dissociative descriptions were used to influence particular groups of people by playing on their supposed fears or dislikes. A Connecticut-born Baptist preacher was probably trying to attract settlers from southern New England when, having described the seasonally 'inundated lands' of Illinois, with their fertile soils but unhealthy miasmas, he claimed that they could 'be reclaimed at much less expense than the swamps and salt marshes of the Atlantic states'.[11] Similarly, an emigrant guide from New York introduced the supposed advantage of the Texan winter by dissociating it from the city where a 'deep gloom settled on the countenances of the poor, as well as on the face of nature ... [and] the cry of the widow and orphan is heard in [the] streets begging for wood and for bread'. At the same season in rural New York

the houseless and pitiless stranger is wading through deep and untrodden snow to seek shelter from the severe cold and the storm – the trees are stripped of their foliage – the fields are all barren and dreary – the produce of the husbandman obtained by severe labor, through the summer months will all be exhausted in the feeding and preserving [of] his stock of cattle etc. before the rays of the sun shall unlock the icy fetters of winter and vegetation re-appear. [But New Yorkers] are not *bound* to endure the rigors of a northern winter ... God in his mercy has created more *genial* climates, where there is neither snow or ice: where nature, clad in her gayest livery, always looks cheerful; and where the earth provides *gratuitously* for herds and flocks, and every thing which can draw sustenance from its bosom. Such a country is Texas.[12]

The description contained few facts but the message was clear.

Dissociation was also used to refute undesirable images by focusing on changes through time in opinion or reality. In the 1870s and 1880s state and railroad promoters were particularly anxious to increase settlement and traffic on the western fringes of the Great Plains by encouraging arable farming where hitherto there had only been extensive cattle ranching. This usually involved either refuting the idea of the Great American Desert or claiming that recent environmental changes had eliminated all or most of it. In 1869, the immigration agent at large for Nebraska claimed that although

until very recently ... a large blank spot simply marked 'American Desert' [had appeared] on every map of our common country ... it has been proven beyond a shadow of doubt that books of history, maps of our country, and official reports to the Government, have been alike inaccurate and unjust; so much so, indeed, that it requires an effort from those who have seen and do know what manner of soil and climate the State of Nebraska really possesses, to comprehend why this rich and unrivaled soil, in the very heart of the American Continent, has remained so long unsettled and unimproved.[13]

The Kansas Pacific Railway, in describing the line's route across western Kansas, admitted that the region had once been thought of 'as a vast sand plain, fit only to be roamed over by savage beasts and more savage men' but described the appearance of it as seen from the railcar as 'a vision of beauty'. The 'rich valleys with their forest-fringed streams, and green prairies dotted here and there with farm houses and fields of corn and wheat speak of anything else but a "dry and desert land"'.[14] This account claimed that an actual change had occurred in the environment and landscape but without stating a cause. Seventeen years later, the Burlington Route likewise admitted that western Kansas, in common with adjacent parts of Nebraska and Colorado, had once been an arid region, which had only produced crops of bankrupts. However, between 1881 and 1887 the 'rain belt' had moved westward, probably as a consequence of changes in the atmosphere induced by the introduction of large-scale irrigation along the eastern fringes of the Rocky Mountains.[15] Others offered different explanations for the disappearance of the Great American Desert, but most explanations hypothesized man as an accidental or indirect initiator of change. An account of improved environmental conditions for which a supposed cause was given would be more persuasive than one without. Ploughing the buffalo-impacted prairie sod had, it was claimed, improved the soil's moisture-retaining capacity and, in so doing, increased the actual 'amount of rainfall and other moisture by the necessary "give and take" principle of plant life'.[16] In this, as in many other temporal dissociations, the author was adopting the rhetorician's practice of *aetiologia* (giving a cause), in an age when education was increasing public awareness of the causal processes involved in environmental change, but before the natural sciences had progressed very far in elucidating them.

Associative descriptions

Associative descriptions of environment and landscape were employed to achieve three somewhat different but not mutually exclusive objectives: first to suggest spatial coincidence or congruity between resources and potentials on the one hand, and other usually observable environmental conditions on the other (a form of *peristatis*: amplifying by describing attendant circumstances); secondly to infer or predict the existence of a property or condition as the consequence of one or more causal factors (a form of *aetiologia*); and thirdly to communicate the characteristics of a place, environment or route by comparing it with another, supposedly better known one (a form of *analogy*).

Spatial associations
The use of spatial coincidence (at a particular site) was rare, but the principle of spatial congruity (within a particular region or area type) was widely employed, especially in publications indicating agricultural potential by associating it with readily observable landscape characteristics. The principle was diffusely but unambiguously stated in one of the earliest emigrant guides dealing with Missouri Territory (then embracing much of the central and northern interior parts of the United States):

The natural geography of these wide regions confines itself to the mountains and rivers; and the details of these, though uninteresting and vapid to the generality of parlour-readers, are of importance to the emigrant, who in choosing from such an immense variety of situations a spot which he can call his own, and leave to his posterity, is willing, in the absence of local descriptions, to put up with general ones; and after due regard to the healthfulness of settlement, will look out for a combination of as many advantages as may be found together on any given point.[17]

An early guide to Texas made a primary distinction between the 75-mile-wide belt of very flat land paralleling the Gulf of Mexico and the 'rolling country' inland. The flat land was said to have the richer soils but the rolling country had better quality water and a 'purer atmosphere'.[18] The guide indicated that the former was suitable for the growth of most of the crops cultivated in the southeastern United States and that it would present no health problems to settlers coming from that region. By implication, the rolling country was better suited to settlement by persons from the more northerly states. This was a large-scale application of selection by association. When applied at a medium scale it was usually with reference to generic land types rather than to specific regions; particularly so for the middle Mississippi valley region. An early guide to the states of Illinois and Missouri recognized four types: river alluvions; bluffs; table land; and rough and uneven land.[19] A later guide to the same states considered this fourfold division unsatisfactory and adopted an eightfold system which took forty pages to describe: inundated lands; river and creek bottoms; level prairies; rolling prairies; barrens; timber and timbered uplands; knobs, bluffs, ravines and sink holes; and stony ground.[20]

Often it was necessary to define ambiguous terms. For example, it was considered important to dispel the

very common notion amongst the people of the Atlantic states, that a prairie is necessarily wet ... *Prairie* is a French word signifying *meadow*, and means any description of surface, covered with grass, and entirely void of timber and of brush wood. Wet, dry, level and rolling, are circumstances merely and apply to prairies in the same sense as they do to timbered land.[21]

The descriptions of each of the eight land types stressed the associated risks and possibilities for settlement. Barrens, for example, were described as 'usually rougher than prairies', combining 'some of the features of timber and prairie'. The term 'barren' was a misnomer as it was not 'poor' but 'second quality' land and, by implication, cultivable. Such lands were healthy and contained many pure water springs. Although the timber was generally scattered, rough and stunted, it would grow to maturity once protected from fires.[22]

At a micro scale there was less need spatially to associate landscapes with potential and hazard. Descriptions of the former and accounts of the latter tended to be juxtaposed rather than linked. For example, a guide to the lands of Iowa Territory contained descriptions of each of the surveyed 6-mile square townships and a map showing the distribution of land types (prairies; marshes; bluffs; hills; and ledges of lime and other rock) down

to the level of the square-mile section. This was based on the Surveyor
General's detailed land surveys. Township T73 R2W was described as

handsomely situated, embracing every variety of soil and timber; there is prairie
and timber sufficiently intermixed to make the whole one of the most valuable
townships in the territory. It is handsomely situated on the Iowa river, which passes
through it, dividing [it into] nearly equal parts. The whole [is] well watered by
numerous small streams which empty themselves into the Iowa; numerous springs
of water issue from the Iowa bluffs ... Growth on upland, white and black oak,
and hickory; on the bottoms cottonwood, maple, sugar and some ash.[23]

Such passages were much closer to independent description. Handsome-
ness, variety and plenty of good water were obviously attractive characteristics but the reader was not advised how to infer the qualities of particular
parts of the townships or to avoid hazards and limitations. This was communicated explicitly in information on land quality given for each square-mile
section according to a threefold classification: first rate timber land; first
rate prairie land; and second rate timber and prairie land. Quite clearly,
spatial association was a more valuable mode where the author was writing
about extensive areas or where detailed systematic evaluations had not
already been made on the ground.

Causal associations
Causal association was a higher order of spatial association which became
commoner as the century progressed. A fairly early example occurred in
the Illinois Central Railroad Company's publicity offering for sale 2.4 million acres of prairie land in Illinois. It first admitted that 'level prairie'
was 'too wet for the profitable cultivation of the several kinds of grain'.
The wetness was a consequence of inefficient run off (implied by 'level')
and a 'compact clay ... subsoil ... through which water settles but slowly'.
Given this cause, the wetness could be almost universally overcome by
manuring and deep ploughing; indeed 'deep ploughing alone will prove
effective in a large majority of instances'.[24] Two years later, the same Company published an expanded version of the booklet illustrated by engravings. One of these, *Breaking Prairie*, was of a landscape in the foreground
of which a man was breaking the prairie with a steel plough drawn by
a team of six oxen, a middle ground with another man ploughing a rail-
fenced field with a team of two horses, near to which were grazing cows,
farm buildings and a neat farmhouse. The background was of virgin prairie
with scattered clumps of trees.[25] The message was fairly clear. The middle
ground had already been transformed and the foreground was in the process
of being transformed. Only the background was ambiguous. Whether it
would also be transformed or conserved as an aesthetic amenity was left

to the imagination. Admitting a limitation, explaining its cause and suggesting a practical remedy was at least as effective, and apparently more honest, than claiming an ideal environment. The technique involved was very similar to the rhetorician's use of *procatalepsis* (anticipating objection).

More than a decade later, the Iowa Railroad Land Company used a different causal association to deprecate 'level prairie', claiming that it was liable 'to fevers and malarious diseases' because the 'drainage is imperfect and the water bad'.[26] The Atchison, Topeka and Santa Fe Railroad Company, whose line followed the Arkansas River in southwestern Kansas, actively promoted the region as 'The Garden of the West'. It claimed that the region had three 'attractive features'. One of these was 'remarkable healthfulness' and this was explained as a consequence of 'the entire absence of stagnant water or anything to breed malaria'.[27] It was commoner, however, to associate health with climatological rather than terrestrial or hydrological conditions. For example, in Minnesota, 'fever and ague, and kindred malarial diseases, are unknown' because of 'a dry atmosphere during the autumn and winter months'.[28] Similarly, the Platte Valley in Nebraska was promoted as 'particularly adapted to persons predisposed to pulmonary diseases' because of the 'dryness of the atmosphere'. Indeed, many of those already afflicted 'rapidly recovered under its influence and became hale and robust'.[29]

Supposed soil conditions and soil–water–atmosphere–plant relationships afforded the bases for some of the most complex causal associations. Stressing the advantages for cultivation of prairies over woods, an early land-company publicity publication claimed that

letting the rays of sun suddenly upon the vegetable deposit of ages, by clearing the woods extensively, is one of the chief causes of the diseases in the western country . . . [whereas] the turning up of the pure loam of the prairies, which has had a similar exposure for centuries . . . is not attended with these deleterious effects.[30]

The soils of Barnes County, North Dakota, were said to be warmer and drier than those on the floor of the Red River Valley to the east where, as a consequence, wheat had to be sown 'dangerously late'. The causal explanation must have impressed many readers at the time. The land within Barnes County had supposedly just been within the limits of glacial Lake Agassiz, first hypothesized only three years before:

and it would appear that the peculiar natural vegetable fertilizer that covers the deep stratum of clay must have been light and have floated to the margin of the lake, there to find lodgement in the shallow places, for we find upon the high prairies a deeper and more unctuous deposit than on the lower lying counties that border on the Red River.[31]

The soil of Knox County in northeastern Nebraska was described as a thick 'dark sandy loam . . . Beneath the soil is found a stratum of porous clay, beneath this a stratum of sand and beneath this a layer of chalk-rock'. The soil was supposedly 'particularly adapted to agriculture' because the sand was sufficiently thick to absorb surplus water in wet periods and to sustain springs when precipitation was light.[32] Most of the outsiders for whom this genre of literature was intended would not have been in a position to distinguish whether causal association was based on speculation, inference or the established findings of science. Providing that it stopped short of being patently ludicrous, even special pleading served to strengthen associations. For example, in promoting western Texas as sheep grazing country the Galveston, Harrisburg and San Antonio Railway Company admitted that, because watering places were far apart, it was necessary every day in hot weather to drive sheep 2 to 4 miles to water. It claimed, however, that this apparent disadvantage was a benefit because the sheep did better 'than when water is abundant in their ranges, for they will drink it when it is better that they should not'.[33] The author, unknowingly, was here combining *peristrophe* (converting an opponent's argument to one's own use) with *procatalepsis*.

Analogous associations
Analogy and *simile* were well known and widely understood rhetorical figures of thought. They were, therefore, particularly suited to communicating the characteristics of areas and places unknown to readers in terms of personally known or familiarly imagined places. Thus, for example, an account of the states of Illinois and Missouri, published in Boston with New England readers in mind, likened their 'River and Creek Bottoms . . . in external appearance, [to] the rich intervals and meadows of the Connecticut river'.[34] Similarly, a guide published for emigrants from Britain indicated that the bluffs which bound the Mississippi River above the Ohio confluence were similar to the 'Chilton Hills [*sic*]' and that the public square in Quincy, Illinois, was about the size of Russell Square, London. The 'scenery of the Thames above Twickenham' supposedly afforded 'a striking resemblance of many sequested spots on the banks of the Upper Mississippi and Des Moines rivers' and the view of the Vale of Worcester as seen from the Malvern Hills was similar to that of the prairies except that the woods were 'more generally distributed in Worcestershire than Iowa . . . [where they] follow the rivulets and water courses'.[35] To reasonably well-informed readers in England in 1844 these analogies must have created an impression of quality. Most analogies were, however, less place specific than these. According to a Scot, who had spent some time in South America and was writing for persons in the Ohio Valley, interior Texas

was excelled in beauty only by Scotland and its coastal plain was second only to Demerara in 'exuberant fecundity'.[36]

Many analogies were with generic types of places. The spires of the several churches of Springfield, Illinois, 'would do honour to some of the most respectable towns in England'.[37] Fillmore County, in common with the Blue River Valley of southeastern Nebraska of which it is a part, abounded 'in long reaches of graceful billowy prairie with intervening valleys covered by clear winding, forest-fringed streams and presents a pastoral landscape as fair and inviting as an oriental garden'.[38]

Sometimes analogy was used predictively. Even the poorest land offered for sale by the Galveston Bay and Texas Land Company was said to be 'admirably suited for vineyards', such that it was 'anticipated [that] in no very remote period [it] would rival the choicest productions of France and Italy in wines and fruit'.[39]

The recognition of generic land types and their use in inferring spatial congruity between one or more natural attributes on the one hand and one or more potentials or limitations on the other, also involved *analogy*. For example, if a particular barren was described as healthy, having many springs of pure water, characterized by second quality land and sustaining the maturation of trees once protected from fire, then it was inferred by analogy that all barrens would possess similar potential. In promoting its lands for sale in Iowa and Nebraska, the Burlington and Missouri River Railroad Company expressed this principle in popular terms: 'He who has seen one [type of] landscape in this region may learn that he can find others as good for the farmer, and bearing similar features. "There are as good fish in the sea as ever were caught," and as good farms in the west as ever were bought.'[40]

During the nineteenth century the number of settlers in the western interior of the United States increased from a few thousand on its eastern fringe to approximately 20 million. Many immigrants were from Europe or from scenically and environmentally quite different parts of the United States. Reasons behind the decision to move were varied. Opportunities to move were consequent upon new legislation, railroad construction, the introduction of new technologies and the opening of new markets. But the decision to migrate to the western interior rather than elsewhere was based on available information about the region. Much of the most effective information was contained in emigrant guides and promotional literature. Whereas its authors did not expect potential immigrants to be influenced entirely – or even mainly – by descriptions of landscape and environment *per se*, they did employ such descriptions to create a general impression of variety and, in doing so, to help dispel prior impressions of monotony and austerity. However, descriptions of landscape and environment were used far more frequently to communicate the supposed advantages of an area, place or route being promoted over better-known or competing ones. These dissociative descriptions were employed in conjunction with associative ones which suggested spatial coincidence or congruity between resources and potentials on the one hand and observable conditions on the other. These modes of describing landscape and environment played an important role in attracting settlers to the region, in shaping their preconceptions of it, in determining where they first settled and what they intended to do when they arrived. Ironically, in promoting a region where landscapes were in no sense spectacular and where environments were problematic, authors effectively deployed both to motivate one of the greatest migrations of people in the nineteenth century.[41]

NOTES

1   The interior was also promoted by means of posters, exhibitions, lectures and excursions; through newspapers and periodicals; and by land agents, immigration commissioners and lobbyists.
2   J. B. Newhall, *The British emigrants' 'hand book' and guide to the United States of America, particularly Illinois, Iowa and Wisconsin* ... (London and Liverpool, 1844), p. 27.
3   Anonymous, *Hand book of Fillmore County, Nebraska* (probably 1883), p. 1.
4   C. A. Higgins, *To California and back* (Chicago, 1893), p. 9.
5   *Ibid.*, p. 150.
6   For a brief review of the decline in the teaching of rhetoric and the contributory causes see R. E. Young, A. L. Becker and K. L. Pike, *Rhetoric: discovery and change* (New York, 1970), p. 5.
7   R. A. Lanham, *A handlist of rhetorical terms: a guide for students* (Berkeley and Los Angeles, 1968), p. 116.
8   First National Bank of Valley City, *Bright, beautiful, bounteous Barnes the banner county of North Dakota* (Valley City, 1882), p. 8.
9   Union Pacific Railway, *Montana. A complete and comprehensive description of the agricultural, stock raising and mineral resources* ... (Omaha, 1889), p. 9.
10   A. Whitney, *A project for a railroad to the Pacific* (New York, 1849), p. 24.
11   J. M. Peck, *A guide for emigrants, containing sketches of Illinois, Missouri, and adjacent parts* (Boston, 1831), p. 94.
12   A.L., *The Constitution of the Republic of Mexico and of the State of Coahuila and Texas* ... (New York, 1832), p. 45.
13   B. M. Davenport, *Resources of Nebraska. A brief account of its soil, agriculture and mineral products* ... (Nebraska City, 1869), pp. 3–4.
14   Kansas Pacific Railway, *Hand book of the Kansas Pacific Railway* ... (St Louis, 1870), p. 66.

15 Burlington Route, *Eastern Colorado. A brief description of the new lands now being opened up* . . . (Omaha, 1887), p. 5.

16 Chicago, Burlington and Quincy Railroad, *The Broken Bow country in central and western Nebraska* . . . (Omaha, 1886), p. 5.

17 W. Amphlett, *The emigrants' directory of the western states of North America* . . . (London, 1819), pp. 194–5.

18 R. S. Hunt and J. F. Randel, *Guide to the Republic of Texas* . . . (New York, 1839), pp. 37–8.

19 L. C. Beck, *A gazetteer of the states of Illinois and Missouri* . . . (Albany, New York, 1823), pp. 11–12.

20 Peck, *A guide for emigrants*, pp. 92–131.

21 *Ibid.*, p. 107.

22 *Ibid.*, p. 118.

23 J. Williams, *A description of the United States lands in Iowa* . . . (New York, 1840), pp. 47–8.

24 Illinois Central Railroad Company, *The Illinois Central Railroad Company offer for sale over 2,400,000 acres selected prairie, farm and wood lands* . . . (New York, 1855), p. 19.

25 Illinois Central Railroad Company, *The Illinois Central Railroad Company offers for sale over 1,500,000 acres selected farming and wood lands* . . . (Boston, 1857), p. 9.

26 Iowa Railroad Land Company, *Choice Iowa farming lands. 1,000,000 acres for sale at low prices* . . . (Cedar Rapids, 1870), p. 8.

27 Atchison, Topeka and Santa Fe Railroad Company, *How and where to get a living. A sketch of 'The Garden of the West'* . . . (Boston, 1876), pp. 25–6.

28 Northern Pacific Railroad Company, *Guide to the Northern Pacific Railroad lands in Minnesota* (New York, 1872), p. 15.

29 Union Pacific Railroad Land Department, *Guide to the Union Pacific Railroad lands. 12,000,000 acres best farming and mineral lands in America* . . . (Omaha, 1870), p. 7.

30 Galveston Bay and Texas Land Company, *Address to the reader of the documents relating to the Galveston Bay and Texas Land Company which are contained in the appendix* (New York, 1831), p. 13.

31 First National Bank of Valley City, *Bright, beautiful, bounteous Barnes*, p. 4.

32 E. A. Fry, *Descriptive pamphlet of Knox County, Neb.* . . . (Niobrara, Nebraska, 1883), unpaged.

33 M. Whilldin, *Immigrants' guide to western Texas* (Galveston, Texas, 1876), p. 87.

34 Peck, *A guide for emigrants*, p. 99.

35 Newhall, *The British emigrants' 'hand book' and guide*, pp. 16, 20, 21 and 37.

36 D. B. Edward, *The history of Texas, or the emigrant's, farmer's and politician's guide* . . . (Cincinnati, 1836), p. 41.

37 Newhall, *The British emigrants' 'hand book' and guide*, p. 20.

38 Anonymous, *Hand book of Fillmore County, Nebraska*, p. 1.

39 D. Woodman Jr, *Guide to Texas emigrants* (Boston, 1835), p. 56.
40 Burlington and Missouri River Railroad Company Land Department, *Views and descriptions of the Burlington and Missouri River Railroad lands* . . . (Burlington, Iowa, and Lincoln, Nebraska, 1872), p. 2.
41 The research upon which this chapter is based was supported by grants from the American Philosophical Society, XXth International Geographical Congress Fund, the Newberry Library, Chicago, and the University of Sheffield Research Fund.

10

Symbolism, 'ritualism' and the location of crowds in early nineteenth-century English towns

MARK HARRISON

There is a theatrical element in almost every large gathering of people, especially if those people happen to be chanting or carrying banners, or if they are listening to oratory projected at them from a platform. Given this element, it is perhaps unsurprising that historians and social commentators have come to see crowds as events of high drama. Massive, disruptive, fiercely acute or wickedly capricious, crowds, it is suggested, load their attention, their corporate cynicism or their mass ebullience onto a select object. That object, commentators would allow, might hold great symbolic significance: the crowd buffets the walls of Parliament during the Gordon riots of 1780, it plucks up the railings from Hyde Park in 1866 or, proverbially, it storms the Bastille.

In the apparently more ritualistic and sectarian urban environment of early modern Europe, the territoriality and symbolic weightiness of crowd locations appears to be a feature almost of everyday life. The various districts of Romans in the late sixteenth century represented both battle lines and foreign soil, to be fought for and captured;[1] youth groups in France attempted, through a sub-culture of ritual and misrule, to transpose the 'biological continuity of the village' onto urban neigh-bourhoods;[2] carnival in the early modern city 'may be seen as a huge play in which the main streets and squares became stages, the city became a theatre without walls and the inhabitants, the actors and spectators, observing the scene from their balconies'.[3] The city-as-stage metaphor is also suggested by the ritualistic activity in English cities in this period.[4]

For the nineteenth century, however, crowd events are seen by historians not so much as elements in a long (even continually) playing drama, but as isolated and melodramatic interventions in urban life. The location of crowds has been seen almost exclusively in terms either of riot action, or of the supposed fear of urban hordes.[5] In the turbulent environment of the early nineteenth century, the argument goes, crowds and gangs assembled or roamed with little rhyme or reason, except their desire to be in the best position from which to gloat at whatever incident or event caught their fancy. Riots were the only mass events that aimed consciously at particular parts of the town.[6] From the second quarter of the nineteenth century, it is generally suggested, English cities, and more especially their suburbs, were designed for privacy and exclusion; there were now to be places in which the individual could enjoy (considerable) personal space, away from the otherwise fearsome suffocation of urban life.[7] The design and policing of such areas attempted to ensure that mass intrusion or disturbance would not take place.

This received history of crowd activity sees a sharp discontinuity between the city as an open stage for the enactment of civic mystery and dispute, and the city as a controlled set of enclosed spheres in which other than officially institutionalised mass activity was incomprehensible and alarming. Undoubtedly, striking changes in the organisation and location of mass events took place in the nineteenth century: the attempt to replace in more 'improving' form the miscellany of outdoor public spaces with halls and theatres and supervised parks, has been well documented.[8] But how sharp and neat was this supposed transition?

The experience of living in a particular place at a particular time is the product not only of personal histories and 'major events', but of repetitive, routinised, patterned social activity. Such activity is what, essentially, constitutes social 'order'. Crowd activity in early nineteenth-century English towns, it is argued here, was a well understood part of this patterning. If the ritualistic dramas of the early modern period were less evident, they were replaced not by inchoate protest, but by more or less quietly theatrical crowd displays around elections, civic events, royal and military celebrations, political meetings and demonstrations. Those events located themselves in such a way within the urban environment as both to give to and gain from their surroundings an extra representational significance. The selection of a particular public square for a mass meeting was a strategic as well as pragmatic decision; the intention of reformers to use a new, hitherto unpursued, processional route could in itself induce panic among the upper classes because of the implications of a break in routine; established patterns of crowd occurrence made crowd events both more comprehensible and, as importantly, avoidable.

This essay analyses the spatial distribution of crowd events of all kinds in four of England's largest provincial towns in the period 1790–1835: Bristol, Liverpool, Norwich and Manchester. The focus of attention will be upon Bristol, since its highly distinctive urban geography and the frequency

of large crowd events gives detailed illustration to arguments that might
be more generally applied to the other locations.

The location of crowds in Bristol 1790–1835

Early nineteenth-century Bristol can be divided into four zones with regard
to crowd events (Fig. 1). The area from Queen Square to Broad Street,
and slightly beyond the river Frome, formed the first. This was the commercial and administrative hub of the city, with public buildings such as the
Guildhall, Mansion House and Council House; with the commercial buildings of the Exchange, Customs and Excise House, the market and the
Merchants' Hall; and with the harbour-side. Residentially, this part of the
town was mixed: the fine Georgian Queen Square standing adjacent to
the overcrowded and poverty stricken Marsh Street. The second zone may
be taken as that stretching up the hill from the docks towards Clifton,
taking in College Green, Park Street, Brandon Hill and Tyndalls Park.
Although the parts of this zone near the docks were poor and overcrowded,
moving up Park Street it became increasingly affluent, predicting the grandeur of the third major area: Clifton. A fashionable place to live, Clifton
was carefully laid out in squares and crescents, and stood up on the hillside
overlooking both the Avon gorge and the city centre. It was both physically
and socially aloof. Its antithesis was the fourth zone, south of the old course
of the Avon,[9] and comprising St Thomas, Temple and Redcliffe parishes,
and going beyond to Bedminster. Temple, St Thomas and Redcliff were
populous, busy and poor. Bedminster was fast growing (with a population
in 1821 of 7,979, and in 1831 of 13,124)[10] and also generally poor, 'comprising principally mechanics, shipwrights, and the families of seafaring
people'.[11]

Each of these zones held a particular significance in terms of crowd events.
The area of the city north of Broadmead, and east of St Peter's Street,
however, experienced few documented crowd occurrences. Most of this
part of town was poor, with the exception of the developing Kingsdown,
which extended uphill from Maudlin Lane and King Street.

Zone one

The first zone, stretching from Queen Square to the river Frome, was
the centre for crowd activity throughout the period under discussion. The
existence of Bristol Corporation buildings in Broad Street and Queen
Square provided an immediate link between the two, with many formal
processions passing through both districts. The annual Corporation procession on 5 November (rarely a crowd event in itself)[12] went from the Council
House, in Broad Street, to the Cathedral, and then to the Mansion House

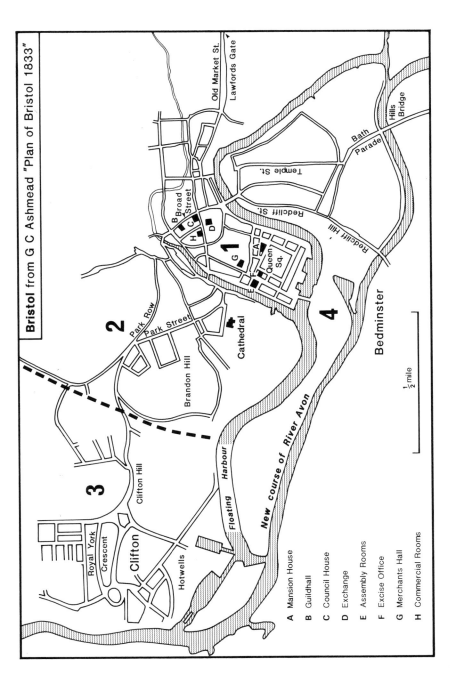

Fig. 1   Bristol: zones and locations of crowd events.

The following labels appear on the map:

Bristol from G C Ashmead "Plan of Bristol 1833"

Old Market St.
Lawfords Gate
Broad Street
Temple St.
Bath Parade
Hills Bridge
Redcliff St.
Redcliff Hill
B Broad Street
H C
D
G 1
A
Queen Sq.
E
Park Row
2
Park Street
Cathedral
Brandon Hill
4
Bedminster
Clifton Hill
3
Royal York Crescent
Clifton
Hotwells
Floating Harbour
New course of River Avon
½ mile

A Mansion House
B Guildhall
C Council House
D Exchange
E Assembly Rooms
F Excise Office
G Merchants Hall
H Commercial Rooms

in Queen Square. Events such as the celebration of military victories during the French wars, in 1797 and 1799, the celebration of the proclamation of peace with France in 1801, 1802 and 1814, George III's golden jubilee in 1809 and the coronation processions of 1821 and 1831 are typical examples of crowd-attracting formal processions which paraded through much of this zone.[13] Parliamentary elections centred on Broad Street, with the Guildhall being the location for the hustings, and the polling also, until Queen Square replaced it in 1830. The Broad Street area contained the party headquarters of the Tories (the White Lion Inn) and the Whigs (the Bush Inn). The chairing processions of victorious candidates frequently took in Queen Square, as in 1790, 1796, 1801, 1830 and 1831.[14] Broad Street and Queen Square were also connected by more continuous activity, such as election rioting against both the Council House and the Mansion House in 1796, assize riots in 1810 and celebrations of the liberation of an individual believed to have been unjustly convicted in 1827.[15]

That part of the zone around Broad Street, Clare Street, High Street and Wine Street was the location for numerous crowd events since it was not only the city centre but also a cross-roads connecting the area south of Bristol Bridge with the northern part of the city, and the eastern streets with the Backs and Queen Square. Queen Square itself held a particular significance. Built in the early eighteenth century, with a character and design actively promoted by the Corporation, it represented an outpost of Clifton-like affluence located adjacent to some of the poorest parts of the city, and surrounded on three sides by water. Although it was the scene for election chairings, patriotic processions, attacks upon the Mansion House, and a number of military displays during the French wars, it was not fully exploited by popular assemblies until 1831. A precedent was set in 1827 when Thomas Redding, convicted on a trifling excise charge, was, on his liberation, led as a hero through the town, and through the square. In 1830, election activity became centred on Queen Square, and the posting of thousands of placards transformed its appearance.[16] A reform meeting to choose parliamentary candidates, convened there in April 1831, con-firmed the challenge to the square's hitherto exclusive image.[17]

Further reform meetings took place in June, and twice in October, 1831.[18] With the square acting as the focus for an election victory by reformers in the same year, it was as if its proprietorship was now open to question.[19] The so-called reform riots of 29–31 October 1831, in which all major public buildings and two sides of Queen Square were systematically plundered and destroyed, represented a climax to the sudden and vigorous challenge. Significantly, in immediately subsequent years Queen Square was not the scene for any popular gathering, with the exception of the election of 1832. The siting of poll booths amid the ruined houses may have contributed to the failure at that election of both the Liberal candidates; certainly the

Tories, who now saw the ruined square as a symbol of reformism, gloried in the belief that Bristol had seemingly disassociated itself from such an evil.[20] Although in the course of the 1832 election a reform meeting was held in the square, it was otherwise shunned by the reformers. When a venue was sought for a dinner to celebrate the passing of the Reform Bill, Queen Square was discussed. The *Bristol Mercury* reported:

We are aware that, as a body, the reformers have been branded as the authors of the mischief which the ruins of the square bear witness to; but we would not, on that account, advise them to forego the use of it on the present occasion, if it should appear to be their interest to assemble there, and thus show how utterly they hold the calumny in contempt.[21]

Nevertheless, Queen Square had become too sensitive, and the meeting was eventually held on Brandon Hill.[22] The trades' reform procession of earlier in the year, although parading around most of the town, studiously avoided Queen Square.[23]

There were repeated negotiations of this kind between power and populace, between the Corporation and its opponents and between rival political parties, over the symbolic control of the heart of the city. Residentially, this area represented a precarious merger of power and deprivation. Its principal buildings, meanwhile, held the ambivalent status common to all civic centres: they were monuments to commercial and Corporation exclusivity, and yet, as public buildings, they were the property of all the inhabitants. Given the restless neutrality of this part of the city, it was relatively simple for one contending group, by undertaking one well-directed and forceful action, to tip the balance of symbolic control in its favour. Since the means by which this might be accomplished were well understood, crowd activity and crowd targeting within the zone possessed a 'ritualistic' element.[24] For example, the popular response to conflict with the city's executive was, repeatedly, to stone Corporation property. Either the Council House or the Mansion House, or both, were attacked in this way in 1793, 1796, 1807, 1810, 1812 and 1831.[25] Three of these occasions were parliamentary elections (1796, 1807 and 1812). The use of Corporation property for the election hustings and the conduct of the poll served to emphasise the thoroughgoing involvement of local government in the broader political process. As a result, the ritualism which surrounded elections (such as the processions of candidates to the Guildhall; the hustings; and the chairing of victorious candidates around the city centre) represented at once the sharing of 'establishment' amenities with the population as a whole, and the intrusion into a supposedly 'open' event of the power which lay behind those amenities.

It was not only Queen Square and Corporation property that were the location for regular and clearly understood acts of assertion. The headquarters of the political parties, situated around Broad Street, would expect, in the course of a contested election, to have to replace their windows after attacks from the opposition.[26] The radical orator and politician, Henry Hunt, for his part, quickly made the area outside the Exchange his regular speaking place; the newspaper press, well understanding the point of such a gesture, soon began to refer to this as his 'favourite' and 'usual' venue.[27]

Zone two

The second zone was that of College Green, Park Street, Brandon Hill, and Tyndalls Park (commonly referred to as simply 'the Park'). This area, with the Cathedral and Bishop's Palace, the prestigious Park Street, Great George Street, and Berkeley Square, and, from 1823, the Philosophical Institution, was highly 'respectable'. It was not exclusive however: the road from Hotwells, and the areas around Limekiln Lane and Denmark Street, were densely populated and poor. The zone was frequently used during the French wars for military displays, and for the firing of cannon from the heights of Brandon Hill and the Park. The Park abruptly ceased to be used for crowd events after 1799, although it is not clear why. Brandon Hill increasingly became the focus for attention although no contentious crowd gathered there until the election of 1807.[28] Its subsequent use by Henry Hunt, in 1816, by the Whig candidate Colonel Baillie during the 1818 election and by radicals in 1819[29] was sufficient for the *Bristol Mirror* to comment, when a religious meeting was held there in 1820, that the Hill was 'famous' for political meetings.[30] This, together with the example of Hunt's use of the Exchange, illustrates well the speed with which a site could gain a reputation, and also indicates the importance attached to crowds and their locations by those who commentated upon them.

The political use of Brandon Hill was, however, short lived, doubtless to the relief of 'respectable' inhabitants who had been made anxious by Henry Hunt's appearance there in 1816.[31] Significantly, no crowd event occurred on the Hill or on Park Street between the coronation celebrations of 1821 and a meeting of the Bristol Political Union (in self-imposed exile from Queen Square) in May 1832.[32] That interregnum, in conjunction with the events of the 1831 riots, also places in context the reform procession of June 1832. In an extraordinary symbolic assertion of power, 10,000 trade society members celebrated the passing of the Reform Bill by walking an 11 or 12 mile route from Lawford's Gate, down to Redcliff Street and back up Temple Street, and then through the city centre to Park Street. At the top of Park Street they detoured to walk around Berkeley Square, before carrying on to Berkeley Place, down to Hotwells, and back through town to Broadmead, and, finally, to Portland Square. With the notable exception of Queen Square, they had covered each significant area of the town. Their visit to the affluent Berkeley Square caused the inhabitants to board up their windows.[33] The single presence in the square of the much loathed Tory alderman, Thomas Daniel, was a permanent liability for the other residents: on the only other occasion on which a contentious crowd ventured to the top of Park Street, during the election of July 1812, it made an attack upon his house.[34]

Zones three and four

The out-parish of Clifton, like the Park Street area, was effectively out-of-bounds for other than casual or recreational crowds. An attack upon the house of Tory parliamentary candidate R. H. Davis in Clifton in 1812, consequently produced a particularly outraged response.[35] Ironically, Clifton, or more specifically the Downs surrounding it, was an area in which the very rich and very poor did both congregate, for sporting events, military displays on Durdham Down and holiday strolls. The years 1817 to 1827 saw a peak in such crowd gathering events. Boxing matches, cricket matches, and horse-racing were frequent and well supported in these years.[36] They generally occurred during working hours, hence the polarised social origins of their attendants. The Downs brought together May Day and Easter holiday crowds, the participation of the young and the poor being described with benign condescension by the press.[37] It was not the case, then, that the bulk of the city population simply did not venture as far as Clifton and the Downs. Indeed, such spectacles as the so-called 'Flyingman's' two attempts to cross the Avon gorge attracted holiday crowds so large that the *Bristol Gazette* was drawn to observe that 'we never witnessed so large a share of the population collected together at one time'.[38] The absence of other than recreational crowds from this zone, therefore, appears to have been a specific policy in the organisation of such events. On the other hand, the coming together for recreational purposes of the socially disparate on the home territory of the wealthy and influential, facilitated the ascription, by reporters, of a consensual meaning to these events.

The other principal crowd function for the Clifton and Park Street zones was as the entry point for visiting dignitaries. The Prince of Wales arrived by this route in 1807, as did Wellington in 1816 and the Duchess of Kent and Princess Victoria in 1830.[39] This contrasts strikingly with other, overtly political, entries, which were made through the fourth zone to be considered here. The road from London and Bath ran into the south-eastern part of the city, via Totterdown and Hills bridge, and then continued to the city centre via Temple Street and Bristol bridge. This route, through a densely populated working-class area of town, was taken by all judges and non-resident parliamentary candidates, without exception. The process of entering the city possessed a ritualistic element: the fact that visitors were entering the city from outside was highlighted by the existence of an established entry point; and their popularity could be measured by the response they received from those on the roadside.

Moving south from Bristol bridge, the suburbs seemed to the 'respectable' more and more remote and dangerous. Formal processions for official proclamations made a token journey across the bridge to Temple Street cross at the end of Bath Street, and to the site of an old cross at the top of Thomas Street, but never beyond.[40] The long detour which the trades' reform procession took in 1832, over the bridge, down to Redcliff Hill, along the New Cut, and back up Bath Parade and Temple Street, appears symbolically deliberate: the reformers were describing the physical and social extent of their constituency.[41]

The out-parish of Bedminster, a mining area, was commonly portrayed as disorderly and brutish. Some of the crowd events there were indeed wild. In 1825 a sortie was made by an anti-Catholic group against the homes of Irish people in Bedminster.[42] In a drawn-out incidence of intimidation, a black-leg shipwright was carried on a pole around Bristol, and south of the river to Bedminster.[43] The Bishop of Bath and Wells received a hostile reception there from reformers in 1831.[44] The Tory newspaper *Felix Farley's Bristol Journal* relished the description of a reform meeting on Bedminster Down in October 1831, depicting the attendants as near imbeciles.[45] Bedminster, the cultural antithesis to Clifton, was, like Clifton, not made use of for organised non-casual crowd events. Crowds were found there only in exceptional instances, or as part of a barely reported autonomous sub-culture; the 'acceptable' nature of recreational events in Clifton, on the other hand, ensured that they were documented.

The visual image of crowds

From the examination of crowd occurrences in these four zones it would seem that the location of crowds could be of great representational significance. Location influenced the context and presentation of crowds at a further level, however: through their visual image and organisational make-up. Spatial distribution was not only symbolic in itself but could influence a crowd's symbolic content. In general, those events attended, organised or greatly opposed by those in authority were subject to the greatest internal or external organisation. Their visual image reflected this involvement. For instance, as the popularity of the Bristol and Clifton races increased, the facilities offered to wealthy spectators improved; the staging of the races became visibly more elaborate.[46] This development served to emphasise both the fact that the races were staged in the territory of the wealthy, and the social demarcation within the event between the affluent and the indigent. When Henry Hunt addressed a meeting on Brandon Hill, in

December 1816, on the other hand, it proved difficult (allegedly because of the intimidation of carpenters by employers) even to have a speaker's platform erected.[47] As the meeting was taking place, 1,000 special constables and the military stood by in the adjacent streets.[48] The meeting was effectively marginalised before it even began. When radical meetings began to take place in Queen Square, they did so with minimum facilities. The speakers' platform was sometimes no more than the back of a wagon.[49] In this instance, the paucity of the facilities was juxtaposed against the grandeur of the square itself.

Most assemblies attended by the wealthy, with the exception of some recreational events, took place indoors, thereby facilitating a high degree of comfort and organisation. Such amenities were officially denied to popular assemblies: the mayor could, and did, deny the use of the Guildhall to such gatherings.[50] Indeed, a Chartist meeting in the Guildhall in 1838 was claimed by its chairman to be 'the first meeting of the working classes ever to be held there'.[51] The very fact that a public meeting took place outdoors indicated the social group at which it was directed.

Celebratory processions (particularly those around the principal streets of the city centre) were a rather more direct declaration both of a crowd's social constituency and its symbolic control of space. The procession for a Corporation-sponsored celebration would include the military, in uniform, and Corporation officials, wearing their ceremonial robes.[52] Such a display, taking place within the civic centre, effectively identified and, at least momentarily, unified the personnel of power.[53] The supporters of a victorious parliamentary candidate, for their part, would include in their procession models and emblems of the city, and of its trade, commerce and industry; they would display colours, banners and mottoes; and the presence of occupational and other societies would indicate the basis of the candidate's support.[54] The claim being made in this instance, of course, was the representation not so much of power as of Bristol. However, it was those political processions which enjoyed widespread popular support which also exhibited the greatest symbolic content. Not only were banners, flags and slogans displayed, and ceremonial costumes worn, but most trades would carry emblems and symbols of their professions.[55] Furthermore, there might be the additional display of the symbols of poverty (such as the carrying of loaves on the ends of sticks), or of personalised hatred (sometimes expressed through the carrying and burning of effigies).[56]

The location in which the various devices of crowd occurrences were deployed influenced the interpretation of those devices by non-participants. The 'right' of a successful parliamentary candidate to be paraded within the city centre was generally acknowledged and effectively institutionalised – whatever the political complexion of the party concerned. The authorities would police the event, but, nevertheless, it would rarely be regarded as posing any kind of threat to the city's social stability. Once the same ingredients of crowd display were carried into a different area, and into a different context, however, their meaning was transformed. The emblems and banners of the trades which celebrated the passing of the Reform Bill became menacing, in the eyes of some of the wealthy, at the moment at which they were carried out of the city centre and into Berkeley Square and Clifton. The political tokens and colours of the Tories became the insignia of racial violence at the moment at which Tory supporters moved off the main thoroughfares and into the back streets, for the purpose of attacking the Irish.[57]

The location of crowds in Liverpool, Norwich and Manchester 1790–1835

Liverpool

The themes of consistency and appropriation which characterised the spatial distribution of crowd events in Bristol apply similarly to Liverpool. They did so within the context of a city expanding rapidly, from a population of 82,000 in 1801 to 286,000 thirty years later. The river Mersey formed a boundary to the west, and Liverpool's expansion took place principally to the south and east (Fig. 2). A striking characteristic of the city in these years was the residential mixing of rich and poor, partly caused by the reluctance of successful merchants and businessmen to move away from the city centre. During the first years of the nineteenth century, however, the new development of Toxteth Park, in the south of the city, was becomingly notoriously poverty stricken and crowded.[58]

Crowd events in Liverpool fell into a very distinctive pattern. The Town Hall was the administrative focal point for the city. About half a mile south-east, however, and reflecting the direction of expansion of the city, Clayton Square was becoming an alternative focus. Clayton Square was developed in the later eighteenth century as a select and secluded residential area.[59] Processional crowds almost invariably 'connected' the new and old centres, and in so doing marked out a central boundary for the city, made up by the Town Hall, Dale Street, Lime Street, Duke Street, Lord Street and Castle Street. The early expansion of the city was acknowledged from about 1820 by major processions, which now extended the easterly boundary out to Seymour Street, Russell Street, Clarence Street and Rodney Street. These routes were so well trodden that they could safely be regarded by contemporaries as the crowd streets. Dale Street was vital in this regard, being officially recognised as the entrance to the city, and widened and improved in 1818 in line with this status.[60]

The central boundary contained a route directly connecting the Town Hall and Clayton Square, which ran along Lord Street and Church Street.

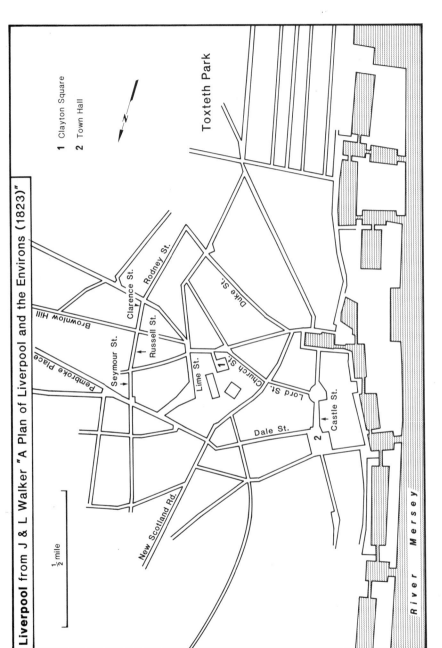

Fig. 2   Liverpool: locations of crowd events.

This was the main passage at election time, and by 1831 could be referred to by the newspapers simply as 'the usual route'.[61] Election crowds rarely processed in from the outskirts,[62] and this confirmed the centralised nature of crowd occurrences. It may be significant that whereas in Bristol and Norwich, both of which were stagnating in this period, many inhabitants showed great interest in the symbolic significance of the city boundary, in fast-growing Liverpool the emphasis was rather more upon stating and restating the outline of the core of the city.

The only two excursions beyond the inner boundary were undertaken by radical processions. The first was the celebration of the abandonment of the Bill of Pains and Penalties in 1820, when a crowd marched out to Mile End in the New Scotland Road.[63] The second was the radical-dominated celebration of the coronation of William IV in 1831, when the procession went out along Brownlow Hill and returned via Pembroke Place.[64] As in Bristol these deviations suggest a radical self-confidence which wanted to express as dramatically as possible its metaphorical and literal domination of the city streets.

More dramatic, however, was the radical appropriation of Clayton Square. A reform meeting held there in February 1817 was the first of five such gatherings in the space of two and a half years.[65] By the early 1830s the residentially exclusive square was, for crowd-gathering purposes, quite simply in the hands of the reformers. It was a powerful expression of the rise of the reform movement.

Norwich

Crowd events in Norwich centred on the castle and market place (Fig. 3). Although the administrative hub of the city, this area was set to the south of the main residential districts. Consequently, participants in crowd events would have travelled up to 2 miles to a no man's land of great crowd activity.

Norwich was a city dominated by elections. Its system of local government provided for ward and mayoral elections, and it was also the location for parliamentary elections not only for the city but also for the county of Norfolk. Candidates for both city and county elections frequently were non-resident; processions into the city, predominantly from the north and west, were a feature of the city's crowd activity. Such processions may have given local residents a sight of large crowds, but the destination for these processions was invariably the market place. Here, in this neutral zone, the contending parties were allocated their territories: the market place was physically divided in two by a chain. The respective groups of supporters, wearing their candidates' colours, threw abuse (or worse) across the dividing line. Sometimes they attempted to capture the opposition

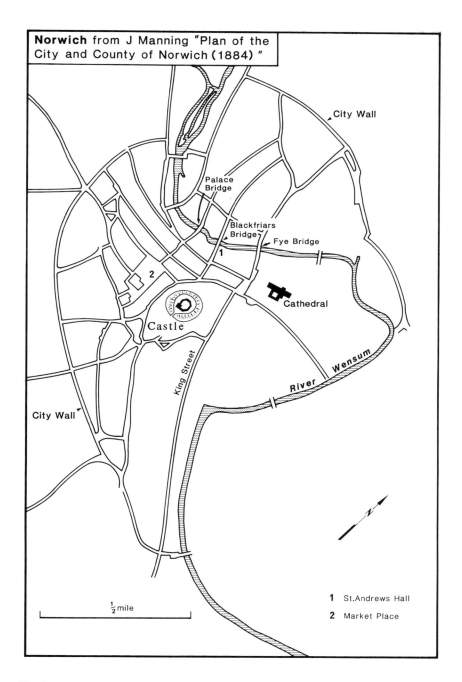

Norwich from J Manning "Plan of the City and County of Norwich (1884)"

City Wall

Palace Bridge

Blackfriars Bridge

Fye Bridge

Cathedral

Castle

King Street

River Wensum

City Wall

½ mile

1 St.Andrews Hall

2 Market Place

Fig. 3   Norwich: locations of crowd events.

ground.[66] It is difficult to avoid comparison with football supporters of the present day.

Rather as in Liverpool, processional crowds of different kinds tended to share well-worn routes. Chairing processions at the end of elections took place within a tight area around the market place and castle. Effectively, crowd events in Norwich took place south of the river. Some non-election processions such as at the proclamation of George IV in 1820,[67] and the proclamation of William IV in 1830,[68] ventured across the river at Fye bridge, but quickly crossed back and down to the market. Living north of the river in Norwich it was possible to give little thought to crowd events.

With major public meetings from 1819 taking place indoors in St Andrews Hall (also situated south of the river) the overwhelming majority of crowd occurrences were linked to elections, and centred on the entrances to the city and the market place. By 1835, and with the exception of occasional official or celebratory processions, large-scale, publicly visible crowd events in Norwich were predictable, semi-official, 'ritualised' incidents of political confrontation.

Manchester

The extraordinarily rapid growth of the unincorporated, unenfranchised town of Manchester makes an adequate examination of crowd occurrences there far beyond the scope of this brief discussion. Two observations can nevertheless be made. First, major public meetings moved south, reflecting the pattern of growth of the town, from St Georges Road to St Peter's Field (Fig. 4) This process had begun before the notorious Peterloo massacre (the trend seems to have taken place from 1816, with a reform meeting in October of that year, followed by the Blanketeers gathering at St Peter's Field in 1817, and an anti-corn law meeting there in January 1819);[69] but Peterloo, inevitably, made St Peter's Field particularly symbolically charged. Second, and perhaps indicative of the speed of change in the size and density of the town, official processions such as for the proclamation of George IV and the coronation of William IV were short, and tied to the acknowledged centre of Manchester: St Anne's Square.[70] Some processions did cut the city east to west (the coronation of George IV and the celebration of the passing of the Reform Bill),[71] or north to south (a reform procession in 1831).[72] But, unlike Liverpool, there was no regular restatement of an inner boundary.

The reason lies in part in lack of opportunity. The absence of parliamentary elections and of a town corporation reduced the occasions on which such displays could take place. Large-scale industrial dispute and riot,

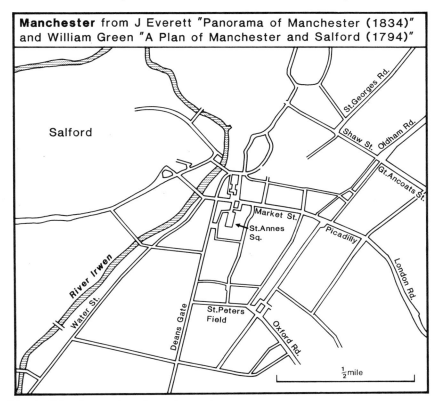

Fig. 4   Manchester: locations of crowd events.

directed at specific work place targets, was as typical a crowd form as any. As Frank Munger has noted for Lancashire in general, contentious gatherings were linked to the demographic distribution of trades.[73] With the exception of St Peter's Field, there was little opportunity for specific locations to gain particular representational significance for crowd events. Furthermore, few locations were designed and built with symbolic aspirations against which crowd occurrences could be pitched.

Conclusions

This essay has examined the representational significance of individual areas and particular buildings in the organisation and conduct of crowd occurrences in early nineteenth-century English towns. Some areas of towns were designed to have a particular symbolic impact. And in some instances patterns of crowd occurrences amplified designed symbolism. But equally, intended symbolism could be compromised: the appropriation of public space gave that space new meanings. The self-confident solidity of Georgian squares became shaky when repeatedly occupied by shabby but sober political aspirants.[74] And repeated activity at crucial crowd venues could create a symbolic significance the architect would never have intended.

More generally, the formation of a crowd in a certain place indicated, for contemporaries, the possible composition and degree of menace of a gathering. Patterns in location invested crowd events, and crowd types, with an image. The existence of such images enabled non-participants to identify a possible and general meaning for crowd occurrences, and influenced their interpretation of the physical appearance of crowds. It was not necessarily the case, of course, that crowd participants would have shared the observer's conclusion.

Herein lies the paradox in crowd presentation. It was the observers and reporters, not the crowd members, who held the monopoly on the final presentation of the crowd. Crowds presented an image which came in part from the surroundings in which they placed themselves. As this essay has demonstrated, there were clear patterns in those presentations which suggest a constancy in crowd occurrence. These provided a common framework for the enactment of contention and made possible and comprehensible the organisation of everyday activities. Those who commentated upon crowds well understood these patterns – clearly so, for it was they who were first to point to changes in crowd routine. Yet they also possessed the power to overlay other presentations, notably ones depicting crowds as fickle. Consequently, there is a double history of crowds. Both histories can be read out of the same sources: crowds as comprehensible, patterned occurrences in the ordering of everyday life; crowds as trivially subservient or wickedly destructive. The symbolism of crowd occurrences may ultimately be determined by selective reportage and refractory interpretation on the part of self-styled social commentators. They have always had the last word.

NOTES

1 Emmanuel Le Roy Ladurie, *Carnival in Romans: a people's uprising at Romans 1579–80*, transl. Mary Feeney (Harmondsworth, 1981).
2 Natalie Zemon Davis, 'The reasons for misrule: youth groups and charivaris in sixteenth-century France', *Past and Present*, no. 50 (Feb. 1971), pp. 41–75.
3 Peter Burke, *Popular culture in early modern Europe* (London, 1978), p. 182.
4 Charles Phythian-Adams, 'Ceremony and the citizen: the communal year at Coventry 1450–1550', in P. Clark and P. Slack (eds.), *Crisis and order in English*

towns 1500–1700 (London, 1972), pp. 57–85; Charles Phythian-Adams, 'Milk and soot. The changing vocabulary of a popular ritual in Stuart and Hanoverian London', in Derek Fraser and Anthony Sutcliffe (eds.), *The pursuit of urban history* (London, 1983), pp. 83–104.

5 The rational nature of targeting by rioters has been widely acknowledged since the pioneering work of Rudé and Thompson: George Rudé, *The crowd in history, 1730–1848* (1964; revised edn London, 1981); E. P. Thompson, 'The moral economy of the English crowd in the eighteenth century', *Past and Present*, no. 50 (Feb. 1971). For discussion of anxieties regarding the urban masses, see Gareth Stedman Jones, *Outcast London: a study of the relationship between the classes in Victorian society* (Oxford, 1971).

6 For example, W. L. Burn, *The age of equipoise: a study of the mid-Victorian generation* (London, 1964), ch. 2; Donald Richter, *Riotous Victorians* (London, 1981).

7 H. J. Dyos and D. A. Reeder, 'Slums and suburbs', in H. J. Dyos and Michael Wolff (eds.), *The Victorian city: images and realities*, 2 vols. (London, 1973), Vol. 1, pp. 359–86; David Cannadine, *Lords and landlords: the aristocracy and the towns 1774–1967* (Leicester, 1980).

8 Hugh Cunningham, *Leisure in the industrial revolution* (London, 1980); H. E. Meller, *Leisure and the changing city 1870–1914* (London, 1976).

9 A harbour improvement scheme in 1804–9 altered the course of the Avon.

10 James Johnson, *Transactions of the corporation of the poor* (Bristol, 1826), appendix F; *Bristol Gazette* (hereafter, *Gazette*), 7 July 1831.

11 *Municipal Corporation Report: 4*, appendix part II, XXIV, p. 1187.

12 1792 and 1807 are the documented exceptions: *Felix Farley's Bristol Journal* (hereafter, *FFBJ*), 10 Nov. 1792; *Bristol Mirror* (hereafter, *Mirror*), 7 Nov. 1807.

13 Routes for these events are described in: *Bristol Mercury* (hereafter *Mercury*), 23 Oct. 1797; *FFBJ*, 7 Sept. 1799; *Bonner and Middleton's Bristol Journal* (hereafter, *BMBJ*), 17 Oct. 1801; *FFBJ*, 8 May 1802; *Mirror*, 2 July 1814; *FFBJ*, 28 Oct. 1809; *FFBJ*, 21 July 1821; *Mercury*, 13 Sept. 1831.

14 For example, *BMBJ*, 26 June 1790; *Gazette*, 2 June 1796; *BMBJ*, 28 Nov. 1801; *Mirror*, 27 June 1818; *Gazette*, 29 July 1830, 5 May 1831.

15 *Gazette*, 2 June 1796; *Mirror*, 21 Apr. 1810; James Acland's *Bristolian*, 11 July 1827.

16 *Mercury*, 3 Aug. 1830.

17 *Gazette*, 28 Apr. 1831; *Mirror*, 30 Apr. 1831.

18 *Gazette*, 11 Aug. 1831, 13 Oct. 1831; *FFBJ*, 15 Oct. 1831.

19 *Gazette*, 5 Aug. 1831, 12 May 1831.

20 *FFBJ*, 15 Dec. 1832.

21 *Mercury*, 30 June 1832.

22 *Mercury*, 18 Aug. 1832.

23 *Mercury*, 23 June 1832.

24 The term 'ritualistic' is used here in a loose sense. These were not ritual actions by the strict definition of the term, since it is unlikely that they possessed any existential element.

25 Mark Harrison, '"To raise and dare resentment": the Bristol Bridge riot of 1793 re-examined', *Historical Journal*, 26, 3 (1983), pp. 557–85.

26 For example: *FFBJ*, 19 June 1790; *Gazette*, 2 June 1796, 7 May 1807; *Mirror*, 4 July 1812, 20 June 1818, 10 June 1826; *Mercury*, 3 Aug. 1830.

27 *Gazette*, 22 Oct. 1812, 14 May 1818.

28 *Mirror*, 9 May 1807; Henry Hunt, *Memoirs*, 3 vols. (London, 1821), Vol. 2, pp. 246–8.

29 *Gazette*, 2 Jan. 1817; *Mercury*, 15 June 1818; *Gazette*, 6 Oct. 1819.

30 *Mirror*, 19 Aug. 1820.

31 *Gazette*, 2 Jan. 1817; Proceedings of Mayor and Alderman, vol. 1785–1820, 19 Dec. 1816, Bristol Record Office (hereafter, BRO); Letters and Miscellaneous papers, Bristol Corporation, Box 1816, BRO.

32 *FFBJ*, 21 July 1821; Serjeant's report book, St Augustine's, 10 May 1832, BRO.

33 *Mercury*, 23 June 1832.

34 *Mirror*, 4 July 1812.

35 *Ibid.*

36 Boxing matches: *Mercury*, 17 Mar. 1817; *Gazette*, 1 July 1822. Cricket matches: *Gazette*, 26 Aug. 1819, 1 May 1820, 14 Aug. 1824, 7 July 1825, 14 July 1825, 10 July 1827. Races: *Gazette*, 29 Mar. 1821; *FFBJ*, 25 May 1821; *Gazette*, 2 June 1823, 18 May 1826.

37 For example, *Gazette*, 5 June 1823, 9 May 1822, 18 May 1826; *Bristol Liberal*, 9 Sept. 1831.

38 *Gazette*, 25 May 1826, 8 June 1826.

39 *Gazette*, 8 Oct. 1807; *FFBJ*, 3 Aug. 1816; *Gazette*, 28 Oct. 1830.

40 Proclamation of peace with France: *Gazette*, 6 May 1802; *Mirror*, 2 July 1814. Proclamation of accession of George IV: *FFBJ*, 5 Feb. 1820. Proclamation of accession of William IV: *Mercury*, 6 July 1830.

41 *Mercury*, 23 June 1832.

42 *Mercury*, 11 July 1825; *Gazette*, 7 July 1825.

43 Sessions Papers, Box 1825–7, 30 Sept. 1826, BRO.

44 *FFBJ*, 29 Oct. 1831; *Gazette*, 26 Oct. 1831.

45 *FFBJ*, 15 Oct. 1831.

46 See 'Vol. of miscellaneous sporting notices 1822–1832', Bristol Reference Library.

47 *Mirror*, 28 Dec. 1816.

48 *Gazette*, 2 Jan. 1817; Letters and Miscellaneous papers, Box 1816, BRO.

49 For example, *Gazette*, 13 Oct. 1819.

50 *Notice from E. L. Fox* (Bristol, 1793), Bristol Reference Library; printed poster, 20 Dec. 1816, in Letters and Miscellaneous papers, Box 1816, BRO; *Mercury*, 11 Oct. 1819.

51 John Cannon, *The chartists of Bristol* (Bristol, 1964), p. 2.

52 W. Mathews, *Bristol guide* (Bristol, 1794), pp. 45–6; J. Mathews, *Bristol guide* (Bristol, 1815), pp. 83–4; *ibid.*, 1829 edition, pp. 80–1; *FFBJ*, 21 July 1821; *Mercury*, 13 Sept. 1831.

53 Abner Cohen, 'Political anthropology: the analysis of the symbolism of power relations', *Man*, new series, 4, 2 (1969), pp. 220–1.

54 For example, *Mirror*, 24 Oct. 1812, 27 June 1818, 11 Mar. 1820.
55 Most dramatically in 1831: *Gazette*, 12 May 1831; *FFBJ*, 7 May 1831.
56 *Gazette*, 21 May 1812, 20 Dec. 1792, 7 Mar. 1793.
57 *Gazette*, 9 Apr. 1829.
58 François Vigier, *Change and apathy: Liverpool and Manchester during the industrial revolution* (Cambridge, Mass., 1970).
59 James Touzeau, *The rise and progress of Liverpool from 1551 to 1835*, 2 vols. (Liverpool, 1910), Vol. 2, pp. 484–5.
60 Touzeau, *Rise of Liverpool*, pp. 783–4.
61 *Liverpool Mercury*, 28 Oct. 1831.
62 For exceptions, see *Liverpool Chronicle*, 6 May 1807; *Liverpool Mercury*, 9 Oct. 1812; *Liverpool Mercury*, 16 June 1826.
63 *Liverpool Mercury*, 24 Nov. 1820.
64 *Liverpool Mercury*, 9 Sept. 1831.
65 *Liverpool Mercury*, 9 Feb. 1817. For subsequent meetings see: *Liverpool Mercury*, 4 July 1817, 3 Sept. 1819, 24 Sept. 1819, 3 Dec. 1819.
66 For example, *Norfolk Chronicle*, 10 July 1802, 20 June 1818, 31 July 1830, 15 Dec. 1832.
67 *Norfolk Chronicle*, 5 Feb. 1820.
68 *Norwich Mercury*, 3 July 1830; *Norfolk Chronicle*, 3 July 1830.
69 *Cowdroy's Manchester Gazette*, 2 Nov. 1816; *Manchester Mercury*, 11 March 1817; *Cowdroy's Manchester Gazette*, 23 Jan. 1819.
70 *Cowdroy's Manchester Gazette*, 12 Feb. 1820; *Manchester Guardian*, 15 Oct. 1831.
71 *Manchester Guardian*, 21 July 1821, 11 Aug. 1832.
72 *Manchester Courier*, 5 Nov. 1831; *Manchester Guardian*, 5 Nov. 1831.
73 Frank Munger, 'Contentious gatherings in Lancashire, England 1750–1893', in Louise A. Tilly and Charles Tilly (eds.), *Class conflict and collective action* (London, 1981), pp. 76–7, 81–2, 86–9.
74 John Berger, 'The nature of mass demonstrations', *New Society*, no. 295 (23 May 1968), pp. 754–5.

11

Symbol of the Second Empire: cultural politics and the Paris Opera House

PENELOPE WOOLF

The essential character of a period can generally be deciphered from its architectural façade, and in the case of the second half of the nineteenth century ... that façade is certainly one of the most wretched in world history. This was the period of eclecticism, of false Baroque, false Renaissance, false Gothic. Wherever in that era Western man determined the style of life, that style tended toward bourgeois constriction and bourgeois pomp, to a solidity that signified suffocation just as much as security. If ever poverty was masked by wealth, it was here.

Hermann Broch, *Hugo von Hofmannsthal and his time*[1]

In 1874 *Le Pays* made the following statement about Charles Garnier's Opera House: 'son gai et splendide édifice répond parfaitement à l'idée qu'on se fera un jour de l'époque impériale'.[2] A century later, Robert Hughes, reconsidering the Beaux-Arts architectural tradition, said of the Opéra: 'no building could have been more symbolic of the Second Empire: quilted with wealth and power, lush of surface, ritually ordered'.[3] Garnier's Opera House was already interpreted by contemporaries as a self-conscious expression of Second Empire Parisian society. A hundred years later, it continues to be viewed as a window on that age. Although work on the Opéra commenced in 1862, following Garnier's success in the 1861 opera house competion, the building was not inaugurated until January 1875, four and a half years after the fall of the Second Empire (Fig. 1).[4] Despite the fact that it was constructed as an expression of his times, the Opéra was never used by Napoleon III. This has not altered the entrenched belief that Garnier's Opéra symbolizes fully the nature of Second Empire Parisian society, that in this monument the richness and diversity of lifestyles at this time found their most perfect expression. This particular view crops up time and again not only in histories of late nineteenth-century architecture, but in guidebooks and historical accounts even today.

The belief that the Opéra mirrors Parisian life between 1852 and 1870 is but one of a number of long-established views about that important episode in the making of modern France which turn out, on closer inspection,

Fig. 1   Postcard of the Place de l'Opéra, c.1900 (the inauguration of the Opera House took place in 1875 and not in 1878 as stated in the caption on the postcard).

to be generalizations and simplifications obscuring complicated historical processes. A large part of our received wisdom about the Second Empire requires more detailed investigation. Alain Plessis' judgement that modern research reveals 'a period astonishingly rich in contrasts' lends credence to Theodore Zeldin's warning that we should be wary of being misled by the hasty and often ill-informed generalizations of contemporaries.[5] Subsequent reports of the actions of historical agents often lack the richness of the historical circumstances surrounding their agency. Zeldin makes this point about one particularly vocal social group, the intellectuals:

> not only have intellectuals played a leading part in these conflicts, but they have also interpreted and labelled them in such a way as to influence all subsequent thought about them . . . Their generalizations became accepted truths, to the extent that they shaped events, for new controversies were fitted into categories they had devised.[6]

In this revisionist mood, I shall examine the received wisdom about the Paris Opéra, not through strands of disembodied evidence floating across the decades from 1861 to the present, but in the historical and social context in which the Opera House was built and viewed by contemporaries. I shall locate this monument in the well-known and ambitious scheme for the rebuilding of Paris devised by the emperor Napoleon III and his Prefect of the Seine, Baron Haussmann. This will lead us to examine ways in

which some common assumptions about the relationship of the Paris Opéra
to its social and historical context distort the kinds of relationship that
actually did then exist between Parisian society and its new Opéra.

Symbol of the Second Empire

The general background to considering the Opera House as a type of social
message is the knowledge, amply documented, that the design of imperial
Paris was explicitly conceived by planners, architects and engineers as a
way of conveying in the built environment an image of those aspects of
French society that were highly valued by these professionals and by the
emperor himself. The urban landscape of Second Empire Paris was intentionally charged with carefully considered and skilfully articulated social meaning. Urban morphology was not simply the translation of architectural
theory into architectural practice, rather it constituted architectural practice
mediated by extra-architectural factors – the pressing demands of social
and political interest. Buildings, bridges, roads and open spaces in the
city conveyed a distinct sense of social order, and a confident belief in
historical destiny.

It is impossible to provide a hard and fast definition of this historical
sense, but it was informed by the romantic view that creative human endeavour was also a projection of historical consciousness. Variously conceived
as the 'spirit of the age' or *Zeitgeist*, the life of the city was believed to
be revealed by the historical circumstances of particular monuments. Architecture was part of the social, economic, political, religious and cultural
fabric which lent to an age its defining characteristics.

Dating from about 1850, but most prominent from the last quarter of
the century, the common coin of celebratory histories of Paris was the
use of monuments as touchstones to immediate historical comprehension.
The author of an 1867 guidebook, R. de Corval, used monuments as historical witnesses: 'étudier les monuments d'une ville, c'est d'étudier son histoire
dans ce que les siècles passés ont laissé de vivant et de palpable'.[7] In the
same year Alfred Normand, architect and director of *Le Moniteur des
Architectes*, wrote a conference report in which he quoted a M. Hermant
as having said: 'l'art de bâtir est un art essentiellement appelé à manifester
les idées générales, les tendances morales et intellectuelles des sociétés'.[8]
Fine buildings were like exemplary lives: a model and a microcosm of
the larger social and historical context.

Just as the past informed the present through the medium of existing
monuments, so the future could be informed of the present through the
construction of new monuments. Furthermore, with careful planning,
monuments could be used to convey certain messages to future generations.
Architecture was recognized by the emperor as a way of communicating

with posterity. The Second Empire would be remembered less for its politics, he prophesied, than for its architecture. But as the emperor well knew, it was not always possible or desirable to separate the two. The built environment could be crafted in such a way as to embody, and pass on, political messages.

The purveyor of the message was understood to be the architect. In Haussmann's scheme, the architect was concerned with individual buildings, while the engineers, the members of the Grands Corps, were responsible for the coordination of city planning (Fig. 2). The relationship of the architect to the building was seen as corresponding to that between a historian and his text. Buildings were described as historical documents. In his *Traité d'architecture* (1858), François Reynaud called architects the interpreters and chroniclers of the age.[9] The influential editor of the *Revue générale de l'architecture et des travaux publics*, César Daly, described the architect as 'la trompette sonore dans laquelle passe le souffle puissant d'une nation; il résonne alors des vibrations qui sortent des poumons de tout un peuple'.[10] Whether he had actively invented the role, or was speaking lines that others had written for him, the architect assumed a star role in the drama of history.

In the same way that a page in a book conveyed a sense of historical narrative, so a building captured a moment in time. Charles Lucas wrote that the history of architecture conveyed the spirit of French civilization.[11] Monuments were also claimed to reveal the nature of the political system in which they were built. An English reviewer of Daly's *L'Architecture privée au XIXe siècle sous Napoléon III* published in *The Builder* (1864) stated that 'all that has been recognized as characteristic of France politically, will be found to extend to its architecture'.[12] An anonymous article in *La Fédération artistique* (1877) made monuments the autobiography of a generation: 'plus que l'histoire, l'architecture est un miroir fidèle des époques qu'elle traverse'.[13]

As a monument, the Opera House in particular would inspire a sense of pride and achievement and testify to the pace of social progress under the Second Empire. The Academy of Music and Dance, or Opéra, was the traditional home of grand opera. Grand opera was a lavish spectacle, a ritual, an escape. A visit to the opera house was an elaborate social occasion. As Paul Lang claimed: 'The new aspirations and political and social preoccupations, the invasion of the bourgeois spirit, the pursuit of money and pleasure, abolished the sincere atmosphere of the first fervours of the romantic movement. The bourgeois spirit found great satisfaction in two genres of art: the pseudo classic drama and the grand opera.'[14] Grand opera was a spectacle in which all the arts – music, dance, painting, architecture – participated. There was thus an intimate link between the architecture of the building and the activity that it was constructed to house.

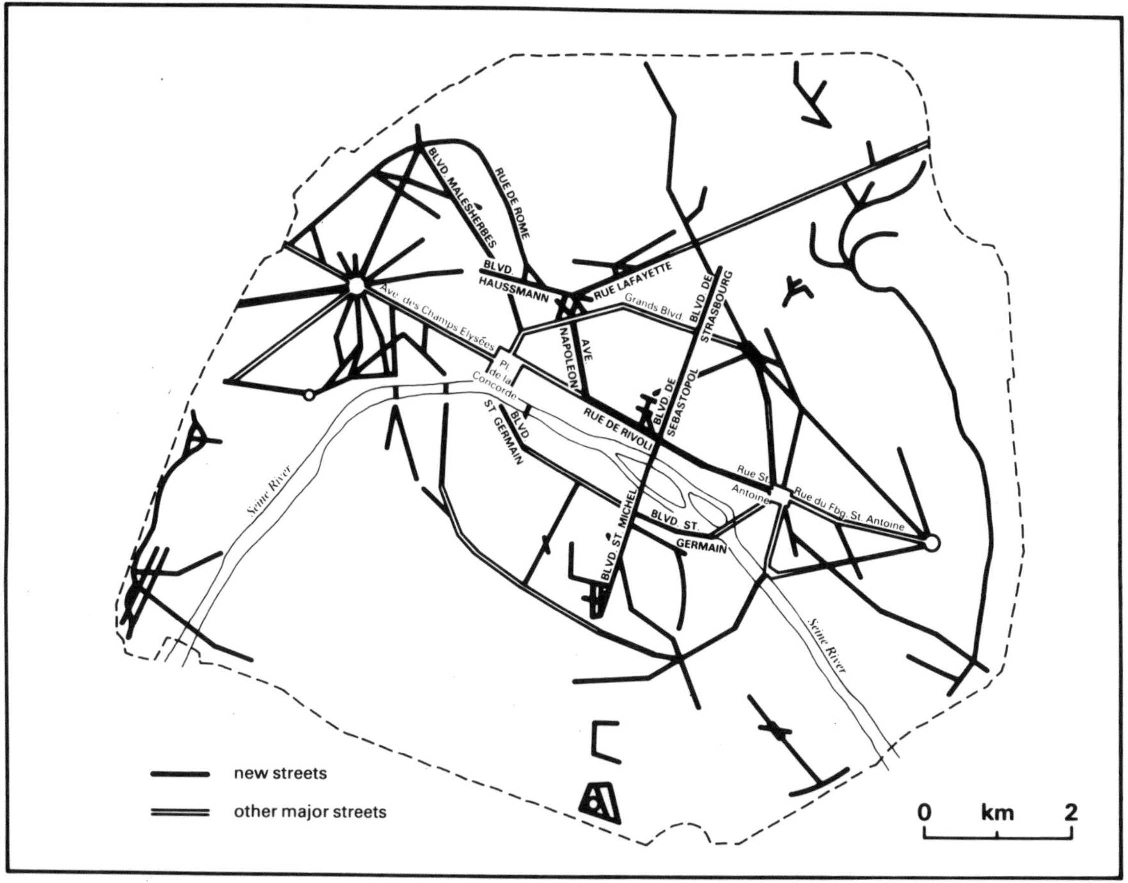

Fig. 2 Principal new streets built in Paris between 1850 and 1870 (based on Département de la Seine, *Les Travaux de Paris,*

Grand opera embraced tradition and novelty, theatrical expertise and great expenditure. It was a mirror for the innovations of the age and a reflection of its prosperity. Because of this, Garnier's Opéra was intended to establish as historical orthodoxy the radical modernity of its age.

One particular novelty of the Opera House, and certain other modern Parisian theatres, was the expectation that they should cater explicitly to the ever-increasing desire for luxury and comfort. Under the Second Empire these were not only expectations but deemed necessities. To the extent that they satisfied these social demands opera houses and theatres acted as barometers of social progress. People judged that if they could not 'vivre là comme on vit dans un foyer familier' then the building had failed.[15]

The Opera house joined banks, market halls, and currency and commodity exchanges as an indicator of opulence and prosperity. Daly ranked opera houses together with churches and railway stations as the most architecturally conspicuous indications of the increased wealth and technological advance issuing from the industrial revolution.[16] He hoped that the Opéra would signify not only wealth, but the sophisticated cultural achievement and refined artistic taste of Second Empire Parisians.

Twentieth-century studies have reinforced this interpretation. A 1941 textbook *Notre France. Son histoire* illustrated the Opera House opposite the title page of the chapter dealing with material progress under the Second Empire (Fig. 3). From *Ecole Primaire* to *Terminale* whether in the form of a crude black and white print or a painstakingly detailed sketch, the Opéra was often the only monument to figure graphically in texts relating the rebuilding of Paris. This view survives to the present. The Opéra is 'the *pièce de résistance*, the symbol of the whole programme of works, and even of the Empire itself with its unashamed, extravagant bad taste';[17] and 'l'édifice le plus parfait et le plus représentatif du Second Empire, le symbole d'une époque brillante, entreprenante et sereine'; or 'an architectural reflection of the gaudy splendour of the Second Empire'.[18]

But these more recent reactions reveal a shift in opinion. The association of monument and Empire has turned sour. This is not an entirely new phenomenon, for nineteenth-century critics had already attacked the emperor or the government through the medium of the Opera House. What has happened in the twentieth century is that heterodoxy has become orthodoxy. The Opéra suffered the stigma of the typical. It fell from crowning glory to 'une des créations caractéristiques du Second Empire'.[19] Not quite banal but no longer a sublime sign of social equipoise, the Opéra became a window on the conspicuous expenditure and corrosive waste of Empire and empire building.

The hostility which many historians have harboured towards the Second Empire and the twentieth-century distaste for ostentatious Beaux-Arts architecture go some way towards accounting for modern tirades against

LE SECOND EMPIRE

(1851-1870)

La prospérité matérielle

SECOND EMPIRE

L'OPÉRA DE PARIS, architecture de Charles GARNIER

Fig. 3   An adaption of the title page of lesson 36 of E. Audrin and L. Baerembach, *Notre France. Son histoire* (Paris, 1941).

the Opera House. The modernist scythe of rational architecture epitomized by Le Corbusier and his disciples robbed Garnier's creation of architectural significance. The rational vision of functional architecture pared of historical purpose and commitment made the Opéra seem an indulgent luxury. Le Corbusier called the building an 'art de mensonge'. The 'événement Garnier est un décor d'enterrement' he declared.[20] In 1941 Sigfried Giedion dubbed Garnier's conception merely transient: the perfect expression of the short-lived glories of the Second Empire.[21] How, he argued, could such a trifle, a decorative trinket, make a lasting contribution to the progress of architectural theory which, surely, consisted in solving the problem of the best fit of form to function?

Despite such modernist criticisms the power of the Opéra as a social statement remains undiminished. Criticisms of the building have been levelled either at Second Empire society, stressing the decadence of its aesthetics as evidenced in this monument; or at the Opéra as an incoherent conglomerate of styles. The fundamental idea that the Opera House articulates a given society has rarely been subject to sustained historical scrutiny. It survives through force of sheer repetition, its strength and frequency of utterance.

Recently, some revisions to this idea have been made. Monika Steinhauser argues that far from symbolizing a unitary Second Empire society, the Opéra conveys an impression of one small segment of it.[22] She calls the Opéra the contrivance of an assertive and ambitious bourgeoisie, working in association with the emperor to further their own class interests. 'En fait, l'Opéra symbolise une tentative de création d'un style nouveau, répondant à la volonté de prestige de Napoléon III et aux ambitions de la bourgeoisie ... Aucune autre création architecturale contemporaine ne reflète autant le "contentement de soi" du Second Empire.'[23] The aim of what follows is to investigate and amplify received wisdom about the Opéra in the light of this revisionist argument.

The Opera House and the transformation of Paris

In order to understand why the Opera House was chosen to crown the reconstruction of Paris we need to consider the qualities that had been attributed to opera houses in Paris ever since they were first introduced from Italy in the late seventeenth century; qualities such as prestige, splendour and glory. A brief consideration of the association between opera and the Baroque period, an association that was later picked up in the choice of Neo-Baroque as a style for many nineteenth-century opera houses, will help to answer the question of what it was about the reign of Napoleon III that made an opera house such an important symbol.

Cultural politics

The use of opera as an art form bestowing cultural prestige has long been exploited politically. This has affected not only the construction of opera houses, but the choice of music and the set designs within them. The importance of the Baroque period (in France the seventeenth and early eighteenth centuries) for opera and theatre cannot be overestimated. To simplify greatly, in this period a building was conceived less as an edifice than a drama. The walls, columns, interior and exterior all figured in the creation of spectacle. Each element was itself a form of expression subordinate to the whole. Opera was at this time considered a decorative art whose appropriate style was characterized by maximum decoration and the interplay of light and shade. Large, complex spaces and a sensuous, decorative style are recognized as typically Baroque.

There was not only a special relationship between opera and Baroque architecture, but also between that architecture and townscape. The sheer size and magnificence of Baroque buildings required that they be viewed from a distance. This conception of city planning and architecture – straight roads connecting monuments – originated in sixteenth-century Italy and Pope Sixtus' commission for the redesigning of Roman streets. This principle of perspective planning in the grand manner led to the *culte de l'axe* (intersecting axes) which dominated nineteenth-century planning in France and is particularly evident in Haussmann's transformation of Paris.

The early association of opera and court life is captured in the word *palais* which is still used to refer to Garnier's Opéra. In the Baroque age, the court was the place where cultural and spiritual activities were secularized. People were brought together at concerts, grand operas and at the theatre. Hence the Baroque conception of secular theatrical cities and the rivalry between the court theatres of Paris and Vienna.[24]

From the seventeenth century, champions of the construction of a new Paris opera house emphasized the glory that such a monument would bring to the reign in which it was built. This argument received a new impetus after the Opera House at the Palais Royal was destroyed by fire in 1781. Although a 'temporary' replacement was built in the rue Le Peletier in 1821, the demand for a new permanent Opera House continued unabated. Following government investigations into the structural soundness of the 'temporary' Opéra in the 1840s, it was condemned by the press as a dangerous liability. The theatre could collapse at any time, it was argued, injuring not only people inside it but also those who lived in neighbouring buildings. An equally powerful source of scorn was that this theatre was architecturally unworthy of Paris. By the time the competition for a new opera house was announced in December 1860, most critics were agreed that the former Opéra was an anachronism, a disgrace to a city internationally respected as the queen of the arts.

Paris' future as an artistic centre was questionable, it was claimed. Edmond Duponchel, the author of a counter-proposal to the official choice of site, architect and more than once director of the Opera House wrote: 'La reconstruction de notre scène lyrique est donc avant tout une question d'art qui, grâce au bruit qui s'est fait autour d'elle, prend les proportions d'une question politique. L'amour national s'y trouve sérieusement et légitimement engagé, et il doit recevoir une complète satisfaction.'[25] The success of the Opera House project was thus directly linked to national self-esteem. The debate over the new theatre was politically charged. The new monument had to be capable of inspiring Frenchmen with pride and foreigners with envy. No one would deny that through the Opera House France would be judged all over the world for her ability to create great works of art and stage magnificent theatrical performances.

Size and magnificence were the criteria by which the new Opera House would be judged. It had to be the largest theatre in Europe, still more exquisite than the new Opera House being built in Vienna. In 1884 F. de Donville reported that 'son aspect rapelle vaguement celui du Colysée de Rome'.[26] The size of the building has been a constant theme in guidebooks over the last hundred years.

The emphasis on a central location

The symbolic importance of the Opéra, and its role as a social centre, were to be emphasized through its geographical location. This in itself was not new. Throughout the nineteenth century many projects for a new opera house sought acceptance for their designs by choosing locations in central Paris. F. Grille offered a design for the Place Vendôme in 1847, and Joseph de Filippi selected the Passage Sandrié in 1858.[27]

What lent more credence to this idea after 1852 was the fact that centrality had become an important concept in Haussmann's scheme to modernize Paris. The *culte de l'axe* gave paramount importance to the centre. The city was redesigned as a network of focal points and radiating arteries. These focal points deployed buildings, fountains, statues – anything that would give prominence to a particular site. The perspective along orthogonals towards monuments became the city's aesthetic code.

In September 1860 the official choice of the Chaussée d'Antin as the site for the Opéra confirmed the rumour that this district was to be graced with the monument. Commonly known as the *grands boulevards* (Fig. 2), it was at the centre of aristocratic Paris and was regarded by contemporaries as the heart of Parisian life. In 1856 Théophile Gautier explained its attraction: 'la vie de Paris s'est de plus en plus transportée de la Seine au boulevard, à mesure que l'argent a dominé la noblesse et que la Chaussée d'Antin a vaincu le faubourg aristocratique'.[28] Gautier explained that migration to the area was linked to the rise of capitalism and to the changes in value that accompanied the creation of a market economy. He, and many others, referred to the Opéra as the 'cathédrale mondaine de la civilisation', thus emphasizing a shift from religious to secular values.[29] As Hermann Broch wrote of Richard Wagner: 'He knew that the age he was born into would choose the operatic as the form for its representative total expression; he saw how the new bourgeois cities were seeking a community center that would replace the cathedral and how they strove to raise the Place de l'Opéra to that honoured status.'[30] By locating the Opéra at the centre of a district that was itself the heart of Paris, just as Paris was the artistic capital of France, Europe and even the world, the imaginative power of the monument would rest on layer upon layer of symbolic meaning.

Contemporary and subsequent writers have seized upon the location

Fig. 4   Aerial view of the Opera House and its environs. Courtesy of the Bibliothèque Nationale.

of the Opera House at the luxurious centre of Paris as something typically
Second Empire. Described variously as the 'centre géographique de la vie
mondaine' or as being at the 'hub of the Parisian's life', the Opera House
lives on in guidebooks and histories as the very focus of life in Paris (Fig.
4).[31]

The question of style

The radical modernity of Napoleon III's reign was to be expressed in more
than merely the location of the Opéra. Throughout the nineteenth century
many architectural writers were preoccupied with the problem of creating
a new style to give fresh impetus to art and reflect the achievements of
the century of progress. It was hoped that the new Paris Opéra would
finally launch the new style. This was what the architect J. Belliol seems
to have had in mind when he wrote that this monument would be 'l'édifice
lyrique et grandiose qui manque à Paris et qui devra enfin être le point
de départ d'une architecture en quelque sorte nouvelle'.[32]

Most critics were confident that Garnier had realized this aim. He was
lauded for having created a monument that was not only typical of his
age but also characteristic of the whole nineteenth century (Fig. 5). Jules
de Précy described modern art as realistic, a response to a materialistic,

Fig. 5   Postcard of the Place de l'Opéra, c.1900.

individualistic era.[33] Gautier believed that Garnier had understood this for these were the qualities that the Opéra displayed. This was 'une architecture élégante, fleurie, coquette et même un peu chargée d'ornements'.[34]

Modern Paris was to proclaim and project the imperial planners' belief in progress. Modernity was to be expressed through the medium of monuments and in the plan of the city, with the Opéra as the supreme embodiment of the values of Second Empire Parisian society. This in turn was linked to the role of Paris as an artistic centre and a city of pleasure both French and international.

The myth of Paris

It was a well-established tradition that opera houses be used to enhance Paris' reputation as a cultural capital. What changed in the nineteenth century, and became a principal reason for using the Opera House as the supreme symbol of Second Empire society, was that Paris had indeed become the capital of pleasure. Its entertainment was not confined to the stage; the city itself was on show. Herein lay its legendary attraction for writers, musicians and artists. The poet Heinrich Heine, who made Paris his home, wrote of his adopted city: 'Paris is not simply the capital of France, but of the whole civilized world, and the rendezvous of its most brilliant intellectuals.'[35] Heine's friend, Heinrich Laube, echoed his enthusiasm referring to Paris as 'the capital of the universe'.[36]

In an article entitled 'Paris, mythe moderne', Roger Caillois defines the mystique associated with Paris: 'Il existe . . . une représentation fantasmagorique de Paris, plus généralement de la grande ville, *assez puissante sur les imaginations pour que jamais en pratique ne soit posée la question de son exactitude.*'[37] Both he and Ellen Taylor-Huppert conclude that the myth of Paris was loosely connected to the transformation of Paris from a medieval city to the capital of a modern state.[38] In Taylor-Huppert's opinion the physical changes, as narrow and crooked medieval streets were replaced by large, open boulevards, corresponded to social changes, with new classes and families replacing traditional communities. The myth was related to the political and social importance of Paris within France.

What is most pertinent to a study of the Paris Opéra as a symbol is the modern dimension to the myth which depicts Paris as a city of pleasure and, integral to this, the idea of Paris as a vast open-air theatre. In his book on Manet T. J. Clark writes about the emergence of Paris as a unit, a spectacle in itself, something that developed in the latter part of the nineteenth century.[39] He considers the 1860s an epoch of transition in which public and private life had not yet been completely separated. The spectacle was disorganized and still mixed up with old forms of sociability. It was almost a cliché for writers in the second half of the nineteenth century to call Paris a stage. They were evoking life on the new boulevards, the displays in shop windows, the cafés, theatres and bars (Fig. 6). Paris had become an international arena in which to parade new clothes and fashions and to display goods which owed their existence to mass production and industrialization. Culture was on show and it attracted an international audience. Contemporary guidebooks described theatres as typically Parisian, characteristic of this phase of Parisian life.[40]

The key to an explanation of why opera flourished at certain times in history, a clue to why the Opera House was chosen to symbolize the Second Empire, can be found in this idea of a society on show, in the concept of a theatrical age.[41] Gilbert Durand attempts to explain the links between culture and society, and to discover why opera thrived at a particular time.

Durand identifies periods of 'socio-cultural intensification'. Opera became a significant socio-cultural fact when it was controlled by a small number of powerful decision-makers. Opera was popular in the seventeenth and eighteenth centuries and again in the second half of the nineteenth century: 'Ces deux moments culturels que signent la souveraineté de l'Opéra sont les points culminants de deux sociétés de l'apparat: les ors et les marbres du palais Garnier font écho à ceux de la Scala de Piermarini en 1776 et un siècle plus tôt à ceux de Versailles.'[42] Opera at these times was the symbol of a society that valued appearance above all: 'Mais rien

Fig. 6   Postcard of the Boulevard des Italiens, c.1900.

ne signe mieux cette intensité socio-culturelle de l'opéra aux XVIIe–XVIIIe siècles comme durant le Second Empire que ses effets si l'on peut dire sur "l'infrastructure": la salle de spectacle.'[43]

Grand opera in the reign of Napoleon III had become what F. Martens refers to as an 'imperial institution'.[44] The glory of the sovereign and his court were reflected in the extravagant scenery, the attention to detail in the fine costumes and the magnificence of the imperial box in the Opera House on the rue Le Peletier. Performances were semi-official court functions attended by dignitaries who were as keen to impress the crowd as to listen to the music. Important foreign visitors normally spent their first evening in Paris at the Opéra. There was a vogue for theatre, much as there was for cinema in the mid-twentieth century, with people striving to imitate the accents that they heard on stage.

The choice of the operas themselves had an important influence on popular opinion about the regime, although, as we have seen, symbols are double-edged, able to be used against the regime they are intended to glorify. Offenbach's celebrated *La Vie Parisienne* (1866), which was written in homage to the emperor and to the society surrounding him, was interpreted as an expression of corruption and became part of the popular conception of, and attack on, *la fête impériale*. Carpeaux's *La Danse*, one of the four principal statues to adorn the façade of the Opéra, suffered a similar fate. When ink was thrown at the statue of dancing Bacchantes whose nakedness caused moral outrage, it was taken as a sign that Bonapartism was at an end. Music and dancing were the *cachet* of the Second Empire.

The two ideas, of Paris as a theatre, and of society as spectacle, come together in many contemporary descriptions of Paris. Louis Véron, director of the Opera House between 1831 and 1835, called Parisian society a great opera and Théophile Gautier, speaking about the rebuilding of Paris, said that the city was being adorned for foreigners.[45] Tourists were the audience for this great spectacle of change and were sufficiently distanced not to feel implicated in the plot. Just as the concept of the centre was significant because it worked on a number of levels, so too that of the stage embraced a multiplicity of meanings. There was the performance and audience in the Opera House. This audience was itself part of the spectacle of the monument as people paraded their finery during the interval, catching a glimpse of themselves in the large mirrors which returned an image of their own self-importance. Paris was a stage which attracted visitors from all over the world. In the Opera House, we are led to believe, the spectacle of Paris was acted out in miniature.

The divided city

Not everyone has accepted the uniform picture of society conveyed by the Opera House. In the unfinished *Passagen-Werk* Walter Benjamin used the built environment as part of an attempt to construct what George Steiner has called a complete 'material and psychological inscape' of a society at a given moment in time.[46] Benjamin argued that far from acting as accurate statements on the lifestyle of Second Empire Parisians, the new monuments of Haussmann's Paris were only the symbolic expression of people's desires. They attributed an air of wealth and prosperity to the city and yet most people did not share in these riches. Benjamin's argument was voiced by contemporaries. In 1872, E. Fribourg described the new cafés and theatres: 'cependant tout cela n'était qu'illusions, ombres trompeuses, masquant l'abîme vers lequel s'acheminait en écervelée la société toute entière'.[47]

In Emile Zola's *Rougon-Macquart* novels, the metaphor of Paris as crumbling city becomes a moral statement on society. Just as the feasting and revelry which he associated with the Second Empire could not go on for ever and people would be forced at some stage to face up to their responsibilities, so Zola believed that the squalor hidden behind the new apartment blocks would eventually break through. The façades were cracking, the Opéra itself was crumbling because these buildings concealed the revolutionary potential of so many Parisians. To Zola, the Opera House was a deceit because its severe façade proclaimed a society of upright, dignified men when in fact the reverse was true. The façade hid the revelry and joviality that filled the building. Rather than reflecting contemporary life, the Opéra deceived in two ways. It was misleading because of what went on inside it and because it spoke for a small part of society.[48]

The question of the segregation of Paris into affluent west and destitute east is vital to the revised thesis that far from articulating the whole of Parisian society, the Opéra speaks for a small minority. Opinion varies as to whether the rebuilding of Paris accentuated the split between east and west, or whether it helped to reverse this process. The balance of critical opinion weighs more heavily on the side of those who believe that an increased segregation occurred between 1852 and 1870. Workmen were forced out of the central areas and were prevented from returning when the building work had finished by the inevitable increases in rent. As the rich migrated to the north-west of the city they abandoned the inner eastern area to the poor. The Opera House, built at the centre of fashionable western Paris, was accused by the press of being constructed for the rich. The government was criticized for wasting money on luxurious monuments rather than attending to the needs of the less well-off by building food markets or hospitals. That this was a sensitive topic is demonstrated by the letter that Napoleon III sent to the city administration in July 1864. He urged that the Hôtel-Dieu be completed before the new Opera House because of the adverse publicity that the government would suffer if a prestigious monument was seen to take precedence over buildings for the sick and the poor.

Not only does the idea that the Opéra conveys a homogeneous society not bear close scrutiny, but much of the received wisdom on the Opéra is either inaccurate or incomplete. Myths have been perpetuated in the histories and guidebooks that bear scant relation to the events that took place.

The forgotten history

One example of such a myth is the idea that Garnier failed to adapt his plans to the restrictive nature of the site (Fig. 7). The architect is depicted as a spoilt child obstinately refusing to see reason. One of many similar comments is Philp Gilbert Hamerton's claim that Garnier failed to tailor the Opera House to a space that had been purposefully created for it.[49]

What Hamerton's and other accounts fail to mention is that the site was planned by Charles Rohault de Fleury and Henri Blondel in 1858, not for Garnier's creation at all but for Rohault de Fleury's Opera House. The latter was the official architect of the new Opéra between 1858 and 1860 and was the man to whom everyone turned for the production of a successful design. It was only when the competition was launched in December 1860 that Rohault de Fleury lost his commission. The detailed

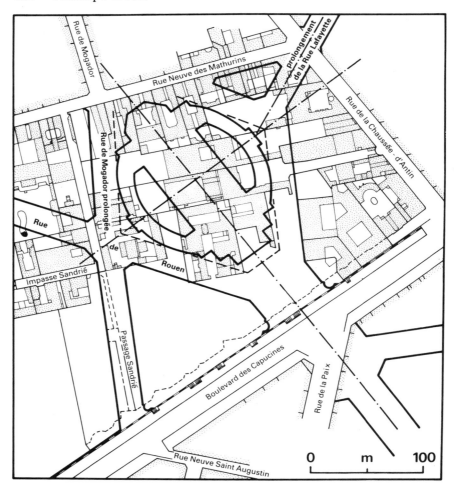

Fig. 7   The site of the new Opera House, October 1860. Courtesy of the Bibliothèque Nationale.

plans for the site had been drawn up for an Opéra that was never to be
built.

Also missing from our received wisdom on the new Opéra is any mention
of Garnier's desperate efforts to have alterations made to the plans for
the surrounding buildings so as not to dwarf the Opera House. As he
recounts in *Le nouvel Opéra de Paris* (1878), he did not expect the neighbouring buildings to exceed 17 m 30 cm, but they finally attained a height
of 23 m. Garnier had obtained the emperor's permission for changes but

these were never carried out.[50] Somewhat bitterly, he vented his feelings: 'c'est alors que j'ai maudit et le préfet et les financiers, qui, sans pitié pour l'Opéra, l'enfermaient comme dans une grande boîte'.[51] A closer look at the evidence vindicates Garnier and shifts the blame for the misfit between the monument and its vicinity to the administration, or, more accurately, to the lack of communication between national and local government. The State was in charge of the construction of the Opera House because this was deemed to be a national concern whereas the City of Paris dictated what was constructed around it.

Inaccuracies relating to the location of the Opéra, though important, do not have the same evocative power as the myth of infinite spending. In an 1886 guidebook *Living Paris and France*, we read that Garnier was given *carte blanche*.[52] *Cassell's guide to Paris* (both 1884 and 1900 editions) stated that 'the new building was constructed regardless of expense, with the evident intention of endowing Paris with the finest theatre in the world'.[53] Similarly in the 'Almanach-Album' (n.d.) we read: 'ainsi des millions ont-ils étés prodigués à l'artiste afin qu'il peut entasser selon sa fantaisie, toutes les richesses de tous les arts à la fois'.[54]

These statements are not borne out by Garnier's careful accounts of his expenditure which can be consulted at the Archives Nationales. These records tell a story of financial struggles, cuts in budgets and of the architect's sadness and disappointment at being forced through lack of money to eliminate some works of art from his plans for the building.

Once implanted, the myth of infinite spending seems to have proliferated, manifesting itself in different ways. It appears in another guise in relation to the use of coloured materials on the exterior and in the interior of the monument. Garnier's use of polychromy has been interpreted as a sign of prodigious wealth, the very impression that it was intended to convey. In *Le nouvel Opéra de Paris*, we learn how Garnier bartered with two Italian craftsmen and how he succeeded in persuading them to reduce their original estimate for the use of coloured materials on the central arch and the two domes from 3,000 fr. to 162 fr.[55] Narratives that inform us that Garnier sent for marble from every corner of Europe without a moment's thought for cost have a hollow ring once the documents concerning polychromy have been consulted. Authors of guidebooks, keen to emphasize Paris' attractions, have unwittingly contributed to the success of the imperial planners who wanted us to believe that no expense was spared on the Opéra.

Conclusion

In the light of the evidence, we can consider the imperial planners' aim of forging a link between the Paris Opéra and Second Empire Parisian society to have been successful. Yet a closer examination of the social, historical, political and economic context in which the monument was constructed reveals some of those contrasts noticed by Alain Plessis. The wealth of the Paris Opéra, and the lifestyle that it symbolized, were restricted to a very small percentage of the Parisian population. In the words of Guy Chaussinand-Nogaret: 'Si les beaux quartiers, la population luxueuse ou aisée, les magnifiques monuments, la vie mondaine et culturelle entretiennent le mythe de la plus belle ville du monde, la misère, le crime et la peur planent comme une gangrène sur le corps purulent de la capitale.'[56]

An analysis of the Opera House in its historical context allows us to redress the balance of the image of Second Empire society that has been passed down to us over the last hundred years. Through an analysis of the links between theatre, opera, the reign of Napoleon III and the rebuilding of Paris we can come to a better understanding of a monument and its epoch and to begin to appreciate that it was 'no wonder an epoch filled with the insatiable desire for decoration sought and found its representation precisely in the opera'. For, 'in the truest sense, or the most correct doublesense of the word, the theater became the showground of the epoch's poverty, masked by wealth'.[57]

NOTES

1 H. Broch, *Hugo von Hofmannsthal and his time. The European imagination 1860–1920*, transl. and ed. M. Steinberg (Chicago and London, 1984), p. 33.

2 'Revue Dramatique', *Le Pays* (5 October 1874), Bibliothèque de l'Opéra, Fonds Garnier Pièce 372C ('his bright and splendid building blends perfectly with the image we will one day hold of the imperial age').

3 R. Hughes, 'The Beaux-Arts tradition reconsidered', *Horizon* (Winter 1976), pp. 64–70.

4 The selection of five competition winners in January 1861 led to a further competition in May 1861.

5 A. Plessis, *The rise and fall of the Second Empire 1852–1871*, transl. J. Mandelbaum (Cambridge, 1985), p. xvii; T. Zeldin, *France 1848–1945*, Vol. 1: *Ambition, love and politics* (Oxford, 1973).

6 Zeldin, *France*, p. 1.

7 R. de Corval, *Paris monumental, artistique et historique* (Paris, 1867) ('to study a city's monuments is to study the palpable and living record of its past centuries').

8 A. Normand, 'Société Impériale et Centrale des Architectes. Conférences Internationales. Première Séance. Compte Rendu', *Le Moniteur des architectes* (1 August 1867), p. 134 ('the essential responsibility of the art of building is to make manifest the general ideas, the moral and intellectual tendencies of a society').

9 F. Reynaud, *Traité d'architecture* (Paris, 1858), p. 604.

10 C. Daly, *L'Architecture privée au XIXe siècle sous Napoléon III* (Paris, 1864), p. 11 ('the sonorous trumpet through which the strong breath of a nation passes; he [the architect] thus resonates to the vibrations emerging from the lungs of an entire people').

11 C. Lucas, 'Charles Garnier', *La Construction moderne*, 46 (13 August 1898), p. 541.

12 'The architecture of Paris under Napoleon III', *The Builder* (4 June 1864), p. 406.

13 'Le Nouvel Opéra de Paris', *La Fédération artistique* (9 September 1877), Bibliothèque de l'Opéra, Fonds Garnier Pièce 372C ('more so than history, architecture accurately mirrors the passage of time').

14 P. H. Lang, *Music in western civilization* (New York, 1941), p. 827.

15 Loirette, 'Des Boulevards et des Théâtres de Paris. Emplacement du nouvel Opéra et de l'Opéra Italien' (15 July 1859), Archives Nationales F21 830 ('to live there as one lives in the family home').

16 C. Daly, 'Concours pour le Grand Opéra de Paris', *Revue générale de l'architecture et des travaux publics*, 19 (1861), p. 79.

17 J. M. and B. Chapman, *The life and times of Baron Haussmann* (London, 1957), p. 189.

18 M. Gaillard, *Paris au XIXe siècle* (Paris, 1981), p. 186 ('the most perfect and representative building of the Second Empire, symbol of a brilliant, enterprising and serene era'); *International Herald Tribune* (Paris) 12 April 1984, p. 11.

19 L. Dubech and P. d'Espézel, *Histoire de Paris* (Paris, 1926), p. 411 (It fell from crowning glory to become 'but one of the characteristic creations of the Second Empire').

20 Le Corbusier, *Almanach d'Architecture Moderne*, Collection de 'L'Esprit Nouveau', Charles Eliot Norton Lectures 1938–9 (Paris, 1955), p. 120 ('a lying art', the 'Garnier movement is a décor of the grave').

21 S. Giedion, *Space, time and architecture. The growth of a new tradition*, 5th edn (Oxford, 1967), p. 754.

22 M. Steinhauser, 'L'Architecture', in *Petite encyclopédie illustrée de l'Opéra de Paris*, Vol. 1 (Paris, 1974).

23 *Ibid.*, p. 11 ('In fact, the Opera symbolizes an effort to create a new style, both a response to Napoleon III's desire for prestige and to the ambitions of the bourgeoisie ... No other contemporary architectural creation so accurately reflects the Second Empire's self-satisfaction').

24 Broch, *Hugo von Hofmannsthal*, pp. 62–3.

25 E. Duponchel, *Déplacement de l'Opéra. Contre-projet par M. Edmond Duponchel* (Paris, 1860), p. 2 ('The rebuilding of our great lyric theatre is thus primarily an artistic question, which, because of the publicity surrounding it, has taken on political proportions. National pride is properly and seriously at stake and patriotism must be satisfied').

26 F. de Donville, *Guide complet de l'étranger dans Paris* (Paris, 1884), p. 297 ('its aspect vaguely recalls that of the Roman Colosseum').

234   Penelope Woolf

27 F. Grille, *Lettre à M. Darreste sur le Louvre, la Bibliothèque et l'Opéra* (Paris, 1847); J. de Filippi, 'Projet de déplacement de l'Opéra', *La Revue municipale* (20 March, 20 December 1858; 10 January 1859).

28 In A. Dumas *et al.*, *Paris et les parisiens au XIXe siècle. Moeurs, arts et monuments* (Paris, 1856), p. 155 ('Parisian life has moved ever closer to the boulevards from the Seine, following the increasing power of money over nobility and the rising popularity of the Chaussée d'Antin compared to the aristocratic districts').

29 T. Gautier, quoted in *Petite encyclopédie illustrée*, p. 17 ('the worldly cathedral of civilisation').

30 Broch, *Hugo von Hofmannsthal*, p. 55.

31 B. Champigneulle, *Paris de Napoléon à nos jours* (Paris, 1969), p. 133; C. Holland, *Things seen in Paris*, 2nd edn (Paris, 1953), p. 73.

32 J. Belliol, Letter to Comte Walewski, 1 March 1861, Archives Nationales F21 830 ('the great lyric building which Paris lacks and which will ultimately become the originating point of a new form of architecture').

33 J. de Précy, 'Le Théâtre par Charles Garnier', *Feuilleton de la Liberté* (20 November [n.d.]), Bibliothèque de l'Opéra, Fonds Garnier Presse, Carton 3.

34 T. Gautier (1861) quoted in *Petite encyclopédie illustrée*, p. 28 ('elegant, fancy, coquetish architecture, even a little too ornamental'). The description recalls the Baroque style.

35 H. Heine, quoted in H. Sutherland Edwards, *Old and new Paris. Its history, its people and its places* (London, 1893), p. 1.

36 R. Bauer, 'Paris, Capitale du XIXe Siècle. Réflexions sur quelques textes de Walter Benjamin', *Revue d'Allemagne*, 4 (1972), pp. 622–37.

37 R. Caillois, 'Paris, mythe moderne', *Nouvelle revue française*, 284 (1 May 1937), p. 684 ('There exists ... a phantasmagorical representation of Paris, more so of the great city in general, which exerts so powerful a hold on our imagination that, in practice, we never question its accuracy').

38 E. Taylor-Huppert, 'The image of the city: Paris of the novelists from Stendhal to Zola' (unpublished Ph.D. dissertation, University of California, Berkeley, 1970).

39 T. J. Clark, 'The view from Notre-Dame', in *The painting of modern life. Paris in the art of Manet and his followers* (London, 1984).

40 *Paris since the war* (1873), p. 11.

41 G. Durand, 'Un sociologue à l'Opéra', *Sociétés*, 1 (1984), pp. 12–18.

42 *Ibid.*, p. 14 ('These two cultural episodes which mark the Opera House's supremacy are the culmination of two societies, devoted to appearances: the palais Garnier's gold and marble recalls that used by Piermarini for La Scala in 1776 and that of Versailles a century before').

43 *Ibid.*, p. 16 ('Nothing marks the socio-cultural intensification of opera in the seventeenth to eighteenth centuries, and again during the Second Empire, quite as well as its effects on what one might call the 'infrastructure': the theatre').

44 F. Martens, 'Music mirrors of the Second Empire', *Music Quarterly*, 16 (1930), p. 419.

45 L. Véron, 'Paris en 1860', *Revue générale de l'architecture et des travaux publics*, 18 (1860), p. 137; T. Gautier, 'Le Nouveau Paris' in Dumas *et al.*, *Paris et les parisiens.*

46 'Baudelaire as contagious conspirator', *The Times Literary Supplement* (8 January 1970), p. 31. This review has been attributed to George Steiner.

47 E. Fribourg, *Du paupérisme parisien. Ses progrès depuis 25 ans* (Paris, 1872), p. 12 ('however, all this was nothing but illusions, deceptive shadows, obscuring the abyss into which the whole of society was unwittingly sliding').

48 E. Zola, 'Une allégorie', *La Cloche* (22 April 1870).

49 P. G. Hamerton, *Paris in old and present times* (London, 1892), p. 288.

50 C. Garnier, *Le Nouvel Opéra de Paris*, 2 vols. (Paris, 1878), Vol. 1, p. 30.

51 *Ibid.*, p. 30 ('thus I cursed both the Prefect and the financiers, who, with no concern for the Opéra, closed it up as if within a great box').

52 A. L. B., *Living Paris and France* (London, 1886), p. 193.

53 J. Cassell, *Cassell's guide to Paris* (London, 1884), p. 57.

54 'Almanach-Album. Charles Garnier', Bibliothèque de l'Opéra, Fonds Garnier Presse, Carton 3 Pièce 2 ('so millions were lavished on the artist so that he could recreate his fantasy by amassing all the wealth of all the arts simultaneously').

55 Garnier, *Le Nouvel Opéra*, Vol. 1, p. 275.

56 G. Chaussinand-Nogaret, 'Urbanisme et société' in G. Duby (ed.), *Histoire de la France urbaine*, 4 vols (Paris, 1980–4), Vol. 3, ed. E. Le Roy Ladurie, *La Ville classique de la Renaissance aux révolutions* (1981), p. 586 ('If all the beautiful *quartiers*, the rich or well-off population, the magnificent monuments, cultured and worldly life support the myth of the world's most beautiful city; misery, crime and fear spread like a cancer over the rotting body of the capital').

57 Broch, *Hugo von Hofmannsthal*, p. 40.

Thanks are due to David Blow and Hugh Clout for comments on earlier drafts of this essay, and to Chris Cromarty for the photographs.

12

The sphinx in the north: Egyptian influences on landscape, architecture and interior design in eighteenth- and nineteenth-century Scotland

ERIC GRANT

Since classical antiquity ancient Egypt has exerted a continuing spell on western civilisation. The Greeks borrowed architectural ideas and symbols from Egypt and, more particularly, the Romans developed a cult of Isis and re-erected Egyptian obelisks in Rome. Sphinxes, pyramids and obelisks, symbolising both death and belief in an after-life, survived as Roman motifs to the end of the middle ages. These three elements reproduced and preserved an image of Egypt as the land of esoteric wisdom and mystery. The Renaissance witnessed a distinct revival of interest in Egypt as part of the wider appreciation of classical and pre-classical antiquity.[1] In the late eighteenth and early nineteenth centuries, the intellectual climate of the Enlightenment and, more specifically, the Napoleonic invasion of Egypt, stimulated an Egyptian revival which left its mark on the landscapes of Britain and America.

Origins of the Egyptian revival

R. G. Carrott identifies two main phases of this revival.[2] The first phase commenced soon after 1750 and was part of a wider Picturesque movement that also incorporated Chinese pagodas, Greek temples and Gothic ruins. While generally there was little thought given to incorporating Egyptian styles and motifs, there was a decorative and a hermetic interest in hieroglyphics. A later, more profound, phase of the revival towards the end of the eighteenth century 'developed within itself from an initial rococo stage to a more consciously archaeological one which was a serious attempt at solving formal aesthetic and symbolical iconographical problems'.[3] An even more scholarly phase in the early nineteenth century was prompted by the important archaeological discoveries made in Egypt at that time.

The most important use of Egyptian motifs was in the iconography of death. Obelisks and pyramids were utilised to symbolise both immortality and social status while tombstones with any form of Egyptian symbolism became popular. Cemetery gates were also a vehicle for the style, with motifs derived from temple constructions. The image of Egypt as the land of ancient wisdom was expressed in various types of institutional buildings, in libraries, museums, masonic lodges, churches, prisons and courthouses. These buildings were usually based on some aspect of temple architecture, including the pylon structures that formed the gateways to temple complexes, and the lotus, papyrus or palm-headed capitals that were found in temple colonnades. Finally, Egyptian symbolism exploited the massiveness and horizontality of Egyptian architecture to convey solidity, performance and dependability in the construction of such civil engineering works as bridges, railway stations and reservoirs.

The rapid growth of interest in Egyptianism in the eighteenth century can be traced to Italy and France. In Italy, Piranesi was the foremost exponent of the decorative or picturesque use of the style, exploiting Egyptian iconography for formalistic reasons and largely applying it to interior design, especially to the design of fireplaces, a distinctly non-Egyptian use. His book *Diverse maniere d'adornare i cammini*, published in 1769, and containing many Egyptian-inspired designs, had considerable impact in Italy and other European countries.[4]

In France, several eighteenth-century writers extolled the virtues of Egyptian architecture and design: its primitivity, massiveness, solidity and simplicity.[5] The pseudo-classical artists of the Louis XVI period borrowed profusely such Egyptian images as sphinxes, caryatids and canopic figurines, applying them to furniture, interior decoration and ceramics. This trend continued through the period of the French Revolution and into the Empire, and a major stimulus for all things Egyptian resulted from Napoleon's Nile campaigns of 1798–9. Napoleon's accompanying savants drew, described and measured the temples and tombs, making many discoveries and scholarly reconstructions and paving the way for the translation of hieroglyphs.

Two French publications in the early nineteenth century were of the greatest significance in promoting Egypt. Published in 1802 (and in an English edition the following year), Denon's *Voyage dans la Basse et la Haute Egypte* (1802) was an account of the French military campaign liberally illustrated with engravings of the country and its ruins.[6] Of more influence still were the 21 volumes of *Description de l'Egypte*, prepared by an army of scholars at the behest of the Emperor and published between 1809 and 1828.[7] This staggering production brought to the attention of a wide public for the first time the architectural wonders of Egypt. The detailed archaeological and architectural descriptions further stimulated this second period of the Egyptian revival by offering architects and designers a much more exact set of motifs from which to borrow.

An increasing number of travellers and artists visited Egypt themselves.[8]

Giovanni Battista Belzoni, an Italian living in England, toured Egypt in 1817, making many important archaeological discoveries and publishing his findings in *Narrative of operations in Egypt* (1830).[9] Britain was a major source of travellers to Egypt, several coming from Scotland. Sir John Maxwell of Pollock House, Glasgow, toured Egypt in 1813–15, recording much detail in his journals about the pyramids and temples, subjects which particularly interested him because of his familiarity with the Egyptian mysteries associated with masonic iconography.[10] Robert Hay of Linplum, a Scottish antiquary and admirer of Belzoni, made several journeys to Egypt between 1824 and 1835, drawing monuments and taking plaster casts.

The traveller who had the greatest influence in Britain in the first half of the nineteenth century was David Roberts. He was the first artist deliberately to set out for Egypt with the intention of making sketches and drawings. Roberts was born in Edinburgh in 1796 and went to London as a successful artist in his twenties but his Scottish connections certainly helped in promoting his art in Scotland. He travelled down the Nile in 1838–9 making detailed sketches as he went, many of them appearing as lithographs in his magnificent set of volumes entitled *Egypt and Nubia*.[11] Roberts's evocative pictures probably appeared a little too late to influence the by then declining Egyptian revival in England, but his work was precisely timed to have an effect in Scotland.

The picturesque phase of the Egyptian revival in Scotland

In eighteenth-century Britain Egyptian-style fireplaces are found in several important houses, while sphinxes adorn the entrances and rooflines. The principal architects and interior designers of the late eighteenth century – including George and Nathaniel Dance, Robert Adam, Sir William Chambers and John Soane – all used Egyptian motifs. The most complete Piranesi-influenced Egyptian schemes appeared in Scotland. James Playfair designed Cairness House, Aberdeenshire, for Charles Gordon during 1791–7. The exterior has primitive doric columns, an order which some writers considered to have Egyptian origins.[12] The interior decoration of the billiard room is the earliest complete Egyptian interior in Britain and several other rooms had Egyptian-inspired fireplaces and doorways (Fig. 1). Its creation by an architect as important as Playfair immediately established Scotland's position in the Egyptian revival.

Other Egyptian elements, notably sphinxes, were introduced into both rural and urban Scotland at this time. Gosford House in East Lothian, designed in 1792–1800 by Robert Adam for the Earl of Wemyss, has the sphinx symbol on the main building and gateposts, while the grounds contain a mausoleum in the shape of a pyramid.[13] Sphinxes became a favourite feature of the new classical landscape in Edinburgh. They occupy each

Fig. 1   Fireplace decorated with hieroglyphics (Egyptian Room, Cairness House, Aberdeenshire). By kind permission of The Royal Commission on the Ancient and Historical Monuments of Scotland.

corner of Charlotte Square, the northern side of which was designed by Robert Adam as one of the most prestigious terraces in the New Town. Commissioned in 1791 it was built piecemeal rather than systematically, and we know that in 1797 a master mason, James Tait, was offering to feu three lots, observing at the same time that 'the front next the square will be built to Mr Adam's elevation . . . it is understood by us that I shall be free from the expense of making and putting up the Sphinx, bulls head, swag husks and ribbon knots'.[14] The old Parliament building reconstructed in 1807–10 to the design of Robert Reid has sphinxes crouching on top of the classical façade. Between 1822 and 1826 William Henry Playfair, the son of James Playfair, designed the first building in Scotland to display battered Egyptian-type doorways, the Royal Institution in Edinburgh (now the Royal Scottish Academy), when the building was enlarged a decade later it was ornamented with the largest tribe of sphinxes in Scotland (Fig. 2).

Whether the sphinx was seen as a specifically Egyptian symbol is unclear. The sphinx motif had been adopted by ancient Greek architects (changing

Fig. 2   Sphinxes over the portals of Playfair's Royal Scottish Academy, Edinburgh. By kind permission of The Royal Commission on the Ancient and Historical Monuments of Scotland.

sex in the process) and its utilisation in classical Edinburgh may have been no more than as a repetitive symbol of the values of the classical world generally. But the main period of its utilisation does coincide with the height of the Egyptian revival and in Scotland, with its strong tradition of freemasonry, symbolic references to ancient Egypt, even by way of Greece, were always acceptable.

Although the picturesque aspects of the revival were widely adopted in Scotland, there was a hiatus in the second decade of the nineteenth century. In England at this time the revival was in full swing and we can identify the more archaeologically influenced phase noted by Carrott. The Egyptian Hall in Piccadilly, built in 1812 as a private museum for William Bullock, and modelled on a drawing in Denon's book, was the earliest conscientious archaeological attempt in England. The Egyptian House in

Penzance is a similar structure, with stepped gable windows, cavetto cornice, torus moulding and winged disc. Although ostensibly following archaeologically based models, the Egyptian House and Joseph Bonomi's flax mill in Leeds (1842) are far from archaeologically pure (the latter has two storeys for example) and were built mainly for their value in attracting general interest and potential custom. The Egyptian revival had reached its ascendancy in England by the 1830s and though Egyptian-influenced buildings were still to be found after that time, the popularity of the style soon declined. In Scotland the revival proved more resilient.[15]

The archaeological phase of the Egyptian revival in Scotland

The Egyptian revival continued well after 1830 in Scotland, indeed its main period was from 1830 to 1870. With about 30 buildings in the genre, Scotland is a country of greater importance to the Egyptian revival than has hitherto been recognised.[16] There can be no doubt that it was the institutional symbolism of Egyptian architecture, especially its connotations of antiquity, permanence, solidity and triumph, that appealed to Scots in the nineteenth century; and arguably one reason for this was the local importance of freemasonry.

Freemasonry has provided a powerful stimulus for the adoption of Egyptian symbolism. Freemasons have frequently claimed to trace their history directly to Egypt, and in particular to mystical connections with the cult of Isis and Osiris.[17] It is unlikely that there is such a direct link, or even, as has also been suggested, an indirect one via Greece. Freemasonry probably originated among the working masons of medieval England to allow them to move freely round the construction sites of churches and abbeys. James I, who was particularly interested in mysticism, revived masonic lodges when he moved from Scotland to become king in England and Inigo Jones, the court architect, was a master mason within the movement. Modern freemasonry originated at a meeting of the London lodges in 1717 when the Grand Lodge of England was formed. Freemasonry also became a major cultural force on the continent where it had strong connections with Rosicrucianism, a cult dominated by hermetic mysticism. Egyptian rites were introduced into continental freemasonry in the late eighteenth century by Count Cagliostro and Carl Friedrich Köppen and quickly followed in Britain.[18] So the Egyptian element in freemasonry was largely invention but it was enthusiastically adopted. It became highly significant in relation to the central masonic symbol, the temple, the built form being seen to reflect the personal construction of an inner, spiritual temple. As more and more ancient Egyptian temples were discovered, and the skills of the temple builders became better appreciated, freemasons were increasingly attracted to the symbolic resonances between geometry, stonemasonry, building and architecture. They constructed an Egyptian genealogy for Solomon's temple and its proportions (already a principal figure in freemasonry), arguing that the Israelites, having built for the Egyptians must surely have brought Egyptian skills to Jerusalem.[19] In addition to architecture, freemasons were also attracted to the more arcane aspects of ancient Egyptian culture, especially the hermetic mysteries of hieroglyphics.

Freemasonry had always been strong in Scotland, with lodges mentioned as early as 1599 at Edinburgh, Kilwinning and Stirling. Though non-craft membership is also recorded early in Scotland (in 1600 John Boswell of Auchinleck, a prominent Scots landowner, was admitted as a freemason) craft masons dominated Scottish freemasonry much longer than in England. The Supreme Grand Royal Arch Chapter of Scotland was founded in Edinburgh in 1816 and other prominent lodges were created about this time in the major cities of Scotland, a period of considerable urban development that embraced both classical and Egyptian revivals. The strength of freemasonry in Scotland and its interest in Egyptian architecture and symbolism offered a fertile environment for the reception of the Egyptian style in architecture and the progress of the Egyptian revival generally. Because of the secrecy maintained by masonic lodges, it is difficult to obtain details of past membership, but it is safe to say that almost every prominent Scots architect, builder, master tradesman and businessman was a freemason. The development of freemasonry can be seen as one aspect of the Scottish Enlightenment that brought continental ideas of art and architecture to a Scottish people desperately trying to overcome a conservative cultural heritage and lay aside its disastrous Jacobite sympathies.

The Egyptian style was widely adopted for funerary monuments and architecture. As in most cultures the celebration of death in Scotland was highly symbolic and there was considerable social pressure among the successful middle classes (many of whom were freemasons) to erect imposing monuments to the deceased. If such monuments had Egyptian symbols or architectural form signifying immortality and eternal wisdom, then so much the better.

The emergence of garden cemeteries in Britain after 1830 as a response to the lack of churchyard burial space presented a rich opportunity for funerary architecture. These garden cemeteries were usually placed at the edge of expanding cities and quickly became popular places of burial for the professional middle classes, and Egyptian-influenced monuments find their greatest expression in them. Perhaps best known is the avenue of Egyptian catacombs constructed in 1839 in Highgate cemetery, London. In Scotland, necropoleis were created in Glasgow, Edinburgh and Dundee, with forests of obelisk memorials. Pyramids are also found (for example the memorial in Dean cemetery, Edinburgh, to Lord Rutherford who died

Fig. 3   Glasgow Necropolis. Photograph from the 1870s by George Washington Wilson. By kind permission of The Royal Commission on the Ancient and Historical Monuments of Scotland.

in 1854) as well as more conventional headstones that have sloping sides and cavetto cornices, motifs with origins in Egyptian temple architecture.

The greatest density of Egyptian influences in funerary architecture is found in the Glasgow Necropolis, a spectacular city of the dead, providing a sepulchral landscape almost unparalleled outside Italy.[20] Instead of simple headstones placed in the ground, the monuments are architect designed, many being veritable miniature houses of the dead occupying a prominent hill-top site near the city centre. Every Glasgow citizen of importance who died between 1832 and 1867 was interred in the Necropolis (Fig. 3). Egyptian architecture was employed on the grand scale with the building of the Egyptian vaults in 1837 for temporary storage of the bodies before the construction of permanent tombs. Also in Glasgow, at Sighthill cemetery, stands the only Egyptian cemetery entrance lodge in Scotland, designed in 1839 by John Stephen, the first Glasgow architect to embrace the Egyptian style.[21] In America cemetery gates in the Egyptian style had been criticised as pagan and anti-Christian but this did not trouble the Scots with their Old Testament beliefs and masonic admiration for Egypt.

Though Aberdeen has no necropolis as such, it was the seat of a significant contribution to funerary architecture. In the mid-nineteenth century it is reputed that a traveller to Egypt brought a piece of polished granite back to Aberdeen, at a time when polishing was unknown in the city's granite industry. Alexander McDonald, an Aberdeen granite merchant, adopted the technique and produced the first polished granite headstone.[22] This rapidly developed into a major Aberdeen trade, and craft masons had a certain social status in the city as well as most being members of masonic lodges. Egyptian influences characterise the design of headstones, with sloping sides and cavetto cornices, but also, and more spectacularly, in the manufacture of complete granite sarcophagi. Queen Victoria and Prince Albert lie in the Royal Mausoleum in Aberdeen granite sarcophagi, and through their patronage such pieces, including the tomb of Napoleon III, were exported throughout Europe. The most spectacular example of Egyptian influence on funerary architecture was in the mausoleum of the Dukes of Hamilton near Glasgow where the tenth duke was laid to rest in a complete copy of a mummy-shaped sarcophagus.[23]

An enthusiasm for the monumentality of Egyptian architecture was responsible for what can be called 'Egyptianising' buildings, that is, buildings which contain no specific Egyptian detail, but are otherwise Egyptian-looking because of their massive proportions and rectangularity and, in the case of Aberdeen, their execution in granite. The North Church, Aberdeen (1829–31), by the city architect John Smith, though classical, has extremely severe proportions, and Carrott notes that it is architecturally very similar in impact to Downtown Presbyterian Church in Nashville, Tennessee, which was built in 1848 with unmistakable Egyptian motifs and proportions.[24] Archibald Simpson, the architect of the beautiful classical exteriors of Aberdeen in native granite, designed the New Market Hall (c.1840) with giant anta order pilasters and a very simple geometrical outline, that also echoes Egyptian proportions and rectangularity.[25]

The use of Egyptian architecture to symbolise solidity, permanence and reliability found wider expression in Scotland. Perhaps the least known example is the series of lighthouses constructed by the Commissioners of Northern Lighthouses between 1846 and 1851. Alan Stephenson, son of Robert Stephenson, was the invited architect and his series of six lighthouses at Noss Head, Covesea, Cromarty, Chanonry, Hoy and Ardnamurchan all have domestic blocks in the Egyptian style (Fig. 4). The towers of the Scottish lighthouses are not Egyptian but there could well be some association with the Pharos of Alexandria, particularly as the Stephenson family were involved in railway construction in Egypt.[26]

The Egyptian churches of 'Greek' Thomson

In Scotland, several churches with Egyptian architectural components and motifs were constructed, the earliest being St Jude's Free Presbyterian

Fig. 4   Noss Head lighthouse, Caithness. By kind permission of The Royal Commission on the Ancient and Historical Monuments of Scotland.

Church in Glasgow, designed in 1838–9 by John Stephen who also designed the entrance lodge of Sighthill cemetery.[27] John Stephen was an important devotee of the Egyptian revival but unfortunately little is known about him, in particular, whether he had any influence on Alexander Thomson, Glasgow's most important Victorian architect.

Alexander Thomson (1817–75) was the architect who most fully embraced the Egyptian style in Scotland. Known as 'Greek' Thomson, in fact 'Egyptian' Thomson would be as apt a nickname. Almost all Thomson's work was in Glasgow and he had a major impact on the architecture of that city from 1849 until his death. There is little doubt that he was the major figure responsible for the survival of the Greek and Egyptian revivals in Scotland through to the 1860s and 1870s. Thomson's early commissions were for villas and country retreats for the burgeoning middle classes of Glasgow and though some of these display a certain structural design owing something to the Egyptian revival – such as an emphasis on horizontality – on the whole they were fairly restrained classical revival houses. He was, however, greatly stimulated by classical revival architects, particularly Thomas Hamilton, architect of the Royal High School in Edinburgh, and William Playfair himself, architect of the Royal

Scottish Academy, National Gallery of Scotland and the Surgeons' Hall in Edinburgh.

At the same time as the wealthy merchants of Glasgow were seeking new villas appropriate to their station, a major event in the history of the Church of Scotland made great demands on architects. In 1843 the Free Church of Scotland broke away from the established Church of Scotland setting up a rival Christian community that required new churches. The Free Church folk, especially in the lowlands, were often the better educated and more energetic sections of the community, bringing both wealth and enthusiasm to their new churches. In 1847 another group of early secessionist churches came together to form the United Presbyterian Church, again with wealthy members who were only too keen to set up independent churches and break the ties between the state and established Church of Scotland with its landowning patrons. The 1840s and 1850s witnessed a period of considerable church building throughout Scotland, a movement that has been somewhat neglected by architectural historians. The classical revival was still in vogue in Scotland and its popularity for many of these new churches was a major factor in ensuring the continuation of the classical revival in Scotland. The Egyptian influence on several of these churches is usually explained in association with the classical revival.[28] However, it is much deeper than that. Although some Gothic churches were built they were not popular with the Old Testament Presbyterians, for Gothic ornamentation suggested Roman Catholic and Anglican associations.

Alexander Thomson was himself a United Presbyterian from a family with deep religious beliefs. Thomson's first church was Caledonia Road United Presbyterian Church in Hutchesontown, Glasgow, 1856. Thomson worshipped at the church so it was not surprising his firm received the commission. The site was a difficult triangular one but Thomson overcame this by lifting the Greek portico on to a large podium with Egyptian-style doorways. The whole lower part of the church is massive and solid with no windows, only doors. Light was introduced by a clerestory arrangement along the sides with simple post and lintel construction, and this emphasis on long horizontal lines held up by short pillars became a feature of his work and certainly owes something to Egypt, perhaps indirectly via the work of the eclectic German architect Karl Friederich von Schinkel, whose work Thomson appears to have admired.[29] Thomson was well aware of the symbolic qualities of architecture and his use of Greek and Egyptian elements in Caledonia Road was not solely ornamental. The heavy Egyptian lower part was to impress the congregation by evoking the solidity and might of antiquity. The Greek portico leads nowhere; it was a small temple in its own right suggesting a gateway to heaven.

Thomson's second church commission was for St Vincent Street United Presbyterian Church, opened in 1859. This is an extraordinary creation bringing Greek and Egyptian symbolism to even greater prominence. The site, though large, was sloping, but Thomson overcame this by constructing a huge stylobate base and placing a Greek temple on top. The podium again has strong Egyptian characteristics and also cyclopean masonry, but the main innovation was to increase the breadth of the church by using side aisles in order to accommodate a congregation of 1500. Although in idea this was sailing close to Gothic practice, Thomson made the aisles distinctively Egyptian with massive pylons rising above the entablature. In a 1916 history of the church, a member of the congregation brought out the masonic connotations of this feature by mentioning that Solomon's temple had side aisles.[30] The tower of the church contains several Egyptian elements – the doorway, bands of pseudo-isodomic masonry, openings with sphinx-like caryatids holding up a lintel, followed by further Egyptian doorway structures and dwarf columns.

In 1867 Thomson was asked to design Queen's Park Church, Glasgow, in competition with an architect who was asked to produce a Gothic design. Here we know that it was the United Presbyterian congregation who made the choice, preferring Thomson's emphatically Egyptian structure to the Gothic one. The main façade, asymmetrical in order to accommodate the church hall, has the form of a propylaeum, with a large pylon entrance. Queen's Park Church was the most archaeological of Thomson's designs with Egyptian elements dominant and the Greek contribution proportionately reduced (Fig. 5).[31]

Thomson produced two designs for churches in Edinburgh, but lost to Gothic designs in each case (sectarian divisions were less deep in Edinburgh) with the result that his work is completely unrepresented in the capital. He was responsible for some smaller churches in Glasgow as well as for office blocks, tenement blocks and modest houses. Although Greek prototypes were his main inspiration, he employed Egyptian forms where he felt them appropriate to the character of the building. The so-called Grecian Chambers (1865) in Sauchiehall Street, for example, are more Egyptian than Grecian, with an Egyptian-style doorway, a colonnade of short Egyptian columns and a massive cornice. The strict geometry and horizontality of the building is distinctly Egyptian and the whole block symbolises a strength, respectability and permanence that no doubt appealed to its commercial owners.

Egyptian revival styles are not normally found in domestic architecture, but Thomson used Egyptian geometric proportions in many of his tenement blocks and houses, while the exquisite villa, Ellisland, is his most overtly Egyptian composition. It was designed towards the end of Thomson's career but we do not know if the purchaser, a manufacturer of gas fittings, ordered the design or if Thomson had a free hand. Ellisland is unique amongst his several houses designed for the growing middle-class suburbs of southern

Fig. 5   Queen's Park United Presbyterian Church, Glasgow. By kind permission of The Royal Commission on the Ancient and Historical Monuments of Scotland.

Glasgow. It is a single storey symmetrical house with central entrance and an emphasis on strong horizontal lines; furthermore the house is finely detailed with Egyptian motifs such as lotus flower chimney pots and lotus flower columns with painted capitals flanking the doorway.

Thomson's contribution to the Egyptian revival in Scotland is paramount. While he appreciated the academic qualities of geometry and proportion in Grecian styles, it is clear that Thomson favoured Egyptian motifs to express moral virtues and to flavour them with a hint of mysticism. Thomson frequently lectured on architecture (to the Glasgow Society of Architects and for the Haldane Institute)[32] and in one of his lectures he offered a detailed summary of Egyptian architecture and his personal interpretation of its symbolic qualities. He examined the pyramid, obelisk and temple in turn, concluding that they respectively symbolised unchangeableness, justice and goodness.[33] Thomson intentionally spurned the Gothic revival with its Roman Catholic associations and indeed gave lectures on its unsuitability as an architectural style. His Presbyterian background with its Old Testament teaching and masonic connections predisposed him to the Egyptian style.

With Thomson's death in 1875 the Egyptian revival in Scotland was essentially over though the style lingered on until the end of the century. Between 1880 and 1893 Robert Thomson (no relation of Alexander Thomson) built several villas at Uddingston and Strathaven near Glasgow that utilise Egyptian motifs both inside and outside. In Edinburgh, where the Egyptian style had been in abeyance since the 1830s (other than for cemetery memorials) the wealth and strength of freemasonry was responsible for a dramatic finale in the employment of Egyptianism. Despite the strength of freemasonry in Scotland, there were few examples of Egyptian architecture incorporated into the design of lodges until the spectacular employment of Egyptian motifs in the interior of the Supreme Grand Royal Arch Chapter Rooms, Queen Street, Edinburgh. The lodge had moved to new headquarters in 1899 and one of its members, the architect Peter Henderson, was asked to design a new chapter room.[34] He drew up a scheme based heavily on Egyptian iconography, including Egyptian columns, hieroglyphics and throne, a scheme that met with acclaim from the lodge members and was duly executed and dedicated in December 1900 (Fig. 6).

Conclusion

The origins and main directions of the Egyptian revival in Britain are well known, but less attention has conventionally been paid to the peculiarities of its progress in Scotland. After 1830, when Egyptian influences were beginning to wane in England, Scotland's part in the Egyptian revival entered a new phase unparalleled elsewhere in Britain. A number of separate developments can be identified which together make Scotland a major contributor to the revival as a whole. Over 30 public buildings, churches, lighthouses, office blocks, masonic halls and domestic constructions display one or more Egyptian structural elements: battered door and window cases, cavetto cornices, dwarf pillars, and papyrus, lotus or palm capitals. Others are ornamented with sphinxes, anthemions,[35] winged discs and even hieroglyphics. The use of massive proportions in certain buildings, particularly those executed in granite, may represent a reworking of Egyptian architectural proportions rather than a direct imitation of the Egyptian style, but there is no doubt about the appeal of these proportions to the nineteenth-century Scottish intellect. Egyptian influences on the iconography of death are found in almost every cemetery in Scotland, with obelisks, pyramids, pylon-inspired tombstones and vaults, granite sarcophagi and other decorative elements dominating the landscape of death in place of the Gothic angels, crosses and similar Christian symbols that predominate in English or catholic cemeteries. Moreover the export of Egyptian-inspired granite tombstones and sarcophagi did extend this influence well beyond Scotland.

There are several reasons for the popularity of the Egyptian style in

Fig. 6   Design for the interior of a new chapter room for the Supreme Grand Royal Arch Chapter of Scotland, Edinburgh. Exhibition drawing, 1901, Robert F. Sherar. By kind permission of The Royal Commission on the Ancient and Historical Monuments of Scotland.

Scotland. The Scottish Enlightenment in the late eighteenth and early nineteenth centuries embraced the classical revival generally and certain Egyptian motifs, particularly the sphinx and anthemion, were embraced in a wider appreciation of classical architecture. Ascetic Scots were also attracted to the solid character of Egyptian architecture. This was particularly evident in the 1840s and 1850s when the secession from the established Church of Scotland required the construction of many new churches whose designers frequently looked to Greek and Egyptian temples for inspiration. That these prototypes were developed in a pre-Christian period of pagan worship did not trouble the Scottish Presbyterians who were heavily imbued with a sense of ancient timelessness from their close adherence to the Old Testament and its moral values. This was further reinforced by the strength of freemasonry in the business communities of Scotland.

There are some interesting parallels between the Egyptian revival in Scotland and that in the United States, where the greatest number of Egyptian-inspired buildings are found. Many of the same social forces favouring the revival were at work. The United States was a self-consciously new nation trying to create a sense of antiquity and solid worth in public buildings as quickly as was possible. Though not a new nation, Scotland was trying to throw off its isolation and Jacobite history by borrowing from a revered and respected antiquity. New churches in America and Scotland both sought ancient prototypes and in both countries freemasonry was strong. Although Scotland cannot compare with the United States in the number of buildings displaying Egyptian influences, the longevity of the Egyptian revival and its striking impact on the urban landscape made Scotland arguably the most important European participant.

NOTES

1 N. Pevsner and S. Lang, 'The Egyptian revival', *Architectural Review*, 119 (1965); reprinted in N. Pevsner, *Studies in art, architecture and design*, Vol. 1 (London, 1968), pp. 213–25.
2 R. G. Carrott, *The Egyptian revival: its sources, monuments and meaning 1808–1858* (Berkeley, 1978), p. 2.
3 *Ibid.*, p. 1.
4 G. B. Piranesi, *Diverse maniere d'adornare i cammini* (Rome, 1769).
5 For example, in the work of A. C. P. Caylus de Thubières, *Recueil d'antiquités Egyptiennes, Etrusques, Grèques et Romaines* (Paris, 1752–67).
6 D. V. Denon, *Voyage dans la Basse et la Haute Egypte pendant les campagnes du Géneral Bonaparte* (Paris, 1802).
7 Commission des Monuments d'Egypte, *Description de l'Egypte, ou recueil des observations et des recherches qui ont été faites en Egypte pendant l'expedition de l'armée française publié par les ordres de Sa Majesté l'empereur Napoléon le Grand* (Paris, 1809–28).

8 P. Clayton, *The rediscovery of ancient Egypt: artists and travellers in the nine-teenth century* (London, 1982). See also: P. Conner (ed.), *The inspiration of Egypt* (Brighton, 1983).

9 G. B. Belzoni, *Narrative of the operations and recent discoveries within the pyra-mids, temples, tombs and excavations of Egypt and Nubia* (London, 1830).

10 'Glasgow and the Cairo connection', *Glasgow Herald*, 7 January 1984.

11 D. Roberts, *Egypt and Nubia*, 3 vols., with notes on the plates by W. Brockedon (London, 1846–50).

12 J. S. Curl, *The Egyptian revival. An introductory study of a recurring theme in the history of taste* (London, 1982), p. 17.

13 National Monuments Record of Scotland, photograph EL 5434.

14 A. J. Youngson, *The making of classical Edinburgh* (Edinburgh, 1966), p. 101.

15 Carrott, *Egyptian revival*.

16 Carrott includes Scotland under his analysis of England and though he notes later buildings in Scotland he does not recognise the strength of the revival in Scotland after it had peaked in England.

17 F. L. Pick and G. N. Knight, *The freemason's pocket reference book*, 3rd edn, revised by Frederick Smith (London, 1983), p. 107.

18 Curl, *Egyptian revival*, p. 88.

19 A. Horne, *King Solomon's temple in the masonic tradition* (London, 1972).

20 J. S. Curl, *A celebration of death. An introduction to some of the buildings, monuments and settings of funerary architecture in the western European tradition* (London, 1980), p. 210.

21 F. Worsdall, *Victorian city: a selection of Glasgow's architecture* (Glasgow, 1982), p. 160

22 J. R. Allen, *The north-east lowlands of Scotland* (London, 1952), p. 128.

23 National Monuments Record of Scotland, photograph LA 2240.

24 Carrott, *Egyptian revival*, p. 77 n. 22.

25 John Betjeman was particularly impressed by the massive use of granite in the New Market Hall façade, but despite his enthusiasm, Aberdeen Corporation allowed it to be demolished.

26 I am grateful to Brian Blouet for this piece of information.

27 Carrott, *Egyptian revival*, pp. 70–7.

28 R. McFadzean, *The life and work of Alexander Thomson* (London, 1979).

29 *Ibid.*, pp. 216–20. There may be a further connection here with freemasonry. Schinkel was a prominent freemason and designed the sets for the 1815 Berlin production of Mozart's *Magic Flute*, the text of which is partly based on a masonic initiation ceremony (Curl, *Egyptian revival*, p. 88). It is not known if Thomson was a freemason but it would be most unlikely if a prominent archi-tect like him was not a freemason. As a Presbyterian, with Old Testament preferences, freemasonry's reverence for Solomon's temple would also appeal to him, as would its anti-catholic prejudice.

30 J. Fleming, *Historical sketch of St Vincent Street United Free Church congrega-tion, Glasgow* (Glasgow, 1916), p. 17. The temple of Solomon was adopted as the principal symbol of freemasonry 'because it was the most stable and magnificent structure that ever existed': C. F. W. Dyer, *Symbolism in craft freemasonry* (London, 1976), pp. 62–3.

31 McFadzean, *Alexander Thomson*, p. 157. Queen's Park Church was Thomson's finest Egyptian creation, but as a result of being destroyed in 1942 by enemy action it has been insufficiently recognised by historians of the Egyptian revival.

32 A. Thomson, 'The Haldane Academy Lectures. Art and architecture: a course of four lectures', *British Architect*, 1 (1874), pp. 274–8, 354–7; 2 (1874), pp. 50–2, 82–4, 272–4, 288–9, 317–18.

33 This echoes the idea that the freemason's lodge is supported on three pillars representing wisdom, strength and beauty. Similarly, Thomson's advocacy of 'the principles of the past' in architecture also has masonic overtones.

34 'Proceedings of the Supreme Grand Chapter and Committee for the year 1899–1900', *The Supreme Grand Royal Arch Chapter of Scotland's Reporter*, 4 (1890–1900), pp. 843–54.

35 The anthemion motif found throughout the New Town of Edinburgh as a decoration on stone, metal and plaster work has its ultimate origin in Egypt where it was used as a decorative representation of the palm or lotus.

13

The geometry of landscape: practical and speculative arts in sixteenth-century Venetian land territories

DENIS COSGROVE

In sixteenth-century Venetian culture landscape was a subject of wide interest and it incorporated meanings that related to contemporary changes in the conditions of life in the Republic. In this essay I examine those conditions, most particularly Venice's increasing strategic and economic interests in the Italian land territories (the *terraferma*, Fig. 1) which it had acquired during the preceding century. The Venetian State was very closely involved in land drainage and reclamation, and many of those directly engaged in the processes of land transformation were equally involved in the artistic representation of landscape. Such a coincidence of interest is to be found in other places and periods, for example in eighteenth-century England where Charles Bridgeman, the Royal Gardener and landscape designer also produced surveys and reports on Fenland drainage.[1] Part of the iconography of landscape is thus to be disclosed by relating it to the material appropriation of land itself. Here I will examine the iconography of Venetian landscape within the context of the technical practices of land survey and reclamation and of late Renaissance literary and philosophical ideas.

Venice and the development of the *terraferma*

Having very nearly forfeited the *terraferma* to the Imperial armies in the first decade of the sixteenth century, Venice directed its efforts over the remaining decades to protecting, administering and exploiting its landed patrimony. By 1600 the *terraferma* rivalled maritime trading in its political, strategic and economic significance to Venice. This growing importance was inevitably reflected in the transformation of the land itself, in building fortifications, redirecting rivers, introducing new crops and above all purchasing, draining, irrigating and improving the productivity of agricultural land. The cultural significance of landscape developed therefore in a society in which land itself was acquiring a new importance.

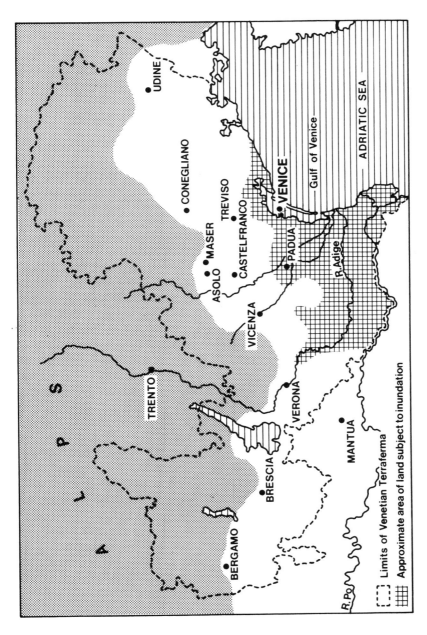

Fig. 1 The Venetian *terraferma* in the sixteenth century.

Materially and culturally the articulating point of Venetian land development was geometry, specifically the geometrical axioms to be found in Euclid's *Elements*. In late Renaissance Italy not only was geometry fundamental to practical activities like cartography, land survey, civil engineering and architecture, but it lay at the heart of a widely accepted neo-platonic cosmology and related esoteric and occult beliefs and practices which found expression in the art of the period. The speculative and the practical are often indissoluble in sixteenth-century culture. They are equally important in understanding the idea of Venetian landscape at this time.

In 1556 the Venetian Senate established a *magistratura*, a ministry, to supervise and regulate hydrological matters in the *terraferma*. The Provveditori ai Beni Inculti (PBI), as the three nobles who ran this office were called, became the key figures in implementing a state policy of land reclamation in areas subject to inundation by the slow rivers that spread the Alpine meltwaters across the Venetian plain, together with irrigation in the higher lands where summer drought burns off the pastures and scorches the crops. The geographical significance of the PBI's work, particularly in the years between 1560 and 1600, is hard to overestimate.[2] Land reclamation reflected the critical need for secure food supplies as Venice's traditional Mediterranean granaries were threatened by the Ottomans. These reclamation activities were closely bound up with the most fundamental change in the course of Venetian economic history, the shift of investment destinations from maritime commerce into agrarian property and rents. During the first fifty years of the PBI's existence the mainland territories witnessed large-scale purchases of land by Venetian nobles, the enlargement and capitalisation of estates, new labour contracts and the introduction of new commercial crops like rice and American corn.[3]

Between 1560 and 1600, under the PBI's supervision, over 150,000 ha of *terraferma* land were reclaimed by drainage and an uncalculated but equally significant area improved by irrigation. The former schemes were generally organised by consortia of landowners, the latter by individual initiatives. Details of both drainage and irrigation schemes were documented in the state archives for every alteration in the flow of water had by law to be notified to their office and approved by the Provveditori. In the process of deciding whether to grant approval, and under what conditions, the most critical agents were the engineers and surveyors, at this time not separate professions but the same men, the *periti* of the PBI.[4] On receipt of a request for irrigation or drainage, itself often accompanied by drawn plans and detailed description, the Provveditori would send out two *periti* to survey, assess, cost and document the scheme and its implications for surrounding areas and water flows. Their written report had to be accompanied by a map (*disegno*) of the area affected by the proposal, and these documents, together with the officers' recommendations, formed the basis for the Provveditori's final decision.

Practical geometry

The *periti* represented a new profession in sixteenth-century Italy. In Europe generally the surveyor was a new and powerful, occasionally mistrusted, figure in the landscape in the eyes of countryfolk, wielding strange instruments and deploying obscure, perhaps even diabolical knowledge to determine land areas and boundaries. We shall see that the folk association of survey skills with esoteric, even occult, practices was not without some foundation. Within their ranks the *periti* of the PBI certainly counted men of considerable and broadly based distinction. Among the very earliest to be employed in this work, in the 1560s, were two of Italy's most important Renaissance cartographers, Giacomo Gastaldo and Cristoforo Sorte.[5] Indeed Sorte, on whose work I shall concentrate, seems to have been a minor example of that Renaissance ideal, the universal man. Not only are his topographical maps memorable (Fig. 2), but together with the major architects of his day like Andrea Palladio, Sorte merited consultation over the restoration of the Ducal Palace, the most important building in the Republic, after the disastrous fire of 1577. He was actually commissioned to design the decorative scheme for the ceilings of the Sala del Gran Consiglio, the very heart of the palace and the symbolic centre of the Republic's government.[6] In the 1580s he was invited to produce a vast wall map of the Venetian dominions for the Ducal Palace, a scheme later altered to a number of smaller, but still sizeable, maps of individual provinces. Sorte also produced schemes for vast reclamation projects and the diversion of rivers, designed pumping engines and sluice locks, and wrote a remarkably advanced theoretical essay on the hydrological cycle.[7] In 1580 he wrote a treatise on painting, *Osservazioni nella pittura*, a work that contains the first theoretical discourse on landscape art.[8]

The routine work of a *perito* like Gastaldo or Sorte for the PBI involved the survey skills of levelling, determining the size and shape of fields, and measuring distances and directions. While the exact methods and instruments employed by any individual surveyor are difficult to establish with certainty, a volume of Sorte's working notes and designs has been preserved in the Venetian state archive – probably because as a designer of strategic maps for Venice Sorte's papers were considered to have security implications.[9] These allow us to reconstruct something of his methods. Sorte's techniques appear to have been those described in contemporary works by the 'mathematical practitioners', as their English equivalents were called, the writers of mathematical and geometrical texts, a large number of which were published in Venice during the course of the sixteenth century.[10] These

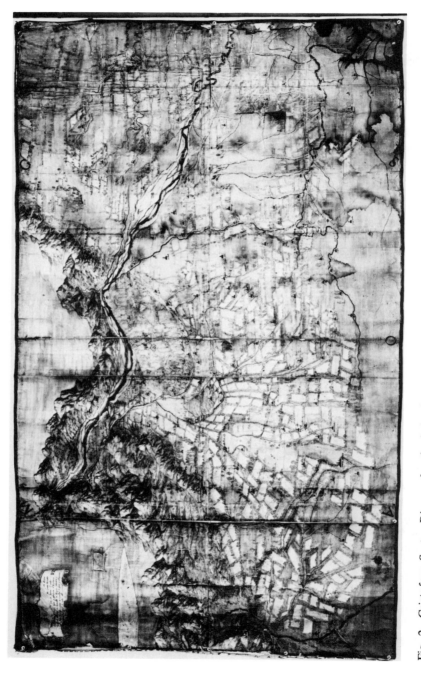

Fig. 2 Cristoforo Sorte, *Disegno* for the irrigation of the province of Treviso, 1556. Watercolour on paper. Archivio di Stato di Venezia: Savi ed esecutori alle acque, Diversi 5.

texts were never purely survey handbooks, rather they were manuals of practical or applied mathematics and geometry in which pride of place was given to Euclid's theorems and their application to a range of practices like mercantile measurement of volumes, navigation and ballistics. Some, like Bartoli's *Del modo di misurare le distantie* . . . (1564), specifically outlined methods for making large-scale maps of provinces. The application of Euclidian concepts to survey was of course an obvious one, particularly when land survey was predominantly based on visual methods using the compass for directional fixes, a quadrant or cross-staff to determine angles and proportional triangles to calculate areas inferentially (Fig. 3). Sorte's unpublished notes and sketches show that these were his methods. For example in calculating the area of an irregular field we can observe him splitting it up into the smallest possible number of triangles and calculating the area of each visually, then summing for the final total, exactly as recommended by Bartoli. The compass, cross-staff, quadrant and astrolabe were the daily tools of Gastaldo's and Sorte's trade, Euclidian geometry its theoretical foundation.

The work of the PBI and its *periti* undoubtedly stimulated advances in survey technique and practice in early modern Venice, as did warfare and defence.[11] In the newly drained and capitalised farming areas of the Polesine, Padovano and Vicentino the straight lines of the canalised rivers and drainage channels and the surveyed boundaries of the reticulated fields produced a regular, geometrical landscape which proclaimed a new conceptual as well as technical mastery over the environment.

Landscape art and the *terraferma*

To the history of those arts that deal with landscape: painting, pastoral poetry and the construction of artistocratic rural dwellings Renaissance Venice made a significant contribution. From the Bellinis, through Giorgione and Titian to Bassano, Tintoretto and Veronese, landscape formed the setting for Venetian paintings, increasing their subject matter.[12] In the poetry of Bembo and Tasso, pastoral and arcadian themes dominate. And in Palladio's villas, 'for the first time in Western architecture, landscape and building were conceived as belonging to each other'.[13] Why the 'vision of landscape' should have been so strong in Venice at this time is difficult, perhaps impossible, to explain. Fashion in the art market and the commercial popularity of Flemish painting, both indicators of the highly developed commercial society Venice was, no doubt played their part. But the rapidly expanding material interest in land among the Venetian patriciate cannot be ignored as an influence. It manifested itself in a rash of treatises on the art of villa living which were as much cultural handbooks as agrarian manuals.[14] Villa living meant both the practical organisation of the estate

LIBRO

Propofitione. vi.

Mi uoglio fabricare uno iftruméto che mi ferua a liuelar un piano, et anchora a conofcere cõ lafpetto, le altezze, larghez- ze profundita, diftantie hipotumiffale & horizontale delle cofe apparente, & che anchora con facilita me lo poffa accomo dar da inueftigar la uarieta di tiri de cadauno pezzo de arte- gliaria, & fimilmente de ogni mortaro.

Piglio una lamina di alcun metallo ben piana groffa una bonà cofta di cortello, cuer una tauoletta di alcun legno fodo e ben fecco groffa al men un dedo grof- fo, & con una rega, & fquadra giufta, ne cauo della detta lamina, ouer tauoletta una fquadra alla fimilitudine della infrafcritta.a b c.d e f.che habbia interchiufo uno per- fettiffimo quadro alla fimilitudine del quadro.e g h i. & luntano una cofta di cortello uel circa da li dui lati.g h.& .h i.tiro tre lince luntane l'una da l'altra un dedo grof- fo uel circa equidiftante alli detti dui lati.g h.& .h i. & cadauna di quelle due che fo- no propinque alli detti dui lati.h g.& .h i.diuido in.1 2.parti eguali & dal angolo.e. a cadauno delli detti.1 2.e.1 2.duifioni,ouer ponti,tiro le lince diuidente li fpaci, che interchiude le tre,e tre lince equidiftanti alli dui lati.g h.& i.in.1 2.fpaci eguali & cofi haro compita la figura gnomonica.k h l.diuifa in.1 2.c.1 2.parti eguali, laqual figura dalli antiqui e chiamata fchala altimetria & la parte h l.é detta ombra retta et la parte.h k.e chiamata ombra uerfa et la linea h e. (cioe il diametro del quadro) é detta linea de l'ombra media & la diuifione.1.de l'ombra retta fe chiama il primo

Fig. 3 Silvio Belli, method of levelling and determining distances, heights, etc., from *Libro del misurar con la vista* (Venezia, 1565).

and, in emulation of classical writers like Pliny and Ovid, a philosophical reflection on the relations between man, society and the natural world.

In 1580 Cristoforo Sorte published *Osservazioni nella pittura*, a systematic consideration of the techniques of landscape painting, an unusually direct example of the link between cartography and landscape art. Sorte had in fact been trained as a painter and architect under Giulio Romano at Mantua. His topographical maps or chorographies are works of landscape art of astonishing informality and directness which owe more to Flemish traditions than to the idealised landscapes of the Venetian school (Fig. 2).[15] It is upon one of these works that Sorte is commenting in his *Osserva- zioni*,[16] written in reply to a series of requests about his method from a friend in Verona. In the text Sorte discusses an astonishing range of issues, both scientific and artistic – the origin of rivers and the hydrological cycle, selection and mixing of pigments, the use of colour as a key to land use on maps, the organisation of the angelic choirs, methods of representing the Divinity on canvas – these indicate something of the range of the essay. Much of the text is concerned with *light*, the critical focus for the landscape painter, with linear and aerial perspective, chiaroscuro and ways of capturing dual light sources on canvas.[17]

For Sorte the foundation of all painting is linear perspective: 'it being the most essential foundation for painters and requiring of them the greatest familiarity, recognising that without it nothing can be depicted of any value'.[18] The last part of *Osservazioni* is a detailed discussion of the means of determining true linear perspective, based on the teachings of Giulio Romano, using the graticule and mirror. Since landscape painting depends upon composing an illusion of real space, some form of perspective is central to it.[19] Perspective in Rennaissance painting was constructed theoretically upon an understanding of the same Euclidian principles as Sorte and his fellow *periti* employed in devising the landscape of Venetian reclamation.[20] Technically and theoretically therefore both the reality and the illusion of Venetian landscape were grounded in Euclidian geometry.

Nowhere is this clearer than in the *terraferma* villas built for Venetian landowners, the beneficiaries of schemes approved by the PBI. These were constructed according to the geometrical and proportional principles of late Renaissance architectural theory[21] and decorated by painters like Paolo Veronese with *trompe-l'oeil* views over arcadian countryside, exercises in perspective which consciously mirrored the harmony of surveyed and often reclaimed fields in which the villas were set. At the Villa Godi at Lonedo for example the internal frescoes depict classical scenes but incorporate recognisable features of the working landscape of the Veneto: farmhouses, watermills and even the weirs constructed for water control. Designed by Palladio and decorated by Veronese, the masterpiece of such landscape art is the Villa Maser, built in the 1560s. Its entire composition, decorative scheme and garden, stretching into the landscape beyond, hinges upon geometry.[22]

Palladio's Villa Rotonda, architecturally the most perfect exercise in applied geometry of cube and sphere, is described in *The four books of architecture* in the terms of a landscape painting:

The site is as pleasant and delightful as can be found, because it is upon a small hill, and is watered on one side by a navigable river, and on the other side it is encompassed with the most pleasant risings, which look like a very great theatre, and all are cultivated and abound with most excellent fruits and most exquisite vines: and therefore, as it enjoys from every part most beautiful views, some of which are limited, some more extended, and others that terminate with the horizon, there are loggias made on all four sides.[23]

Foreground, middleground and distance composed a landscape over the fields and farms of a working estate even in this, the least apparently functional of the villas.[24]

Speculative geometry

This geometry – of architecture, of perspective, of landscape composition, survey and mapping – was at one level a very practical affair, merely the common foundation for a series of techniques appropriate to different aspects of a society and economy exercising new degrees of material and cultural control over its environment. In the manuals referred to earlier it is generally treated in such a way, but not entirely. *Scala grimaldella: libro d'aritmetica, e geometria speculativa e practicale* was the title of one by Francesco Feliciano. For some the speculative side of geometry was more critical than the practical.[25] Geometry and number theory underlay a complex esoteric culture and cosmology in the sixteenth century, one that found particular favour among educated Venetians. Pythagorean and neo-platonic philosophy had been given a huge stimulus in the High Renaissance by Ficino's translation of the hermetic corpus, a group of mystical and magical texts believed to predate and prefigure the ideas of both Plato and Christ.[26] With Pico della Mirandola's contemporary introduction of Cabalistic number theory,[27] Renaissance magic became acceptable to many devout Christians. Much of its practice was bound up with astronomy and astrology, spherical calculations, zodiacal predictions and related theories, all of which involved complex geometrical knowledge. While this 'religion of the world' was taken much further by some thinkers than conventional doctrine would allow, for example by Cornelius Agrippa and Giordano Bruno, in dilute form it had very widespread appeal. The texts of the mathematical practitioners that we have considered integrate speculative ideas quite comfortably alongside their practical concerns.[28]

The unity of practical and speculative geometry is made explicit in the frontispiece of Nicolo Tartaglia's *La nuova scienzia*, a text on mathematical arts and specifically artillery and ballistics, published in Venice in 1550 (Fig. 4). It shows Euclid opening the gate to a circular enclosure. In this space are collected around Tartaglia himself a group of figures who symbolise the sciences dependent upon geometry. They include astronomy, perspective, arithmetic, music, astrology, hydromancy, geomancy, necromancy, pyromancy, horoscopy, geography, chorography and architecture.[29] The 'new science' as such, ballistics, is represented by two firing cannons whose trajectories may be calculated by applied geometry using the straight line and circle. An inner enclosure, guarded by Plato and Aristotle leads to a throne upon which is seated Philosophia, indicating the exalted

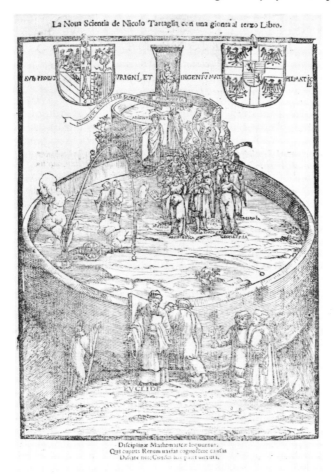

Fig. 4 Nicolo Tartaglia, *La nova scientia* (Venezia, 1550), frontispiece.

dignity of Tartaglia's subject matter. The meaning of this picture is made explicit in the introduction to Tartaglia's 1543 Italian translation of Euclid's *Opere*. Both the liberal and the mathematical arts depend on geometry. In ancient times both sets of sciences 'were revered, sought out and celebrated by all the most discerning and talented men, for through them not only are earthly things necessary to us mortals brought to our notice and understanding, but equally by their means we come to understand things divine'.[30]

Indeed the speculative side of geometry was regarded as far more exalted than the practical, for only in theoretical discourse is certainty possible. Thus speculative geometry is the 'pure food of intellectual life' ('il puro cibo della vita intelletuale') because it deals with figures in the mind rather than the eye, in Platonic terms with pure, unchanging forms rather than their dull reflection in material reality. Thus, says Tartaglia, Plato demanded that anyone entering his academy should know geometry, 'because he knew that in this geometrical science every other occult science was to be found'. Among Tartaglia's sources are Plato, Pythagoras, Hermes Trismegistus and the key text of Renaissance magic, Cornelius Agrippa's *De occulta philosophia*.[31] Speculative geometry contemplated the beauty and regularity of points, lines, areas and the theorems that related them, for herein was the measure of the Divine and of its order throughout creation. Through astrology, 'the pure essential science', it sought to know that cosmic order with which we should seek harmony in living our human lives.

There is no direct evidence that Cristoforo Sorte actually read Tartaglia. But it would be surprising if he did not know the work, for Tartaglia was a military engineer in Sorte's home town of Verona when the latter was himself a young engineer and artist in the 1530s. However, Sorte certainly knew another of the practitioners, Silvio Belli, author of two books on practical and theoretical geometry and proportion, for both men were engaged in a long wrangle over a survey Sorte had completed in the Alpine borders of the northern Veneto, a survey Belli claimed was inaccurate, partly because of Sorte's inadequate compass technique.[32] Belli was a co-founder with Palladio and others of the Olympic Academy at Vicenza, a humanist, neo-platonic group whose founding declaration stated that 'The Olympic Academicians are all of one mind and one wish ... that each of them desires to improve all the sciences, and especially mathematics, which is the true grace of the noble and virtuous soul.'[33] Belli's books, *Della proportione e proportionalità* (1573) and *Libro del misurar con la vista* (1565), are heavily influenced by Francesco Giorgio's *De harmonia mundi*, one of the critical cabalistic texts of the Venetian Renaissance. Belli understood the uses of the mystical compass[34] and the complex harmonics of the celestial spheres. Close reading of Sorte's *Osservazioni nella pittura* suggests that he too had some familiarity with the esoteric discourse of speculative geometry.

In the opening part of his essay Sorte describes himself as a pure practitioner ('un puro prattico'). Sorte thus implicitly acknowledges the speculative aspect of his work while disclaiming any authority to speak about it. However, when he discusses the artistic representation of Divine themes, Sorte describes the angelic choirs in relation to the celestial spheres, a cabalist theme. He speaks of nature as the mother of all things and mover of the circling heavens, while God he refers to as 'the eternal father ...

an omnipotent, invisible essence, incorporeal and incomprehensible'.[35] While it would be wrong to claim *Osservazioni nella pittura* as in any way an esoteric text, there are a number of examples of hermetically informed language in this early discourse on landscape.

Landscape and the 'religion of the world'

It is worth remembering that Sorte's teacher, Giulio Romano, whose authority is cited more than once in the essay, was the painter of the Sala dei Venti in the Palazzo del Tè at Mantua with its complex zodiacal iconography. That speculative considerations were by no means far removed from the interests of cartographers is indicated in the work of a map-maker contemporary with Sorte, Antonio Campi, whose 1571 map of the Cremonese, bordering on the regions mapped by Sorte, quite explicitly combines accurately surveyed geography, from a vertical perspective, and distances correct from Cremona, with obliquely viewed decorative landscape elements. Either side of the Spanish royal arms are a design of the Empyreum, *primum mobile* and ten heavenly spheres, balanced by a world map based on an azimuthal projection with diagrammatic representation of astronomical fixing of terrestrial location (Fig. 5).[36]

From this juncture, founded in geometry, between practical chorography and a speculative philosophy, I think we can discern a deeper iconography of landscape than the study of land developments or artistic tastes alone can disclose. This is the idea of landscape symbolising an achieved harmony between human life and the hidden order of creation, landscape as an expression of a 'religion of the world', as Yates has termed the hermetic vision of the Renaissance. Landscape painting, Sorte claims, can capture the beauty and harmony of nature particularly by addressing itself to two types of natural condition, that is to the periods of dawn and dusk and to the seasons. A long passage is devoted in his *Osservazioni* to the 'aurora', the moment of the rising sun and the wonders of its light across the landscape. A similar praise of dawn landscapes appears consistently in the agricultural treatises of the period when discussing the pleasures of villa living – interestingly different from later artistic emphasis on evening scenes.[37] At dawn and dusk the sun, that focus of hermetic symbolism, newly located centre of the Copernican universe and basis of astronomical calculation, performs its most obvious and spectacular daily duties and its light is at its most diffuse and mysterious. A religion of the world turns naturally to such moments as the holiest of all and nature or landscape is at those times most permeated with sacred meaning.

The seasons too express the revolutions of the spheres, the cycles of the heavens, indeed they are the most powerful evidence for them in the natural landscape. The landscape painter, Sorte claims, must capture

Fig. 5 Antonio Campi, map of the province of Cremona, 1571. Woodcut. Università degli studi di Bologna, Instituto di geografia.

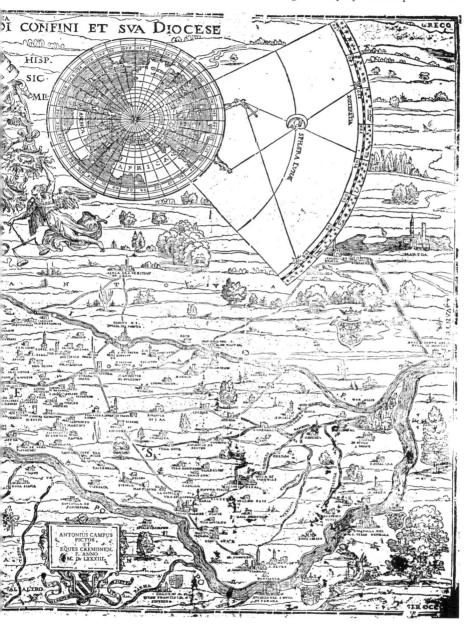

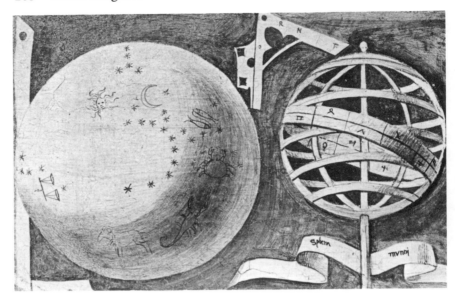

Fig. 6   Giorgione of Castelfranco, frieze of the liberal arts, detail showing astrolabe, global sphere and zodiacal signs, c.1500. Fresco, Casa Marta-Pellizari, Castelfranco, Veneto.

the variety of the four seasons of the year: In the gentle spring we see the earth dressed in the most beautiful and diverse shades of green, adorned in pinks and a thousand varieties of flowers, with the newest leaves of the trees, and with every kind of bush and plant which, scarcely emerged from their maternal buds but begin to green. In the broad fields of summer we see the oceans of grain bleaching as their crop ripens, and, in parts, the leaves of the trees turning to orange while the earth burns in the heat, as if its vital spirit were exhausted. Autumn reveals other charms and varieties of colours, for we see the leaves turning russet and gold with age and begin to fall. Then follows naked winter, abandoned by all the sweetness of both colour and air, which for the most part is overtaken by mists and rains and the earth by frost and snow, whose horror is never more clearly revealed than in the blasted trees and the earth shorn of all beauty.[38]

Painting the seasons is of course the oldest of all the traditions of landscape painting, and its links with hermetic and zodiacal themes are already firmly established by the end of the fifteenth century in the frescoes of the Palazzo Schifanoia at Ferrara.[39] In chorography and in landscape painting, Sorte seems to be implying, by capturing the seasons or the aurora, we can touch the revolutions of the great machine of the world, revolutions that reflect the divine harmony, and thus capture that harmony in paint.

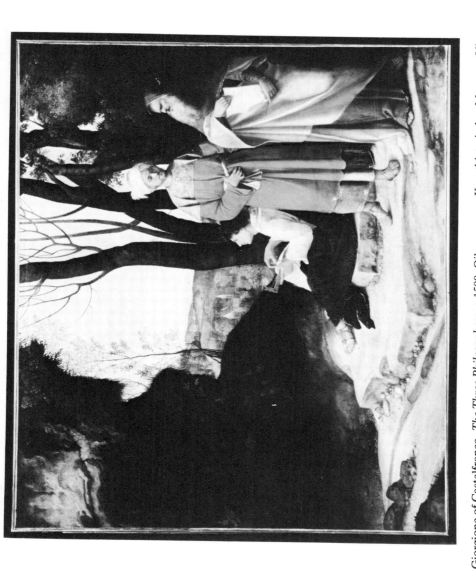

Fig. 7 Giorgione of Castelfranco, *The Three Philosophers*, c.1500. Oil on canvas. Kunsthistorisches Museum, Vienna.

Fig. 8   Giorgione of Castelfranco, *Adoration of the Magi*, c.1500. Oil on canvas.
The National Gallery, London.

Perhaps this is the message and meaning offered to us in the works
of one of the most ambiguous landscapists of the Venetian school, Giorgione of Castelfranco. In his native town, deep in the *terraferma*, frescoes
only recently attributed to Giorgione confirm his interest in the humanist
concepts of the mathematical arts, whose unification of practical and speculative knowledge is founded in geometry (Fig. 6).[40] In Giorgione's landscapes geometry may again be a key element. Are those men in *The Three
Philosophers* (Fig. 7), so obviously of different ages, all the same person?
Could he be perhaps the thrice-holy Hermes – king, priest and philosopher?
Certainly the young man whose quadrant shares with the setting sun the
very centre of the painting is taking a bearing on the heavens, and the
oldest holds an astrological chart. While the traditional interpretation of
the subject matter is that these are the magi seeking signs of Christ's coming,
in Giorgione's *Adoration of the Magi* (Fig. 8) in the National Gallery in
London their representation is very different. The issue is not particularly
important for, as Johannes Wilde puts it, the real content of the painting
is 'man's communion with nature',[41] that is it expresses the idea that under

certain conditions humans can touch the deepest rhythms of creation and achieve a unity between their own spirit and that of the living universe. Compositionally the perspective focuses through a verdant landscape to the sun, whose mysterious light determines the mood of this, like so many of Giorgione's pictures. But the landscape like its staffage is also a triple composite, for the great trees to the right of the middleground are bare and wintry while to the left a young sapling has a spring-like look and a fig hidden in the recesses of the rock pushes new leaves. The background landscape is in full summer foliage. Setting sun, seasons, magi and the archetypal geometrical instrument here anticipate the landscape iconography of later sixteenth-century Venice, an iconography which bound together the practical world of survey and mapping then spreading a new rational order across the fields of the *terraferma*, and a speculative, philosophical culture whose esoteric intellectualism acts as a sophisticated veneer upon a very ancient universal religion of the world. For sixteenth-century Venice a key to this unity of material and cultural change, of the practical and the speculative, lies in the geometry of landscape.[42]

NOTES

1 Peter Willis, *Charles Bridgeman and the English landscape garden* (London, 1977), p. 36. Although the words *paese* and *paesaggio* were applied to paintings in Renaissance Venice they generally referred to Flemish works and in most Venetian paintings landscape is represented as background to religious or mythological subject matter. However there is little doubt that landscape representation was enjoyed for its own sake and painted with exquisite care by Giovanni Bellini and those who followed him, particularly Giorgione and Titian. For a summary view of Venetian landscape art during the sixteenth century see A. R. Turner, *The vision of landscape in Renaissance Italy* (Princeton, NJ, 1963), and on the broader social context of the landscape idea in sixteenth-century Venice see D. E. Cosgrove, *Social formation and symbolic landscape* (London, 1984), pp. 102–41.

2 The most comprehensive overview of the reclamation work undertaken by Venice in the second half of the sixteenth century remains Angelo Ventura's 'Considerazioni sull'agricoltura veneta e sulla accumulazione originaria del capitale nei secoli XVI e XVII', *Studi Storici*, 9 (1968), pp. 674–722. More detailed specific studies have subsequently been undertaken on particular aspects or areas of the work, for example Salvatore Ciriacono, 'Scrittori d'idraulica e politica delle acque', in *Storia della cultura veneta. Dal primo quattrocento al Concilio di Trento* (Vicenza, 1980); 'Investimenti capitalistici e cultura irrigue. La coniuntura agricola nella terraferma veneta (secoli XVI e XVII)', in A. Tagliaferri (ed.), *Atti del convegno: Venezia e la terraferma attraverso le relazione dei rettori* (*Trieste, 1980*) (Milano, 1981), pp. 123–58, on irrigation; and G. Borelli (ed.), *Uomini e acqua nella republica veneta tra secolo XVI e secolo XVIII: il tratto veronese dell'Adige* (Verona, 1979), on drainage schemes along the river Adige.

3 Since the last discussion published in English on the investment shift of Venetian capital from maritime commerce to landed property in the sixteenth century in B. Pullan (ed.), *Crisis and change in the Venetian economy in the 16th and 17th centuries* (London, 1968), a great deal of research has been published in Italy on aspects of the problem. A useful recent summary is contained in G. Barbieri, 'Tendenze della storiografia veneta degli ultimi decenni', in Tagliaferri (ed.), *Atti del convegno*, pp. 47–64. On land purchase see D. Beltrami, *Penetrazione economica dei veneziani in terraferma: forze di lavoro e propretaria fondiaria nelle campagne venete dei secoli XVII e XVIII* (Venezia, 1961); on labour contracts see G. Corazzol, *Fiti e livelli a grano. Un aspetto del credito rurale nel veneto del '500* (Milano, 1979); on new crops see M. Fassina, 'Elementi e aspetti della presenza del mais nel Vicentino: con particolare riferimento a Lisiera e alla zona attraversata dal fiume Tesina', in C. Povolo (ed.), *Lisiera: immagini, documenti e problemi per la storia e coltura di una communità veneta* (Vicenza, 1981), pp. 309–26.

4 U. Mozzi, *I magistrati venete alle acque ed alle bonifiche* (Bologna, 1927). There were two types of *periti*: *periti ordinarii*, permanent employees of the State, and *periti straordinarii*, skilled men contracted for specific schemes.

5 R. Almagia, *Monumenta italiae cartographica* (Firenze, 1929), p. 26.

6 Cristoforo Sorte remains one of the least-studied cartographers and geographers of the sixteenth century. Other than some essays on his map-making by the Italian cartographic historian and geographer R. Almagià in the earlier part of this century, the only interest in his work has come from art historians. The most recent writings on Sorte's life and work have been those of Juergen Schultz where reference to earlier studies on Sorte may be found. Sorte's papers and sketches at the ASV were first brought to light by Schultz and discussed in 'New maps and landscape drawings by Cristoforo Sorte', *Mitteilungen des kunsthistorischen institutes in Florenz*, 20 (1976), pp. 107–26. On Sorte's reclamation work see Silvino Salgaro, 'Il governo delle acque nella pianura veronese da una carta del XVI secolo', *Bollettino della società geografica italiana*, Ser. 10 (Roma, 1980), pp. 327–50, fn. 7.

7 J. Schultz, 'Cristoforo Sorte and the ducal palace of Venice', *Mitteilungen des kunsthistorischen institutes in Florenz*, 3 (1962), pp. 193–208.

8 C. Sorte, *Osservazioni nella pittura* (1580), reprinted in P. Barocchi (ed.), *Trattati d'arte del cinquecento: fra manierismo e contrariforma*, Vol. 1 (Bari, 1960), pp. 271–301. E. H. Gombrich refers to the significance of this essay for the history of landscape in 'The Renaissance theory of art and the rise of landscape', in E. H. Gombrich, *Norm and form: studies in the art of the Renaissance* (London, 1966), pp. 107–21, quotation on p. 118.

9 My own brief survey of the two archival folders and of the many other *disegni* by Sorte scattered throughout the archive supports Schultz's comment in 'New maps' that these documents need to be examined from a cartographical and geographical perspective (ASV: Provv. Camera ai Confini, Generali, B.260, 262).

10 The earliest of these works was Fra Luca Pacioli's *Summa di aritmetica, proportione e proportionalità* (1494), and among the most influential in terms of survey were Francesco Feliciano's *Scala grimaldella: libro d'aritmetica, e geometria speculativa, e practicale* (1518), and Cosimo Bartoli's *Del modo di misurare le distantie . . .* (1564). There is no recent history of surveying in Italy, the most comprehensive is still G. Rossi, '*Groma e squadro*' *ovvero storia dell'agrimensura italiana dai tempi antichi al secolo XVIIo* (Torino, 1877). Rossi selects the invention of the cross-staff which he dates from about 1485 as the critical moment for the development of modern surveying. The first writer to discuss this instrument explicitly was Feliciano, whom Rossi calls 'the true founder of modern surveying in Italy' (p. 121).

11 J. R. Hale, 'The development of the bastion 1440–1534', in J. R. Hale *et al.*, *Europe in the late middle ages* (London, 1965).

12 Turner, *The vision of landscape*.

13 N. Pevsner, *An outline of European architecture* (Harmondsworth, 1957).

14 Paola Lanoro Sartori, 'Gli scrittori veneti d'agraria del cinquecento e del primo seicento tra realtà e utopia', in Tagliaferri (ed.), *Atti del convegno*, pp. 261–310.

15 Gombrich, *Norm and form*, p. 118; Schultz, 'New maps', p. 121.

16 The treatise was written in reply to a letter from Bartolomeo Vitali of Verona dated 1573 thanking Sorte for a 'chorografo' of the Veronese accompanied by a history of the city's ancient history. The map has not to my knowledge been traced, and Schultz who has recovered a number of Sorte's maps previously thought uncompleted or lost, including one of the Veronese produced later than the one referred to here, makes no mention of it.

17 Perhaps the most memorable part of the treatise is a highly poetic passage describing a fire which Sorte watched from a bridge over the Adige river under moonlight in Verona in 1561. In its combination of picturesque sensibility and technical interest in competing light sources and reflections the passage anticipates the painterly concerns of landscape artists into the nineteenth century. Sorte, *Osservazioni nella pittura*, pp. 289–91.

18 *Ibid.*, p. 296: 'essendo ella necessarissimo fondamento de'pitturi e convenendo essere loro molto familiare, consciosa che niuna cosa sensa di lei si possa dipingere che sia bene'.

19 On the relations between perspective theory and landscape in the Renaissance see D. Cosgrove, 'Prospect, perspective and the evolution of the landscape idea', *Institute of British Geographers, Transactions*, NS, 1 (1985), pp. 45–62. Curiously, in his topographical mapping Sorte did not use a full triangulation and theoretical graticule to construct his plans.

20 Perspective is treated as one of the mathematical arts in the treatises mentioned above. In the introduction to his Italian translation of *Euclid* (1543), Nicolo Tartaglia discusses perspective in this way, as later did John Dee in a similar preface to the English translation of *Euclid* (1570). See also the discussion in F. Yates, *Theatre of the world* (London and Henley, 1969), pp. 47–8.

21 R. Wittkower, *Architectural principles in the age of humanism* (London, 1962).

22 One of the two brothers who commissioned Palladio to design the villa at Maser, Daniele Barbaro, both wrote a commentary on Euclid and translated Vitruvius into Italian: *I dieci libri dell'architettura di M. Vitruvio tradutti et commentati da Monsignor Barbaro* (Vinezia, 1556). Palladio drew the illustrations for Daniele's translation. See the discussion in Wittkower, *Architectural principles*, pp. 65ff. On the general significance of Vitruvian theory for Renaissance philosophy and speculative arts, see Yates, *Theatre of the world*, pp. 21ff.

23 A. Palladio, *The four books of architecture* (1570; transl. Isaac Ware, 1738; facs. New York, 1965), p. 41.

24 The Rotonda was in fact not merely a belvedere as is often supposed from the description provided by Palladio in *The four books*. The sale documents relating to its transfer, uncompleted, in 1590 make it clear that it was the centre of a working estate and its inventory suggests that the cellars of the building stored agricultural produce.

25 The discussion which follows is closely dependent upon the work of Frances Yates who has pioneered contemporary study of the role of magic and the occult in sixteenth-century Renaissance culture. Of particular relevance to this paper are her *Theatre of the world; Giordano Bruno and the hermetic tradition* (London, 1964); *The art of memory* (London, 1966) and *The occult philosophy in the Elizabethan age* (London, 1979). The influence of Yates' work on Italian

studies of Venetian sixteenth-century culture is revealed in G. Barbieri, *Andrea Palladio e la cultura veneta del rinascimento* (Roma, 1983).

26 Yates, *Giordano Bruno*, pp. 12–19.

27 Yates, *The occult philosophy*, pp. 17–22.

28 Luca Pacioli's *De divina proportione*, for which Leonardo da Vinci drew the illustrations, is one example. Cosimo Bartoli was also interested in aspects of hermeticism, and the best-known English mathematical practitioner, John Dee, was deeply involved in mystical mathematics and the occult generally. For Pacioli, see Yates, *Theatre of the world*, pp. 36–7; for Bartoli, see Judith Bryce, *Cosimo Bartoli (1503–1572): the career of a Florentine polymath* (Génève, 1983), pp. 61–4 and 213–14; for Dee, see Peter J. French, *John Dee: the world of an Elizabethan magus* (London, 1972).

29 N. Tartaglia, *La nuova scienzia, con una giunta al terzo libro* (Venezia, 1550).

30 N. Tartaglia, *Euclide magarense philosopho: solo introddutore delle scientie mathematice diligentissimente reassettato, et alla integrità ridotto* (Venezia, 1543), fo. III ('antiquamente furono reverite, cercate, e celebrate da tutti li perspicacissimi ingegni, mediante lequali non solo son pervenuti alla notitia e cognitione delle cose terrene, a noi mortali necessarie, ma etiam per mezzo di quelle son venuti in cognitione delle divine'). In sum the disciplines listed by Tartaglia are those of the mathematical arts as understood in the Renaissance Vitruvian tradition. It may be that John Dee, in his own *Preface* to the English translation of Euclid some 27 years after Tartaglia, drew upon the Italian's work. In her discussion of the provenance of Dee's ideas (*Theatre of the world*, pp. 20–41) Yates makes no mention of Tartaglia although Dee actually refers to both of Tartaglia's books in his *Preface*. Certainly there are strong superficial resemblances in the structure and content of the two essays.

31 Tartaglia, *Euclide*, fo. iiir. On the significance of Cornelius Agrippa's book as the key magical text in the Renaissance see Yates, *The occult philosophy*, pp. 37–47.

32 Sorte, ASV: Provv. Camera ai Confini, Generali, B.260, fasc.1–9. The dispute is discussed in Schultz, 'New maps', pp. 113–14.

33 On Belli, see Yates, *Theatre of the world*, pp. 35–6, and Wittkower, *Architectural principles*, p. 141. Whittkower also discusses the foundation and nature of the Olympic Academy, *ibid.*, p. 141. See also Yates, *Art of memory*, pp. 172–3.

34 Yates, *Giordano Bruno*, Plate 16a. Compass and set-square were fundamental to the iconography of the mathematical arts, and later for freemasonry.

35 Sorte, *Osservazioni nella pittura*. On the angelic choirs: 'And according to the writings of scholars and even holy theology, the heavens are nine in number, and equally there are nine choirs or grades of angels, they [artists] must attempt by opening a sweet vista through the centre of these heavens, to reveal the supreme divinity and most perfect beauty, and then the angels, choir upon choir or step by step according to their nature and character, sweetly with imagined colours.' ('E secondo che scrivono i savi et anco i santi teologi, che i cieli sono per numero nove e che parimente sono nove i cori, overo i gradi degli angeli, doverebbono sforzarsi, con una dolce apertura di tutti essi cieli nel centro, di quella suprema divinità et eccellentissima bellezza dimostrarlo,

et appresso gli angeli di coro in coro, overo di grado in grado, secondo la natura e proprietà loro dolcemente con i colori imaginare') p. 295; on Nature: 'mother of all things and governor of the continuous revolution of the heavens' ('madre di tutte le cose et operatrice col continovo girar de'cieli') p. 286; on God: 'and the same eternal Father ... an omnipotent, invisible essence, incorporeal and incomprehensible' ('e esso eterno Padre ... una omnipotente essenza invisibile, incorporea et incomprehensibile'), p. 294.

36 Antonio Campi, 'Tutto il Cremonese et suoi confini et sua Diocese' (1571; repr. 1583). The map was produced originally to accompany a history of Cremona written by Campi, referred to by Almagià (*Monumenta*, p. 37) as a painter and scholar. It is reproduced in Almagià as Tav. XXXIX. Only one copy is known, at the Institute of Geography, University of Bologna, with whose generous permission it is reproduced here.

37 See for example Agostino Gallo, *Le dieci giornate della vera agricoltura e piacere della villa* (Vinegia, 1565), Bk 8, fo. 165v, where he speaks of watching the sunrise as one of the greatest joys of villa living.

38 Sorte, *Osservazioni nella pittura*, pp. 288–9.

39 Yates, *Giordano Bruno*, p. 57, discusses the hermetic content of the Schifanoia frescoes.

40 The frescoes form a frieze around one of the upper rooms of a house adjacent to the duomo in Castelfranco, now named Giorgione's house and devoted to a permanent exhibition of the artist's work, although there is no direct evidence of Giorgione having lived there. The church at Castelfranco contains Giorgione's masterpiece: *The Virgin with Child, St Francis and St Liberale*. The attribution of the frieze to Giorgione was made in 1966 by Adriano Mariuz.

41 Johannes Wilde, *Venetian art from Bellini to Titian* (Oxford, 1981), p. 66. Wilde also points out that X-ray analysis of the painting reveals that the head dress of the oldest man originally had a specifically oriental character.

42 I would like to acknowledge with gratitude the assistance of the British Academy's Research Fund in the Humanities and the Gladys Krieble Delmas Foundation for supporting research in Venice. I am grateful also to colleagues who commented on drafts: Helen Wallis, David Coffin, Brian Harley and Stephen Daniels

14

Maps, knowledge, and power

J. B. HARLEY

Give me a map; then let me see how much
Is left for me to conquer all the world, . . .
Here I began to march towards Persia,
Along Armenia and the Caspian Sea,
And thence unto Bithynia, where I took
the Turk and his great empress prisoners.
Then marched I into Egypt and Arabia,
And here, not far from Alexandria
Whereas the Terrene and the Red Sea meet,
Being distant less than full a hundred leagues
I meant to cut a channel to them both
That men might quickly sail to India.
From thence to Nubia near Borno lake,
And so along the Ethiopian sea,
Cutting the tropic line of Capricorn,
I conquered all as far as Zanzibar.

Christopher Marlowe, *Tamburlaine*, Part II (V.iii.123–39)

A book about geographical imagery which did not encompass the map[1] would be like *Hamlet* without the Prince. Yet although maps have long been central to the discourse of geography they are seldom read as 'thick' texts or as a socially constructed form of knowledge. 'Map interpretation', usually implies a search for 'geographical features' depicted on maps without conveying how as a manipulated form of knowledge maps have helped to fashion those features.[2] It is true that in political geography and the history of geographical thought the link is increasingly being made between maps and power – especially in periods of colonial history[3] – but the particular role of maps, as images with historically specific codes, remains largely undifferentiated from the wider geographical discourse in which they are often embedded. What is lacking is a sense of what Carl Sauer understood as the eloquence of maps.[4] How then can we make maps 'speak' about the social worlds of the past?

Theoretical perspectives

My aim here is to explore the discourse of maps in the context of political power, and my approach is broadly iconological. Maps will be regarded as part of the broader family of value-laden images.[5] Maps cease to be understood primarily as inert records of morphological landscapes or passive reflections of the world of objects, but are regarded as refracted images contributing to dialogue in a socially constructed world. We thus move the reading of maps away from the canons of traditional cartographical criticism with its string of binary oppositions between maps that are 'true and false', 'accurate and inaccurate', 'objective and subjective', 'literal and symbolic', or that are based on 'scientific integrity' as opposed to 'ideological distortion'. Maps are never value-free images; except in the narrowest Euclidean sense they are not in themselves either true or false. Both in the selectivity of their content and in their signs and styles of representation maps are a way of conceiving, articulating, and structuring the human world which is biased towards, promoted by, and exerts influence upon particular sets of social relations.[6] By accepting such premises it becomes easier to see how appropriate they are to manipulation by the powerful in society.

Across this broad conceptual landscape I shall pinpoint three eminences from which to trace some of the more specific ideological contours of maps. From the first I view maps as a kind of language[7] (whether this is taken metaphorically or literally is not vital to the argument).[8] The idea of a cartographic language is also preferred to an approach derived directly from semiotics which, while having attracted some cartographers,[9] is too blunt a tool for specific historical enquiry. The notion of language more easily translates into historical practice. It not only helps us to see maps as reciprocal images used to mediate different views of the world but it also prompts a search for evidence about aspects such as the codes and context of cartography as well as its content in a traditional sense. A language – or perhaps more aptly a 'literature' of maps – similarly urges us to pursue questions about changing readerships for maps, about levels of carto-literacy, conditions of authorship, aspects of secrecy and censorship, and also about the nature of the political statements which are made by maps.

In addition, literary criticism can help us to identify the particular form of cartographic 'discourse' which lies at the heart of this essay. Discourse has been defined as concerning 'those aspects of a text which are appraisive, evaluative, persuasive, or rhetorical, as opposed to those which simply name, locate, and recount'.[10] While it will be shown that 'simply' naming or locating a feature on a map is often of political significance, it nevertheless can be accepted that a similar cleavage exists within maps. They are a class of rhetorical images and are bound by rules which govern their codes and modes of social production, exchange, and use just as surely as any other discursive form. This, in turn can lead us to a better appreciation of the mechanisms by which maps – like books – became a political force in society.[11]

A second theoretical vantage point is derived from Panofsky's formulation of iconology.[12] Attempts have already been made to equate Panofsky's levels of interpretation in painting with similar levels discernible in maps.[13] For maps, iconology can be used to identify not only a 'surface' or literal level of meaning but also a 'deeper' level, usually associated with the symbolic dimension in the act of sending or receiving a message. A map can carry in its image such symbolism as may be associated with the particular area, geographical feature, city, or place which it represents.[14] It is often on this symbolic level that political power is most effectively reproduced, communicated, and experienced through maps.

The third perspective is gained from the sociology of knowledge. It has already been proposed that map knowledge is a social product,[15] and it is to clarify this proposition that two sets of ideas have been brought to bear upon the empirical examples in this essay. The first set is derived from Michel Foucault who, while his observations on geography and maps were cursory,[16] nevertheless provides a useful model for the history of map knowledge in his critique of historiography: 'the quest for truth was not an objective and neutral activity but was intimately related to the "will to power" of the truth-seeker. Knowledge was thus a form of power, a way of presenting one's own values in the guise of scientific disinterestedness.'[17]

Cartography, too, can be 'a form of knowledge and a form of power'. Just as 'the historian paints the landscape of the past in the colours of the present'[18] so the surveyor, whether consciously or otherwise, replicates not just the 'environment' in some abstract sense but equally the territorial imperatives of a particular political system. Whether a map is produced under the banner of cartographic science – as most official maps have been – or whether it is an overt propaganda exercise, it cannot escape involvement in the processes by which power is deployed. Some of the practical implications of maps may also fall into the category of what Foucault has defined as acts of 'surveillance'[19] notably those connected with warfare, political propaganda, boundary making, or the preservation of law and order.

Foucault is not alone in making the connection between power and knowledge. Anthony Giddens, too, in theorising about how social systems have become 'embedded' in time and space (while not mentioning maps explicitly) refers to 'authoritative resources' (as distinguished from material resources) controlled by the state: 'storage of authoritative resources involves above all *the retention and control of information or knowledge*. There can be no doubt that the decisive development here is the invention

of writing and notation.'[20] Maps were a similar invention in the control
of space and facilitated the geographical expansion of social systems, 'an
undergirding medium of state power'. As a means of surveillance they
involve both 'the collation of information relevant to state control of the
conduct of its subject population' and 'the direct supervision of that conduct'.[21] In modern times the greater the administrative complexity of the
state – and the more pervasive its territorial and social ambitions – then
the greater its appetite for maps.

What is useful about these ideas is that they help us to envisage cartographic images in terms of their political influence in society. The mere
fact that for centuries maps have been projected as 'scientific' images –
and are still placed by philosophers and semioticians in that category[22]
– makes this task more difficult. Dialectical relationships between image
and power cannot be excavated with the procedures used to recover the
'hard' topographical knowledge in maps and there is no litmus test of their
ideological tendencies.[23] Maps as 'knowledge as power' are explored here
under three headings: the universality of political contexts in the history
of mapping; the way in which the exercise of power structures the content
of maps; and how cartographic communication at a symbolic level can
reinforce that exercise through map knowledge.

Political contexts for maps

TSAR
My son, what so engrosses you? What's this?

FYODOR
A map of Muscovy; our royal kingdom
From end to end. Look, father,
Moscow's here
Here Novgorod, there Astrakhan.
The sea there,
Here is the virgin forestland of Perm,
And there Siberia.

TSAR
And what may this be,
A winding pattern tracing?

FYODOR
It's the Volga.

TSAR
How splendid! The delicious fruit of
    learning!
Thus at a glance as from a cloud to scan
Our whole domain: its boundaries, towns,
    rivers.

Alexander Pushkin, *Boris Godunov*

In any iconological study it is only through context that meaning and influence can properly be unravelled. Such contexts may be defined as the circumstances in which maps were made and used. They are analogous to the 'speech situation' in linguistic study[24] and involve reconstructions of the physical and social settings for the production and consumption of maps, the events leading up to these actions, the identity of map-makers and map-users, and their perceptions of the act of making and using maps in a socially constructed world. Such details can tell us not only about the motives behind cartographic events but also what effect maps may have had and the significance of the information they communicate in human terms.

Even a cursory inspection of the history of mapping will reveal the extent to which political, religious, or social power produce the context of cartography. This has become clear, for example, from a detailed study of cartography in prehistoric, ancient and medieval Europe, and the Mediterranean. Throughout the period, 'mapmaking was one of the specialised intellectual weapons by which power could be gained, administered, given legitimacy, and codified'.[25] Moreover, this knowledge was concentrated in relatively few hands and 'maps were associated with the religious elite of dynastic Egypt and of Christian medieval Europe; with the intellectual elite of Greece and Rome; and with the mercantile elite of the city-states of the Mediterranean world during the late Middle Ages'.[26]

Nor was the world of ancient and medieval Europe exceptional in these respects. Cartography, whatever other cultural significance may have been attached to it, was always a 'science of princes'. In the Islamic world, it was the caliphs in the period of classical Arab geography, the Sultans in the Ottoman Empire, and the Mogul emperors in India who are known to have patronised map-making and to have used maps for military, political, religious, and propaganda purposes.[27] In ancient China, detailed terrestrial maps were likewise made expressly in accordance with the policies of the rulers of successive dynasties and served as bureaucratic and military tools and as spatial emblems of imperial destiny.[28] In early modern Europe, from Italy to the Netherlands and from Scandinavia to Portugal, absolute monarchs and statesmen were everywhere aware of the value of maps in defence and warfare, in internal administration linked to the growth of centralised government, and as territorial propaganda in the legitimation of national identities. Writers such as Castiglione, Elyot, and Machiavelli advocated the use of maps by generals and statesmen.[29] With national topographic surveys in Europe from the eighteenth century onwards, cartography's role in the transaction of power relations usually favoured social elites.

The specific functions of maps in the exercise of power also confirm the ubiquity of these political contexts on a continuum of geographical scales. These range from global empire building, to the preservation of the nation state, to the local assertion of individual property rights. In each of these contexts the dimensions of polity and territory were fused in images which – just as surely as legal charters and patents – were part of the intellectual apparatus of power.

Maps and empire

As much as guns and warships, maps have been the weapons of imperialism. Insofar as maps were used in colonial promotion, and lands claimed on paper before they were effectively occupied, maps anticipated empire. Surveyors marched alongside soldiers, initially mapping for reconnaissance, then for general information, and eventually as a tool of pacification, civilisation, and exploitation in the defined colonies. But there is more to this than the drawing of boundaries for the practical political or military containment of subject populations. Maps were used to legitimise the reality of conquest and empire. They helped create myths which would assist in the maintenance of the territorial *status quo*. As communicators of an imperial message, they have been used as an aggressive complement to the rhetoric of speeches, newspapers, and written texts, or to the histories and popular songs extolling the virtues of empire.[30]

In these imperial contexts, maps regularly supported the direct execution of territorial power. The grids laid out by the Roman *agrimensores*, made functional in centuriation, were an expression of power 'rolled out relentlessly in all directions ... homogenizing everything in its path',[31] just as the United States rectangular land survey created 'Order upon the Land' in more senses than merely the replication of a classical design.[32] The rediscovery of the Ptolemaic system of co-ordinate geometry in the fifteenth century was a critical cartographic event privileging a 'Euclidean syntax' which structured European territorial control.[33] Indeed, the graphic nature of the map gave its imperial users an arbitrary power that was easily divorced from the social responsibilities and consequences of its exercise. The world could be carved up on paper. Pope Alexander VI thus demarcated the Spanish and Portuguese possessions in the New World.[34] In the partitioning of North America, itself 'part of a vast European process and experiment, an ongoing development of worldwide imperialism', the

very lines on the map exhibited this imperial power and process because they had been imposed on the continent with little reference to indigenous peoples, and indeed in many places with little reference to the land itself. The invaders parceled the continent among themselves in designs reflective of their own complex rivalries and relative power.[35]

In the nineteenth century, as maps became further institutionalised and linked to the growth of geography as a discipline, their power effects are

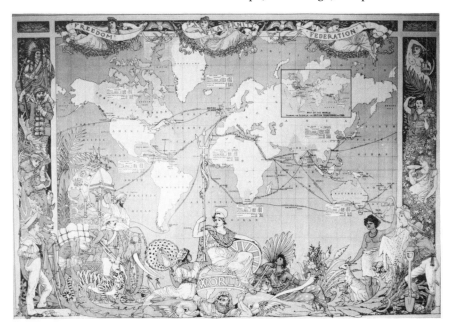

Fig. 1   *Imperial Federation – map of the world showing the extent of the British Empire in 1886* was first published as a supplement to the *Graphic* newspaper. Mercator's projection, a pink tint for empire territory, and decorative emblems showing Britannia seated on the world are used to articulate the message of the 'New Imperialism'. By courtesy of the Mansell Collection.

again manifest in the continuing tide of European imperialism. The scramble for Africa, in which the European powers fragmented the identity of indigenous territorial organisation, has become almost a textbook example of these effects.[36] And in our own century, in the British partition of India in 1947, we can see how the stroke of a pen across a map could determine the lives and deaths of millions of people.[37] There are innumerable contexts in which maps became the currency of political 'bargains', leases, partitions, sales, and treaties struck over colonial territory and, once made permanent in the image, these maps more than often acquired the force of law in the landscape.

Maps and the nation state
The history of the map is inextricably linked to the rise of the nation state in the modern world. Many of the printed maps of Europe emphasised

the estates, waterways, and political boundaries that constituted the politico-economic dimensions of European geography.[38] Early political theorists commended maps to statesmen who in turn were among their first systematic collectors.[39] The state became – and has remained – a principal patron of cartographic activity in many countries.[40]

Yet while the state was prepared to finance mapping, either directly through its exchequer or indirectly through commercial privilege, it often insisted that such knowledge was privileged. In western Europe the history of cartographic secrecy, albeit often ineffective, can be traced back to the sixteenth-century Spanish and Portuguese policy of *siglio*.[41] It was the practice to monopolise knowledge, 'to use geographic documents as an economic resource, much as craft mysteries were secreted and used'.[42]

A major example of the interaction between maps and state polity is found in the history of military technology. In military eyes, maps have always been regarded as a sensitive sort of knowledge and policies of secrecy and censorship abound as much today in the 'hidden' specifications of defence and official map-making agencies as in the campaign headquarters of the past.[43] At a practical level, military maps are a small but vital cog in the technical infrastructure of the army in the field. As the techniques of warfare were transformed from siege tactics to more mobile strategies, especially from the eighteenth century onwards, so too were the maps associated with them transformed.[44] Even in these active contexts, however, there were subtler historical processes at work. Map knowledge allows the conduct of warfare by remote control so that, we may speculate, killing is that more easily contemplated.[45] Military maps not only facilitate the technical conduct of warfare, but also palliate the sense of guilt which arises from its conduct: the silent lines of the paper landscape foster the notion of socially empty space.

Not all military maps are silent; many stridently proclaim military victory. Just as there were military parades, songs, and poems, so too, at least from the fifteenth century onwards in Europe, there have been battle plans designed to commemorate the sacred places of national glory.[46]

Maps and property rights

Cadastral or estate maps showing the ownership of property reveal the role of mapping in the history of agrarian class relations. Here the map may be regarded as a means by which either the state or individual landlords could more effectively control a tenant or peasant population.[47] In Roman society the codified practices of the *agrimensores* may be interpreted not just as technical manuals of land division in a theoretical sense but also as a social apparatus for legally regulating appropriated lands and for exacting taxation.[48] The maps themselves, whether cast in bronze or chipped in stone, were designed to make more permanent a social order in which there were freemen and slaves and for which the territorial division of land was the basis of status.[49] In early modern Europe, too, though the sociological context of mapping was different, some of the same forces were at work. The extent to which the mapping of local rural areas was locked into the process of litigation can leave us in no doubt about its socio-legal context and as a means by which conflict between lords and peasants over private rights in land could be more effectively pursued.[50] Maps fitted as easily into the culture of landed society as they had into the courtly diplomacies and the military manoeuvres of European nation states in the Renaissance.

In similar terms maps can be seen to be embedded in some of the long-term structural changes of the transition from feudalism to capitalism. The world economy and its new geographical division of labour was produced with the aid of geographical documents including maps.[51] Accurate, large-scale plans were a means by which land could be more efficiently exploited, by which rent rolls could be increased, and by which legal obligations could be enforced or tenures modified. Supplementing older, written surveys, the map served as a graphic inventory, a codification of information about ownership, tenancy, rentable values, cropping practice, and agricultural potential, enabling capitalist landowners to see their estates as a whole and better to control them.[52] Seeing was believing in relation to the territorial hierarchies expressed in maps. Whether in the general history of agricultural improvement, of enclosure, of the draining or embankment of fens and marshes, or of the reclamation of hill and moor, the surveyor ever more frequently walks at the side of the landlord in spreading capitalist forms of agriculture.[53]

Maps impinged invisibly on the daily lives of ordinary people. Just as the clock, as a graphic symbol of centralised political authority, brought 'time discipline' into the rhythms of industrial workers,[54] so too the lines on maps, dictators of a new agrarian topography, introduced a dimension of 'space discipline'. In European peasant societies, former commons were now subdivided and allotted, with the help of maps, and in the 'wilderness' of former Indian lands in North America, boundary lines on the map were a medium of appropriation which those unlearned in geometrical survey methods found impossible to challenge. Maps entered the law, were attached to ordinances, acquired an aureole of science, and helped create an ethic and virtue of ever more precise definition. Tracings on maps excluded as much as they enclosed. They fixed territorial relativities according to the lottery of birth, the accidents of discovery, or, increasingly, the mechanism of the world market.

Fig. 2 Large-scale estate maps, and the written cadastres they accompanied, became a tool in the rise of agrarian capitalism in England from the sixteenth century. In this portion of Samuel Walker's map of the estate of Garnetts, Essex (1622), details of ownership (DN = Edward Naylor's desmesne, DL = Richard Lavender's desmesne, etc.), precise delineation and accurate measurement (in acres, roods, perches) translate property rights into a tangible and legally binding image. By permission of the

Map content in the transaction of power

'Is that the same map?' Jincey asked. She pointed to the large map of the world that hung, rolled up for the summer, above the blackboard behind Miss Dove. 'Is China still orange?' 'It is a new map,' Miss Dove said. 'China is purple.' 'I liked the old map,' Jincey said. 'I like the old world.' 'Cartography is a fluid art,' said Miss Dove.

Frances Gray Patton, Good Morning, Miss Dove

Cartographers and map historians have long been aware of tendencies in the content of their maps that they call 'bias', 'distortion', 'deviance', or the 'abuse' of sound cartographic principles. But little space in cartographic literature is devoted to the political implications of these terms and what they represent, and even less to their social consequences. Such 'bias' or 'distortion' is generally measured against a yardstick of 'objectivity', itself derived from cartographic procedure. Only in deliberately distorted maps, for example in advertising or propaganda, are the consequences discussed.[55] 'Professional' cartography of the Ordnance Survey, the USGS, Bartholomew or Rand McNally or their predecessors would be regarded as largely free from such politically polluted imagery. That maps can produce a truly 'scientific' image of the world, in which factual information is represented without favour, is a view well embedded in our cultural mythology. To acknowledge that all cartography is 'an intricate, controlled fiction'[56] does not prevent our retaining a distinction between those presentations of map content which are deliberately induced by cartographic artifice and those in which the structuring content of the image is unexamined.

Deliberate distortions of map content

Deliberate distortions of map content for political purposes can be traced throughout the history of maps, and the cartographer has never been an independent artist, craftsman, or technician. Behind the map-maker lies a set of power relations, creating its own specification. Whether imposed by an individual patron, by state bureaucracy, or the market, these rules can be reconstructed both from the content of maps and from the mode of cartographic representation. By adapting individual projections, by manipulating scale, by over-enlarging or moving signs or typography, or by using emotive colours, makers of propaganda maps have generally been the advocates of a one-sided view of geopolitical relationships. Such maps have been part of the currency of international psychological warfare long before their use by Nazi geopoliticians. The religious wars of seventeenth-century Europe and the Cold War of the twentieth century have been fought as much in the contents of propaganda maps as through any other medium.[57]

Fig. 3   Even simple thematic maps can carry subtle propaganda messages. This
school atlas map, from *Geschichtsatlas ... Deutsch* (1933), represents Germanic
elements in Europe and (inset) overseas but omits a key to the values of the three
sizes of symbol. While the distribution pattern is realistic, German minorities in
European countries were usually very much smaller (under 4 per cent of total
population) than the use of ranked symbols suggests. By permission of the British
Library.

Apparently objective maps are also characterised by persistent manipulation of content. 'Cartographic censorship' implies deliberate misrepresentation designed to mislead potential users of the map, usually those regarded
as opponents of the territorial *status quo*. We should not confuse this with
deletions or additions resulting from technical error or incompetence or
made necessary by scale or function. Cartographic censorship removes from
maps features which, *other things being equal*, we might expect to find
on them. Naturally this is less noticeable than blatant distortion. It is justi-
fied on grounds of 'national security', 'political expediency', or 'commercial
necessity' and is still widely practised. The censored image marks the boundaries of permissible discourse and deliberate omissions discourage 'the
clarification of social alternatives', making it 'difficult for the dispossessed
to locate the source of their unease, let alone to remedy it'.[58]

The commonest justification for cartographic censorship has probably always been military. In its most wholesale form it has involved prohibiting the publication of surveys.[59] On the other hand settlement details on eighteenth-century maps were left unrevised by Frederick the Great to deceive a potential enemy, just as it has been inferred that the towns on some Russian maps were deliberately relocated in incorrect positions in the 1960s to prevent strategic measurements being taken from them by enemy powers.[60] Since the nineteenth century, too, it has been almost universal practice to 'cleanse' systematically evidence of sensitive military installations from official series of topographical maps.[61] The practice now extends to other features where their inclusion would be potentially embarrassing to the government of the day, for example, nuclear waste dumps are omitted from official USGS topographical maps.

Deliberate falsification of map content has been associated with political considerations other than the purely military. Boundaries on maps have been subject to graphic gerrymandering. This arises both from attempts to assert historical claims to national territory,[62] and from the predictive art of using maps to project and to legitimate future territorial ambitions.[63] For example, disputed boundaries, whether shown on official maps, in atlases, or in more ephemeral images such as postage stamps, have been either included or suppressed according to the current political preference.[64] Nor do these practices apply solely to political boundaries on maps. It is well documented how the geographies of language, 'race', and religion have been portrayed to accord with dominant beliefs.[65] There are the numerous cases where indigenous place-names of minority groups are suppressed on topographical maps in favour of the standard toponymy of the controlling group.[66]

'Unconscious' distortions of map content

Of equal interest to the student of cartographic iconology is the subtle process by which the content of maps is influenced by the values of the map-producing society. Any social history of maps must be concerned with these hidden rules of cartographic imagery and with their accidental consequences.[67] Three aspects of these hidden structures – relating to map geometry, to 'silences' in the content of maps, and to hierarchical tendencies in cartographic representation will be discussed.

Subliminal geometry

The geometrical structure of maps – their graphic design in relation to the location on which they are centred or to the projection which determines their transformational relationship to the earth[68] – is an element which can magnify the political impact of an image even where no conscious distortion is intended. A universal feature of early world maps, for example, is the way they have been persistently centred on the 'navel of the world', as this has been perceived by different societies. This *'omphalos'* syndrome',[69] where a people believe themselves to be divinely appointed to the centre of the universe, can be traced in maps widely separated in time and space, such as those from ancient Mesopotamia with Babylon at its centre, maps of the Chinese universe centred on China, Greek maps centred on Delphi, Islamic maps centred on Mecca, and those Christian world maps in which Jerusalem is placed as the 'true' centre of the world.[70] The effect of such 'positional enhancing'[71] geometry on the social consciousness of space is difficult to gauge and it would be wrong to suggest that common design features necessarily contributed to identical world views. At the very least, however, such maps tend to focus the viewer's attention upon the centre, and thus to promote the development of 'exclusive, inward-directed worldviews, each with its separate cult centre safely buffered within territories populated only by true believers'.[72]

A similarly ethno-centric view may have been induced by some of the formal map projections of the European Renaissance. In this case, too, a map 'structures the geography it depicts according to a set of beliefs about the way the world should be, and presents this construction as truth'.[73] In the well-known example of Mercator's projection it is doubtful if Mercator himself – who designed the map with navigators in mind to show true compass directions – would have been aware of the extent to which his map would eventually come to project an image so strongly reinforcing the Europeans' view of their own world hegemony. Yet the simple fact that Europe is at the centre of the world on this projection, and that the area of the land masses are so distorted that two-thirds of the earth's surface appears to lie in high latitudes, must have contributed much to a European sense of superiority. Indeed, insofar as the 'white colonialist states' appear on the map relatively larger than they are while 'the colonies' inhabited by coloured peoples are shown 'too small' suggests how it can be read and acted upon as a geopolitical prophecy.[74]

The silence on maps

The notion of 'silences' on maps is central to any argument about the influence of their hidden political messages. It is asserted here that maps – just as much as examples of literature or the spoken word – exert a social influence through their omissions as much as by the features they depict and emphasise.

So forceful are the political undercurrents in these silences that it is sometimes difficult to explain them solely by recourse to other historical or technical factors. In seventeenth-century Ireland, for example, the fact that surveyors working for English proprietors sometimes excluded the

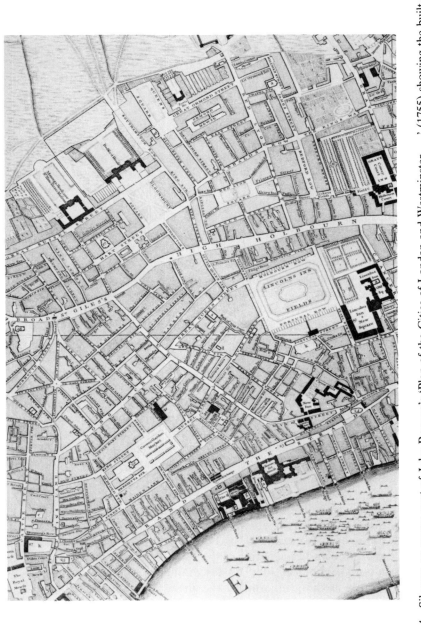

Fig. 4 Silences on maps: part of John Rocque's 'Plan of the Cities of London and Westminster . . .' (1755) showing the built-up area west of the City of London and the prestigious new green field developments of Bloomsbury. While districts to the north of Covent Garden and around Broad Street and St Giles were rapidly becoming slums, the cartographer has produced an idealised view of the city which emphasises the gracious rurality of the main squares but fails to convey urban squalor. By permission of the British Library.

cabins of the native Irish from their otherwise 'accurate' maps is not just a question of scale and of the topographical prominence of such houses, but rather of the religious tensions and class relations in the Irish country-side.[75] Much the same could be said about omissions on printed county surveys of eighteenth-century England: the exclusion of smaller rural cottages may be a response as much to the ideal world of the map-makers' landed clients as to the dictates of cartographic scale.[76] On many early town plans a map-maker may have unconsciously ignored the alleys and courtyards of the poor in deference to the principal thoroughfares, public buildings and residences of the merchant class in his conscious promotion of civic pride or vaunting commercial success.[77] Such ideological filtering is a universal process. In colonial mapping, as in eighteenth-century North America, silences on maps may also be regarded as discrimination against native peoples. A map such as Fry and Jefferson's of Virginia (1751) suggests that the Europeans had always lived there: where 'Indian nations' are depicted on it, it is more as a signpost to future colonial expansion than as a recognition of their ethnic integrity.[78] In this way, throughout the long age of exploration, European maps gave a one-sided view of ethnic encounters and supported Europe's God-given right to territorial appropriation. European atlases, too, while codifying a much wider range of geographical knowledge, also promoted a Eurocentric, imperialist vision, including as they did a bias towards domestic space which sharpened Europeans' perception of their cultural superiority in the world system.[79] Silences on maps – often becoming part of wider cultural stereotypes – thus came to enshrine self-fulfilling prophecies about the geography of power.

Representational hierarchies

The role of the map as a form of social proclamation is further strengthened by the systems of classification and modes of representation – the so-called 'conventional' or cartographic signs[80] – which have been adopted for landscape features. It has long been one of the map-maker's rules that the signs for towns and villages – whether depicted iconically or by abstract devices – are shown proportionally to the rank of the places concerned. Yet the resulting visual hierarchy of signs in early modern maps is often a replica of the legal, feudal, and ecclesiastical stratifications. Indeed, the concept of a tiered territorial society was by no means lost on contemporary map-makers. Mercator, for example, had hoped in his 1595 atlas to show 'an exact enumeration and designation of the seats of princes and nobles'.[81] Like other map-makers before him, he designed a set of settlement signs which, just as truly as the grids which have already been discussed, reify an ordering of the space represented on the map by making it visible. On other maps, towns occupy spaces on the map – even allowing for cartographic convention – far in excess of their sizes on the ground.[82] Castle

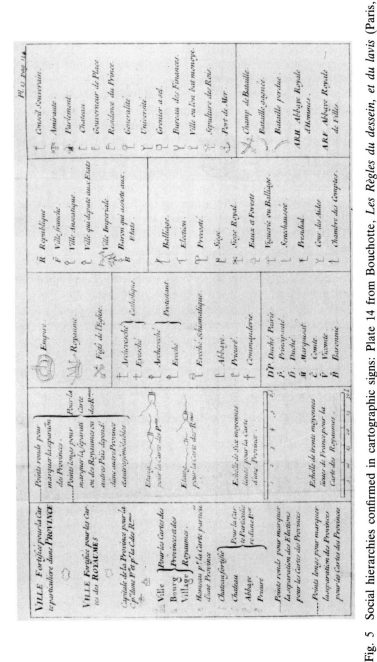

Fig. 5 Social hierarchies confirmed in cartographic signs: Plate 14 from Bouchotte, *Les Règles du dessein, et du lavis* (Paris, 1721). By permission of the British Library.

signs, too, signifying feudal rank and military might, are sometimes larger than signs for villages, despite the lesser area they occupied on the ground. Coats of arms – badges of territorial possession – were used to locate the *caput* of a lordship while the tenurially dependent settlements within the feudal order were allocated inferior signs irrespective of their population or areal size. This was particularly common on maps of German territory formerly within the Holy Roman Empire. Such maps pay considerable attention to the geography of ecclesiastic power. The primary message was often that of the ubiquity of the church. Whether in 'infidel' territory held by the Turk, in lands under the sway of the Papacy, in areas dominated by protestants in general, or by particular sects such as the Hussites, maps communicated the extensiveness of the temporal estate within the spiritual landscape. As a secondary message, not only do these maps heighten the perception of the power of the church as an institution within society as a whole, but they also record the spatial hierarchies and conflicting denominations within the church itself. On the former point, we may note that on Boazio's map of Ireland (1599), an exaggerated pictorial sign for 'a Bishopes towne' is placed at the head of its key,[83] just as on the regional maps of Reformation England the signs for church towers and spires often rose far above the requirement of a notional vertical scale. On the matter of hierarchy, individual signs for archbishoprics and bishoprics, in arrays of single or double crosses, or croziers, mitres, and variations in ecclesiastical headgear, testify to the social organisation of religion.[84] Here again, the selective magnifications of cartographic signs were closely linked to the shifting allegiances of opposing faiths. They survive as expressions of the religious battlegrounds of early modern Europe.

But if map signs sometimes reacted to changing religious circumstances they also tended to favour the *status quo*, legitimising the hierarchies established on earlier maps. They were a socially conservative vocabulary. In France, for example, map-makers, as servants of the crown, inscribed images as a form of state propaganda, emphasising the administrative mechanisms of its centralised bureaucracy and depicting aspects of the legal code of the *Ancien Régime*.[85] In 1721, when Bouchotte codified the signs to be used on regional maps (*cartes particulières*), for the territories which gave holders their titles, no less than seven of these are listed (*Duché Pairie, Principauté, Duché, Marquisat, Comté, Vîcomté, Baronnie*) as well as five ecclesiastical ranks (archbishopric, bishopric, abbey, priory, *commanderie*).[86]

The cartographic symbolism of power

> The earth is a place on which England is found,
> And you find it however you twirl the globe round;

RELPAX®
(eletriptan HBr)

For the spots are all red and the rest is all grey,
And that is the meaning of Empire Day.

> G. K. Chesterton, 'Songs of Education: 11 Geography', *The collected poems of G. K. Chesterton*

In the articulation of power the symbolic level is often paramount in carto-graphic communication and it is in this mode that maps are at their most rhetorical and persuasive. We may consider the symbolic significance of the group of maps found within paintings, where maps are *embedded in the discourse of the painting*. Alternatively we may assess how artistic emb-lems – which may not be cartographic in character but whose meaning can be iconographically identified from a wider repertoire of images within a culture – function as signs in decorative maps where they are *embedded in the discourse of the map*. Having linked the meaning of particular emb-lems with the territory represented on the map, we may consider how non-decorative maps may equally symbolise cultural and political values.

Maps in painting

The use by artists of globes and maps as emblems with their own specific symbolism can be traced back to the classical world. As a politically laden sign the globe or orb has frequently symbolised sovereignty over the world.[87] From Roman times onwards – on coins and in manuscripts – a globe or orb was held in the hand of an emperor or king. In the Christian era, now surmounted by a cross, the orb became one of the insignia of the Holy Roman Emperors and, in religious painting, it was frequently depicted held by Christ as *Salvator Mundi*, or by God the Father as *Creator Mundi*.[88] Such meanings were carried forward in the arts of the Renaissance. By the sixteenth century, globes which like maps had become more common-place in a print culture,[89] were now shown as part of the regalia of authority in portraits of kings, ambassadors, statesmen, and nobles. But now they were primarily intended to convey the extent of the territorial powers, ambitions, and enterprises of their bearers. These paintings proclaimed the divine right of political control, the emblem of the globe indicating the world-wide scale on which it could be exercised and for which it was desired.[90]

Maps in painting have functioned as territorial symbols. The map mural cycles of the Italian Renaissance, for example, may be interpreted as visual *summa* of contemporary knowledge, power, and prestige, some of it reli-gious but most of it secular.[91] In portraits of emperors, monarchs, states-men, generals, and popes, maps also appear as a graphic shorthand for the social and territorial power they were expected to wield. It is apt that Elizabeth I stands on a map of sixteenth-century England; that Louis XIV is portrayed being presented with a map of his kingdom by Cassini;[92] that

Fig. 6 The map as territorial symbol: in this painting of Thomas 14th Earl of
Arundel and his wife Alethea (Van Dyke, ca.1639), the Earl points to a colonial
venture in the island of Madagascar which he was promoting. By courtesy of the
Duke of Norfolk.

Pope Pius IV views the survey and draining of the Pontine marshes;[93] and
that Napoleon is frequently shown with maps in his possession, whether
on horseback, when campaigning, or seated and discussing proposed or
achieved conquest.[94] Even when the medium changes from paint to photo-
graphy and film the potent symbolism of the map remains, as the makers
of films about Napoleon or Hitler readily grasped.[95] In newspapers, on
television screens, and in innumerable political cartoons, military leaders
are frequently shown in front of maps to confirm or reassure their viewers
about the writ of power over the territory in the map. Map motifs continue
to be accepted as geopolitical signs in contemporary society.

The ideology of cartographic decoration

Since the Renaissance, map images have rarely stood alone as discrete
geographical statements, but have been accompanied by a wide range of
decorative emblems.[96] From Jonathan Swift onwards these elements have
been dismissed as largely incidental to the purposes of cartographic communication.[97] Decorative title pages, lettering, cartouches, vignettes, dedi-

Fig. 7   Atlas title-page as geopolitical affirmation: in that of the 1573 edition of Abraham Ortelius' *Theatrum Orbis Terrarum*, Europe, personified as ruler of the world, is enthroned above the other three continents. By courtesy of the American Geographical Society Collection, University of Wisconsin-Milwaukee.

cations, compass roses, and borders, all of which may incorporate motifs from the wider vocabulary of artistic expression, helped to strengthen and focus the political meanings of the maps on which they appeared. Viewed thus, the notion of cartographic decoration as a marginal exercise in aesthetics is superannuated.

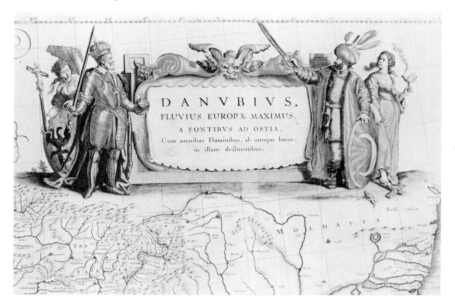

Fig. 8   Religious and territorial conflict is epitomised in the cartouche to the map of the Danube in *Mayor o Geographia Blaviana*, Vol. 3: *Alemania* (Amsterdam, 1662). Here, the Holy Roman Emperor (left), vested with emblems of power and the Christian faith, confronts the infidel Sultan, enemy of Christendom and spoiler of the cross. By courtesy of the American Geographical Society Collection, University of Wisconsin-Milwaukee.

Such a symbolic role for decoration can be traced through much of the history of European cartography. The frontispieces and titlepages of many atlases, for example, explicitly define by means of widely understood emblems both the ideological significance and the practical scope of the maps they contain.[98] Monumental arches are an expression of power; the globe and the armillary sphere are associated with royal dedications; portraits of kings and queens and depictions of royal coats of arms are incorporated into the design; royal emblems such as the *fleur de lys* or the imperial eagle also triggered political as well as more mundane geographical thoughts about the space mapped. The figures most frequently personified are those of nobles, bishops, wealthy merchants, and gentry. On English estate maps, microcosmic symbols of landed wealth, it is the coats of arms, the country house, and the hunting activity of the proprietors which are represented.[99] To own the map was to own the land.

In atlases and wall maps decoration serves to symbolise the acquisition of overseas territory. European navigators – portrayed with their cartographic trade symbol of compasses or dividers in hand[100] – pore earnestly over *terrae incognitae* as if already grasping them before their acts of 'discovery', conquest, exploration, and exploitation have begun. Indeed, it is on the maps of these overseas empires that we find some of the most striking examples of ideological reinforcement through decoration. Whether we are looking at the French explorer's maps of South America in the sixteenth century[101] or nineteenth-century British maps of African territories decoration plays a part in attaching a series of racial stereotypes and prejudices to the areas being represented. This is manifestly so with Africa. The decoration on maps produced in Europe disseminated the image of the Dark Continent. Some of the motifs employed suggest that Europeans found it hard to accept that African humanity *was* different. Thus, in the margins of many maps African faces stare out with European features. African men were given 'ideal' physiques and poses found in the iconography of figures in classical Greece and Rome; and African rulers – in obedience to the assumption that the political systems of Europe were universal – were usually depicted on maps as 'kings'.

In other cases the symbols of 'otherness' assumed the form of a bizarre racism. Natives are shown riding an ostrich or a crocodile, engaged in cannibal practices, located in captions as 'wild men', or, as on one French map of the eighteenth century, include 'a race of men and women with tails'. Female sexuality in depictions of African women and allegories for America and the other continents is often explicit for the benefit of male-dominated European societies.[102] Nor are the symbols of European power ever far from African space. European ships, castles, forts, and soldierly figures in European uniforms are deployed on maps in coastal regions; African 'kings' are subject to European authority; and allegorical angels, the Bible, or the cross, bring to the 'barbarous' Africans the benefits of Christianity as part of a colonial package of enlightenment. Sometimes, too, cartouches and vignettes symbolise the colonial authority of individual nations: on a French map of 1708, black Africans are shown with a lion below the arms of France.[103]

Cartographic 'fact' as symbol

It is a short step to move back from these examples of artistic expression to consider another aspect of 'real' maps. Having viewed maps in metaphorical contexts, it is easier to realise how a map which lacks any decorative features or even caption and explanation, can nevertheless stand on its own as a symbol of political authority. Such maps are characterised by a 'symbolic realism', so that what appears at first sight to be cartographic 'fact' may also be a cartographic symbol. It is this duality of the map which encompasses much cartographic discourse and is a principal reason why maps so often constitute a political act or statement.

Once the ubiquity of symbolism is acknowledged, the traditional discontinuity accepted by map historians, between a 'decorative' phase and a 'scientific' phase of mapping, can be recognised as a myth.[104] Far from being incompatible with symbolic power, more precise measurement intensified it. Accuracy became a new talisman of authority. For example, an accurate outline map of a nation, such as Cassini provided for Louis XIV, was no less a patriotic allegory than an inaccurate one, while the 'plain' maps of the Holy Land included in Protestant Bibles in the sixteenth century, in part to validate the literal truth of the text, were as much an essay in sacred symbolism as were more pictorial representations of the region.[105]

These are not exceptional examples of the historical role of measured maps in the making of myth and tradition.[106] Estate maps, though derived from instrumental survey, symbolised a social structure based on landed property; county and regional maps, though founded on triangulation, articulated local values and rights; maps of nation states, though constructed along arcs of the meridian, were still a symbolic shorthand for a complex of nationalist ideas; world maps, though increasingly drawn on mathematically defined projections, nevertheless gave a spiralling twist to the manifest destiny of European overseas conquest and colonisation. Even celestial maps, though observed with ever more powerful telescopes, contained images of constellations which sensed the religious wars and the political dynasties of the terrestrial world.[107] It is premature to suggest that within almost every map there is a political symbol but at least there appears to be a *prima facie* case for such a generalisation.

Conclusion: cartographic discourse and ideology

I have sought to show how a history of maps, in common with that of other culture symbols, may be interpreted as a form of discourse. While theoretical insights may be derived, for example, from literary criticism, art history, and sociology, we still have to grapple with maps as unique systems of signs, whose codes may be at once iconic, linguistic, numerical, and temporal, and as a spatial form of knowledge. It has not proved difficult to make a general case for the mediating role of maps in political thought and action nor to glimpse their power effects. Through both their content and their modes of representation, the making and using of maps has been pervaded by ideology. Yet these mechanisms can only be understood in specific historical situations. The concluding generalisations must accordingly be read as preliminary ideas for a wider investigation.

The way in which maps have become part of a wider political sign-system has been largely directed by their associations with elite or powerful groups and individuals and this has promoted an uneven dialogue through maps. The ideological arrows have tended to fly largely in one direction, from

Fig. 9   Maps came to serve as surrogate images for the nation state itself. In this engraving from *The Polish captivity* (Vol. 1, London, 1863), the partition of Poland is signified by the tearing of the map. The act is witnessed with distress by its onlookers, while an angel, representing the Catholic Church, turns away in horror and sounds a trumpet in alarm. By courtesy of the American Geographical Society Collection, University of Wisconsin-Milwaukee.

the powerful to the weaker in society. The social history of maps, unlike that of literature, art, or music, appears to have few genuinely popular, alternative, or subversive modes of expression. Maps are preeminently a language of power, not of protest. Though we have entered the age

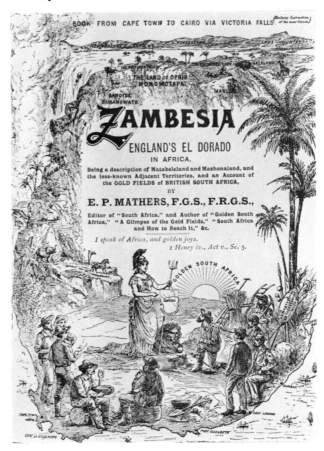

Fig. 10   Title-page from *Zambesia, England's El Dorado in Africa* (London, 1891). The scene is set on an outline map of southern Africa. Britannia, displaying a map of Zambesia, entices white colonists to take advantage of the economic wealth of the country while the indigenous African population is excluded from the stage. By courtesy of the American Geographical Society Collection, University of Wisconsin-Milwaukee.

of mass communication by maps, the means of cartographic production, whether commercial or official, is still largely controlled by dominant groups. Indeed, computer technology has increased this concentration of media power. Cartography remains a teleological discourse, reifying power, reinforcing the *status quo*, and freezing social interaction within charted lines.[108]

The cartographic processes by which power is enforced, reproduced, reinforced, and stereotyped consist of both deliberate and 'practical' acts of surveillance and less conscious cognitive adjustments by map-makers and map-users to dominant values and beliefs. The practical actions undertaken with maps: warfare, boundary making, propaganda, or the preservation of law and order, are documented throughout the history of maps. On the other hand, the undeclared processes of domination through maps are more subtle and elusive. These provide the 'hidden rules' of cartographic discourse whose contours can be traced in the subliminal geometries, the silences, and the representational hierarchies of maps. The influence of the map is channelled as much through its representational force as a symbol as through its overt representations. The iconology of the map in the symbolic treatment of power is a neglected aspect of cartographic history. In grasping its importance we move away from a history of maps as a record of the cartographer's intention and technical acts to one which locates the cartographic image in a social world.

Maps as an impersonal type of knowledge tend to 'desocialise' the territory they represent. They foster the notion of a socially empty space. The abstract quality of the map, embodied as much in the lines of a fifteenth-century Ptolemaic projection as in the contemporary images of computer cartography, lessens the burden of conscience about people in the landscape. Decisions about the exercise of power are removed from the realm of immediate face-to-face contacts.

These ideas remain to be explored in specific historical contexts. Like the historian, the map-maker has always played a rhetorical role in defining the configurations of power in society as well as recording their manifestations in the visible landscape. Any cartographic history which ignores the political significance of representation relegates itself to an 'ahistorical' history.[109]

NOTES

1 Geographical maps are but one aspect of the wider discourse of maps which extends to embrace other genres such as cosmological and celestial representations and maps of fictional areas.

2 Historians are also primarily concerned with the extent to which the evidence of maps can be evaluated as a 'true' record of the facts of discovery, colonisation, exploration, or other events in space.

3 On this view Margarita Bowen, *Empiricism and geographical thought from Francis Bacon to Alexander von Humboldt* (Cambridge, 1981); and D. R.

Stoddard (ed.), *Geography, ideology and social concern* (Oxford, 1981), esp. pp. 11, 58–60.

4 Carl O. Sauer, 'The education of a geographer', *Annals of the Association of American Geographers*, 46 (1956), pp. 287–99, esp. p. 289.

5 W. J. T. Mitchell, *Iconology: image, text, ideology* (Chicago, 1986), pp. 9–14.

6 Cf. the analysis of art in 'Art as ideology', in Janet Wolff, *The social production of art* (London, 1981), p. 49.

7 How widely this is accepted across disciplines is demonstrated in W. J. T. Mitchell (ed.), *The language of images* (Chicago, 1980).

8 Arthur H. Robinson and Barbara Bartz Petchenik, *The nature of maps: essays toward understanding maps and mapping* (Chicago, 1976), discuss the analogy at length. It is rejected by J. S. Keates, *Understanding maps* (London, 1982), p. 86, although he continues to employ it as a metaphor for the ways maps 'can be studied as ordered structures'. Another recent discussion is C. Grant Head, 'The map as natural language: a paradigm for understanding', in Christopher Board (ed.), *New insights in cartographic communication*, Monograph 31, *Cartographica*, 21, 1 (1984), pp. 1–32, and Hansgeorg Schlichtmann's 'Discussion' of the Head article, *ibid.*, pp. 33–6.

9 Jacques Bertin, *Semiology of graphics: diagrams, networks, maps*, transl. William J. Berg (Madison, 1983); see also Hansgeorg Schlichtmann, 'Codes in map communication', *Canadian Cartographer* 16 (1979), pp. 81–97; also Hansgeorg Schlichtmann, 'Characteristic traits of the semiotic system "Map Symbolism"', *Cartographic Journal*, 22 (1985), pp. 23–30. A humanistic application of semiology to maps is found in Denis Wood and John Fels, 'Designs on signs: myth and meaning in maps', *Cartographica*, 23, 3 (1986), pp. 54–103.

10 Robert Scholes, *Semiotics and interpretation* (New Haven, 1982), p. 144.

11 In accepting that maps can be regarded as an agent of change in history we can draw on the ideas of Lucien Febvre and Henri-Jean Martin, *The coming of the book: the impact of printing 1450–1800*, transl. David Gerard (London, 1976); see also Kenneth E. Carpenter (ed.), *Books and society in history: papers of the Association of College and Research Libraries Rare Books and Manuscripts Preconference 24–28 June 1980, Boston, Massachusetts* (New York, 1983).

12 Erwin Panofsky, *Studies in iconology: humanistic themes in the art of the Renaissance* (Oxford, 1939).

13 A preliminary discussion is in M. J. Blakemore and J. B. Harley, *Concepts in the history of cartography. A review and perspective*, Monograph 26, *Cartographica*, 17, 4 (1980), pp. 76–86, and in J. B. Harley, 'The iconology of early maps', *Imago et mensura mundi: atti del IX Congresso internazionale di Storia della Cartographia*, ed. Carla Marzoli, 2 vols. (Rome, 1985), 1, pp. 29–38. A narrower context is found in J. B. Harley, 'Meaning and ambiguity in Tudor cartography', in Sarah Tyacke (ed.), *English map-making 1500–1650: historical essays* (London, 1983), pp. 22–45. For another application see Patricia Gilmartin,'The Austral continent on 16th century maps; an iconological interpretation', *Cartographica*, 21, 4 (1984), pp. 85–90. See also Brian S. Robinson, 'Elizabethan society and its named places', *Geographical Review*, 63 (1973), pp. 322–33.

14 W. H. Stahl, 'Representation of the earth's surface as an artistic motif', in *Encyclopedia of world art* (New York, 1960), 3, cols. 851–4.

15 Mitchell, *Iconology*, p. 38.

16 See 'Questions on geography', in Colin Gordon (ed.), *Power/knowledge: selected interviews and other writings 1972–1977 of Michel Foucault*, transl. Colin Gordon, Leo Marshall, John Mepham, Kate Soper (Brighton, 1980), pp. 63–77, esp. pp. 74–5.

17 Mark Poster, 'Foucault and history', *Social Research*, 49 (1982), pp. 116–42, esp. pp. 118–19.

18 *Ibid.*

19 M. Foucault, *Discipline and punish*, transl. Alan Sheridan (London, 1977), esp. pp. 195–228.

20 Anthony Giddens, *The contemporary critique of historical materialism: power, property and the state* (London, 1981), p. 94 (emphasis added).

21 *Ibid.*, p. 5.

22 See, for example, Nelson Goodman, *Languages of art: an approach to a theory of symbols* (Indianapolis and New York, 1968), pp. 170–3.

23 These arguments will be more fully developed in J. B. Harley, *The map as ideology: knowledge and power in the history of cartography* (London, forthcoming).

24 Oswald Ducrot and Tzvetan Todorov, *Encyclopedic dictionary of the sciences of language*, transl. Catherine Porter (Oxford, 1981), pp. 333–8.

25 J. B. Harley and David Woodward, 'Concluding remarks', in J. B. Harley and David Woodward (eds.), *The history of cartography*, Vol. 1: *Cartography in prehistoric, ancient, and medieval Europe and the Mediterranean* (Chicago, 1987), p. 506.

26 *Ibid.*

27 Islamic cartography is most authoritatively described in E. van Donzel, B. Lewis and Ch. Pellat (eds.), *Encyclopaedia of Islam* (Leiden, 1978), Vol. 4, pp. 1077–83.

28 Joseph Needham, *Science and civilisation in China*, Vol. 3, sec. 22 (Cambridge, 1959).

29 B. Castiglione, *The courtier* [1528], transl. George Bull (Harmondsworth, 1967), p. 97; Thomas Elyot, *The boke named the gouernour*, ed. from the first edn of 1531 by H. H. S. Croft, 2 vols. (London, 1880), Vol. 1, pp. 45, 77–8; Machiavelli, *Arte della guerra* [1521], ed. S. Bertelli (Milan, 1961), pp. 457–8.

30 For the classical empires see O. A. W. Dilke, *Greek and Roman maps* (London, 1985), pp. 41–53 (on Agrippa's map) and pp. 169–70 (on the world map of Theodosius II). Maps of the British Empire became popular during the Victorian era: see Margaret Drabble, *For Queen and country; Britain in the Victorian age* (London, 1978), where the map by Maclure & Co., London, 1886, is reproduced. The geopolitical message of such maps and globes is unequivocably conveyed by G. K. Chesterton, 'Songs of Education: II Geography', quoted on pp. 294–5 above.

31 Samuel Y. Edgerton, Jr., 'From mental matrix to *mappamundi* to Christian

empire: the heritage of Ptolemaic cartography in the Renaissance', in David Woodward (ed.), *Art and cartography* (Chicago, 1987), p. 22.

32 Hildegard Binder Johnson, *Order upon the land. The U.S. rectangular land survey and the upper Mississippi country* (New York, 1976).

33 Claude Raffestin, *Pour une géographie du pouvoir* (Paris, 1980), p. 131.

34 Alexander's bull regarding the demarcation line is given in Anne Fremantle (ed.), *The papal encyclicals in their historical context* (New York, 1956), pp. 77–81.

35 D. W. Meinig, *The shaping of America: a geographical perspective on 500 years of history*, Vol. 1: *Atlantic America, 1492–1800* (New Haven, 1986), p. 232. A similar point is made by Robert David Sack, *Human territoriality: its theory and history* (Cambridge, 1986), p. 11.

36 See P. A. Penfold (ed.), *Maps and plans in the Public Record Office*, Vol. 3: *Africa* (London, 1982), *passim*; J. Stengers, 'King Leopold's imperialism', in Roger Owen and Bob Sutcliffe (eds.), *Studies in the theory of imperialism* (London, 1972), pp. 248–76.

37 For a vivid reconstruction of Radcliffe's partition of India employing relatively small-scale maps see Larry Collins and Dominique Lapierre, *Freedom at midnight* (London, 1982), pp. 245–8.

38 Chandra Mukerji, *From graven images: patterns of modern materialism* (New York, 1983), p. 83. See also Giuseppe Dematteis, *Le metafore della terra: la geografia umana tra mito e scienzia* (Milan, 1985), pp. 54–9.

39 On early map collections see R. A. Skelton, *Maps: a historical survey of their study and collecting* (Chicago, 1972), pp. 26–61; Harley, 'The map and the development of the history of cartography', in Harley and Woodward (eds.), *History of cartography*, pp. 6–12.

40 For early examples of state involvement in topographical mapping see Lloyd A. Brown, *The story of maps* (Boston, 1949), esp. pp. 241–71.

41 Daniel J. Boorstin, *The discoverers* (New York, 1983), pp. 267–9; on the Dutch East India Company's policy see Gunter Schilder, 'Organization and evolution of the Dutch East India Company's hydrographic office in the seventeenth century', *Imago Mundi*, 28 (1976), pp. 61–78; for an English example, Helen Wallis, 'The cartography of Drake's voyage', in Norman J. W. Thrower (ed.), *Sir Francis Drake and the famous voyage, 1577–1580* (Los Angeles and London, 1985), pp. 133–7.

42 Mukerji, *From graven images*, p. 91; see also Chandra Mukerji, 'Visual language in science and the exercise of power: the case of cartography in early modern Europe', *Studies in Visual Communications*, 10, 3 (1984), pp. 30–45.

43 Official map-making agencies, usually under the cloak of 'national security', have been traditionally reticent about publishing details about what rules govern the information they exclude especially where this involves military installations or other politically sensitive sites.

44 Christopher Duffy, *Siege warfare. The fortress in the early modern world 1494–1660* (London, 1979), esp. p. 81; and *The fortress in the age of Vauban and Frederick the Great 1660–1789* (London, 1985), esp. pp. 29, 72, 142. On the effect of cartography on more mobile warfare see R. A. Skelton, 'The

military surveyor's contribution to British cartography in the 16th century', *Imago Mundi*, 24 (1970), pp. 77–83.

45 Phillip C. Muehrcke, *Map use: reading, analysis, and interpretation* (Madison, WI, 1978), pp. 299–301.

46 Probably the majority of published battle plans and campaign maps issued 'after the event' in Europe down to the end of the eighteenth century fall either into this category or illustrated histories justifying the conduct of warfare.

47 A comparison can be made here with written documents; see, for example, M. T. Clanchy, *From memory to written record: England 1066–1307* (London, 1979), esp. pp. 149–265.

48 O. A. W. Dilke, *The Roman land surveyors. An introduction to the Agrimensores* (Newton Abbot, 1971).

49 P. Anderson, *Passages from antiquity to feudalism* (London, 1974), esp. pp. 147–53, 185, 188–9, 207–8.

50 P. D. A. Harvey, *The history of topographical maps: symbols, pictures and surveys* (London, 1980), *passim*.

51 Mukerji, *From graven images*, p. 84; Immanuel Wallerstein, *The modern world-system*, Vol. 2: *Mercantilism and the consolidation of the European world economy, 1600–1750* (New York, 1980), offers many clues to this process. Appropriately enough, the frontispiece to the volume is a world map by Jan Blaeu (1638).

52 J. R. Hale, *Renaissance Europe 1480–1520* (London, 1971), pp. 52–3.

53 F. M. L. Thompson, *Chartered surveyors: the growth of a profession* (London, 1968).

54 David S. Landes, *Clocks and the making of the modern world* (Cambridge, Mass., 1983), pp. xix, 2, 25, 228–30, 285–6; and Stephen Kern, *The culture of time and space* (London, 1983), pp. 10–35.

55 There is an extensive literature on maps in the pre-war German school of geopolitics. See, for example, Hans Speir, 'Magic geography', *Social Research*, 8 (1941), pp. 310–30; Louis O. Quam, 'The use of maps in propaganda', *Journal of Geography*, 42 (1943), pp. 21–32; Louis B. Thomas, 'Maps as instruments of propaganda', *Surveying and Mapping*, 9 (1949), pp. 75–81; and John Ager, 'Maps and propaganda', Society of University Cartographers, *Bulletin*, 11 (1977), pp. 1–14.

56 Muehrcke, *Map use: reading, analysis, and interpretation*, p. 295.

57 Geoffrey Parker, *The Thirty Years' War* (London, 1984), plates 10, 13.

58 T. J. Jackson Lears, 'The concept of cultural hegemony: problems and possibilities', *American Historical Review*, 90 (1985), pp. 567–93.

59 Harry Margary, *The old series Ordnance Survey maps*, Vol. 3 (Lympne Castle, 1981), p. xxxiv.

60 Speir, 'Magic geography', p. 320; F. J. Ormeling, Jr, 'Cartographic consequences of a planned economy – 50 years of Soviet cartography', *The American Cartographer*, 1, 1 (1974), pp. 48–9; 'Soviet cartographic falsifications', *The Military Engineer*, 62, 410 (1970), pp. 389–91.

61 For 'security' reasons not even the existence of these practices is reported, although in Britain, for example, in recent years they have been unearthed

by investigative journalism: see *New Statesman*, 27 May 1983, p. 6, which reported that 'Moles within the Ordnance Survey have sent us a most interesting secret manual which lists and defines the places in Britain which do not officially exist, and therefore cannot appear on maps.'

62 For example, in West Germany, the publishers of atlases have been obliged to obey a set of detailed ministerial regulations relating to political boundaries for maps that are to be used in schools. These did not receive approval for publication unless they showed the 1937 boundaries of Germany as well as those of today: K. A. Sinnhuber, 'The representation of disputed political boundaries in general atlases', *The Cartographic Journal*, 1, 2 (1964), pp. 20–8.

63 Numerous examples occur in the eighteenth-century British and French maps of North America: Percy G. Adams, *Travelers and travel liars 1660–1800* (New York, 1980), pp. 64–79, who, however, misses the ideological significance of the cartographic falsification he describes. See also J. B. Harley, 'The bankruptcy of Thomas Jefferys: an episode in the economic history of eighteenth century map-making', *Imago Mundi*, 20 (1966), pp. 28–48, esp. pp. 33–40. For a nineteenth-century example see Charles E. Nowell, *The rose-coloured map: Portugal's attempt to build an African empire from the Atlantic to the Indian Ocean* (Lisbon, 1982).

64 For political aspects of carto-philately see Bruce Davis, 'Maps on postage stamps as propaganda', *Cartographic Journal*, 22, 2 (1985), pp. 125–30.

65 H. R. Wilkinson, *Maps and politics. A review of the ethnographic cartography of Macedonia* (Liverpool, 1951).

66 F. J. Ormeling, *Minority toponyms on maps: the rendering of linguistic minority toponyms on topographic maps of western Europe* (Utrecht, 1983).

67 The idea of the hidden rules of cartography comes from Michel Foucault, *The order of things, an archaeology of the human sciences* (London, 1966; repr. 1970).

68 These geometrical elements also include the manipulation of scale and orientation and the use of cartographic grids to organise space. On the wider social significance of these geometries see Robert Sack, *Conceptions of space in social thought: a geographic perspective* (London, 1980), *passim*.

69 The phrase is that of Edgerton, 'From mental matrix to *mappamundi*', p. 26.

70 On European examples see Harley and Woodward, *The history of cartography*, Vol. 1; on Chinese maps, Needham, *Science and civilisation in China*, Vol. 3; and on Islamic maps, *Encyclopaedia of Islam*, Vol. 4.

71 The concept is E. H. Gombrich's *The sense of order* (Ithaca, 1979), pp. 155–6.

72 Edgerton, 'From mental matrix to *mappamundi*', p. 27. For potential insights into how maps could have contributed to the infrastructure of social cosmologies, see Michael Harbsmeier, 'On travel accounts and cosmological strategies: some models in comparative xenology', *Ethnos*, 50, 3–4 (1985), pp. 273–312.

73 Denis E. Cosgrove, *Social formation and symbolic landscape* (London, 1984), p. 8.

74 Arno Peters, *The new cartography* (New York, 1983), p. 63; see also Terry Cook, 'A reconstruction of the world: George R. Parkin's British Empire

map of 1893', *Cartographica*, 21, 4 (1984), pp. 53–65, for the deliberate use of Mercator's projection in a map promoting the 'New Imperialism' of the pan-Britannic world of the late nineteenth century. The recent reaction of cartographers towards the 'unscientific' nature of the alternative 'Peters' projection', which adjusts some of these distortions in favour of the Third World, provides a contemporary gloss on the entrenched scientism among map-makers which still gives credibility to the mathematically constructed map while ignoring the possibility of the social and political effects of its imagery. For example, see the comments by John Loxton, 'The Peters' phenomenon', *The Cartographic Journal*, 22, 2 (1985), pp. 106–8, which attempt to discredit Peters as a 'Marxist' and 'Socialist'. 'The so-called Peters' projection', in *ibid.*, pp. 108–10, which is presented as the considered view of the German Cartographical Society is in some respects more polemical than Peters in its 'defence of truthfulness and pure scientific discussion'. See also A. H. Robinson, 'Arno Peters and his new cartography', *American Cartographer*, 12 (1985), pp. 103–11, and Phil Porter and Phil Voxland, 'Distortion in maps: the Peters' projection and other devilments', *Focus*, 36 (1986), pp. 22–30.

75 J. H. Andrews, *Plantation acres: an historical study of the Irish land surveyor and his maps* (Belfast, 1985), pp. 157–8.

76 J. B. Harley, 'The re-mapping of England 1750–1800', *Imago Mundi*, 19 (1965), pp. 56–67; Paul Laxton, 'The geodetic and topographical evaluation of English county maps, 1740–1840', *The Cartographic Journal*, 13, 1 (1976), pp. 37–54.

77 Cf. Juergen Schulz, 'Jacopo de' Barbari's view of Venice: map making, city views and moralized geography before the year 1500', *Art Bulletin*, 60 (1978), pp. 425–74; J. B. Harley, 'Meaning and ambiguity in Tudor cartography', pp. 28–32.

78 For the development of this argument see J. B. Harley, 'Society, ideology, and the English geographical atlas in the eighteenth century', in John A. Wolter (ed.), *Images of the world: the atlas through history* (Washington, D.C., forthcoming).

79 James R. Akerman, 'National geographical consciousness and the structure of early world atlases', Paper presented at the Eleventh International Conference on the History of Cartography, Ottawa, Canada, July 1985.

80 I am indebted to Catherine Delano Smith for discussion and the sight of a draft manuscript on 'Cartographic signs in the Renaissance', to be published in J. B. Harley and David Woodward (eds.), *The history of cartography*, Vol. 3: *Cartography in the age of Renaissance and discovery* (Chicago, forthcoming).

81 Catherine Delano Smith, 'Cartographic signs on European maps and their explanation before 1700', *Imago Mundi*, 37 (1985), pp. 9–29, where Mercator's *Advice for the use of maps: atlas sive cosmographicae. Meditationes de fabrica mundi et fabricati figura* (1595) is quoted, pp. 25–6.

82 See Christian Sgrothen's maps of the Netherlands (1573) where towns such as Bruges, Brussels, and Ghent are depicted in high oblique in such a way – and with so large a sign – as to ensure ample scope for the detailed display of the attributes of their commercial success and civic pride.

83 Edward Lynam, 'Boazio's map of Ireland', *British Museum Quarterly*, 11 (1937), pp. 92–5.

84 François de Dainville, *Le Langage des géographes: termes, signes, couleurs des cartes anciennes, 1500–1800* (Paris, 1964), pp. 236–44.

85 François de Dainville, 'Le Signe de "justice" dans les cartes anciennes', *Revue Historique de Droit Français et Etranger*, 4th ser., 34 (1956), pp. 111–14. For a broader context see Yi Fu Tuan, *Landscapes of fear* (Oxford, 1980).

86 Buchotte, *Les Règles du dessin et du lavis* (Paris, 1721), plate facing p. 124.

87 Helen Wallis, 'Globes in England up to 1660', *The Geographical Magazine*, 35 (1962–3), pp. 267–79.

88 David Woodward, 'Medieval *mappaemundi*', in Harley and Woodward (eds.), *The history of cartography*, Vol. 1, pp. 334–42.

89 Victor Morgan, 'The literary image of globes and maps in early modern England', in Tyacke (ed.), *English map-making 1500–1650*, pp. 46–56.

90 For other meanings of the globe see James Hall, *Dictionary of subjects and symbols in art* (London, 1974), p. 139; and J. E. Cirlot, *A dictionary of symbols*, 2nd edn, transl. Jack Sage (London, 1971), pp. 118–19.

91 Juergen Schulz, 'The map mural cycles of the Renaissance', in Woodward (ed.), *Art and cartography*, pp. 97–120.

92 Reproduced in *Arte e scienza per il disegno del mondo* (Milan, 1983), p. 57; see also the plate on p. 56.

93 Roberto Almagià, *Monumenta cartographica vaticana*, 4 vols. (Vatican City, 1952), Vol. 3: *Le pitture murali della galleria delle carte geografiche*, pp. 7, 12.

94 *Cartes et figures de la terre* (Paris, 1980), p. 354; *A la decouverte de la terre. Dix siècles de cartographie* (Paris, 1979), facing p. 57.

95 Abel Gance, *Napoleon* (France, 1927); *The Great Dictator* (US, 1940). On the Gance film see Peter Pappas, 'The superimposition of vision: *Napoleon* and the meaning of Fascist art', *Cineaste. A Magazine on the Art and Politics of the Cinema* (1983), pp. 5–13.

96 A. G. Hodgkiss, *Understanding maps: a systematic history of their use and development* (Folkestone, 1981), pp. 184–98; MacDonald Gill, 'Decorative maps', *The Studio*, 128 (1944), pp. 161–9.

97   So Geographers in *Afric*-Maps
        With Savage-Pictures fill their Gaps;
        And o'er unhabitable Downs
        Place Elephants for want of Towns.

                                        Jonathan Swift, *On poetry: a rhapsody*

'Savage-Pictures', 'Elephants', and a 'want of Towns' (towns being one of the hallmarks of European civilisation), suggest that a stereotype of African geography, promoted by maps, was already in existence. On present-day attitudes towards decoration, see R. A. Skelton, *Decorative printed maps of the 15th to 18th centuries* (London, 1952), p. 1.

98 These have been treated as decorative ephemera for collectors: R. V. Tooley, *Title pages from 16th to 19th century* (London, 1975). Historians of cartography

still have to attempt the depth of iconographic analysis revealed in M. Corbett and R. Lightbown, *The comely frontispiece: the emblematic title-page in England 1550–1660* (London, 1979), or, F. A. Yates, *Astraea: the imperial theme in the sixteenth century* (London, 1975), p. 63.

99 Harley, 'Meaning and ambiguity in Tudor cartography', pp. 37–8; Hilda Marchant, 'A "Memento Mori" or "Vanitas" emblem on an estate map of 1612', *Mapline*, 44 (1986), pp. 1–4.

100 In different contexts compasses have other meanings: see Hall, *Dictionary of . . . Symbols*, p. 73.

101 H. Wallis, *The boke of idrography of Jean Rotz* (Oxford, 1982), esp. pp. 67–72; Bernadette Bucher, *Icon and conquest: a structural analysis of the illustrations of de Bry's Great Voyages* (Chicago, 1981).

102 On the female personifications for America see Hugh Honour, *The new golden land: European images of America from the discoveries to the present time* (New York, 1975), pp. 85–117, and Clare Le Corbeiller, 'Miss America and her sisters: personifications of the four parts of the world', Metropolitan Museum of Art, *Bulletin*, 19, New Series (1961), pp. 209–23. I owe these two references to Howard Deller.

103 Oscar I. Norwich, *Maps of Africa: an illustrated and annotated carto-bibliography* (Johannesburg, 1983). For comparison see Leonard Bell, 'Artists and empire: Victorian representations of subject people', *Art History*, 5, 1 (1982), pp. 73–86.

104 R. Rees, 'Historical links between cartography and art', *Geographical Review*, 70 (1980), pp. 60–78; David Woodward, 'Introduction', in Woodward (ed.), *Art and cartography*, Vol. 2.

105 The continued symbolic significance of the map is indicated by Louis XIV's dismay in the thought that his kingdom had shrunk as a result of more accurate survey. Brown, *Story of maps*, facing p. 246. On biblical maps see the prefatory 'epistle' to the 1559 Geneva Bible of Nicolas Barbier and Thomas Courteau where the usefulness of the maps in interpreting the scriptures is explained: I owe this reference to Catherine Delano Smith.

106 Göran Therborn's argument in *The ideology of power and the power of ideology* (London, 1980), pp. 81–4, about 'affirmative symbolism or *ritual*' is relevant to maps; see also Eric Hobsbawm and Terence Ranger (eds.), *The invention of tradition* (Cambridge, 1983), esp. pp. 1–100, 211–62.

107 Deborah J. Warner, *The sky explored: celestial cartography 1500–1800* (New York and Amsterdam, 1979), pp. xi–xii, discusses the iconographies of constellations produced by astronomers supporting the Reformation and the Counter Reformation respectively.

108 There is a parallel here to some of the tendencies identified by Robert David Sack, 'Human territoriality: a theory', *Annals of the Association of American Geographers*, 73, 1 (1983), pp. 55–74; the ideas are more fully developed in Sack, *Human territoriality: its theory and history*.

109 This paper was given in a preliminary form at a meeting of the 'Visual Documentation Group' of the History Workshop Centre for Social History, held at Ruskin College, Oxford, in February 1984. It has subsequently been presented

in seminars at the Department of Art History and Theory in the University of Essex and at the Department of Geography at the University of Wisconsin at Madison. I am grateful for the constructive suggestions received on those occasions and, for helpful comments, to John Andrews, Peter Barber, Mark Blacksell, Mark Cleary, Catherine Delano Smith, Anne Godlewska, Derek Gregory, Nicola Gregson, Roger Kain, Richard Oliver, Raphael Samuel, and David Woodward.

Index